Worlds of Consumption

Series Editors
Hartmut Berghoff
Institute for Economic & Social History
University of Göttingen, Göttingen, Germany

Uwe Spiekermann
Institute for Economic & Social History
University of Göttingen, Göttingen, Germany

Published in association with the German Historical Institute, Washington, DC. This series brings together historical research on consumption and consumerism in the modern era, especially the twentieth century, and with a particular focus on comparative and transnational studies. It aims to make research available in English from an increasingly internationalized and interdisciplinary field. The history of consumption offers a vital link among diverse fields of history and other social sciences, because modern societies are consumer societies whose political, cultural, social, and economic structures and practices are bound up with the history of consumption. Worlds of Consumption highlights and explores these linkages, which deserve wide attention because they shape who we are as individuals and societies.

More information about this series at
http://www.springer.com/series/14382

Regina Lee Blaszczyk • Uwe Spiekermann
Editors

Bright Modernity

Color, Commerce, and Consumer Culture

palgrave
macmillan

Editors
Regina Lee Blaszczyk
School of History
University of Leeds
Leeds, United Kingdom

Uwe Spiekermann
Institute for Economic & Social History
University of Göttingen
Göttingen, Germany

Worlds of Consumption
ISBN 978-3-319-50744-6 ISBN 978-3-319-50745-3 (eBook)
DOI 10.1007/978-3-319-50745-3

Library of Congress Control Number: 2017940258

Cover illustration: Shade card for spring 1901, J. B. Chambeyron fils, St. Etienne and Lyon, France, Hagley Museum and Library, Wilmington, DE, accession 2188: Papers of the Inter-Society Color Council, item 118. Courtesy of Hagley Museum and Library.

Printed on acid-free paper

This Palgrave Macmillan imprint is published by Springer Nature
The registered company is Springer International Publishing AG
The registered company address is: Gewerbestrasse 11, 6330 Cham, Switzerland

Contents

List of Contributors

Joyce Bedi Lemelson Center for the Study of Invention and Innovation, Smithsonian Institution, Washington, DC, USA

Regina Lee Blaszczyk School of History, University of Leeds, Leeds, United Kingdom

Alexander Engel Institute for Economic and Social History, University of Göttingen, Germany

Mary Lisa Gavenas Journalist and independent scholar, New York, NY, USA

Nicholas Gaskill Department of English, Rutgers University, New Brunswick, NJ, USA

Ingrid Giertz-Mårtenson Centre for Business History, Stockholm, Sweden

Dominique Grisard Center for Gender Studies, University of Basel, Switzerland

Charlotte Nicklas College of Arts and Humanities, University of Brighton, United Kingdom

Margaret Maile Petty School of Design, Creative Industries Faculty, Queensland University of Technology, Brisbane, Queensland, Australia

Melissa Renn Harvard Business School, Boston, MA, USA

Michael Rossi Department of History, The University of Chicago, Chicago, IL, USA

Uwe Spiekermann Institute for Economic & Social History, University of Göttingen, Göttingen, Germany

List of Figures

CHAPTER 1

Bright Modernity: Color, Commerce, and Consumer Culture

Regina Lee Blaszczyk and Uwe Spiekermann

The year 1856 was a watershed moment in the history of color. That spring in the East End of London, William Henry Perkin, a teenaged student of the German chemist August Wilhelm von Hoffmann at the Royal College of Chemistry (now Imperial College), accidentally discovered a way to synthesize the color mauve in the laboratory using coal tar, a waste product generated in the manufacture of gas for streetlamps. The gaslight era's invention of "mauveine"—also called "aniline purple" and "Perkin's mauve" at the time—helped to launch the synthetic organic chemicals industry, the high-technology industry that later produced aspirin and other pharmaceuticals, photochemicals, high explosives, and miracle fibers such as nylon, acrylic, polyester, and spandex. For visual and material culture, the most important developments to come out of this "high-tech" cauldron were synthetic dyes, lacquers, paints, pigments, and varnishes. These remarkable colorants changed the look of the modern world and—with other new technologies such as plastics and electricity—ushered in a period of what we might call bright modernity.

Bright modernity transformed material life in Western Europe, Central Europe, and North America from the mid-nineteenth century into the late twentieth century. The pioneers in this development were France, Germany, Great Britain, Sweden, Switzerland, and the United States, whose industrial economies depended heavily on the rise of the synthetic organic chemicals industry and whose consumer societies were considerably advanced by the

R.L. Blaszczyk
School of History, University of Leeds, Leeds, United Kingdom

U. Spiekermann (✉)
Institute for Economic & Social History, University of Göttingen, Göttingen, Germany

R.L. Blaszczyk, U. Spiekermann (eds.), *Bright Modernity*, Worlds of Consumption, DOI 10.1007/978-3-319-50745-3_1

availability of a bright palette of new colorants that were standardized, reliable, and durable. In textile manufacturing, the mills that produced silk, cotton, wool, and rayon fabrics for use in ladies' dresses and men's suits relished brilliant hues that did not fade in the sun and blacks that were truly black. Retail shops created eye-catching window displays using electric lights and brightly colored fabric backdrops to attract window shoppers after dark. There were new opportunities for product diversification through color in factories that made appliances, automobiles, fashion, and other consumer goods; art education and art supply stores; and media businesses such as magazine publishers and Hollywood movie studios.

In 1930, the inaugural issue of *Fortune* magazine contained an article entitled "Color in Industry," which described major transformations in the material and visual culture of the United States since World War I.[1] Everything from cooking pots to kitchen appliances, women's dresses, and the family car appeared to have been dipped in a pot of bright paint. A new group of color professionals, often associated with the nascent advertising industry of Madison Avenue or with the burgeoning chemical industry of the Delaware River valley, appeared on the scene in the 1920s and took charge of managing the rainbow. Sizing up the situation, *Fortune* dubbed it "the color revolution." Some eight decades later, Regina Lee Blaszczyk used that phrase for the title of a monograph. That book explored the background, birth, growth, and maturation of America's newfound passion for color in consumer products, interior design, and architecture with reference to the many colorful personalities who made up the army of professional color revolutionaries that ushered in the new world of bright modernity.[2]

Bright Modernity builds on this work and extends research on color in exciting new directions. While the color revolution was an American phenomenon, it had deep European roots and the color revolutionaries had strong ties to Europe. The transatlantic and multidisciplinary nature of the color revolution connects this historical topic to ongoing research in transatlantic history.[3] Researchers concerned with transatlantic cultural and economic connections initially focused on the transfer of American culture and expertise to Europe after World War II, writing under the rubric of the "Americanization" theme developed within foreign policy studies and business history by scholars exploring the impact of the Marshall Plan.[4] More recently, triggered by the rise of transnational history, researchers have argued for a more nuanced, multidirectional interpretation of transatlantic history in the twentieth century.[5] The color revolutionaries who created the era of bright modernity would have been in total agreement with this perspective. There were no "color dictators" commanding industries to accept one single hue each season. Color management was a complex cultural phenomenon, and color choices were often determined by multidirectional information flows. The color revolutionaries fully understood that color for commerce was best approached from a holistic perspective and from multiple disciplines. This anthology is crafted with that legacy in mind.

Color and Consumption

Despite its relevance to modern consumer societies and consumer cultures, color is one of the most neglected topics in the expanding field of consumption history. This fact is astonishing because other disciplines have dealt with color in a sophisticated way. Art history has not only opened a perspective onto the materiality of painting, but art historians also acknowledge that color is important for understanding how art links to broader cultural, social, and technological frameworks.[6] On the other side of the spectrum, science and technology studies have contributed to our understanding of the physiology of colors and color perception. Most scientific studies of color, however, are not really interested in history and offer linear stories of inventions and scientific progress.[7] More nuanced are several contributions to the history of the dyestuffs industry that offer a good overview of fundamental technological and industrial breakthroughs in the second half of the nineteenth century.[8] Helpful amendments to such branch studies are books on the history of individual dyestuffs such as mauveine and madder red. These works offer a better understanding of the complex developments in the multiplex worlds of color.[9] Finally, the contributions of individuals and organizations in the color prediction industry have been examined, and there is also growing scholarly interest in the materiality of colors.[10]

Color is the elephant in the room of consumption history, whether the approach is cultural or socio-economic. Of course, this does not mean that scholars of modern consumer societies are unaware of color as a discrete research topic, but in most cases they subsume color under more general concepts. Stuart Ewen's pioneering book, *Captains of Consciousness,* for instance, discusses the "aesthetic of mass industrialism" but does not mention color as a core feature of twentieth-century consumer culture.[11] Textbooks on consumer society routinely describe colorful consumer settings, such as the home and the department store, without analyzing the symbolism or the psychology of color in those settings.[12] The same oversight is evident in countless books on commercial architecture and roadside advertising.[13] Some researchers argue that "colors have a precise significance" for representation and identity without probing deeper. Even the best researchers make these types of assumptions and move on to new territory without further discussion. This is particularly striking in the case of Gary Cross, one of the most distinguished historians of modern consumer culture. His books on toys, on pleasure places, and on commercial memories and traditions chronicle changes in twentieth-century color schemes without exploring the cultural significance of those palettes as they evolved over time.[14] This blind spot is also evident in the work of other cultural historians. Even a history of lipstick takes the role of color in the creation of feminine beauty as a given.[15]

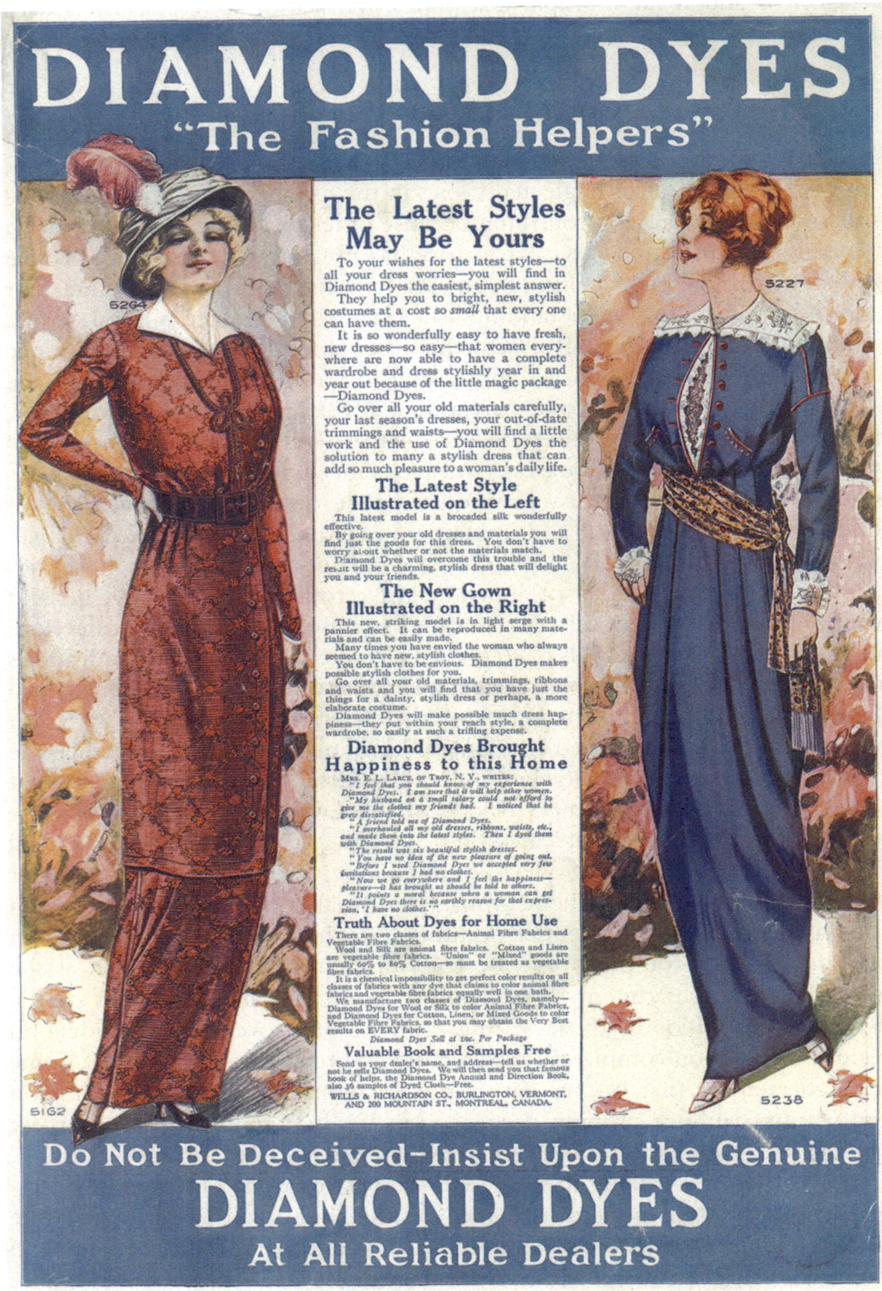

Fig. 1.1 Magazine advertisement, 1913, for Diamond Dyes, made by Wells & Richardson Co., Burlington, Vermont

Color is a ubiquitous phenomenon hiding in plain sight, and in most cases it is not analyzed seriously. This is surprising because university textbooks on marketing and consumer behavior almost always include some discussion of the visual dimensions of consumer culture.[16] The sheer volume of change from the mid-nineteenth century to the early twentieth century—a period in which the number of synthetic dyes grew from less than fifty in 1870 to around 1,300 by 1913—resulted in a new quality of visual culture and in a new consumer experience. Colors became an integral part of consumer culture in the years between 1880 and 1930, changing the design, production, and marketing of consumer goods. Many Westerners shopped in colorful spaces, purchased colored products, and lived in colorized environments. These consumers used colors to express their identities (Fig. 1.1).[17] The growing number of economical pigments and dyes led to a level of upward social mobility and democratization of consumption never before seen in history.[18] As Gary Cross reminds us, "Color lithography revolutionized packaging and must have been quite astonishing to consumers unaccustomed to such exciting sights."[19] But this and many other color-related topics have yet to be integrated into the broader historiography of consumption and consumer culture.

Of course, there are some exceptions to this general neglect of color in consumption history. Some three decades ago, two pioneering cultural historians, Roland Marchand and Neil Harris, pointed to the importance of color in advertising imagery and packaging, urging researchers to explore modern America's chromatic appetite.[20] One example of how color figured prominently in everyday life is the role of color in clothing as a marker of social identity. In the early twentieth century, recent immigrants to the United States deliberately chose to wear certain styles and colors of clothing so as to fit in with mainstream American society.[21] Color has also served as a marker for more general changes in society, namely, in gender relations.[22] Art history has recently offered a nuanced interpretation of the French experience by examining color in tapestries, posters, fireworks, and gardens during the age of Impressionism.[23] Design history has also ventured into color territory with studies of color and dress in Victorian women's magazines, white in the British

Fig. 1.1 (Continued)
Pitched at women of modest or moderate means, this advertisement proclaims, "It is so wonderfully easy to have fresh, new dresses—so easy—that women everywhere are now able to have a complete wardrobe and dress stylishly year in and year out because of the little magic package—Diamond Dyes." The text includes testimony from a housewife: "My husband on a small salary could not afford to give me the clothes my friends had. I noticed that he grew dissatisfied." But then a friend told her about Diamond Dyes, and she went to work on her "old dresses, ribbons, waists, etc." The result pleased her to no end. "You have no idea of the new pleasure of going out. Before I used Diamond Dyes we accepted very few invitations because I had no clothes."

Source: *Collier's, The National Weekly*, ca. 1913, collection of Regina Lee Blaszczyk.

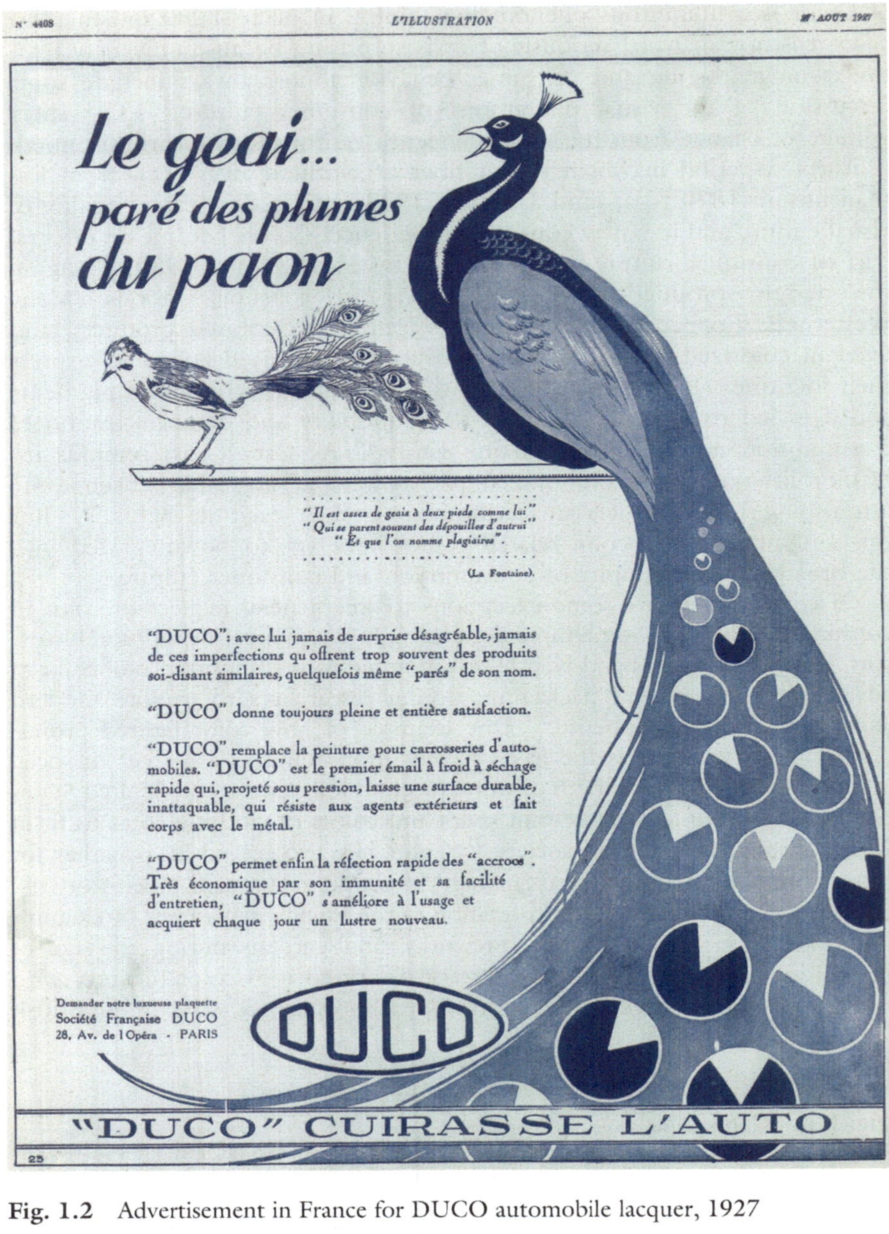

Fig. 1.2 Advertisement in France for DUCO automobile lacquer, 1927

This stylish advertisement of a DuPont product for refinishing cars targets the refined consumer, emphasizing that DUCO is the genuine article, the product that gives your car "a durable, watertight [*inattaquable*] surface that resists the elements and is integral [*fait corps*] to the metal." The text pitches the product as "very economical because of its immunity and its easy maintenance," but it was aimed at a prosperous audience. Readers are told to "request" the company's "luxurious booklet" from Société Française DUCO at a prestigious Parisian address, 28 Avenue de l'Opéra. If the text aesthetic interior, the cultural significance of day-glow paint, and Chinese color schemes in Australian architecture.[24] But most of the historiography has yet to follow these leads.[25]

Color, Design, and Changing Patterns in Manufacturing, Selling, and Living

Modern consumer cultures are driven by a "perpetual motion machine" in which modes, manners, morals, and markets are consistently reconfigured.[26] Colors connect our visual perception, cognitive performance, and everyday experience—even if we rarely take time to think about it. Color can be used as a tool to link individual consumer practices with the rapidly changing commercial environment of Western societies.

Until the mid-nineteenth century, bright colors were mainly the preserve of the wealthy, the only people who could afford them. The development of synthetic dyes enabled more shades to be created in brighter, longer-lasting, and more affordable hues. Middle-class consumers purchased goods in the vivid fade-proof—or "color-fast"—shades that were new on the scene. They bought different clothes, upgraded their furniture, improved their homes, and kept their cars looking good (Fig. 1.2). Colors continued to mark social hierarchies, to embody social, cultural, and material capital. The growing number of colors, however, supported very different lifestyles and representations. The wealthier classes chose more subtle shades, while the masses preferred bright hues. Color schemes could signal inclusion or exclusion in mainstream culture—but they could also serve as symbols for countercultures, as shown by the case of white as the favorite hue of radical design reformers in late Victorian Britain.[27] The public discourse on color usage was divided and contradictory. Although most people welcomed the new chromatic options provided by the marketplace, warning voices focused on threats to the human eye, the commercialization of everyday life, and the general decline of taste and distinction.[28]

The changing significance of color, however, was unmistakable. The *New York Times* summed up the Victorian perspective: "Color culture, it may be said, is sometimes wonderfully developed."[29] If this voice from the 1880s noted shifts in limited sectors of private bourgeois life, comparable voices from the 1920s celebrated a "new enlightenment." The *Christian Science Monitor* was upbeat: "Variety of color is creeping in where drab monotony was once the rule." Fabrics and shoes, cars and coats, furniture, kitchen and bath utilities—they all produced a "gay array" of colors, including influences from foreign decors.[30] (See, for example, Figs. 1.3 and 1.4.)

Fig. 1.2 (Continued)
places protection front and center, the beautiful drawing of a large peacock plume suggests in an understated, tasteful way the great variety of shades available. And the text itself ends with the assertion that DUCO "takes on a new luster every day."

Source: *L'Illustration,* August 1927, collection of Regina Lee Blaszczyk.

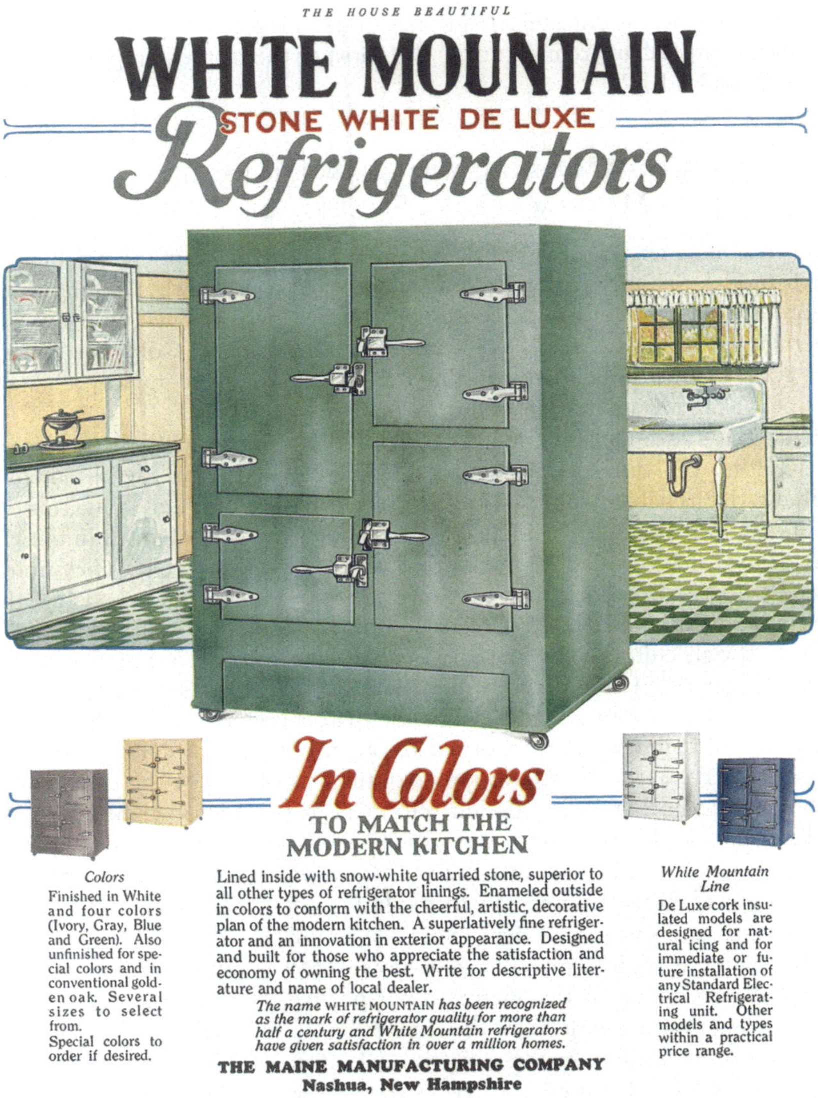

Fig. 1.3 Advertisement for White Mountain Refrigerators "in colors to match the modern kitchen," 1927

This icebox advertisement used the modern word r*efrigerator*. It also mentioned an important practical issue: these units could be cooled with "natural icing" or they could have an electrical refrigeration system installed, whether right away or in future. But the main focus of the advertisement is color. One could now have a kitchen—and a refrigerator—that was color-coordinated, presumably by the middle-class woman who read the magazine *House Beautiful*, in which this appeared. This multi-colored advertising strategy employed by the Maine Manufacturing Company in Nashua, New Hampshire, was used for a wide variety of modern products, ranging from telephones and cars to elastic garters.

Source: *House Beautiful*, May 1927, collection of Regina Lee Blaszczyk.

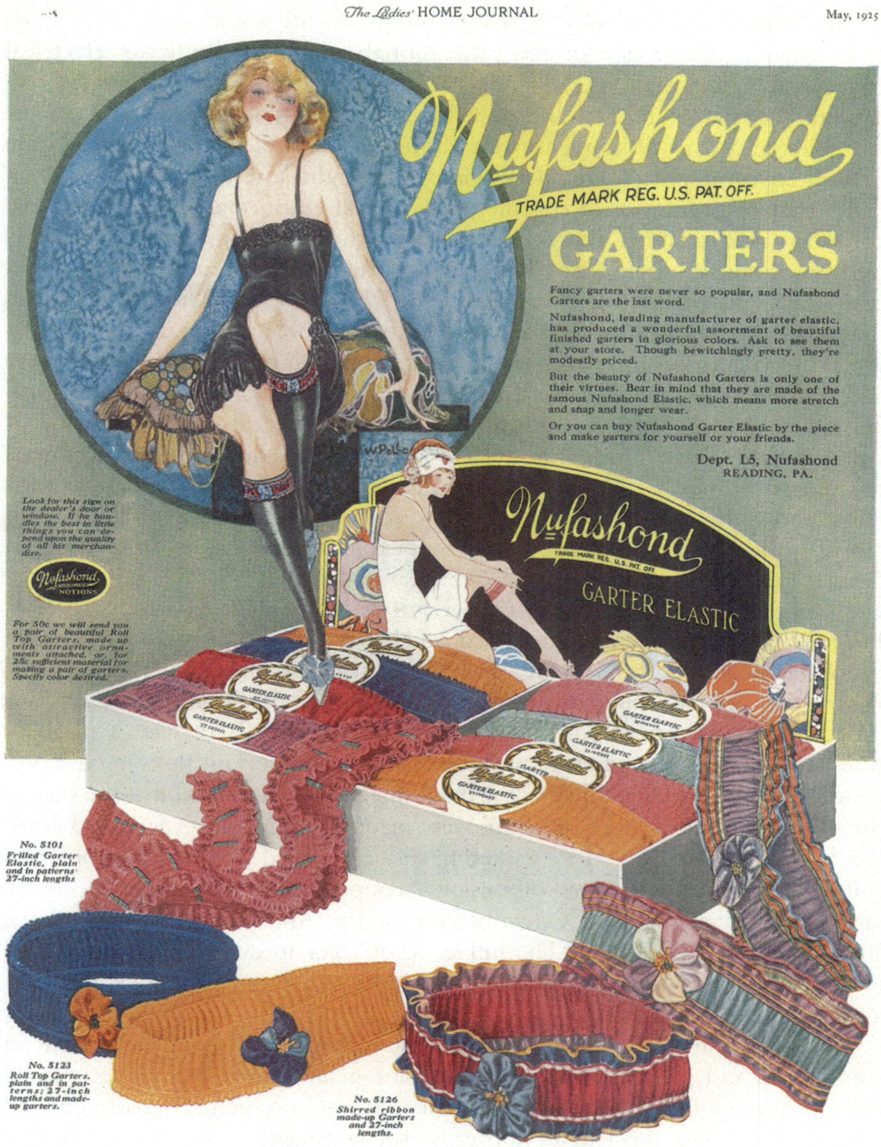

Fig. 1.4 Nufashond Garters advertisement, 1925

The ubiquitous theme of color in advertising and retailing is front and center in this advertisement in the *Ladies' Home Journal*. "Nufashond... has produced a wonderful assortment of beautiful finished garters in glorious colors," announces the text. "But the beauty of Nufashond Garters is only one of their virtues. Bear in mind that they are made of the famous Nufashond Elastic, which means more stretch and snap for longer wear." As with so many other products designed as life-enhancing for the consumer, women could enjoy garters made of elastic, and they could do so in a color of their choosing, according to this advertisement from Nufashond in Reading, Pennsylvania.

Source: *Ladies' Home Journal*, May 1925, collection of Regina Lee Blaszczyk.

The new presence of color in private and public life was a result of decisions and innovations by a slew of new professionals: chemists, physicists, electrical engineers, mechanical engineers, psychologists, product designers, retail stylists, and early consumer engineers. Chemical research not only produced new pigments and dyestuffs but also established a new reflexive distance to the natural environment.[31] This development brought an end to the traditional belief that colors imparted specific physical and emotional properties to the consumer and enabled the refurnishing of the outer appearance of many traditional consumer goods. Nineteenth-century practical men and their successors, the engineers, were responsible for cheaper manufacturing processes that allowed the print media to spread color via chromolithography.[32] Early visual merchandisers improved the decoration in commercial window displays and shop interiors through the creative combination of colorful paints, chromatic artifacts, and electrical illumination.[33] The emerging science of behavioral psychology found a new field of study in examining consumers' perceptions of goods, shop interiors, and advertising images.[34] These experts knew about the sensory and hedonistic qualities of color and integrated this "most salient aspect of the visual appearance" of goods into product development.[35]

In the new age of color, consumer goods became materialized expertise. Product design was increasingly based on abstract ideas of accepted and useful forms, tastes, and colors. Apparently easy questions became business questions. When the popular German consumer magazine *Frauengenossenschaftsblatt* (Women's Cooperative Journal) asked what color and flavor were typical for true bee honey, it was referring to one of the most important tasks in entrepreneurial decision-making.[36] When the magazine posed this question at the start of the twentieth century, such decisions were made by individual experts and firms. But in the following decades, marketing specialists tried to establish more general schemes and new ways of business cooperation to meet the needs of saturated buyers' markets. One observer of the American advertising scene after World War II noted, "The influence of color in everything from supermarkets and plane and ship interiors to shirts and fountain pens is assuming greater importance yearly."[37]

New colors and new color management strategies had a major impact on commercial and private environments. Color management techniques shaped the appearance of the new public spaces of consumption such as department and chain stores. Color also had an impact on the arrangement and illumination of products in those retail spaces, and on the advertising of goods on billboards, on trade cards, and in magazines.[38] Whereas color applications in the commercial environment remained the bailiwick of male experts, women brokered color in the home (Figs. 1.3 and 1.4). Middle-class consumers educated themselves on market options while looking through the shops; and, as one observer noted, they returned home "with pleasant dreams of color schemes which they are impatient to carry out."[39] At the same time, there were some transatlantic differences. American housewives took to expert ideas of "color harmony" that were rooted in the industrial arts tradition,[40] whereas German homemakers read about the new functional schemes of the Bauhaus and the International Style.[41] In the United States in the 1920s, expert color prescriptions were met by the rise of the "new woman," who decked herself out in color according to her social position and self-image.[42] "Every woman should be a picture," advised one psychologist, Orcella Rexford. "Moreover, she can be if she chooses her colors wisely."[43] Cosmetics, clothes, shoes, jewelry, and other consumer goods helped the American woman look smart and up-to-date.[44] Colorful dress and a colorful home were the modern woman's tools for expressing her colorful personality, as was often stated in the parlance of the twenties.[45] Immigrants adopted the colorful new styles, as did African American women, who started using skin whiteners and hair straighteners to put on an "acceptable" appearance and a "white," European American persona.[46]

These private endeavors were complemented by a growing emphasis on the part of professionals on training and educating the consumer. Even before World War I, salespeople were sensitized to the need to develop a commercial knowledge of color so as to assist their clients in making chromatic choices.[47] It was especially important for stores to guide male customers if their wives could not help them select the right shade of suit or the right color of cravat. Salespeople were expected to entice consumers to use new color schemes and embrace changing fashions.[48] This would not only improve sales figures but also strengthen the fortitude of the United States as a nation. "The use of color is gradually increasing in America," wrote one household columnist in the *Washington Post* in 1924. "It is a step up and will make us a happier, gayer and more imaginative nation."[49] This type of advice triggered negative responses from critics, who decried consumer manipulation and behavioral conditioning. But at the same time, the transfer of knowledge from experts to consumers was a salient feature of consumer culture as it matured from the 1920s onward. In America, this effort was closely related to the work of the Textile Color Card Association of the United States and the rise of other color management experts.[50]

Knowledge Transfers and Entanglements

Although the United States played a leading role in the development of a modern network of creative industries that applied expert knowledge to the realm of color, the use of color was part of a broader swath of Western history dating from the 1880s, the height of the Second Industrial Revolution. The rise of the synthetic dyestuffs industry and the use of color in consumer products was a story of knowledge transfers between and entanglements among several important industrial economies of the late nineteenth century—France, Germany, Great Britain, Switzerland, and the United States. From this perspective, the histories of globalization and Western cultural, economic, and technological supremacy can be retold with the story of color.

European and American middle-class consumers of the late nineteenth century were proud of the technological and economic progress of the era. Color emerged as a demarcator of space and place, as a means by which one city was differentiated from another. The fact that different European cultural capitals had distinctive visual features was a commonplace by this period. Paris was not only perceived as the world capital of fashion but also as a metropolis with a particular color scheme.[51] Paris was the City of Light, made pale and warm through the widespread use of a distinctive cream-grey limestone in its buildings, whether in the glorious Place de la Concorde or in the creative bohemian enclave of Montparnasse. A new illuminating technology—electricity—enhanced the streets, the cream-colored buildings, and magnificent new monuments, including the Eiffel Tower, the wrought-iron lattice marvel built in 1889 for the Exposition Universelle, the world's fair held during the centenary of the French Revolution.[52] The bourgeois elites of Paris had distinctive ideas on color harmony, especially regarding the beauty of women.[53] Before World War I, Paris set the standard for fashion and for the fashionable use of colors.[54] American society ladies went to France to purchase gowns and returned home to present themselves in accordance with elaborate bourgeois norms of style and taste.[55] At the same time, American advertising and marketing were recognized all over Europe, even if the comments were predominantly critical.[56] By the interwar years, there occurred a role reversal as American color management practices and the American predilection for bright hues inspired emulation in British textiles and French fashion.[57]

Although Germany remained by far the unchallenged market leader in the production of pigments and dyestuffs, the United States became the country with independent color experts in business management and marketing, intermediaries who consulted with a variety of companies instead of being employed exclusively by one firm and serving only that firm's leadership.[58] Whereas in Germany men in production and sales dominated marketing discourses into the late 1920s, in the United States there emerged a distinctive culture of color experts, some of them women.[59] Their work was based in part on the American color system developed by the Boston art educator Albert H. Munsell before World War I.[60] From the 1920s onward, these experts fueled the establishment of American methods in color management, which were respected, if not adopted, in Europe. Pioneering specialists in the application of color to product design, forecasting, and marketing—Hazel Adler, Faber Birren, Louis Cheskin, Frank Alva Parsons, Margaret Hayden Rorke, and H. Ledyard Towle—helped to create a worldwide reputation for American know-how in the business of color styling and color management.[61]

The years after World War I saw the institutionalization and global diffusion of Western ideas of color. Artificial dyes represented the ability of Western nations to develop synthetic chemicals and a formerly unknown range of dependable colors. Synthetic dye manufacturing was perfected in Germany, while some of the first theories on color harmonies and color contrasts in textiles were developed by Michel-Eugène Chevreul at the French state tapestry works, the Manufactures Nationales des Gobelins, in Paris. But the United States pioneered the use of color as a marketing tool, combining production, design, consumer and market research, retailing, and advertising. Higher incomes were a crucial factor in developing American consumer society as an attractive model for the rest of the world.[62] Westerners, especially Americans, were perceived as the "people of plenty," people who enjoyed an unrivaled standard of living. They "made their power felt around the world and, wherever they could, advocated their vision of society."[63]

Color was one factor that helped American consumer culture to achieve exemplary status across the globe commencing in the twenties.[64] This apparent global ascendancy, in turn, triggered ideas of national supremacy in the United States and led to ethnocentric discussions about "primitive man." Cultures that preferred a bright palette to the subtle hues in vogue in advanced industrial societies were compared to young children with their penchant for primary colors.[65] The use of color in marketing was always an expression of the relative power of the protagonists.[66] The global success of the Munsell Color System, which had been developed for elementary education but eventually found applications in science and commerce, is one aspect of a much broader history that has yet to be examined.[67]

In This Book

This book brings together eleven original essays on the relationship between color and consumer society in Europe and North America from the nineteenth century to the present. It looks at the organizations, institutions, and individuals who helped to make color an essential element in consumer culture over the *longue durée*.

Organized around four thematic sections, the volume examines the history of color through the lenses of production, distribution, and value creation. Part I deals with the nineteenth century and juxtaposes dye production and art education to stress the interconnectedness of color practices in seemingly disparate areas. Part II homes in on cultural dimensions by examining relationships among color in consumer products and gender identity. Part III provides insight into major technological innovations in printing, advertising, and movie making that allowed for the widespread dissemination of color in visual culture during the mid-twentieth century. Part IV shifts to the inner workings of commerce to explore the hidden history of color forecasting, the practice of designing and coordinating color palettes across product categories, industries, and nations to achieve manufacturing efficiencies while satisfying consumers' aesthetic appetites. Overall, the book considers how various types of actors, from dye manufacturers to forecasting organizations, interacted with the marketplace, and it examines how consumers responded to the color revolution's new hues.

To explore the multifaceted history of bright modernity, this book brings together research from contributors rooted in the academy, museums, fashion journalism, and fashion practice. The fusion of their diverse perspectives allows us to examine the rich legacy of color in ways that might well have been appreciated by the color revolutionaries themselves. After all, these men and women recognized no fixed boundaries between art, business, history, philosophy, psychology, and science; and the history of color needs to take a similarly interdisciplinary approach.

Foundations: Industry and Education

The book begins with Alexander Engel's chapter on German dyestuffs marketing in the nineteenth and early twentieth centuries. Conventional wisdom on the chemical industry holds that German dyestuffs manufacturers captured the global dye market by virtue of their superior scientific skills. For many years, the research laboratory and the research chemist in a white lab coat were held up as symbols of German excellence in synthetic organic chemicals. Although historians such as John Beer understood that marketing prowess contributed to the success of the German companies in the global market, before Engel wrote his doctoral dissertation in economic history, no one had gathered quantitative evidence on the dissemination of synthetic dyes versus natural dyes.[68] In the absence of such data, the image of the chemist in the lab coat continued to dominate the picture.

Engel's chapter draws on an in-depth analysis of trade statistics to discuss the marketing innovations of the five major German chemical companies that came to dominate the global dye market by the early twentieth century. He demonstrates that synthetic dyes gradually pushed natural dyes out of the picture due to a combination of technical improvements to the dyes and the intervention of sophisticated internal corporate marketing departments. Demonstrating that marketing was just as important as chemistry, Engel allows us to replace the image of the chemist in a lab coat with a picture of a globetrotting salesman with a suitcase full of dye sample books.

Another important business innovation for color, albeit on a smaller scale, was introduced in Springfield, Massachusetts, in the late nineteenth century. In this manufacturing center about ninety miles west of Boston, the famous board game magnate Milton Bradley saw the need for easy-to-use materials for color lessons for schoolchildren, as did his rival Albert Munsell. Bradley accumulated a fortune through sales of his famous board game *The Checkered Game of Life,* which he used to advance his pet project, the kindergarten movement, following the ideas of the German pedagogue Friedrich Fröbel. With a printing plant at his disposal, Bradley developed colorful teaching aids that were adopted by the Massachusetts state school system, then the most advanced in the United States. Nicholas Gaskill takes us to school with Milton Bradley in Chapter 3, where we learn about the fierce debates over human perception that preoccupied scientists, businesspeople, and educators during the early color revolution. Educators disagreed over what colors children could see, and whether muted hues or bright hues were best for them. Bright modernity won out in the end, as Milton Bradley's recommended colors became the industry standard for crayons, watercolor paints, and other teaching materials for art in the classroom.

Gender and Color

Contemporary global brands such as Hello Kitty (a cartoonish, catlike girl introduced by the Sanrio company of Tokyo in 1974 that appears on a variety of consumer products from school supplies to fashion accessories) follow a gender convention for colors, wherein blue is for boys and pink is for girls. Although Jo Paoletti tells us that these gender color codes were not widely adopted until after World War II, there are plenty of examples from earlier periods in Western culture.[69] Two iconic British oil paintings, *The Blue Boy* (1770) by Thomas Gainsborough and *Sarah Barrett Moulton: Pinkie* (1794) by Thomas Lawrence, were purchased by the American railroad magnate and art collector Henry E. Huntington, who added them to the collection of The Huntington in San Marino, California, in the late 1920s. The most famous painting at the Huntington, *The Blue Boy,* depicts an anonymous subject in fancy seventeenth-century Dutch dress, including a blue satin doublet and matching knee britches. The subject of the other painting was Sarah Moulton, the eleven-year-old daughter of a wealthy Jamaican plantation family whose grandmother had nicknamed her "Pinkie." The portrait was painted when Pinkie was in England for her education. In it she is wearing a white dress ornamented with a large pink ribbon at the waist; on her head is a large pink bonnet.[70] Although *Blue Boy* and *Pinkie* were not conceived as a pair, they are often mentioned in the same breath. As Melissa Renn notes in Chapter 9, color reproductions of the paintings were published for a mass audience in *Life* magazine in 1938. Their fame, and widespread dissemination in popular culture, did much to solidify gender stereotypes in color.

In Chapter 4, Dominique Grisard blends history and theory in a sweeping synthesis about the gendered coding of colors. Her essay traces the cultural association of men with form and women with color back to Renaissance Italy and forward, through the French court of the early modern era, into the twentieth century. The French association of women with pastels, including pink, laid the foundation for the creation of gendered color codes for fashionable clothing in the nineteenth and twentieth centuries, wherein pastels and bright colors were associated with frivolity, fashion, and femininity. In our own time, the persistence of this gendering has spurred theoretical debates over the meaning of transgressions by little boys who like pink. Significantly, Grisard suggests that the cultural meanings associated with color are rooted in long-standing Western traditions. The color revolution did little to challenge these stereotypes. Instead, the new dyes, paint schemes, and forecasts extended these gender color codes to a wider swath of the population.

If the pink and blue of Grisard's story are culturally familiar to us, the next two essays examine some now-forgotten aspects of the nexus between gender and color. In Chapter 5, Charlotte Nicklas does a thorough reading of nineteenth-century women's magazines and advice literature to examine relationships between women in the home and men in the chemical laboratory or at the editor's desk. Nicklas shows how Victorian women in both Great Britain and the United States were expected to develop a sophisticated understanding of dyes, fashion, and color as part of their domestic responsibilities. On the other hand, men working in dye houses had to develop marketing strategies to sell the proliferation of new hues made possible by organic chemistry. On both sides of the Atlantic Ocean, men and women developed a new vocabulary to describe the rich assortment of novel dyes and colors. Although they operated in separate spheres, the boundary between them was porous. Information about science reached women, and information on fashion reached men. In this way, color served as a means for breaking down gender barriers in one tiny corner of the Victorian world. This development occurred even as the feminization of color in fashion, as described by Grisard, took hold.

The association of fashion colors with feminine frivolity was only surpassed by the association of women with shopping. Shopping was a favorite pastime for Victorian upper-middle-class and wealthy women, but critics warned that excess exposure to the world of goods would cause women to lose their heads—and their husbands' hard-earned money.[71] In Chapter 6, by Michael Rossi, we see two well-known Victorian scientists take to the dry-goods department at A. T. Stewart, the most famous palace of consumption in New York City in the Gilded Age. The novice male shoppers were Ogden N. Rood, a physics professor at Columbia College (precursor to Columbia University) and the author of the color treatise *Modern Chromatics* (1879), and Charles Sanders Peirce, a science polymath, who was helping to define color for the *Century Dictionary*. As pioneers in the field of color science, both men were keen to learn how their emerging understanding of color as a physical phenomenon differed from the cultural sphere's apprehension of color in terms of emotion, sensation, and meaning. Their investigations hinged on their quest for a fabric sample of the fashion color "Isabel," and the tale of their ill-fated shopping expedition delineates the lines being drawn between color as a science and color as culture. This case study stands in contrast to the essay by Nicklas (Chapter 5), which demonstrates the free flow of information between homemakers and dyehouse technicians. In the world of color, there were no hard-and-fast rules.

Ringmasters to the Rainbow: Color Inventions and Visual Culture

Color innovation for the media has been long associated with the Technicolor sections of the 1939 Hollywood film *The Wizard of Oz*, when Dorothy leaves the dreary black-and-white farmland of Kansas for a dazzling place called Oz beyond the rainbow. The Land of Oz can serve as a metaphor for the bright modernity of the color revolution. Just as Dorothy and her troop pulled back the drapes to reveal the little man behind the great and powerful Wizard of Oz, the essays in this section look beyond the glittery façades of movie-making, publishing, and advertising to reveal technological and marketing innovations that put color within reach of twentieth-century American consumers.

In Chapter 7, Joyce Bedi brings the perspective of the history of technology to bear on the evolution of color in the movies, from the colorized films of the early years of the century through the development of Technicolor in the interwar years. Bedi shows that the story of Technicolor—a process for using dyes to colorize movies—is not limited to the invention of the technology itself. Her analysis of the simultaneous invention of many types of color processes demonstrates the multiple pathways that characterize technical innovation, and her discussion of the Technicolor method itself provides insight into the difficulties encountered by inventors and innovators. By the time Technicolor hit the market, the film industry had seen many successes and failures with color processes. Moreover, Technicolor was an extremely complex process, making it difficult for its inventor, Herbert Kalmus, to convince studios to adopt.

Two North American studio innovators—Jack L. Warner of Warner Brothers (born in Ontario, Canada, to Jewish immigrants from Poland) and the cartoonist Walter E. Disney (born in Chicago to a Canadian father and an American mother)—saw the potential in the new color process. Disney, in particular, was quick to embrace new movie-making technologies that would give his cartoons an edge in theaters. He was the first cartoonist to adopt the Technicolor process, and he secured the exclusive right among cartoonists to use the new technology for a period of two years in the early 1930s. Yet when movie directors tried Technicolor in films that starred real people, they found it incompatible with the lights and stage sets that had been perfected for the silver screen. The innovative cosmetician Max Factor, a Polish Jewish immigrant to the United States, rose to the occasion, creating a line of makeup expressly for use with Technicolor. Another innovator was Natalie Kalmus, the former spouse of the inventor Herbert Kalmus. After her divorce from Herbert, Natalie worked behind the scenes on Technicolor movie projects to ensure that sets, costumes, draperies, and furnishings were selected with the peculiarities of the Technicolor process in mind. Her entrepreneurial venture, called the Technicolor Color Advisory Service, may have been a nod to the Duco Color Advisory Service, established in the twenties by E. I. du Pont de Nemours & Company to advise industrial customers on the proper selection and use of the new colorful automotive lacquers.[72] Technicolor, Bedi shows, was more than a miracle invention. It was part of a complex technological system that depended on ancillary inventions in cosmetics, color theory, lighting, set design, and sound reproduction.

In Chapter 8, Margaret Maile Petty takes up the intersection of domestic life and electrical marketing in the American home after World War II. These were the glory years of American consumer society, with the United States having emerged largely undamaged from the global conflict. Electricity was common in American households by this time. Commercial promotions in the 1920s, combined with federal initiatives in the 1930s, had led to the widespread electrification of American homes before World War II, much more so than in Europe. In the competitive business environment of the postwar years, electrical manufacturers looked for new ways to sell electrical goods, and they turned to color as a marketing tool.

During the 1950s, the three major electrical manufacturers—the General Electric Company, Sylvania Electric Products, and the Westinghouse Electric Corporation—invested in extensive advertising and marketing campaigns to promote electric light bulbs in pastel colors. The new hues were expressly designed to complement the decor of the middle-class home and the complexions of white middle-class homemakers. In many ways, the leading electrical corporations and their Madison Avenue advertising agencies looked back to the prescriptions of Chevreul, the important nineteenth-century Parisian color theorist at the Gobelins tapestry works. Chevreul had developed the principles of chromatic complementarity for use in textile design, but he extended the rules of color harmony to the female toilette. His writings included descriptions of how to use the principles of chromatic complementarity to make the best fashion color choices for blondes, brunettes, and redheads. In the postwar era, the large electrical manufacturers modified Chevreul's color rules to suit their marketing needs. Rather than emphasizing color harmony as a tool for the improvement of one's physical appearance to reflect one's character, the advertisements touted the pastel bulbs as unique tools for expressing one's personality. This shift in color practice embodied one of the great transformations in American culture as documented by the historian Warren I. Susman. Whereas the Victorians had valued an individual's "character," the moderns placed emphasis on the individual's "personality."[73] The Victorians expressed their character through religious, family, and community activities, while the moderns showed off their personalities through the judicious selection and display of consumer goods, including automobiles, fashion, furnishings, and homes. Color was an element of distinction in all of these products.

The advertising campaigns for light bulbs in colors such as pearl pink and glamour pink built on the pioneering work of the electrical engineer Matthew Luckiesh, who directed General Electric's research on illumination at Nela Park, outside Cleveland, and who was widely known as the "Father of the Science of Seeing." A prolific writer of popular and scientific texts, Luckiesh had laid the foundation for the application of color psychology to lighting installations well before World War II. His ideas influenced the lighting designs at the Century of Progress exhibition in Chicago in 1933 and at subsequent world's fairs; and they shaped the work of "mood conditioners" like Faber Birren and H. Ledyard Towle, who used colored paints and electric lights to improve factory floors and office interiors during and after World War II.[74] By introducing incandescent bulbs in pastel hues, the electrical manufacturers had found a way to move "mood conditioning" from public spaces (a subject of Chapter 10) to private spaces and thereby capitalize on the growing interest in the expression of one's personality through the artful display of consumer goods in the home.

Chapter 9 shifts to another aspect of color and visual culture in postwar America. Here, Melissa Renn examines the role of *Life*, one of the most popular magazines in mid-twentieth-century America, in using color-printing technology to make art a vital part of everyday experience. From the magazine's decision to become a photographic pictorial weekly in 1936, the editors were committed to expanding the horizons of ordinary Americans by helping them to "see life" via images of humanity's accomplishments—its discoveries, architecture, and artworks, all in color. The reproduction of artistic masterpieces on the pages of *Life* was designed to whet the public's appetite for fine art and to make the United States into the art capital of the world, thereby fulfilling the goal of the new owner, Henry Robinson Luce, an Asian-born American, to make the twentieth century "The American Century."

New printing technology perfected by R. R. Donnelley & Sons in Chicago enabled *Life* to present the world in color. For the first time, a magazine reproduced works of art for public enlightenment, focusing on pictures in American collections. During World War II, the color reproduction of artists' renderings proved a more effective documentary tool than color photography, which was still a novelty and not refined enough to use for action shots. The editors at *Life* commissioned twenty-nine artists to capture life on the front, and reproduced their dramatic paintings in full color. After the war, *Life* sent photographers around the world to photograph art and architectural treasures, such as the Forbidden City, the imperial palace in Beijing, and the Sistine Chapel at the Vatican in Rome. *Life*'s investment in color reproductions provided many Americans with their first exposure to fine art. Renn shows how many writers and artists treasured the issues of *Life* that first exposed them to the heritage of human creativity. In the capable hands of editors like Henry Luce, color was a tool for educating Americans and uplifting the nation.

Predicting the Rainbow

Every fashionista remembers the color scene in the 2006 Hollywood comedy-drama film *The Devil Wears Prada*. The aspiring journalist Andrea Sachs, working as an assistant to the editor-in-chief of a fashion magazine, Miranda Priestly, rolls her eyes as the magazine staff debates which "stuff" to put in a photo shoot. Priestly sizes up Sachs's lumpy blue sweater and explains that it isn't *just* blue or turquoise or lapis, but cerulean blue, introduced by the Dominican-American fashion designer Oscar de la Renta in 2002. Following its appearance on the Paris catwalk, cerulean blue attracted the attention of other designers and brands and eventually found its way to American malls, where bargain hunters like Sachs paw through the sales racks. "It's sort of comical how you think you've made a choice that exempts you from the fashion industry," Priestly concludes, "when in fact, you're wearing a sweater that was selected for you by the people in this room."[75]

Cerulean blue is a striking name for a striking hue, but it is not a color that Oscar de la Renta invented. In 1999, the American color authority Pantone, Inc., selected cerulean blue, described as the color of the sky on a serene day, as the "official color for the millennium." Pantone is one of several global color consultancies, which like the trade fair Première Vision and the subscription service Worth Global Style Network (WGSN), help the creative departments in all types of businesses make color choices for product design and development. The color scene from *The Devil Wears Prada* is important for this book because it shows how the media promotes the idea of a color conspiracy of elites who select the colors that we will wear next season.[76] The reality is quite different.

As colorists forecast the new fashion palette, they must anticipate changes in taste several years in advance. They take into consideration the advance time needed for dye or pigment manufacturers to secure raw materials and negotiate contracts with suppliers, and the relentless shifts in consumer tastes. So, when Oscar de la Renta draped his fabulous cerulean blue gown, he may have been inspired by a Pantone color chip created before the millennium. What seemed cutting edge on the Paris catwalk had, in fact, been imagined years earlier by color forecasters laboring over fabric swatches and paint chips somewhere in New Jersey.[77] The three chapters in Part IV look beyond stereotypes of color dictators like Miranda Priestly to explore the history of color forecasting.

In Chapter 10, Regina Lee Blaszczyk examines the transfer of color forecasting methods and color psychology theories from the United States to Great Britain in the mid-twentieth century. The color revolution that transformed American color practice during the interwar years inspired and influenced British industries. The Textile Color Card Association of the United States, the leading American agency for color forecasting, was the model for the British Colour Council, founded in 1930. American color conditioning—the practice of colorizing assembly-line equipment and interior workspaces according to the principles of color psychology—also gained favor in Britain. But after this warm welcome, the British turned a cold shoulder on American colorists. Several factors, including a generational shift within the British design community and irreconcilable differences between the free enterprise system and the social democratic state, figured into the equation.

Chapter 11 offers an ethnography and business history of Modeurop, a leather industry organization that predicted color trends for the European shoe and leather industry from 1960 to 1998. Using interviews and business records, Ingrid Giertz-Mårtenson also draws on her own experience in the European fashion industry, which included a stint as director of the Swedish Shoe Fashion Council. She sets the stage for a discussion of Modeurop as a pan-European project by first examining the history of several national trade associations.

The chapter begins with the history and rationale of the Swedish Shoe Fashion Council, established in 1945 to reconcile government restrictions on the use of materials with the need to address wider trends in the American,

British, and continental European fashion industries. Soon, the Swedish Shoe Fashion Council joined forces with comparable councils in Norway, Denmark, and Finland to form the Nordic Fashion Council to coordinate color and fashion trends for tanners, shoe and accessory manufacturers, and retailers in Scandinavia.

In 1960, the establishment of the European Free Trade Association (EFTA) to stimulate commerce between Austria, Denmark, Norway, Portugal, Sweden, Switzerland, and the United Kingdom led the various national organizations dedicated to leather market trends to consolidate their efforts under one umbrella: Euro-Mode, which later became Modeurop. Composed of national organizations representing the leather and shoe industry, Modeurop was founded at a time when fashion trends were becoming more complex and difficult to predict. Older forecasting models, as embodied by two subscription services, the Textile Color Card Association and the British Colour Council, collected data from their constituencies and digested that information to produce color standards and seasonal forecasts. Increasingly, however, the fashion press, the triumph of the ready-to-wear industry, the rise of powerful retail chains, and consumer-driven street fashion rendered this model obsolete. New forecasting agencies such as Peclers Paris and Promostyl were founded by female entrepreneurs, and these faster-paced enterprises were poised to interpret the new mass-market styles that often bubbled up from the streets.

Modeurop worked through a system of committees that met annually to decide on upcoming trends. Because of her participation in these activities, Giertz-Mårtenson paints one of the most detailed and nuanced pictures of how a trend-forecasting agency did its job. We read vivid descriptions of color stylists at work—poring over fabric swatches, magazine tear sheets, and leather cuttings to discuss where color had been and which colors were likely to find favor among consumers in the new season. We also learn how women, considered to be endowed with fashion savvy by the shoe manufacturers, had been relegated to the margins of this forecasting organization, working as style consultants until a new generation, led by Giertz-Mårtenson, made inroads commencing in the late 1960s. This stands in contrast to the United States, where Margaret Hayden Rorke helped to pioneer the field of color forecasting as managing director of the Textile Color Card Association shortly after World War I.

In Chapter 12, finally, Mary Lisa Gavenas, a senior editor with more than three decades of experience in the New York fashion press, tells the story of fashion color prediction from the 1970s onward. As the influence of trade associations such as the Textile Color Card Association and the British Colour Council on color prediction waned, a group of silk manufacturers from Lyon, France, saw the need for a European-based organization to coordinate color trends for the fashion industry. Founded in the early 1970s, the Première Vision trade show was also a response to widespread frustration with Interstoff, the large European textile fair in Frankfurt am

Main, Germany. Utilitarian in character, Interstoff was the bane of some of the more high-end textile mills and fabric customers, who longed for a textile fair that was more concerned with fashion. Initially held in Lyon, Première Vision soon moved to a convention space in Paris, near the Porte de Versailles, in 1974 and then the Parc des Expositions near the Charles de Gaulle Airport in 1984. Première Vision gradually expanded its scope beyond silk to include all types of fabrics, and paid ever-greater attention to the needs of ready-to-wear manufacturers and global brands.

Drawing on her experience as a fashion editor, Gavenas provides unique insight into the rationale behind the establishment of Première Vision and its role as the most important color-forecasting organization of the late twentieth and early twenty-first centuries. Eschewing the hierarchical color forecasting methods of earlier trade associations, Première Vision learned to predict the next season's colors through a group activity called "concertation." Shortly before each semiannual show, a select group of representatives from participating mills attended this gathering, where they shared their expert opinions on the new trends. These ideas were used by the management at Première Vision to create a theme for the upcoming show and to create a single color card that showed the trend forecast for the upcoming season. Whereas earlier forecasting efforts were national in focus—tied to French, American, British, or Swedish markets, for example—the Première Vision forecasts originated in France but were geared to the international fashion industry. Gavenas's chapter, which benefits from her decades-long career as a fashion journalist and editor, is not only an enjoyable read, but also provides a direct counterpoint to the image of the omnipotent color dictator in *The Devil Wears Prada*.

Bright Modernity's Contradictions: Brave New World of Color

No anthology can cover all aspects of a topic, and the essays in this book mainly focus on color's positive impact on modern life. In closing this introduction, however, we draw the reader's attention to the shady underbelly of color and consumer culture. There are countless avenues for research on this topic. Recent work in fashion studies has pointed to the health hazards posed by some of the new synthetic dyes introduced in Victorian times. Pundits never failed to mock the follies of fashion, as they did in the 1850s with jokes on how women who dressed in the new purple hues looked as if they had "mauve measles."[78] Humor aside, some of the new textile dyes, including those that produced brilliant greens, actually were poisonous.[79]

Color troubles began in production and extended to consumption. The synthetic organic chemicals industry that produced the new dyestuffs and the textile industry that used them to manufacture cloth were major polluters of nearby waterways. Further down the supply chain, many of the compounds behind the color revolution could have adverse health effects on the individual consumer. Beginning as early as the 1870s, these dangers attracted the attention of health officials and inspired a new breed of expert, the consumer advocate, to lobby for consumer protection laws. In part, the regulatory state emerged in response to the expanding dyestuffs industry, whose contributions to the creation of a brilliant fashion palette and foods that looked appetizing were not without risks to the consumer. Here we draw on Uwe Spiekermann's evolving research on dyestuffs and food colorants in Germany to show the darker aspects of the color revolution. We hope these preliminary findings will inspire a new generation of researchers to think carefully about the many dimensions of color history.

***

If Aldous Huxley's dystopian novel *Brave New World* (1932) is perhaps no longer a fresh read, its premise still offers an important insight for historians of twentieth-century commerce and consumption. In the novel, mass production makes possible an affluent society in which all types of individual behaviors—including human reproduction—are closely regulated. Critical thinking is prohibited. Conformity is imposed through the ubiquitous use of pharmaceuticals and psychological techniques to manage one's mood and one's sense of well-being. Huxley was responding to the adverse consequences of modern consumer society and the rise of advanced psychological methods in marketing and purported mass manipulation.[80] With his warning in mind, we point to "the brave new world of color" as the dark side of bright modernity.

Without question, the German dyestuffs industry was on the leading edge of industrialization and modernization in the second half of the nineteenth century.[81] At the same time, however, the large-scale manufacture of synthetic dyes and their use in textile processing demonstrated the fundamental environmental hazards that these innovative products posed. Unregulated and inefficient waste disposal led to widespread water pollution. Rivers stained in the colors of the newest dyestuffs as well as the killing of fish and wildlife epitomized the risks of innovation, especially in the late-nineteenth and early-twentieth centuries, when factories abounded, unhindered by environmental regulations.[82] The German dye industry was predominantly clustered along the Rhine River and its tributaries, the Neckar, the Main, and the Wupper rivers. The textile industry was necessarily located in proximity to these rivers because it needed water to process cloth and to wash away countless chemicals, including dyestuffs. The coal and coal tar industry of Westphalia also needed fresh water from the Ruhr River and the Rhine River for processing materials and cheap transportation to major ports.[83] As a consequence of this regional cluster, the Rhine, celebrated by many as a symbol of the German nation, often shimmered in the colors of the rainbow. The color of the river might change, depending on what kinds of materials the chemical industry and other polluters dumped in it. Nineteenth-century mills and factories understood rivers mainly as sewage canals conveniently

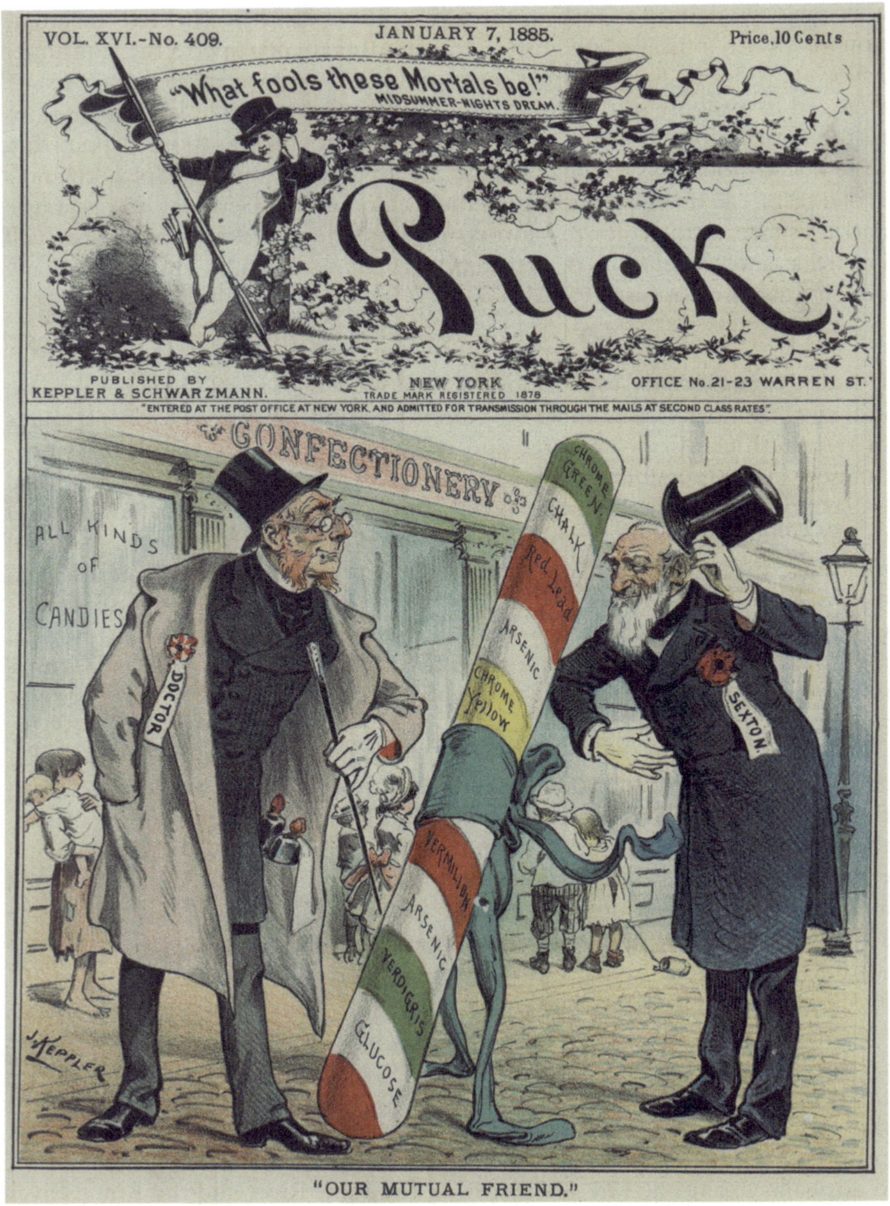

Fig. 1.5 Cartoon from 1885 criticizing the colorful but unhealthy, even dangerous, substances in a candy store's wares

Note the consumers portrayed outside the store, four respectably dressed children with shoes (center and right). Whether the poorer barefoot girl holding the baby (left) could hope for such sweets was another matter, but she is looking at the other kids, presumably wanting candy herself. The only two adults present are a doctor (left) and a gravedigger (right), who figure as the primary beneficiaries of the provided by Mother Nature. In their minds, water pollution was a reasonable price to pay for what became the global hegemony of the German dye industry.[84] But such arguments fooled neither the general public nor the growing number of government health officials.[85] More efficient wastewater treatment practices and regulatory interventions by the state reduced the environmental costs of dye production in the years leading up to World War I. Despite these early cleanup efforts, however, efficient regulatory structures for water protection were not installed in Germany—or in the United States—before the early 1970s. Modern color production was therefore always linked with growing health risks and other environmental costs.

A second area of intense debate among experts, manufacturers, and consumers was food coloring. From the 1860s, changes in food manufacturing, the extension of traditional supply chains, and the rising expectations of bourgeois consumers in the aesthetics of foodstuffs created a health-sensitive market that favored the introduction of new dyes. Natural colorants, often used for representative dishes and prestigious goods, were replaced by inorganic mineral pigments and synthetic coal tar colors.[86] The unregulated use of these new materials, however, caused serious health problems. There were poisonings and even fatalities (Fig. 1.5). In Germany, the so-called color law of 1887 was one of the first national consumer protection laws, but it was only a "purely defensive law to fight obvious abuses."[87] The law prohibited the use of the most important pigments and coal-tar colors and some individually named chemicals that were used to colorize food and furnishings. But the 1887 law did not provide for the regulation of all new synthetic colorants and was therefore limited in its effectiveness because prohibitions could be sidestepped with new recipes.

What followed was quite typical for modern regulatory practice. First, food chemists could establish themselves as independent experts fighting against deception and defining risks related to the use and consumption of food dyes. These food chemists cooperated with food manufacturers to establish regimes of voluntary declarations and thresholds for safety levels. Second, food producers mostly accepted these regulatory regimes because these practices created trust among consumers. In crucial cases, however, food producers put their own business interests before the majority of expert opinions. A good example was the greening of canned vegetables, for which copper sulfate (also called blue vitriol) was used. The ingestion of the copper caused health hazards, particularly if one ate canned vegetables on a regular basis. Although Germany's color law of 1887 prohibited the use of this additive, the food industry continued to use it because there was no alternative or substitute.

Fig. 1.5 (Continued)
chemicals listed on an attractive confection containing chrome green, chalk, red lead, arsenic, chrome yellow, vermillion, verdigris, and glucose. Most of these eight substances were used as colorants.

Source: J. Keppler, "Our Mutual Friend," cartoon, *Puck*, vol. 16, no. 409, January 7, 1885, title page, Library of Congress Prints and Photographs Division, https://lccn.loc.gov/2011661809.

Years of intense struggles between chemists, the Federal Department of Health, and manufacturers resulted in the 1896 edict of tolerance, which allowed the use of copper sulfate up to a specific threshold. Third, consumers were quite concerned about the health risks related to colored foods, although only the life reform movement and the consumer cooperatives made this a topic of public discussion.[88] Public debates about additives resulted in a certain level of uncertainty about colored foodstuffs. These concerns triggered debates among experts over possible revisions to the color law, and led to a new regulatory regime for dealing with coal tar dyes in the consumer sphere.[89] But these regulatory efforts failed because the brilliant, if hazardous, coal tar dyes were cheaper and brighter than "natural" colorings, which were limited to red, yellow, green, brown, and black.

German debates over the proper use of dyes in processed food continued into the 1920s. Ultimately, the deliberations resulted in the inclusion of mineral pigments and synthetic coal tar dyes in the revised German food law of 1927. The new law permitted the use of a larger number of colorants in processed foods. Moreover, whereas the manufacturers were made responsible for producing safe products, the federal food chemists and physicians who monitored the market could adjust the regulatory framework as necessary.[90] At the same time, food reformers drew on scientific studies to question the conclusions of these official regulatory experts and to screen for new risks related to food coloring, especially those dyes associated with cancer. Under the Nazi regime, strong factions among official health experts favored a new regulatory framework that would only allow safe colors. In general, however, business interests trumped consumer health. Regulators banned only a few very obvious health hazards, such as yellowed egg pasta in 1934 and yellowed butter in 1939. At this point in time, it was difficult to test products and make direct links to health hazards. As a result, the prevention of deception in consumer markets was still more important than fighting health hazards that might have resulted from the coloring of foods. In Germany, this pattern changed only with the 1958 food law, which prohibited all food additives that had not been tested and proven safe for consumers. Along these lines, food colors were permitted only after a scientific examination guaranteed their harmlessness for consumers.

In the United States, the regulatory situation was even more complex due to the varying powers of the historical actors. The individual states had a strong say in the regulation of the food market, courts had substantial power, and food manufacturers took a moderate stance on the topic.[91] The Progressive Movement, with its emphasis on reforming industry for the greater good of society, combined with numerous scandals in the food sector, led to the passage of the federal Pure Food and Drug Act in 1906 and to the creation of the regulatory agency that became the Food and Drug Administration (FDA) in 1930. The Pure Food and Drug Act approved a mere seven dyes as safe for food coloring, a number that was later changed according to business needs and risk analysis.[92] However, similar to Germany, the main concern of America's reform-minded chemistry experts was to prevent coloring as an aid to deception that stemmed from an "eagerness for pecuniary gain."[93] In contrast to consumers, food chemists were willing to accept uncolored foodstuffs. "It is an interesting question how far, since a bright color appeals to the aesthetic sense, the manufacturer shall be allowed to take advantage of this psychological fact," wrote one concerned scientist in the *American Food Journal*. "Probably we have to thank the food manufacturers for the present condition of our taste in regard to color in foods, and it may take some time to undo the evil to accept nature unadorned."[94] This did not happen, because food manufacturers used colors to create new products and to differentiate their products from the competition in marketing. For example, Coca-Cola remained a dark-colored soft drink, while 7 Up, born as a dark beverage, became a clear, colorless drink in 1929. Consumers learned to think of Coke and other colas as always being a dark brown liquid and to associate cola alternatives with colorlessness. In the long run, the American regulatory regime was more successful than the German regulatory regime in guaranteeing that only relatively harmless dyes would be used in foodstuffs. Passed in 1938, the Federal Food, Drug, and Cosmetic Act enabled the Food and Drug Administration to establish strict scientific standards for the safety of food additives.

This short history of food colorants in Germany and the United States shows that colorized goods often follow a long complicated trajectory from manufacturer to consumer. This vignette has drawn back the curtain on color additives in foodstuffs to reveal some of the more sobering dimensions of color history. Foodstuffs garnered special attention among regulators because people understood that anything ingested could have an effect on the body. Fashion was considered to be frivolous and health officials were slow to understand that the skin was an organ by which foreign substances could be absorbed into the body. The comparison between Germany and the United States also shows how national cultures were manifested in attitudes about color and laws to govern dyes, paints, and pigments. In both countries, new groups of professionals, whether food chemists in Germany or nutritional scientists in the United States, took it upon themselves to explore the impact of artificial colorants on the food chain. If corporate innovators such as Milton Bradley and Margaret Hayden Rorke invented new color regimes for crayons and cloth, the regulation of colorized foodstuffs fell to yet another group of professionals, who defined themselves as guardians of or spokesmen for the consumer. Bright modernity had many faces.

Conclusion: Visibly Invisible

The goal of this volume is to make color and the material world visible within the history of consumer society. The essays place color in a broad analytical and historical context. Historians cannot isolate color as a restricted field of study, as scientists and physiologists have done. Neither can they eschew color as subservient to form nor deem the color choices of immigrants to be in poor taste, as did early art historians and social workers, respectively. Historians must sidestep the chromophobia that dominates tastemaking circles and seek to comprehend, analyze, and explain the chromophilia that has fired the popular imagination since the Second Industrial Revolution.[95] They must grapple with the very real challenge of understanding color as a visible technology that invisibly connects so many puzzling aspects of modern consumer societies—research and development, manufacturing and selling, presenting and seeing goods, creating a distinct environment or a unique persona, and more.

Color cannot be avoided. It is omnipresent in our lives, manifest in everything from felt-tip markers and fashion to magazines and foodstuffs. The historical study of color has the potential to link very different specialized fields of research—chemistry and psychology, engineering and marketing, fashion history and business history, communication and the arts, visual culture and architecture, and the public and private spheres. The study of color can provide researchers with a new way to examine the operations of the consumer societies created by the Second Industrial Revolution and the ways in which people deal with commodified environments. We hope this book will inspire researchers to explore the many dimensions of color, commerce, and consumer culture in greater depth.

* * *

This book originated in a workshop called “Bright Modernity: Color, Commerce and Consumption in Global Perspective,” held at the German Historical Institute, Washington, DC.[96] We are grateful to the GHI for the generous support that it has lent to the workshop and this book, first under the directorship of Hartmut Berghoff and then under the directorship of Simone Lässig, and to Mark Stoneman for his painstaking editorial work.

Notes

1. “Color in Industry,” *Fortune*, February 1930, 85–86.
2. Regina Lee Blaszczyk, *The Color Revolution* (Cambridge, MA, 2012).
3. See Egbert Klautke, *“Amerikanisierung” in Deutschland und Frankreich (1900–1933)* (Stuttgart, 2003); Christof Mauch and Kiran Klaus Patel, eds., *The United States and Germany During the Twentieth Century: Competition and Convergence* (Cambridge, UK, 2010); Mary Nolan, *The Transatlantic Century: Europe and America, 1890–2010* (Cambridge, UK, 2012).
4. Detlef Junker, ed., *Die USA und Deutschland im Zeitalter des Kalten Krieges 1945–1990: Ein Handbuch*, 2 vols. (Stuttgart, 2001).
5. Daniel T. Rodgers, *Atlantic Crossings: Social Politics in a Progressive Age* (Cambridge, MA, 1998); Ian Tyrell, *Transnational Nation: United States History in Global Perspective since 1789* (Houndmills, 2007); Emory Eliott, “Diversity in the United States and Abroad: What Does It Mean When American Studies Is Transnational?,” *American Quarterly* 59 (2007): 1–22.
6. Recent examples: Katie Greenwood, *100 Years of Color: Beautiful Images and Inspirational Palettes from a Century of Innovative Art, Illustration and Design* (London, 2015); Victoria Finlay, *The Brilliant History of Color in Art* (Los Angeles, CA, 2014); Victoria Finlay, *Color: A Natural History of*

the Palette (New York, 2004). Individual colors have been analyzed by Michel Pastoureau in his *Blue: The History of a Color* (Princeton, NJ, 2001); *Black: The History of a Color* (Princeton, NJ, 2008); and *Green: The History of a Color* (Princeton, NJ, 2014).

7. Mary Virginia Orna, *The Chemical History of Color* (Heidelberg, 2013); Gudrun Wolfschmidt, *Farben in Kulturgeschichte und Naturwissenschaft* (Hamburg, 2011); Manlio Brusatin, *Histoire des colouers* (Paris, 2009); Jakob Steinbrenner and Stefan Glasauer, eds., *Farben: Betrachtungen aus Philosophie und Naturwissenschaften* (Frankfurt am Main, 2007); Bernard Guineau and Francois Delemare, *Colors: The Story of Dyes and Pigments* (New York, 2000); Robert A. Crome, *A History of Color: The Evolution of Theories of Light and Color* (Alphen, 1999).
8. John Joseph Beer, *The Emergence of the German Dye Industry*, rev. ed. (North Stratford, 1981); Arne Andersen and Gerd Spelsberg, eds., *Das blaue Wunder: Zur Geschichte der synthetischen Farben* (Cologne, 1990); John Edmonds and Alan Dronsfield, *The Transition from Natural to Synthetic Dyes* (Little Chalfont, 2001); Alexander Engel, *Farben der Globalisierung: Die Entstehung moderner Märkte für Farbstoffe 1500–1900* (Frankfurt am Main, 2009).
9. Simon Garfield, *Mauve: How One Man Invented a Color That Changed the World* (New York, 2002); Robert Chenciner, *Madder Red: A History of Luxury and Trade* (London, 2000).
10. Léatrice Eiseman and Keith Recker, *Pantone: Le XXe siècle en couleurs* (Paris, 2011); Leatrice Eisemen and Keith Recker, *Pantone: The Twentieth Century in Color* (San Francisco, 2011); Léatrice Eiseman and E. P. Cutler, *Pantone on Fashion: A Century of Color in Design* (San Francisco, 2014); Regina Lee Blaszczyk and Ben Wubs, eds., *The Fashion Forecasters: A Hidden History of Color and Trend Prediction* (London, 2018, forthcoming); Andrea Feeser, Maureen Daly Goggin and Beth Fowkes Tobin, eds., *The Materiality of Color: The Production, Circulation, and Application of Dyes and Pigments, 1400–1800* (Farnham, UK, 2012).
11. Stuart Ewen, *Captions of Consciousness: Advertising and the Social Roots of the Consumer Culture* (New York, 1977).
12. For example: Lawrence B. Glickman, ed., *Consumer Society in American History: A Reader* (Ithaca, NY, 1999).
13. Martin Treu, *Signs, Streets, and Storefronts: A History of Architecture and Graphics along America's Corridors* (Baltimore, MD, 2012).
14. Gary Cross, *Kids' Stuff: Toys and the Changing World of American Childhood*, 2nd ed. (Cambridge, MA, 2001); Gary Cross and John K. Walton, *The Playful Crowd: Pleasure Places in the Twentieth Century* (New York, 2005); Gary Cross, *Men to Boys: The Making of Modern Immaturity* (New York, 2010).
15. Mag Cohen Ragas and Karen Kozlowski, *Read My Lips: A Cultural History of Lipstick* (San Francisco, CA, 1998).
16. Michael R. Solomon, *Consumer Behavior: Buying, Having, and Being*, 7th ed. (Upper Saddle River, NJ, 2007), 51–55.
17. All of these dimensions are discussed in Cheryl Krasnick Warsh and Dan Malleck, eds., *Consuming Modernity: Gendered Behavior and Consumerism before the Baby Boom* (Vancouver, 2013), albeit without a particular emphasis on color and the visual culture of modernity.
18. For a striking example, see C. Anne Wilson, "Ritual, Form and Colour in Mediaeval Food Tradition," in *The Appetite and the Eye: Visual Aspects of Food*

and Its Presentation Within Their Historic Context, ed. C. Anne Wilson (Edinburgh, 1991), 5–27.
19. Gary S. Cross and Robert N. Proctor, *Packaged Pleasures: How Technology and Marketing Revolutionized Desire* (Chicago, IL, 2014), 67.
20. Roland Marchand, *Advertising the American Dream: Making Way for Modernity, 1920–1940* (Berkeley, CA, 1985); Neil Harris, *Cultural Excursions: Marketing Appetites and Cultural Tastes in Modern America* (Chicago, IL, 1990).
21. Jenna Weissman Joselit, *A Perfect Fit: Clothes, Character, and the Promise of America* (New York, 2001), esp. 92–94 and 152.
22. References to color are often made in more popular books; see, for instance, Elizabeth Ewing, *History of Twentieth Century Fashion* (Totowa, NJ, 1986); Elizabeth Ewing, *Everyday Dress, 1650–1900* (New York, 1989); James Laver, *Costumes and Fashion: A Concise History*, 4th ed. (London, 2002).
23. Laura Kalba, "How Media Were Made: Chromolithography in Belle Époque France," *History and Technology* 27, no. 4 (December 2011): 441–53; Laura Kalba, "Blue Roses and Yellow Violets: Flowers and the Cultivation of Color in Nineteenth-Century France," *Representations* 120, no. 1 (Fall 2012): 83–114; and Laura Kalba, "Fireworks and Other Profane Illuminations: Color and the Experience of Wonder in Modern Visual Culture," *Modernism/Modernity* 19, no. 4 (November 2012): 657–76.
24. Regina Lee Blaszczyk, ed., "Colour and Design," special issue of the *Journal of Design History* 27, no. 3 (September 2014), 203–308.
25. We are interested in the role of color in the modern world of man-made goods, architecture, and spaces. Our work generally does not extend to the topic of skin color, race, racial classifications, or racism. This important subject has been studied by several generations of distinguished historians. See, for example, Winthrop D. Jordan, *White Over Black: American Attitudes Toward the Negro, 1550–1812* (Chapel Hill, NC, 1968), and Mia Bay, *The White Image in the Black Mind: African-American Ideas about White People, 1830–1925* (New York, 2000).
26. Regina Lee Blaszczyk, "Rethinking Fashion," in *Producing Fashion: Commerce, Culture, and Consumers*, ed. Regina Lee Blaszczyk (Philadelphia, PA, 2008), 2.
27. Sally-Anne Huxtable, "White Walls, White Nights, White Girls: Whiteness in the British Artistic Interior, 1850–1900," *Journal of Design History* 27, no. 3 (September 2014): 237–55.
28. "Vision of City Dwellers," *Washington Post*, June 1, 1902.
29. "Home Studies in Color: Economic Methods of Floor Decoration," *New York Times*, May 8, 1881.
30. "The Rising Tide of Color," *Christian Science Monitor*, May 22, 1928.
31. "Die blaue Farbe der reifen Wacholderbeeren," *Prometheus* 11 (1900): 303.
32. Michael Kriegeskorte, *100 Jahre Werbung im Wandel: Eine Reise durch die deutsche Vergangenheit* (Cologne, 1995), 32–41.
33. Uwe Spiekermann, "Display Windows and Window Displays in German Cities of the Nineteenth Century: Towards the History of a Commercial Breakthrough," in *Advertising and the European City: Historical Perspectives*, ed. Clemens Wischermann and Elliot Shore (Aldershot, 2000), 160–64.
34. Dirk Reinhardt, *Von der Reklame zum Marketing: Geschichte der Wirtschaftswerbung in Deutschland* (Berlin, 1993), 87–99.

35. Armand V. Cardello, "The Role of Human Senses in Food Acceptance," in *Food Choice, Acceptance and Consumption*, ed. H. L. Meiselman and H. J. H. Macfie (London, 1996), 11.
36. "Welche Farbe und welchen Geschmack muß echter Bienenhonig haben?," *Frauengenossenschaftsblatt* 3 (1904): 136.
37. James J. Nagle, "News of the Advertising and Marketing Fields," *New York Times*, August 23, 1953.
38. Jan Whitaker, *Service and Style: How the American Department Store Fashioned the Middle Class* (New York, 2006). This study, too, includes plenty of information on color but does not explicitly discuss the subject.
39. "Modern Color and Old Furniture," *Christian Science Monitor*, October 3, 1919.
40. "Introducing More Color into the Home," *Christian Science Monitor*, September 21, 1923.
41. "Das wohnliche Heim," *Hamburger Anzeiger*, June 5, 1929, suppl. 1, 3.
42. There was, of course, a long prehistory; see Annelie Ramsbrock, *The Science of Beauty: Culture and Cosmetics in Modern Germany, 1750–1930* (New York, 2015).
43. Quoted in Myra Nye, "Four Necktie Changes Daily," *Los Angeles Times*, March 29, 1921. Orcella Rexford (1887–1946) was a professional lecturer on spiritual topics related to the Bahá'í faith; see "Orcella Rexford" at *Bahá'í Chronicles: A Journey to the Past and Present*, http://bahaichronicles.org/orcella-rexford/. Her oeuvre included two self-published booklets, *The Joy and Symbolism of Color* and *The Psychology of Color: Its Effects upon Health, Happiness and Finances*, both from 1925.
44. "When the College Girl Shops for Color," *Christian Science Monitor*, May 29, 1929.
45. Blaszczyk, *Color Revolution*, 141.
46. Gary Cross, *An All-Consuming Century: Why Commercialism Won in Modern America* (New York, 2000), 41.
47. "Der Verkäufer als Erzieher," *Berliner Volks-Zeitung*, December 7, 1913, suppl. 5, 1.
48. "In the Shops," *New York Times*, September 16, 1902.
49. Helen Barton Friez, "Influence of Color in Rooms Given a High Estimate," *Washington Post*, March 31, 1924.
50. "Color Standards Praised by Reyburn," *New York Times*, February 27, 1926. For a history of the Textile Color Card Association and the many varieties of color experts in early-twentieth century America, see Blaszczyk, *Color Revolution*.
51. "Colors of Paris Shops," *Washington Post*, January 29, 1888.
52. "The Stones of Paris," *The Independent*, September 21, 2007.
53. "The Influence of Color," *Chicago Daily Tribune*, July 14, 1889.
54. Blaszczyk, *Color Revolution*; "Plaids to Follow Persians," *Christian Science Monitor*, July 15, 1914.
55. Cynthia Amnéus, *A Separate Sphere: Dressmaking in Cincinnati's Golden Age, 1877–1922* (Cincinnati, 2003), 85–77.
56. Harold Morré, "Amerikanische Reklame," *Berliner Volkszeitung*, October 18, 1907.
57. Blaszczyk, *Color Revolution*; Regina Lee Blaszczyk, "The Rise of Color Forecasting in the United States and Great Britain," in *The Fashion Forecasters*.

58. Best known are the "scientific management" experts. See Robert Kanigel, *The One Best Way: Frederick Winslow Taylor and the Enigma of Efficiency* (New York, 1999). The early reception of American marketing in Germany is discussed in Uwe Spiekermann, "'Der Verbraucher muss erobert werden!' Marketing in Landwirtschaft und Einzelhandel in Deutschland in den 1920er und 1930er Jahren," in *Marketinggeschichte: Die Genese einer modernen Sozialtechnik,* ed. Hartmut Berghoff (Frankfurt am Main, 2007) 123–47. For the United States, see Pamela Walker Laird, "The Business of Consumer Culture History: Systems, Interactions and Modernization," in *Decoding Modern Consumer Societies,* ed. Hartmut Berghoff and Uwe Spiekermann (New York, 2012), 89–109.
59. Wilhelm Ostwald developed a color system that rivaled the Munsell Color System in Germany in 1914. See Wilhelm Ostwald, *Die Farbenfibel* (Leipzig, 1917) and Albrecht Pohlmann, "Von der Wissenschaft und zurück: Farbenlehre und Ästhetik bei Wilhelm Ostwald (1853–1932)," (PhD diss., Martin Luther University of Halle-Wittenberg, 2012), http://digital.bibliothek.uni-halle.de/hs/urn/urn:nbn:de:gbv:3:4–8878.
60. Albert H. Munsell, *A Color Notation* (Boston, MA, 1905); Blaszczyk, *Color Revolution*, 45–70.
61. Blaszczyk, *Color Revolution*; "Ideas Expressed in the Colors Used," *New York Times,* March 2, 1922; "Visibility Tests for' 25 Auto Plate," *New York Times,* February 3, 1924; "Acclaims New Mode at Shoe Conference," *New York Times,* October 16, 1929; Frances Mangum, "Color Choice Has Important Beauty Effect," *Washington Post,* October 5, 1934; Alfred E. Clark, "Louis Cheskin, 72; Studied Motivation And Effects of Color," *New York Times,* October 10, 1981.
62. Alys Eve Weinbaum et al., *The Modern Girl around the World: Consumption, Modernity, and Globalization* (Durham, NC, 2008); Regina Lee Blaszczyk, *American Consumer Society, 1865–2005: From Hearth to HDTV* (Hoboken, NJ, 2009).
63. Quotations: David M. Potter, *People of Plenty: Economic Abundance and the American Character* (Chicago, IL, 1954); and Olivier Zunz, *Why the American Century?* (Chicago, IL, 1998), 92.
64. Nonetheless, the United States was not exceptional. See Thomas Bender, *A Nation among Nations: America's Place in World History* (New York, 2006). Merritt Ierley, *The Comforts of Home: The American House and the Evolution of Modern Convenience* (New York, 1999), discusses the American model, but does not explicitly focus on color.
65. Friez, "Influence of Color."
66. Global markets have colors, although books such as Alexander Nützenadel and Frank Trentmann, eds., *Food and Globalization: Consumption, Markets and Politics in the Modern World* (Oxford, UK, 2008), do not discuss this topic.
67. Blaszczyk, *Color Revolution*; "How Color Revolutionized Our World: An Interview with Regina Lee Blaszczyk," parts 1–4, Munsell Color Blog, April–July, 2015, http://munsell.com/color-blog/author/regina-lee-blaszczyk/.
68. Beer, *Emergence of the German Dye Industry.*
69. Jo B. Paoletti, *Pink and Blue: Telling the Boys from the Girls in America* (Bloomington, IN, 2013).

70. Thomas Lawrence, *Sarah Barrett Moulton: Pinkie*, oil on canvas, 1794; and Thomas Gainsborough, *The Blue Boy*, oil on canvas, 1770—both at The Huntington, San Marino, CA, http://huntington.org.
71. For frivolity and shopping in the British context, see Erika Rappaport, *Shopping for Pleasure: Women in the Making of London's West End* (Princeton, NJ, 2000). This was also a theme in Émile Zola's 1883 novel about a Parisian department store, *Au Bonheur des Dames (The Ladies' Delight)*, trans. and ed. Robin Buss (London, 2001).
72. Blaszczyk, *Color Revolution*, 115, 121–26. For her earlier research on the Duco Color Advisory Service, see Regina Lee Blaszczyk, "The Importance of Being True Blue: The DuPont Company and the Color Revolution," in *Cultures of Commerce: Representation and American Business Culture, 1877–1960*, ed. Elspeth H. Brown et al. (New York, 2006), 27–50, and Regina Lee Blaszczyk, "True Blue: DuPont and the Color Revolution," *Chemical Heritage* 25, no. 3 (Fall 2007): 20–25, https://www.chemheritage.org/distillations/article/true-blue-dupont-and-color-revolution.
73. Warren I. Susman, *Culture as History: The Transformation of American Society in the Twentieth Century* (New York, 1984).
74. Blaszczyk, *Color Revolution*, 190–240.
75. *The Devil Wears Prada*, DVD, directed by David Frankl (Los Angeles: Twentieth Century Fox, 2006); Regina Lee Blaszczyk, "The Color of Fashion," *Humanities* 29, no. 2 (March/April 2008), http://www.neh.gov/humanities/2008/march april/feature/the-color-fashion.
76. Blaszczyk, "The Color of Fashion."
77. Ibid.
78. Blaszczyk, *Color Revolution*, 26.
79. Alison Matthews David, *Fashion Victims: The Dangers of Dress Past and Present* (London, 2015).
80. Kenneth Lipartito, "Subliminal Seduction: The Politics of Consumer Research in Post–World War II America," in *The Rise of Marketing and Market Research*, ed. Hartmut Berghoff, Philip Scranton, and Uwe Spiekermann (New York, 2012), 215–36.
81. Anthony S. Travis, *The Rainbow Makers: The Origins of the Synthetic Dyestuffs Industry in Western Europe* (Bethlehem, PA, 1993); Kathryn Steen, *The American Synthetic Organic Chemicals Industry: War and Politics, 1910–1930* (Chapel Hill, NC, 2014).
82. John Robert McNeill, *Something New under the Sun: An Environmental History of the Twentieth-Century World* (New York, 2000), 118–48; Arne Andersen, "Pollution and the Chemical Industry: The Case of the German Dye Industry," in *The Chemical Industry in Europe, 1850–1914: Industrial Growth, Pollution, and Professionalization*, ed. Ernst Homburg, Anthony S. Travis, and Harm G. Schröter (Dordrecht, 1998), 183–201.
83. Marc Cioc, "The Rhine as a World River," in *The Environment and World History*, ed. Edmund Burke III and Kenneth Pomeranz (Berkeley, CA, 2009), 165–90.
84. Thomas Rommelspacher, "Das natürliche Recht auf Wasserverschmutzung. Geschichte des Wassers im 19. und 20. Jahrhundert," in *Besiegte Natur: Geschichte der Umwelt im 19. und 20. Jahrhundert*, ed. Franz-Josef Brüggemeier and Thomas Rommelspacher (Munich, 1987), 42–63.

85. Jürgen Büschenfeld, *Flüsse und Kloaken: Umweltfragen im Zeitalter der Industrialisierung (1870–1918)* (Stuttgart, 1997); Friedemann Schmoll, *Erinnerung an die Natur: Die Geschichte des Naturschutzes im deutschen Kaiserreich* (Frankfurt am Main, 2004).
86. Eberhard Schmauderer, "Wandlungen in der Lebensmittelbeurteilung im 19. Jahrhundert. Modellbetrachtung am Beispiel der künstlichen Färbung," *Technikgeschichte* 41 (1974): 201–26.
87. Bernhard Wurzschmitt, "Lebensmittelfärbung—Ein Problem der Lebensmittelindustrie," *Zeitschrift für Lebensmitteluntersuchung und -Forschung* 89 (1949), suppl., 145–55, here 148; "Gesetz, betreffend die Verwendung gesundheitsschädlicher Farben bei der Herstellung von Nahrungsmitteln, Genußmitteln und Gebrauchsgegenständen. Vom 5. Juli 1887," in *Reichs-Gesetzblatt 1887* (Berlin), 277–80. The United States saw similar discussions, especially on the use of arsenic; see, for example, "Protection for Consumers," *New York Times*, December 16, 1884.
88. Uwe Spiekermann, "Die Normalität des (Lebensmittel-)Skandals. Risikowahrnehmungen und Handlungsfolgen im 20. Jahrhundert," *Hauswirtschaft und Wissenschaft* 52 (2004): 61–63. At that time, it was still common to use copper bowls for the preservation of vegetables. Housewives added vinegar to obtain an appealing green result.
89. Theodor Weyl, "Zur Revision des Reichgesetzes betr. die gesundheitsschädlichen Farben," *Deutsche Nahrungsmittel-Rundschau* 9 (1911): 92–94, 101–103.
90. Adolf Beythien, "Über das Färben von Lebensmitteln," *Zeitschrift für die Untersuchung der Lebensmittel* 70 (1940): 13–18; A. Wingler, "Über Farbstoffe von Lebensmitteln: Zur Frage der Krebsgefährdung," *Zeitschrift für Krebsforschung* 59 (1953): 134–55.
91. Uwe Spiekermann, "Redefining Food: The Standardization of Products and Production in Europe and the United States, 1880–1914," *History and Technology* 27, no. 1 (2011): 19–23.
92. Adam Burrows, "Palette of Our Palates: A Brief History of Food Coloring and Its Regulation," *Comprehensive Reviews in Food Science and Food Safety* 8, no. 4 (October 2009): 398–99.
93. Julius Hortvet, "Restrictions of Artificial Color in the Preparation of Food Products with Specific Recommendations," *American Food Journal* 2, no. 8 (1907): 40.
94. Edgar H. S. Bailey, "The Importance of Prohibiting the Use of Artificial Coloring Where It Is Used for the Purpose of Deception," *American Food Journal* 2, no. 8 (1907): 42.
95. Regina Lee Blaszczyk, "Chromophilia: The Design World's Passion for Colour," *Journal of Design History* 27, no. 3 (September 2014): 203–17.
96. See Uwe Spiekermann, conference report, "Bright Modernity: Color, Commerce, and Consumption in Global Perspective," German Historical Institute, Washington, DC, June 21–23, 2012, in *Bulletin of the German Historical Institute* 52 (Spring 2013): 141–47, http://www.ghi-dc.org/fileadmin/user_upload/GHI_Washington/Publications/Bulletin52/bu52_141.pdf.

PART I

Foundations: Industry and Education

CHAPTER 2

Coloring the World: Marketing German Dyestuffs in the Late Nineteenth and Early Twentieth Centuries

Alexander Engel

In the late nineteenth and early twentieth centuries, the dye business underwent a fundamental transformation.[1] The traditional natural dyestuffs procured from agriculture and foresting had been increasingly displaced by industrially produced artificial dyestuffs since the 1860s. These so-called coal tar dyes provided the starting point for the rise of the modern chemical industry. And although the new industry had its origins in France and Britain, newly emerging German chemical companies took the lead in the 1870s and 1880s and ended up, by 1913, controlling three-quarters of the world market for artificial dyes, equivalent to about two-thirds of the world market for all dyes (natural and industrial combined).[2] From this position of strength, the German dye companies diversified, becoming dominant global players in the pharmaceutical and fertilizer industries and also contributing massively to Germany's military power in the two world wars by fabricating explosives and chemical weapons. As this chapter sets out to show, the success of the German dye industry was to a considerable degree connected to the ways in which the companies marketed their products to textile manufacturers.

Other studies have attributed the success of the German dye industry mainly to its chemists, who are said to have profited from superior university educations, organization into research and development (R&D) laboratories, and an advantageous patent law context, all of which meant—in this narrative—they could create dyes more inexpensively and undercut the prices of both natural dyes and

A. Engel (✉)
Institute for Economic and Social History, University of Göttingen,
Göttingen, Germany

R.L. Blaszczyk, U. Spiekermann (eds.), *Bright Modernity*, Worlds of Consumption, DOI 10.1007/978-3-319-50745-3_2

their competitors' artificial dyes.[3] In fact, the success story of the German industry could not have occurred without these innovations, but they comprise only half the story. It will be shown that artificial dyes in the aggregate did not have a noticeable price advantage over the bulk of natural dyes, and it becomes evident that early artificial dye producers aimed at specific high-end markets. The later ousting of natural dyes came by conquering the mass market, which required adaptation to a completely different business context. Consequently, this chapter studies and weighs the marketing efforts of the German dye manufacturers. It provides an overview of the transformation of the dye markets and characterizes different stages of that process. Then it describes the structure and peculiarities of the German dye industry. Finally, it relates German marketing efforts to an overall interpretation of the shift from natural to artificial dyes.

Marketing, here, denotes the attempts of a company to bring its supply and customer demand into alignment. These efforts may include (1) the establishment of a suitable distribution system in order to reach customers and communicate with them, thus linking supply and demand; (2) the adaptation of one's product range to meet better the perceived wants of one's customers, thereby making supply fit demand; and (3) efforts to influence customers and reconfigure their preferences toward one's own products, making demand match supply. In the case of the industrial dye producers of the late nineteenth and early twentieth centuries, these efforts were for the most part activities known in today's marketing theory as business-to-business marketing, as opposed to business-to-consumer marketing. Consumers were targeted only indirectly by the marketing endeavors of the chemical companies, as they usually bought cloth or, increasingly, ready-made clothing that had already been dyed.[4] Hence, the dye producers sold their products mostly to professional dyers or textile manufactures with dye houses.

The central thesis of this chapter is that winning over this business of dyeing for industrially produced dyestuffs was a three-stage process. First, the highly expensive new dyes succeeded in the high-end segment of fashionable silk dyeing. Second, scaling up production and bringing down manufacturing costs, as well as producing an ever-wider range of dyes, enabled the dye industry to penetrate the mass market of ordinary cotton dyeing. Finally, the mass-market cotton segment was won over by companies' providing extensive services to dyers, thus binding them to the dyes of a single firm. Whereas British and French companies enjoyed success in the first stage, and for good reasons, German companies were better equipped to succeed in the specific circumstances of the second stage and nearly monopolize the business for good in the third stage.

The Transformation of the Dye Markets

The rise of industrial dyes is often traced backed to the accidental discovery of aniline purple—also known as "mauveine"—in 1856 by the budding English chemist William Henry Perkin, but this development has to be put in a wider context.[5] Beginning in the late eighteenth century, natural dyes were no longer seen as holistic, unalterable gifts of divine creation but as substances that could be manipulated by human efforts.[6] The same was true not only for dyes but also for foodstuffs and raw materials in general.[7] Blurring boundaries between the "natural" and the "artificial," purified dyes, extracts, blends, and preparations became more important. Some "wholly artificial" colorants were even created before Perkin's discovery, notably in the 1840s and 1850s.[8]

Next to the production of dyes and their consumption in the dye houses, a third technological sphere emerged. A new group of specialists took over the refinement and processing of natural dyestuffs.[9] Some of these specialists started out as chemists or druggists who experimented with natural dyestuffs in order either to deconstruct them to find the "true coloring matter" (that is, to remove impurities and "foreign matter") or even to alter their properties by transforming them chemically. If promising results could be repeated on a commercial scale, the experiment could be turned into a business. The majority of those specialists, however, were retailers with experience in the dyestuffs trade, who had to repack larger consignments of dyes bought from wholesalers before selling them on to dyers. By further processing them for the dyers' use, whether by grinding dyewoods, for example, or by purifying and even blending dyestuffs, they could easily add value to their merchandise.

When it became obvious that a whole range of different aniline dyes could be generated along the lines used by Perkin to produce aniline purple, many of the new dye processor-traders engaged in this aspect of the business too, integrating it into their other activities.[10] The successful Swiss company J. R. Geigy of Basel, Switzerland, for instance, started as a natural dyes supplier, but then incorporated a dyewood mill, an extraction plant, and finally a factory for making coal tar dyes.[11] Prominent German chemical companies like Friedr. Bayer & Co. of Elberfeld and Farbwerke Meister, Lucius & Brüning of Höchst (near Frankfurt, whereby the company came to be known simply as Hoechst) were co-founded by merchants originally trading in natural dyes.[12]

The aniline dyes of the late 1850s and the 1860s were extremely costly and usually employed in the dyeing of luxury silks, for which new fashionable colors and startling shades were worth almost any price.[13] Compared to cotton—the basic fiber from which most textiles were made at the time—silk occupied a niche in the textile markets, but it was a niche for the well off. In 1860, a pound of raw silk cost about thirty shillings in the London wholesale markets, a pound of cotton only about half a shilling.[14] In the same year, the British textile industry processed about 450,000 metric tons of cotton, but only 4,200 metric tons of silk.[15] The early market leaders in aniline dye production were British and French firms, which were well connected to the European centers of silk dyeing in Mulhouse, Lyon, and Manchester and their accumulated expertise in high-end dyes and dyeing.

The character and fate of the dyeing industry changed in the late 1860s, when both Perkin and the two German chemists Carl Graebe and Carl Liebermann independently discovered a way to synthesize alizarin, the main dyeing compound of madder, the most important dyestuff to give cotton cloth a fast red.[16] Graebe and Liebermann, who were affiliated with the Königliche Gewerbe-Akademie (Royal College for Vocational Studies) in Berlin, cooperated with Heinrich Caro of the Badische Anilin- und Sodafabrik (Baden Aniline and Soda Factory, or BASF) in Mannheim and Ludwigshafen to develop a procedure to produce the dye on an industrial scale.[17] Perkin worked it out on his own; both of the competing parties finished in 1869. In this instance, artificial dye on an industrial scale indeed had a notable cost advantage over its natural counterpart, so much so that madder red was ousted from the markets within a few years. The well-organized and well-connected BASF, along with some German competitors, was notably more successful in grabbing market shares than Perkin's comparatively humble dye plant in Greenford Green, just northwest of London. Perkin finally gave up and sold his firm, G. F. Perkin and Sons, in 1874.[18]

The alizarin innovation marked the entrance of the synthetic dye industry into the mass market of cotton textile production. This step promised turnover on a far greater scale, but it necessitated acquiring a new customer base, that is, connecting to "ordinary" dye houses instead of exclusive silk dyers. The requirements of these new customers were different. In particular, cost efficiency became a more significant factor. This was especially true for the low-cost segment of the market for natural dyes, a segment made up primarily of dyewoods and carriers of tannic acid for dyeing black. In Germany in the early 1870s, these low-cost dyes had a market share of 30 percent in terms of value but 75 percent in terms of the sheer quantity of textiles dyed with them.[19] Prime natural dyes like indigo, cochineal, and madder—the last one rapidly vanishing from the markets—together possessed a market share of up to 50 percent, but these dyes were used on not much more than a tenth of all textiles. The remaining market share of 20 percent by value fell to the coal tar dyes, in large part to alizarin (see Figs. 2.1 and 2.2).

As one would expect, BASF aimed to repeat its success to replace madder with alizarin by focusing on the most important remaining prime dye, indigo. The synthesis of indigo in laboratory conditions succeeded in the late 1870s, but it took years of research into neighboring fields as well as enormous investments to come up with a way to synthesize indigo on a commercial scale profitably.[20] "BASF indigo pure" did not launch until 1897 and—unlike alizarin—did not have a significant price advantage over its natural competitor. Yet it ousted this competitor equally quickly from the markets.

The delays in the indigo project notwithstanding, industrial dye producers targeted the prime segment of the natural dyes from the 1870s to the 1890s. Only from the late 1880s or even the early 1890s did the industry make inroads

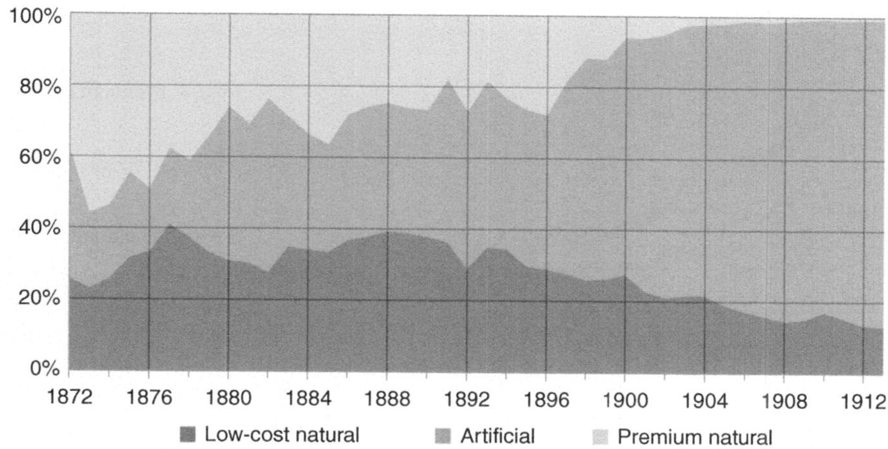

Fig. 2.1 Market shares of dyes in Germany in terms of their monetary value, ca. 1872–1912

Source: Alexander Engel, *Farben der Globalisierung: Die Entstehung moderner Märkte für Farbstoffe 1500–1900* (Frankfurt, 2009), 152–56, 190–91.

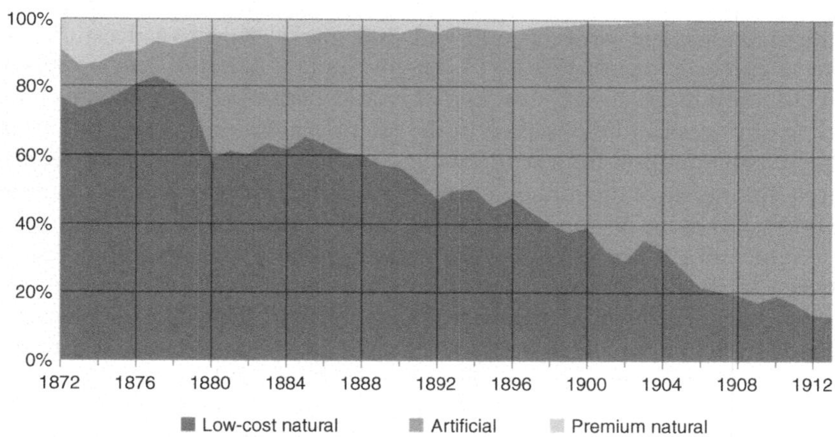

Fig. 2.2 Market shares of dyes in Germany in terms of the quantity of textiles dyed, ca. 1872–1912

Source: Engel, *Farben der Globalisierung*, 152–62, 190–91.

into the low-cost segment of the German market as well. The transformation of international markets was a longer process that depended on how effectively the German firms penetrated them.

In the late nineteenth and early twentieth centuries, dyeing a metric ton of textiles in a customary, middling shade with a prime natural dye

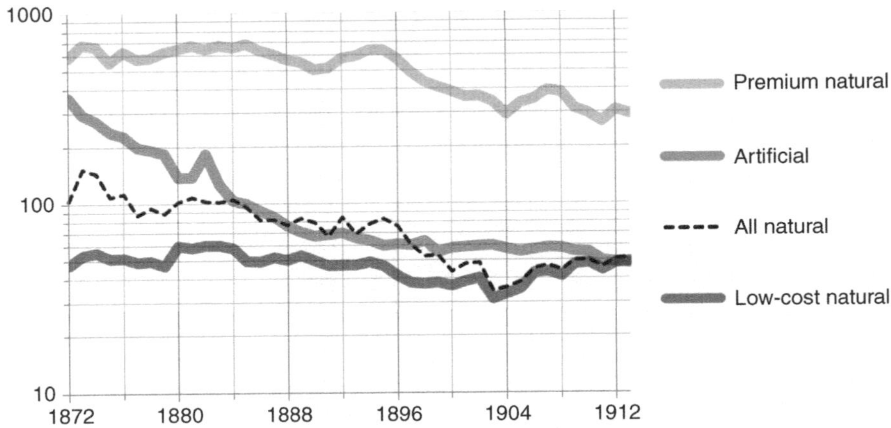

Fig. 2.3 Average cost of dyestuffs to color a metric ton of textiles in Germany, ca. 1872–1912 (marks, logarithmic scale)

Source: Engel, *Farben der Globalisierung*, 193–98.

required on average between 600 and 700 marks' worth of dyestuffs—for some dyes more, for others less.[21] Low-cost natural dyestuffs cost on average only 30 to 60 marks for a metric ton of textiles. For both segments, a certain decline of prices can be observed in the later decades, most likely due to the increased competition from artificial dyes (see Fig. 2.3). The general decrease in freight rates since the middle of the century did not play into this because, in contrast to grain or iron, all dyestuffs had a comparatively very high value-to-weight ratio. All in all, prices for natural dyestuffs remained fairly stable between 1870 and 1914 (as did the general level of prices at the time, so there was hardly inflation or deflation to account for). The cost of procuring artificial dyes, on the other hand, fell heavily, from on average 300 to 400 marks for a metric ton of textiles in the early 1870s (and far more exorbitant prices back in the 1860s) to around 50 marks on the eve of World War I. All the figures cited in this paragraph obviously combine cheaper and more expensive dyes within each of the three groups (low-cost natural dyes, prime natural dyes, artificial dyes), especially in the case of artificial products. Still, it is clear that in the aggregate artificial dyes began to compete against prime natural dyes in the early 1870s—or even the late 1860s—and only gradually turned to target the low-cost segment, albeit without undercutting it.

In their conquest of the low-cost market segment, the German dye firms only synthesized two of the roughly twenty commercially viable natural dyes, madder's alizarin and indigo's indigotine. The chemical synthesis of madder marked the entry of artificial dyes into the prime segment of the mass market, and the synthesis of indigo the virtual elimination of natural dyes from that segment. For the most part, however, artificial dyes rose to dominance not by replicating the chemical substances of natural dyes but by offering new substances (even though some of them derived from alizarin, and later also indigotine). At the same time, few of these new dyes could claim a notable market share in the way even minor natural dyestuffs had; instead, an extraordinary number of dyes and colors emerged. Before 1870, fewer than fifty dyes were known in the market; by 1913, there were around 1,300—marketed in close to 9,000 major varieties (see Fig. 2.4).

In the late 1870s, the annual number of new dyes began to rise steeply. This trend continued until the early 1890s, when the pace of innovation slowed down, ultimately coming more or less to a standstill with World War I. (The peak around 1910 was a one-off, marking a single new family of extremely colorfast, prime quality dyes derived from indigotine, so-called indanthrene dyes.) The period of accelerating innovation corresponded with the process of ousting the prime natural dyes and bringing prices down to the level of the low-cost segment. Around 1900, the market positions that could be achieved had been more or less achieved, which is evident from the fact that the main German firms started to cartelize the dye business and began to diversify more decidedly into pharmaceuticals, agrochemicals, explosives, and other neighboring fields.[22] An all-out fight against the remaining low-cost natural dyes did not promise substantial additional profits, so research capabilities were redirected to these newer fields. Nevertheless, even with the much slower pace of dyestuff innovation, the chemical companies still gained further advantage over the producers of natural dyes.

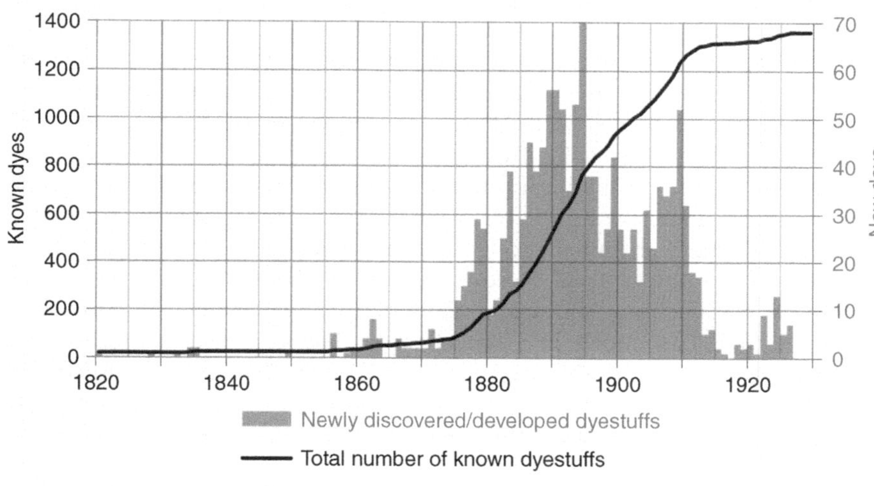

Fig. 2.4 Growth in the number of dyestuffs, 1820–1930

Source: Calculated on the basis of the extensive dye catalogue by Gustav Schultz, *Farbstofftabellen*, 7th ed. (Leipzig, 1931).

The German Dye Industry

The structure of the artificial dye industry differed notably from the structure of the natural dye business. The production of natural dyestuffs was accomplished by a multitude of mostly small-scale producers who specialized in a single dyestuff: Indian indigo planters, Central American dyewood cutters, Mexican and Canarian cochineal raisers, Dutch and French madder farmers, and so on.[23] They were connected to the dyers, mainly European, by chains of independent merchants.[24] Wholesale merchants bought the foreign dyestuffs overseas, often after local traders had collected the output of several producers. In the target markets, retailers combined different dyestuffs into an assortment, or they bought from middlemen who did so. A dye house usually worked with more than one vendor to procure its materials. Obtaining suitable dyestuffs required a good deal of effort, proficiency, and foresight. With the quality and prices of natural dyes fluctuating and the complex stream of goods always shifting within flexible and changing webs of intermediaries, no steady supply of dyeing materials with stable, predictable characteristics by a single vendor could be expected.

The producers of natural dyes had no choice but to confine themselves to just one kind of dyestuff. There were apparently no gains to be had from combining very different production methods (agriculture, forestry, or even insect cultivation in the case of cochineal). Moreover, natural dyestuffs were tied to different, usually non-overlapping geographical spaces. The number of dyestuffs offered by nature that could be utilized commercially was limited, and their modes of production were well established. Less than a handful of new dyes entered the scene over the course of decades and centuries, and it was reasonable to expect a steady demand for an established dye over the long term.[25] In other words, forced specialization and lack of product and process innovation initially meant no great risk for the producer, as he had good reason to believe he would find a market for his product in the future as well. This was only true, of course, until the competition from industrially produced dyes emerged.

Quite the opposite of all this was true for the early producers of coal tar dyes. The family of aniline dyes grew relatively quickly, and fashionable new ones often turned out high initial profits, only to quickly lose their significance. Focusing on just one artificial dyestuff was not a viable strategy, as the case of the Société La Fuchsine showed, a monopolistic joint-stock company with enormous capital, founded in Lyon, France. The epic failure of this firm seriously impeded the development of the French coal tar dye industry.[26] Producing different aniline dyes promised economies of scope and mitigated the risk of changing demand, thus making variety the first prerequisite to staying in the market.

Second, it was important to keep pace with dyestuffs innovations, which could be accomplished either by copying successful new dyes and producing them more efficiently, especially in markets like Germany, which had no effective patent system at the time (this also became a primary Swiss strategy until 1904), or better still by developing new dyes oneself, especially in markets with patent protection such as Great Britain.[27] Whether one turned to imitation and process innovation or preferred product innovation, a combination of technological and chemical expertise was prerequisite to success. Indeed, it can be argued that the ability of German universities to generate a mounting torrent of well-educated young chemists and engineers was a precondition for the success of the growing German dye industry, which employed these new experts in a variety of functions, above all as works managers.[28]

A third requirement for a firm to survive came with the synthesis of alizarin, when artificial dye makers began to enter the market segment held by the prime natural dyes. The demand for alizarin was far larger than for any industrially produced dye to that point and prompted the dyestuffs industry's fast growth. Potential economies of scale came into play, opportunities that could be tapped by process innovation—a specialty of the German firms and one that even found its way into the German patent law of 1877, which in the case of chemicals, protected production processes, not products. Consequently, the pursuit of economies of scale in the European dyestuffs industry translated into the growth of a few German firms, not growth in the total number of firms.

A distinct process of concentration emerged and continued into the early twentieth century. In 1882, there were twenty main German companies producing coal tar dyes, employing on average about 150 people.[29] Seventy-five percent of all employees worked for the four largest companies with more than 200 employees (on average about 750 in those four). In 1907, there were sixteen companies left, with an average of 500 workers. Six dye makers had more than 200 workers, and those six combined for around 90 percent of the industry's workforce. Almost all fell to the "big five"—the three giants BASF, Hoechst, and Bayer, as well as Leopold Cassella & Co. (later Cassella Farbwerke Mainkur) of Frankfurt, and the Berlin Aktiengesellschaft für Anilinfabrikation (Joint-Stock Company for Aniline Production, or AGFA). British dyeing companies, on the other hand, did not manage such growth. Even the three most successful Swiss firms, all in Basel—Geigy, Ciba (Gesellschaft für Chemische Industrie Basel), and Sandoz (Chemische Fabrik vormals Sandoz)—were notably smaller than the three German giants.

Entering the mass market in the 1870s and utilizing economies of scale thus proved to be a turning point. It led to the considerable growth of a few market leaders, and then continued growth helped these leaders to maintain their relative market positions. Being a certain size had allowed firms to extend economies of scope further because resources could be set aside to collaborate extensively with academic researchers who helped in product innovation. From the 1880s onwards, the size of such companies allowed them to internalize the generation of innovation by building up their own R&D capacities.[30] In 1912, for instance, BASF employed no less than 463 chemists and engineers (4.7 percent of all employees) while Hoechst employed 381 chemists (4.2 percent of its employees).[31] About half of these chemists and engineers were works managers, a third were employed in laboratories, and a sixth worked in experimental dyeing works and in sales. Indeed, a good portion of the qualified personnel worked in sales—611 (6.8 percent) at Hoechst and 768 (7.8 percent) at BASF.

The strong emphasis on distribution at these two dye makers and by the other major German producers was also something of a German specialty, perhaps attributable to the fact that most successful German (and Swiss) companies were to a considerable degree rooted in the dye trade, whereas earlier British pioneers such as G. F. Perkin and Sons, I. Levinstein and Co. of Manchester, Read Holliday and Sons of Huddersfield, and Simpson, Maule and Nicholson of South London all lacked a mercantile background. For the most part, chemists had founded and led these enterprises.[32] Although the brilliance of those few outstanding chemists undoubtedly gave British companies a boost in the early phase of the new industry, chemical genius proved insufficient for gaining entry to mass markets.

By building one large R&D apparatus to generate dye inventions and develop production processes on a commercial scale and another apparatus to connect to the markets, the big German companies managed to routinize product and process innovation so as to generate a seemingly endless stream of new dyes, mordants, and other textile chemicals. The Germans took upon themselves the imperative of the early dye business—constant product or process innovation to compete in the fickle market for fashionable high-end dyes—and, outpacing and outdistancing their European competitors, applied this strategy to the larger, much more settled mass market dye business. In doing so, they confronted the producers of the well-established handful of commercially viable natural dyes.

The natural dye makers, as sketched at the outset of this section, operated in a completely different, rather static framework and followed a different logic in their business. Dyewood extractors were an exception to a certain extent, but otherwise each of the natural dye producers focused on a single dye and lacked capacities for R&D or marketing, which left them ill-prepared to defend their positions vis-à-vis the aggressive German dye makers. The latter's activities, as has been shown, cannot be attributed solely to the ingenuity of their chemists and engineers, who worked in the laboratory and the manufacturing plant to produce cheaper artificial substitutes and alternatives to natural dyes. For a long time, undercutting the agricultural competitors was possible only for some of the most desirable high-end colors. The chemists and engineers required a long learning curve to achieve price parity, more or less, with the low-cost natural dyes. Instead, the marketing apparatus of the German firms played a decisive role.

Dye Marketing

Whereas traditional dye makers left distribution to independent merchants, those industrial dyestuffs suppliers who achieved enduring success combined production and distribution into a single company. Some started out as dye-trading businesses, as was the case for many of the German and Swiss companies. Others acquired marketing expertise, as BASF did within only a few years of its establishment by merging with two small-scale dye producers and former trading houses that were already handling the distribution of BASF products, that is, performing the functions of a sales department.[33] With extensive distribution networks and the widespread deployment of traveling salesmen, industrial dye makers maintained close contact with their customers, namely, the professional dyers and the dye houses of textile manufacturers. Other than in the case of traditional dye markets, in which producers and consumers were separated by independent intermediaries, there was a strong bidirectional communications link between the dyers and the dye-producing chemical companies.

At first, the important direction of this communication was from the dye producer to the dye works. Natural dyes in their different varieties were well established and known to the dyers, but the new artificial dyes were not. An initial obstacle faced by the producers was the need to convince dyers to try and use a new dye in the first place. Before Perkin started a business to market his aniline purple, he contacted dyers and asked for their opinions about the new dye. In the same fashion, any new aniline dye in the late 1850s and 1860s was first presented to one or a few potential customers in the hope that it might enable them to create a sensational fashion effect that generated attention and demand for that dye.[34] This strategy was no longer feasible in the second stage of the new industry's development, that is, its entry into the mass market. The number of customers was far greater, making it impossible to generate attention for a dye by having just one or two dyers use it. Here it became increasingly important to target all potential customers and induce them to try a new dye. That task would obviously be fulfilled more insistently and efficiently by someone who more or less exclusively presented the dyes of a certain producer than by an independent distributor who hawked them as a minor part of his assortment.

Additional problems arose when dye works actually liked one of the new colorants and decided to use it on a regular basis. In the case of the natural materials, dyers had been forced to test the dyeing products they were about to procure from an independent middleman for purity, quality, and usability. To this end, certain procedures had evolved, including trials of dye samples or by subjecting a sample to a certain treatment, such as burning.[35] For the experienced buyer, much could be determined by the "look and feel" of a lump of indigo or a piece of dyewood. If dyers had to put some effort into testing what they wanted to buy, they were at least able to develop some certainty about what they were getting. Industrially produced coal tar dyes, on the other hand, possessed far fewer reliably consistent identifying characteristics. They came as powders or pastes with arbitrary hues, meaning their outer appearance did not offer any clues as to their usefulness and applicability. None of the traditional testing methods worked, with the exception of treating some cloth with a sample of the new dye. So a dyer might be satisfied with the results of a new coal tar dye, but how could he be sure he was obtaining that same product again, not a fake or a substandard alternative?

If the new dye could be bought directly from the firm or one of its traveling sales representatives, it would obviously heighten the dyer's trust. In addition, the German industrial dye producers strove to develop their products into brands, selling them in sealed tin containers with unique, usually quite elaborate and colorful labels.[36] The chances of succeeding with this branding strategy increased as the dye industry consolidated, leaving just a few well-known companies. Those big companies enjoyed high visibility in the markets, especially when the number of products they offered grew dramatically in the 1880s and 1890s. The plethora of dyes, in turn, made it increasingly interesting and effective for the dye works to deal with the companies' sales representatives.

For one thing, dyers could use the communications link to the producer to give feedback and express their requirements, knowing that the industrial producers could modify and develop their range of products accordingly. By contrast, the producers of natural dyes could not respond to customer needs, never mind that there was no effective communications link to the market. The producers of natural dyes increasingly saw the lack of these feedback loops as a serious drawback. Faced with the competition from BASF's synthetic indigo after 1897, the Indian indigo planters considered levying an export duty on indigo in order to finance a marketing board.[37] One possible activity by the board was be to employ salesmen as reconnaissance agents:

> Our commercial travellers besides pushing our stuff might also act as an intelligence department which is sorely needed. They could keep us informed as to the work being done by the Badische [BASF]. Might possibly tell us what their bottom price was. Whether the report that the Synthetic people were making indigotine at a loss was true or false. They might also advise us as to whether the suggestion, often put forward, that we should sell some of our indigo in powder or paste would really find to increase consumption or not.[38]

Obviously, the producers of natural indigo struggled with basic decisions regarding the enhancement of their product due to a complete lack of knowledge of distant markets.

The chemical companies were much better informed and able to adapt their products, but they too had their limits. While it posed no serious problem to combine different dyestuffs into a blend and to present a dye as powder or paste, chemists were far from able to design dyes with pre-defined processing attributes, color shades, and fastness. Thus, the strategy of the industrial dye makers was unrestrained diversification. Still, before putting a new dye on the market, the chemical companies ascertained its dyeing and fastness characteristics by intensive testing in their trial dyeing factories to see if it would fit the demand as perceived through the eyes of the salesmen. This testing and coordination reduced the likelihood of failing products.

With the assortment offered by the big dye makers growing evermore comprehensive, dyers were increasingly tempted by "one-stop shopping." This approach to sourcing made the procurement of dyeing materials a lot easier, all the more as the homogeneity of artificial dyes and their comparatively stable prices made extensive stock-keeping by the dye works obsolete. Moreover, as the application of industrial dyes yielded predictable, repeatable results, the production processes in the dye works also changed. To start with, the delicate process of adjusting the dye bath in order to cope with the changeable characteristics of natural dyes could now be skipped.[39]

In fact, the industrial dye manufacturers began pushing for a new regime of standardized industrial dyeing in the 1890s. Experimental dye works within these companies put potential new dyes through their paces before they were marketed. The experimental dye works also developed standardized and optimized procedures to apply each new dye. The resulting technical information for viable products was conveyed to business customers via manuals (each covering a distinctive part of the firm's product line), traveling technicians, and even special classes.[40] This effort had a twofold effect. On the one hand, by bundling the dyes with expert knowledge and service, the dye producers made their products not only more attractive to customers but also more specific, meaning satisfied customers could only get them again from the manufacturer in question, not one of its competitors. In this way, growing specificity meant increased customer loyalty. On the other hand, by inducing dyers to subject themselves to external expertise and a regime of standardized, rationalized, or so-called scientific dyeing, which entailed changes both in work processes and equipment, they effectively locked out traditional dyes, unless these were available in a highly processed form with steady and reliable properties, like dyewood extract. In this way, rather than by simple price competition, and in spite of the very much reduced pace of innovating new dyes, the German dye makers were able to slowly but steadily take over the market segment of low-cost natural dyes.

Summary

The transition from a regime of natural dyes to a world of industrially produced artificial dyes in Europe can be divided into three stages. The first stage comprised the long formation process of the new artificial dye industry, which culminated in the 1860s. From the late eighteenth century onward, the rise of modern chemistry went hand in hand with a reinterpretation of natural dyes. Processes of extraction, purification, and even modification led to the rise of a new technological sphere between traditional dye production and dye consumption. From time to time, wholly new coloring substances were discovered, among which the aniline dyes proved most important for the further development of the industry. British and French aniline-producing firms, driven by individual ingenious chemists, made an impact on the high-end market for luxury dyeing in the late 1850s and early 1860s. As the industry in France fell behind, German firms entered the scene—mainly as imitators with a knack for process innovation and a stronger grounding in dye trading.

These characteristics of the German competitors proved beneficial, when in the early 1870s the transition from natural to artificial dyes entered a second stage, in which industrially produced dyes penetrated the mass markets. The commercially successful synthesis of alizarin and the ousting of madder from the markets marked the beginning of this stage. BASF and other German firms capitalized on their facility for scaling up and improving production processes, and they leveraged their distribution experience to reap economies of scale and grow quickly, outdistancing smaller competitors, especially the British ones. Their size also enabled the leading German companies to set aside resources for product innovation, which resulted in a rapidly growing flow of dozens, then hundreds of new coal tar dyes, produced by increasingly better organized and capable R&D apparatuses. Combined with the well cultivated capacity to improve production processes and thus bring down costs considerably, industrial dye producers in Germany and Switzerland were increasingly able to compete against the prime natural dyes, largely ousting them from the market by the early 1890s. This development culminated in the relatively belated synthesis of indigo around 1900 after gigantic efforts and investments.

By then, a third stage had already begun as the pace of product innovation slowed down considerably in the 1890s. The chemical companies' progress into the low-cost segment of the dye market, which had started in the 1880s, was accomplished not so much by price competition as by perfecting marketing machinery that was well integrated with the companies' innovation apparatuses. Extensive networks of sales representatives scouted the markets and explored the demands and needs of the dye works so that the product assortments offered by the dye makers could be developed, adjusted, or tailored to suit the customers. These networks helped to tie customers to a single dye manufacturer because each producer marketed its dyes not as individual products but as parts of a system of dyes. Such a system included the dissemination of optimized application processes, developed by the dye makers' own experimental dye works, which served as a link between innovation and the marketing apparatus. In effect, a regime of scientific dyeing had been imposed, changing routines, processes, and equipment in dye houses in a way that made natural dyes largely unusable, unless they were offered in a standardized, homogenous form such as a highly processed extract.

In the first stage of the transition from natural to artificial dyes, an industry evolved that—owing to its target markets—had to adopt a dynamic approach. One could only survive in the volatile markets for fashionable high-end dyes by constant product innovation or at least process innovation.

Success in the second stage, in the confrontation with the prime natural dyes, came to those who carried that approach most effectively into the mass market, by putting sufficient emphasis on process innovation (in scaling and cheapening production) and on distribution capacities. These requirements favored the German latecomers over the British pioneers because the former frequently had roots in the dye trade and started out as imitators focusing on process innovation, whereas the latter were in most cases founded and led by inventor-chemists, and their strength was in product innovation. Success in the third stage was secured (and this could only be done from an already acquired position of strength) by carrying the principles underlying the innovation and production of artificial dyes—a rational, calculating, standardizing, science-based approach—into the realm of their application, adapting not only supply to demand but also somewhat reorienting demand by creating path dependencies that tied dyers to standardized products and even to the products of a single manufacturer.

Notes

1. This paper is based on Alexander Engel, *Farben der Globalisierung: Die Entstehung moderner Märkte für Farbstoffe 1500–1900* (Frankfurt, 2009). It extends some arguments brought forth in Alexander Engel, "Colouring Markets: The Industrial Transformation of the Dyestuff Business Revisited," *Business History* 54, no. 1 (2012): 10–29. A few considerations are repeated from Alexander Engel, "Selling Indian Indigo in Traditional and Modern European Markets, 1780–1910," in *The Rise of Marketing and Market Research*, ed. Hartmut Berghoff, Philip Scranton, and Uwe Spiekermann (New York, 2012), 27–47.
2. Franz Thissen, *Die Stellung der deutschen Teerfarbenindustrie in der Weltwirtschaft vor, in und nach dem Kriege* (Eupen, 1924), 18.
3. John Joseph Beer, *The Emergence of the German Dye Industry* (Urbana, IL, 1959); Johann Peter Murmann, *Knowledge and Competitive Advantage: The Coevolution of Firms, Technology, and National Institutions* (Cambridge, GB, 2003); Anthony S. Travis, *The Rainbow Makers: The Origins of the Synthetic Dyestuffs Industry in Western Europe* (Bethlehem, PA, 1993).
4. Beverly Lemire, "Developing Consumerism and the Ready-Made Clothing Trade in Britain, 1750–1800," *Textile History* 15, no. 1 (1984): 21–44; Christopher Breward, Edwina Ehrman, and Caroline Evans, eds., *The London Look: Fashion from Street to Catwalk* (New Haven, CT, 2004), 47–68.
5. Anthony S. Travis, "Perkin's Mauve: Ancestor of the Organic Chemical Industry," *Technology and Culture* 31, no. 1 (1990), 51–82; Simon Garfield, *Mauve: How One Man Invented a Colour that Changed the World* (London, 2000).
6. Robert Fox and Agustí Nieto-Galan, eds., *Natural Dyestuffs and Industrial Culture in Europe, 1750–1880* (Canton, MA, 1999); Augustí Nieto-Galan, *Colouring Textiles: A History of Natural Dyestuffs in Industrial Europe* (Dordrecht, 2001); Engel, *Farben der Globalisierung*, 79–95.
7. Jakob Vogel, *Ein schillerndes Kristall: Eine Wissensgeschichte des Salzes zwischen Früher Neuzeit und Moderne* (Cologne, 2008); Alessandro Stanziani,

"Negotiating Innovation in a Market Economy: Foodstuffs and Beverages Adulteration in Nineteenth-Century France," *Enterprise and Society* 8, no. 2 (2007): 375–412; see also Uwe Spiekermann's forthcoming book *Künstliche Kost.*

8. Wilfred V. Farrar, "Synthetic Dyes before 1860," *Endeavour* 33, no. 120 (1974): 149–55.
9. Sarah Lowengard, *The Creation of Color in Eighteenth-Century Europe* (New York, 2006), http://www.gutenberg-e.org/lowengard/index.html; Curt Schuster, *Vom Farbenhandel zur Farbenindustrie: Die erste Fusion der BASF* (Ludwigshafen, 1973).
10. Willem J. Hornix, "From Process to Plant: Innovation in the Early Artificial Dye Industry," *British Journal for the History of Science* 25, no. 1 (1992): 65–90.
11. Alfred Bürgin, *Geschichte des Geigy-Unternehmens 1758–1939* (Basel, 1958).
12. Ernst Bäumler, *Farben, Formeln, Forscher: Hoechst und die industrielle Chemie in Deutschland* (Munich, 1989); Anne Nieberding, *Unternehmenskultur im Kaiserreich: Die Gießerei J. M. Voith und die Farbenfabriken vorm. Friedr. Bayer & Co.* (Munich, 2003).
13. Regina Lee Blaszczyk, *The Color Revolution* (Cambridge, MA, 2012), 22–24; Engel, *Farben der Globalisierung*, 234.
14. Wholesale prices for raw Friuli silk and New Orleans cotton, taken from the *London Mercantile Price Current.*
15. Brian R. Mitchell, *Abstract of British Historical Statistics* (Cambridge, 1962).
16. Anthony S. Travis, "Between Broken Root and Artificial Alizarin: Textile Arts and Manufactures of Madder," *History and Technology* 12, no. 1 (1994): 1–22; Garfield, *Mauve*, 89–99; Elisabeth Vaupel, *Carl Graebe (1841–1927): Leben, Werk und Wirken im Spiegel seines brieflichen Nachlasses* (München, 1987).
17. Carsten Reinhardt and Anthony S. Travis, *Heinrich Caro and the Creation of Modern Chemical Industry* (Dordrecht, 2000).
18. Blaszczyk, *Color Revolution*, 27–28.
19. The concepts and data on which the following considerations are based are discussed more fully in Engel, "Colouring Markets."
20. Arnold Reissert, *Geschichte und Systematik der Indigo-Synthesen: Mit specieller Berücksichtigung der einschlägigen Patentliteratur* (Berlin, 1898); Adolf von Baeyer, "Zur Geschichte der Indigo-Synthese," *Berichte der Deutschen Chemischen Gesellschaft*, special issue (1900): L–LXX; Fritz Jenke, *Die volkswirtschaftliche Bedeutung des künstlichen Indigo* (Karlsruhe, 1909).
21. See again Engel, "Colouring Markets," for details.
22. Werner Abelshauser et al., *German Industry and Global Enterprise: BASF: The History of a Company* (Cambridge, UK, 2004), 127–36.
23. Engel, *Farben der Globalisierung*, 246–67.
24. Ibid., 267–72.
25. Ibid., 61–79.
26. Henk van den Belt, "Why Monopoly Failed: The Rise and Fall of Société La Fuchsine," *British Journal for the History of Science* 25, no. 1 (1992): 45–63.
27. Ludwig F. Haber, *The Chemical Industry 1900–1930: International Growth and Technological Change* (Oxford, 1971), 198–204; Murmann, *Knowledge and Competitive Advantage*, 84–92; Arndt Fleischer, *Patentgesetzgebung und chemisch-pharmazeutische Industrie im deutschen Kaiserreich (1871–1918)* (Stuttgart, 1984).

28. Ernst Homburg, "The Emergence of Research Laboratories in the Dyestuff Industry, 1870–1900," *British Journal for the History of Science* 25, no. 1 (1992): 91–111; Murmann, *Knowledge and Competitive Advantage*, 51–60.
29. Data in this paragraph stems from Fritz Redlich, *Die volkswirtschaftliche Bedeutung der deutschen Teerfarbenindustrie* (Munich, 1914), 16.
30. Homburg, "Research Laboratories"; Georg Meyer-Thurow, "The Industrialization of Invention: A Case Study from the German Chemical Industry," *Isis* 73, no. 3 (1982): 363–81.
31. Redlich, *Teerfarbenindustrie*, 60.
32. Maurice Rayner Fox, *Dye-Makers of Great Britain 1856–1976: A History of Chemists, Companies, Products and Changes* (Manchester, UK, 1987).
33. Abelshauser et al., *BASF*, 31–36.
34. Blaszczyk, *Color Revolution*, 25.
35. Engel, *Farben der Globalisierung*, 302–7.
36. Ibid., 312–16.
37. Engel, "Selling Indian Indigo," 39–41.
38. British Library, India Office Records, L/E/7/522, no. 2662: Memorandum of the Sirsiah Research Committee (Sirsiah Research Station), November 7, 1906.
39. Sydney Herbert Higgins, *Dyeing in Germany and America: With a Chapter on Colour Production* (Manchester, UK, 1907), 71–72.
40. Ibid., 103–105.

CHAPTER 3

Learning to See with Milton Bradley

Nicholas Gaskill

In a 1914 editorial for the *School Arts Magazine*, Henry Turner Bailey celebrated the "educational revolution" that had brought color into the schoolroom at the end of the nineteenth century. Commenting on the dramatic nature of this "great transition," he supposed that "the modern teacher can hardly imagine the dreary gray desert stretches of a drawing exhibition in the early 80s," when exercises in form and shading dominated the curriculum and "the lead pencil reigned supreme."[1] Such somber days, he explained, had given way by the 1890s to a brighter era, one in which children played with colored chalk, crayons, construction paper, variously hued wools, and other colorful materials made available by advances in print and dye technology. Bailey credited several pedagogues for accomplishing this revolution in art instruction—among them Louis Prang, Albert H. Munsell, and Denman Ross—but it was Milton Bradley, the toy and board game manufacturer, whom he called "the god-father of color instruction in elementary schools."[2]

And with good reason. The man who made his fortune from *The Checkered Game of Life* (1860, now simply *The Game of Life*) devoted decades of his career and large portions of his business to shaping the way that American children perceived color. He not only developed a precise system of color nomenclature and a controversial theory of color standards but also used these innovations to manufacture a full line of chromatic materials that made those "dreary gray desert stretches" a thing of the past. To instruct educators in how best to use these colorful instruments—many of which had only just been invented, all of which were new to the public classroom—he published several books, in which he introduced his theories, defined key terms, and described exercises for training the "color sense" in young students. In 1914, Bailey singled out the first of these, *Color in the School-Room* (1890), as "epoch-marking" for its insistence on

N. Gaskill (✉)
Department of English, Rutgers University, New Brunswick, NJ, USA

R.L. Blaszczyk, U. Spiekermann (eds.), *Bright Modernity*, Worlds of Consumption, DOI 10.1007/978-3-319-50745-3_3

the place of color in early education.[3] Through these efforts, Bradley played a crucial role in making bright hues an unquestioned fixture in the life of the child.

That the "god-father" of color education also happened to manufacture an array of colorful goods for classroom consumption has given the few historians who have written about him pause. Was Bradley only in it for the money? The internal accounts by the Milton Bradley Company suggest not—the educational initiatives of the business were never profitable, and Bradley's successor shut them down soon after assuming charge.[4] What should we make of the interlacing of manufacturing interests and art education objectives exemplified in Bradley? What, in other words, was the relation between the "educational revolution" that brought color into the classroom and the concurrent "color revolution" that brightened the spaces of turn-of-the-century capitalism and made the materials of color instruction widely available? Bailey's "modern teacher," unable to imagine a school without color, surely resembles the modern consumers, designers, and advertisers that Regina Lee Blaszczyk details in her account of late-nineteenth- and twentieth-century color professionals. Like them, this teacher expected color in places, and in quantities, that previous generations had not. And Bradley, for his part, belongs among those who sought to bring order to the proliferation of commercial colors in the wake of synthetic dyes and pigments, though he focused less on adult consumers and more on child students (consumers-to-be).[5]

Taking the imbrication of these related "revolutions" as its starting point, this essay investigates the deeper affinities between color pedagogy and consumer culture that Bradley's work and writings reveal. It argues that the ways of seeing fostered in the Bradley system prepared students to enter the emerging world of consumerism both as efficient producers and as ready consumers. On the one hand, children trained in Bradley's course came to understand color as an abstract quality, reducible to its quantitative properties; they learned to see the hues of the natural world as composites of the pure colors of the manufacturer. On the other hand, their greater sensitivity to the laws underlying color harmonies cultivated a refined "color feeling" that prepared them to respond to the increasingly colorful displays of advertisers and merchants. In this way, the guiding assumptions of Bradley's method of color instruction bespoke a manufacturing interest more subtle than any profit motive. Only by examining the objectives of his pedagogy can we grasp the meaning of his claim in *Color in the School-Room* that "we should teach the child color not only for the sake of beauty but also for the sake of business."[6] After establishing the industrial problems that prompted Bradley to compose his educational system, this essay discusses what it was that a graduate of his course would perceive, as well as what sorts of tasks and experiences that graduate's color-educated perceptions made possible. In so doing, this chapter explains how the color revolution in education both participated in and reacted to wider developments in marketing and business.

* * *

Bradley was not the first to link art education and manufacturing. In fact, the earliest design-training initiatives in the United States were developed to improve the quality of American-made goods by refining the aesthetic sensibilities of those who would produce them. Bradley's home state of Massachusetts, a leader in these efforts, went so far as to pass the Drawing Act of 1870, which required all public schools to include "industrial drawing" courses as part of their curriculum.[7] Art instruction techniques received unprecedented attention in the subsequent decades, expanding beyond the narrow strategies of industrial design into the more expressive and colorful approaches associated with the romantic pedagogy of Friedrich Froebel (1782–1852), inventor of the kindergarten. As we will see, Bradley came to education through the latter movement, but his innovation was to connect business interest in industrial drawing with the kindergarten's emphasis on color. Before discussing the implications of this combination, though, let us trace the path by which Bradley the manufacturer came to be known as Bradley the color educator.

In 1860, Bradley attended a lecture on the fledgling kindergarten movement delivered by the educational reformer Elizabeth Peabody in his hometown of Springfield, Massachusetts. He left a convert. Peabody had spoken on Froebel's method of instruction and its emphasis on the natural curiosity and activities of the child. Froebel's system required a series of objects he called "gifts" (six worsted balls of different colors, for example, or sets of wooden cubes, spheres, and cylinders) and a series of activities he called "occupations," such as weaving, paper folding, wood carving, and clay modeling. If the kindergarten movement were to gain a foothold in America, the components of these gifts and occupations would need to be manufactured domestically. Here is where Bradley thought he could help. With advice from Peabody and from Edward Wiebé, whose illustrated manual for kindergarteners, *The Paradise of Childhood*, had been published by the Milton Bradley Company in 1869, Bradley began producing the standard line of Froebel materials. (Before long, he also began issuing "improvements" and additions, some of which rankled die-hard Froebelians.) The occupations posed what came to be a fruitful challenge for the manufacturer. Many of the activities called for colored paper, but "the existing supply was uncertain and entirely inadequate to meet the growing demand, consisting of odds and ends of stock found in stores and warehouses," none of which followed any particular color standards.[8] One supplier's red was different from another's. Even worse, the same paper mill often failed to provide steady hues, and so Bradley "found it impossible . . . to insure his customers that any color he had furnished them could be duplicated."[9]

In the process of solving this problem for manufacturing, Bradley formulated his educational program. He established a system of color standards designed to communicate colors between warehouse and factory, and then used this system to ground the student's engagement with the chromatic world. In his three major manuals on color pedagogy—*Color in the School-Room* (1890), *Color in the Kindergarten* (1893), and *Elementary Color* (1895) —he articulated the need for such standards in education in ways that promised to expand Froebel's accomplishments into the increasingly important realm of color. "To Froebel must be given the honor of introducing logical form study into primary education," he wrote, "but in color no corresponding advance has been made because there have been no generally accepted standards in color to correspond to the sphere, cube, cylinder, circle, ellipse and triangle in form."[10] Froebel himself had acknowledged the primary importance of color when he "included [it] as part of the first material used in his system of elementary education"—the first gift of six worsted balls in red, yellow, orange, green, blue, and violet.[11] Yet the lack of standards and, presumably, of the means to manufacture such materials in a cheap and durable way had prevented the German pedagogue from making the most of color. This gap in the kindergarten system had been rendered all the more acute by the influence of child study and of psychological investigations into the mental development of infants, which attested to an early sensitivity to color that required proper training to progress fully.[12] Bradley appealed to these ideas in each of his books, reasoning that "color is one of the earliest subjects which should be taught in any education course" because of the psychological "fact that some bright color is the first thing to attract the infant's eye, winning his notice before he pays any attention to form."[13] Bradley proposed to build on this basic attraction to color through a system of colored materials that, thanks to late-nineteenth-century advances in synthetic colorants (see Chapter 2), could be manufactured for the mass market in a way unthinkable in Froebel's own day. For Froebel's approach to be updated for the 1890s, Bradley implied, it had to become more colorful.

After all, the turn of the century in America was an especially colorful time—so colorful, in fact, that the sheer number of new synthetic dyes and pigments adorning consumer goods made talking about modern color particularly difficult. Reviewing the previous year's "riotous abundance" of dress goods, a *New York Times* writer in 1890 marveled at "the gamut of color" that "embrace[d] every shade and variation of shade heretofore conceived for feminine adornment, and not a few that were never before seen on sea, nor land—nor woman."[14] The author went on to note the fashion not just for new colors but also for new color names, which were generated at the same breakneck pace as the goods they sought to describe. "Eiffel red," in particular, enjoyed a vogue that season, so much so that "if any doubtful shade of red with a tone of lavender, pink, or brown is left undesignated, it is unhesitatingly denominated Eiffel red, and so offered to the public, who accept it with unquestioning faith."[15] But not everyone observed such loose color nomenclature with the same amusement. Bradley, for instance, regarded confused color language as one of most formidable impediments to a proper chromatic education. As he bemoaned in *Color in the Kindergarten*, "[a]ll color terms used by artists, naturalists, manufacturers, tradesmen, milliners and the members of our households are as indefinite as one might naturally expect from the utter lack of a logical basis for the whole subject of color."[16]

Several of Bradley's contemporaries also fretted over the imprecision of color terms. The ornithologist Robert Ridgway, the lithographer Louis Prang, the polymath Herbert Spencer, and Bradley's sometimes collaborator J. H. Pillsbury, a high school teacher from Springfield, all complained of the confusion characterizing color names in the absence of a definite standard, and each attempted to provide a logical solution.[17] Like the *Times* writer, these figures attributed this "chaos of colour-names" to the spectacular increase of colored consumer goods at the end of the century and, more precisely, to the inventive color names developed to sell them.[18] Pillsbury, for instance, worried that the vagueness of color nomenclature would increase "as the revelations of chemistry disclose hues more and more brilliant, for which new names are constantly coined," ridiculous names such as "elephant's breath," "eminence," "baby blue," and "ashes of roses."[19] Bradley too, citing many of the same names, noted a further complication: that even though "the [new color] names will no doubt occur each season," the hues to which they refer "will change with the fickle demands of the goddess of fashion and the interests of the manufacturers and dealers."[20] The primary constituents of the new consumer economy—including the creation of new and expanding markets, the development of the fashion industry, and so on—had created a shifting terrain of color terms in which neither the colors nor the terms stood still. Bradley and Pillsbury set out to tame this wild landscape, not in order to curb its growth but to promote it through better organization.

At this point, before examining the specific techniques and reasoning Bradley developed to sort out our thoughts on color, we should emphasize how problems in both manufacturing and consumer culture spurred Bradley to create his educational system. That is, the troubles that plagued Bradley as he worked to keep kindergarten teachers supplied with consistent colors had their roots not only in the lack of color standards used to produce goods but also in the frenzy of color names developed to sell them. His efforts combined the two most prominent art education initiatives of his day—the industrial drawing program of the British immigrant Walter Smith and the kindergarten movement championed by Peabody—to create a pedagogical program as suited to the colorful, playful enticements of turn-of-the-century consumer capitalism as Smith's techniques had been for Victorian-era manufacturing concerns. Bradley's curriculum set out to equip students with the visual and manual skills required to produce the colorful goods of the modern economy, and thus to give visual order to the increasingly chaotic consumer environment. But how were the color perceptions of students to be thus trained?

The first step, as we noted above, was to set color on a firm foundation by establishing clear color standards, as definite and stable as the "circle, ellipse and triangle in form"[21] (see Fig. 3.1). The so-called primary colors, with their secondary and tertiary combinations, would not do since the Young-Helmholtz

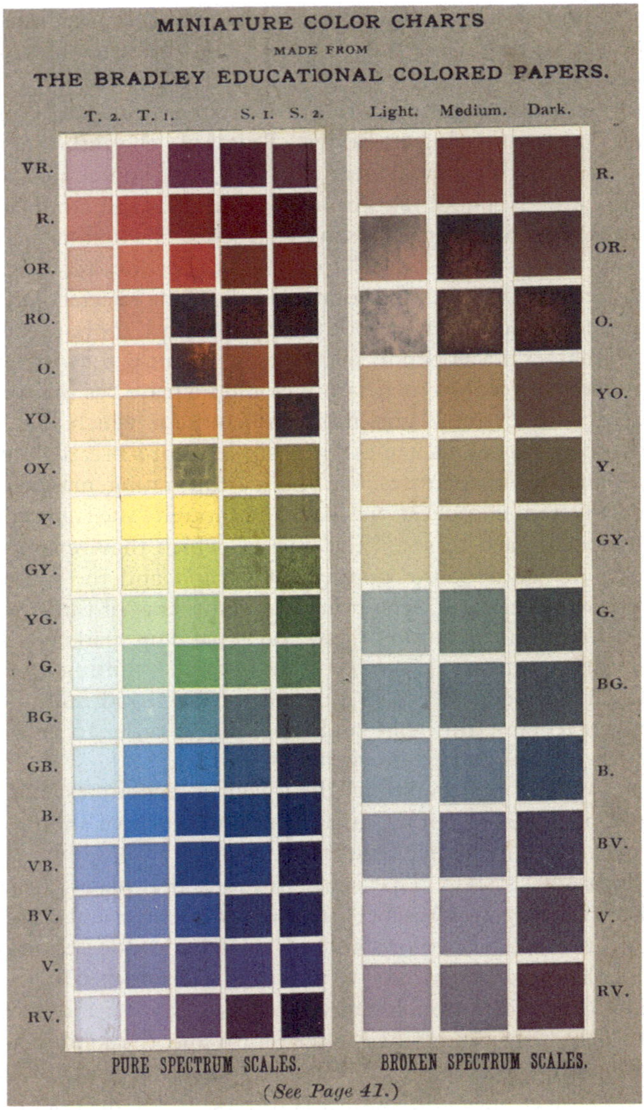

Fig. 3.1 Color charts based on a selection of Milton Bradley's colored papers ("pure" and "broken" spectrums)

Source: Milton Bradley, *Elementary Color*, rev. ed. (Springfield, MA: Milton Bradley Co., 1895), unpaginated front matter, RB 603471, The Huntington Library, San Marino, California.

theory had discredited David Brewster's notion that red, blue, and yellow were the basic hues of vision.[22] Moreover, Bradley worried that no mixture of pigments could yield a hue as vivid as it appeared in nature—for example, no combination of yellow and blue pigments could produce a green as green as that of the rainbow. As such, he argued, the three-primary system not only failed to accord with the most recent science but also hampered the practical work in paints and dyes it was designed to enhance. This double failing also highlighted a different problem, namely, the widening gap between scientific knowledge about color—as both a physical and a psychological phenomenon—and practical wisdom about colorants. As Bradley explained in *Elementary Color*, his "system of color instruction . . . is based on the results of careful study and experiment for many years in which the attempt has been made to bring the scientist and the artist on common ground, where they may work in sympathy with each other instead of at cross purposes."[23]

Bradley reasoned that the only standard of color capable of harmonizing theory and practice, the only one stable and objective enough to place color knowledge on a sure footing, was the solar spectrum, as displayed in both the rainbow and the colors refracted through a prism. Yet this natural standard immediately posed a problem, for even though most people could distinguish six separate hues in the rainbow—red, orange, yellow, green, blue, and violet—the spectrum itself consisted of a continuum of varying wavelengths of light rather than a series of discrete units. How, from this seamless progression of hues, could one carve out color standards? To solve this problem, Bradley and Pillsbury convened a panel of experts tasked with determining the "reddest red, the greenest green, etc." and then matching those psychological perceptions with a physical wavelength of light.[24] Bradley never failed to emphasize how much experimentation and scientific effort went into the determination of his six standards. In *Elementary Color,* he recounted the long battle from obscurity to scientific precision in dramatic terms: "after much experimenting and many conferences with artists and scientists a basis for operation was decided upon and at the end of fifteen years the efforts begun in doubt have resulted in a definite system of color instruction."[25] Pillsbury, on the other hand, told a less glamorous story. In one of his many articles in *Nature* arguing for the spectrum standards, he assured his reader that "to obtain the agreement of six or eight persons well skilled in the use of colours as to exactly what portion of a projected spectrum of eight or ten feet should be selected for each standard was a much less difficult task than would first have been supposed"; in fact, "it was found that very great unanimity of judgment prevailed when the comparison was made."[26]

Whether the trials conducted by this cabal of experts spanned multiple disciplines and many months or simply involved eight people reaching a prompt agreement, the point of these narratives—especially in Bradley's writing—was to show readers that the transition from the physical, measurable spectrum to the slippery realm of human perception (where, after all, the trouble about color began) had been made with full scientific rigor. As Bradley explained, his was "the only system of artistic color instruction based on the scientific truths of color."[27] Yet such an appeal to expert opinion was not as straightforward as it might appear, given that the question of *who* was an expert in color was precisely the issue. Physicists, psychologists, artists, textile manufacturers, and any number of other contributors to the color revolution could all claim authority in their respective realms, and so the invocation of expertise was not akin to "four out of five dentists agree . . . " in contemporary toothpaste marketing, where the topic under discussion has already been assigned to a realm of recognized professionals. Instead, Bradley and Pillsbury used their committee to create a consensus, to produce expert agreement. They enlisted "the psychological color perceptions *of* experts" (or, in Pillsbury's phrase, of "persons well skilled in the uses of colours"), not the judgments of experts in color perception, if such experts even existed.[28] In this way, the origin story of the Bradley system, which Bradley himself never tired of telling, captured the distinctive mix of concern and enthusiasm that characterized the discourse around color at the turn of the century—concern that color had become riotous and enthusiasm that the rationalizing effects of scientific inquiry could organize and direct the insurgence.[29]

Yet the task of calming the chaos of color discourse required more than abstract standards. The trouble, after all, was about ordering colored materials for use in the classroom, and this meant that the standards would have to be given a stable physical embodiment and a reliable set of names. To this end, Bradley's factory manufactured a line of papers covered in pigments that, "as nearly as possible," displayed the "same kind of color" as the spectral hues.[30] Papers rather than paints were preferred because, as evidenced by the products of the three-primary system, mixtures of paints resulted in dulled hues. In his quest for color specificity, Bradley turned to an apparatus that was popular among the emerging practitioners of "chromatics" or color science (some of whom appear in Chapter 6). Instead of mixing materials, he used the device commonly called the "Maxwell disk" (so named after its inventor, the British physicist, James Clerk Maxwell) to combine colors in the eye. The Maxwell disk consisted of a color wheel mounted on a hand-cranked rotating platform on which variously colored disks could be placed in adjustable proportions (Figs. 3.2 and 3.3). When the wheel turned quickly, the hues juxtaposed on its face would appear to blend into a new, solid color: the mixture of the various disks.[31] Bradley divided the circumference of the wheel into 100 parts, thus making for an easy system of nomenclature. For any desired color, one only needed to specify the proportions of hues necessary to produce it on the color wheel, using the six spectral hues (represented by their first letters: R for red, Y for yellow, and so on) and white (W) and black (N). With this method, vague and uncertain terms like "Ashes of Roses" or "Styx" became sturdy names that doubled as recipes for producing the colors they signified, "R.8 ¼, V. 2 ¼, W. 15 ½, N. 74" and "R.10, W.21, N.69," respectively.[32]

In this way, Bradley solved the problem that had started him on his inquiry into color. Using the nomenclature derived from the six standards (plus white and black) and the color wheel, companies could order a precise color from a factory and expect consistency from one order to the next. "As a manufacturer of

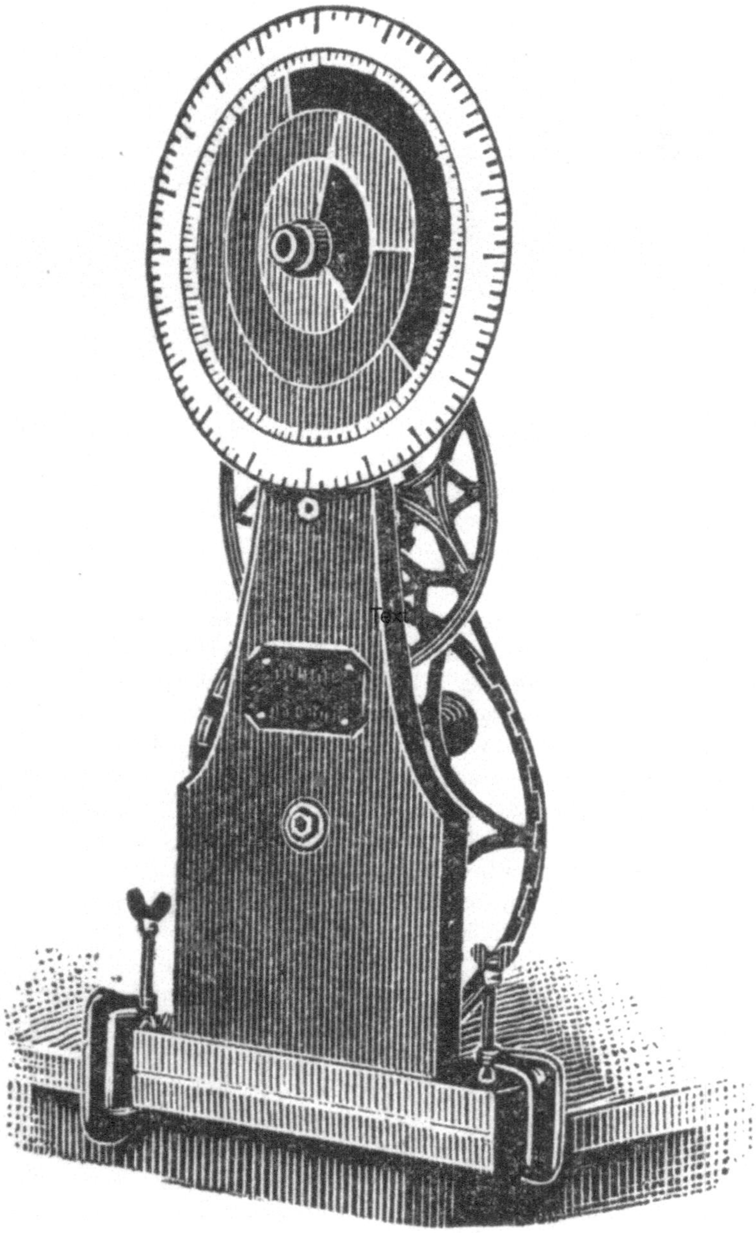

Fig. 3.2 The Milton Bradley color wheel, which teachers and students used to mix colors

Source: Milton Bradley, *Elementary Color,* rev. ed. (Springfield, MA: Milton Bradley Co., 1895), 31, RB 603471, The Huntington Library, San Marino, California.

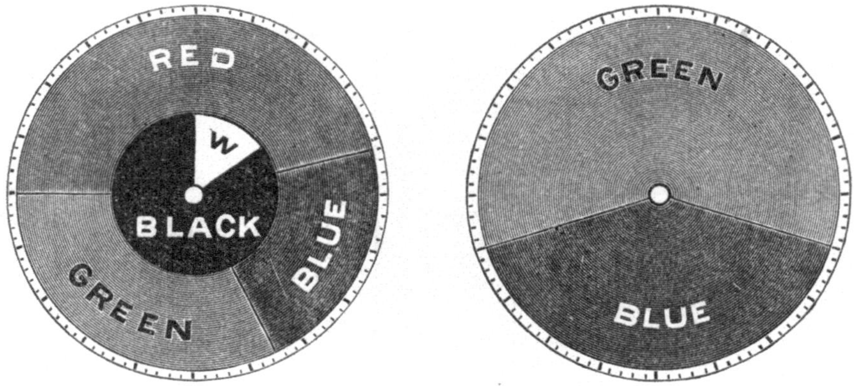

Fig. 3.3 Color disks, which were placed on the color wheel and spun during classroom exercises in mixing and analyzing colors

Source: Milton Bradley, *Elementary Color*, rev. ed. (Springfield, MA: Milton Bradley Co., 1895), 51, RB 603471, The Huntington Library, San Marino, California.

an extended line of colored papers," Bradley wrote in one of his articles for *Science*, "I am constantly putting this proposed nomenclature to a severe test by ordering new colors by telephone." That is, he created a desired color on a wheel in his office; then called the factory, located ten miles away, to give them the formula; and they used their own wheel to reassemble the color on site. Bradley concluded, "under this plan we are liable to have occasion to 'telephone a color' frequently"—and could even "cable colors to Europe."[33] To arrive at this solution, Bradley approached color not as a visual property of specific materials, objects, or activities but rather as an abstract quality capable of moving unchanged through the transformations involved in creating his standards—from the spectral hues of physics to the material hues of pigments, via the committee of experts, and from colored papers to psychological color perceptions, via the color wheel. The Maxwell disks that Bradley used, for instance, were to be treated not as "particular colored objects" but, Michael Rossi explains, as "archetypical abstractions of the sensations referred to by color terms."[34] In the end, one did not even need to see a color to understand its meaning. Reading "G. 18 ½, B. 11, W. 16 ½, N. 53" was enough.

My point here is not to criticize Bradley for producing color as an immaterial property tied only to a standardized, quantitative system. For the purposes of "telephoning colors," after all, this innovation is especially useful, and the labors of coordinating, translating, and inscribing that Bradley orchestrated were especially impressive.[35] Rather, my interest in dwelling at such length on the origins of Bradley's system is to sharpen our ability to ask how an understanding of color that was developed for business worked when it was applied to education. How was this model of perception transferred to the classroom, and to what effect? Not that the needs of business and the needs of education necessarily differed—on the contrary, we have seen how art education developed to address concerns about industrial production. But color instruction at the end of the nineteenth century not only provided students with practical skills but also instilled in them a notion of what color *is* and how it should be seen, and it was in this general understanding of color that Bradley's system differed from that of other color pedagogues. Albert Munsell, for instance, argued that the bright hues of the spectrum were inappropriate for impressionable young eyes, and he offered his toned-down "middle hues" as standards for color instruction, not because they represented nature's palette but because they could regulate the student's developing taste.[36] Louis Prang, on the other hand, joined Bradley in championing bright colors for classroom use; however, unlike Bradley, he and his co-authors justified this position by appealing to the "primitive" perceptual abilities of children, which their course aimed to draw out and refine.[37] Other teachers opposed the very notion of color instruction based on an abstract color system rather than on the particular hues and tints of the natural world. Within this context, Bradley stands out as the pedagogue who most clearly built the assumptions of the manufacturer into his educational exercises. In what follows, then, I will show how Bradley's program of instruction trained students to view the world as a composite of abstract, spectral hues, and I will suggest that this way of seeing not only readied pupils to perceive the world as manufacturers but also to experience it as consumers.

Before tackling the hues of the landscape, household objects, clothing, or flowers, students in a Bradley classroom mastered the six spectral colors. To that end, teachers began the course of color instruction by using a glass prism to disclose the basic colors of nature. Not only were such exercises aimed at quickening the child's natural interest (a requisite for Progressive Era educators); they also provided the phenomenal means for students to form concepts of the standard colors and thus align themselves with the work of the expert committee. "Observation of the spectrum enthuses the children with a feeling for color which can be developed in no other way," Bradley explained. Moreover, "by studying [the prism] the mental image of each of the six colors becomes as distinct as that of the cube after it has been handled and modeled."[38] Through repeated exposure students were meant to internalize the six basic colors as "fixed standards, the child's own property," and to facilitate this process, teachers used the Bradley colored papers to familiarize students with each hue, in proper succession: "If the child thinks when he sees red, 'This is like my spectrum red,' and forms a correct conclusion, he is ready for orange, and so with each of the colors."[39] Once students familiarized themselves with the individual hues, they could begin to study their relations, the way that each gradually bled into its neighbors through a process of mixing, as demonstrated through the color wheel. Thus, they became friendly not only with red and orange but also with red-orange and orange-red.

"Up to this time," Bradley reminded instructors, "we have not suggested the practice of introducing natural objects or calling attention of the children to various colors found in their surroundings."[40] For everyday colors introduce tints, shades, and "broken" colors—mixtures with black, white, or grey—and so require more complicated analytical skills. To ease the transition from the spectrum to the world, Bradley advised teachers to "ask the children to bring from home samples of the color which they are studying," for instance "[b]its of worsted and silk or of cloth or paper, together with plants, leaves and flowers." Next, he instructed,

> Allow the children to group the colors that are similar and develop the idea of resemblance and difference of colors and bring out the fact that while there are many similar colors there is only one standard of a color, and to the standard colors we give the names red, orange, yellow, green, blue and violet, and by these standards all colors are tested and classified, and hence the importance of training the eye to recognize the spectrum standards readily.[41]

Teachers should not be lenient in this exercise, Bradley explained. If a bit of cloth or paper did not match the spectrum hue, they needed to say so. Otherwise, they would perpetuate the same loose talk and confusion that had set Bradley working in the first place. But having insisted on the purity and priority of the standards, the teacher could then proceed to use the color wheel to illustrate for the students how the hues around them expressed varied combinations of R, O, Y, G, B, V, W, and N, the visual components of the natural world. An apple was never 100 percent red, the students learned, but rather R.85, W.5, N.10. Bradley recommended a number of related activities aimed at helping students to see the composite colors around them in terms their constituent parts. For instance, the teacher might use trial and error to match the color of a flower, fruit, or vegetable on the color wheel, or, in more advanced cases, the instructor might create a mixture on the wheel, set it spinning, and then ask the students to analyze its parts.[42]

Through such practice, it was hoped, students would abandon the vague color terms of common discourse, which so often had the object world as their point of reference, and learn to speak—and to see—with precision. Bradley illustrated this process with an anecdote:

> A little child who had become somewhat familiar with the color wheel one day said to the teacher, "What color do you think that dress is," referring to a suit of the so-called "mahogany color." Wishing to test the judgment of the child the reply was, "What do you think it is?" The child replied, "Well, I rather think it is a shade of red orange," which was a very close description of the color. And why is it not better to say a dark red orange than "mahogany color," if any definite expression is required?[43]

The child in this story had traded an understanding of color predicated on real world referents ("mahogany") for one tied to an abstract chart based on a particular notion about nature's "basic" colors. The chromatic world thus appears as the stuff of commerce, susceptible to harnessing and configuring by modern technology. The colors we would assume to be natural—those that surround us in nature—have been carefully displaced through a series of activities that shape the student's mode of attending to the world and, in the process, produce new chromatic experiences. Color instruction, Bradley wrote, "should lead the pupil to closer observation, to see color where he has never thought of looking for it."[44] Color perception here was a learned skill. But what kinds of perceptions did these exercises equip students to have? More to the point, what were such perceptions good for? The decontextualized vision of color cultivated in the Bradley course prompted students to treat hues as abstract elements to be combined and arranged in commercial goods. It is in this regard that we can understand Bradley's boast that "the graduate from a two year's course in the kindergarten may have a better color sense than is at present enjoyed by the average business or professional man."[45]

Not all educators were so enthusiastic about the idea of color that this program promoted. A San Francisco teacher, Katherine M. Ball, worried that "after playing with colored balls, working with colored papers, drawing with wax crayons, always using the same fixed hues—color comes to mean the unvarying qualities of the normal" rather than the splendid and shifting hues of the world.[46] But this shift in the meaning of colors was right at home alongside the conceptual reconfigurations of nature and culture prompted by the emergence of synthetic dyes, which allowed organic chemists to cook up the world's colors on demand. What's more, as the nineteenth- and early-twentieth-century studies of color harmonies and their psychological effects revealed, these abstract colors were not without their pleasures (as we shall see in Chapters 5, 6, and 8 on fashion, shopping, and domestic interiors, respectively). In fact, historians of consumption have amply demonstrated that the laws of color harmony guided the display strategies and marketing campaigns of modern department stores and fashion designers.[47] One prominent example of this practice comes from L. Frank Baum, another late-nineteenth-century American who straddled the realms of childhood entertainment and consumer culture. In *The Art of Decorating Dry Goods Windows and Interiors* (1900), Baum recommended the "bright and varied colorings" of cheesecloth for the backgrounds of window arrangements. Easily harmonized and arranged, these hues "make a window attractive enough to stop pedestrians, who, glancing at the display, unconsciously note that the goods on exhibition are thrown prominently into the foreground, while the coloring that made them pause has modestly retired and serves only as a foil for the articles of merchandise."[48] Though undetected, colors here performed the most essential work of advertising and marketing: that of "arrest[ing] the eye of the passive throng and so direct[ing] attention to the goods themselves."[49] Similarly, Bradley himself noted that "the harmonious combinations and contrasts of different colors constitute one of our greatest sources of pleasure," and, he continued, "in numerous lines of business an understanding of the correct use of color is of great commercial service."[50]

So it was only fitting that Bradley included in his program exercises in the production and enjoyment of color harmonies, especially since "we are confronted with the sad reality that half the people of the present day have no true perceptions of the value of colors, or of the effects" they have on one another.[51] The threat of this sad reality was not simply that without color training the flood of consumer goods would continue to sully the visual environment with jarring chromatic combinations (the problem, to modify Walter Smith, of "Industrial Coloring") but also that people—as potential customers—were unable to appreciate the harmonious colors appealing to them. As a remedy, Bradley suggested "the work of cutting and pasting designs in educational colored papers," which, he explained, "affords the earliest and best practical expression of the color feeling which has been acquired and stimulates the further development of color perception"[52] (see Fig. 3.4). To guide teachers in nurturing this "color feeling," he described a series of tasks that required students to arrange various shapes and colors cut from the Bradley Papers and to learn, with the help of the instructor, to feel the effects of the arrangements. Continued study would bring increased understanding and, more importantly, "added enjoyment."[53] In this regard, we can see the "great commercial service" of Bradley's pedagogical program as inhering not only in its professed objective of training more aesthetically accomplished producers—and of providing the nomenclature to facilitate their production—but also, more subtly, in its efforts to develop the habits of receptiveness and attention required for these products to be sold. In Bradley's classroom, learning to see beauty and to take pleasure in chromatic harmonies, especially when situated alongside exercises that presented the visual world as material to be broken down and reassembled in manufactured goods, contributed to the aestheticized economic practices of the late nineteenth century.

This, then, is how the "god-father of color instruction" reveals the techniques and assumptions that link the "educational revolution" in the 1890s with the wider "color revolution" that continued to drive business practices even after systematic color education fell out of fashion.[54] In particular, Bradley's color education emerged from his concerns as a manufacturer and enshrined ways of seeing that were suited first and foremost for industrial production. He began with a particular notion of abstract color qualities, and to give this abstraction weight—to transform the spectral colors into the concrete material of nature—he oversaw an elaborate process of mediation that aligned the discordant color logics of physics, psychology, and art through a committee of experts. This concept of color then guided the types of exercises in analysis and combination outlined in Bradley's teaching manuals. When viewed within the larger framework of consumer

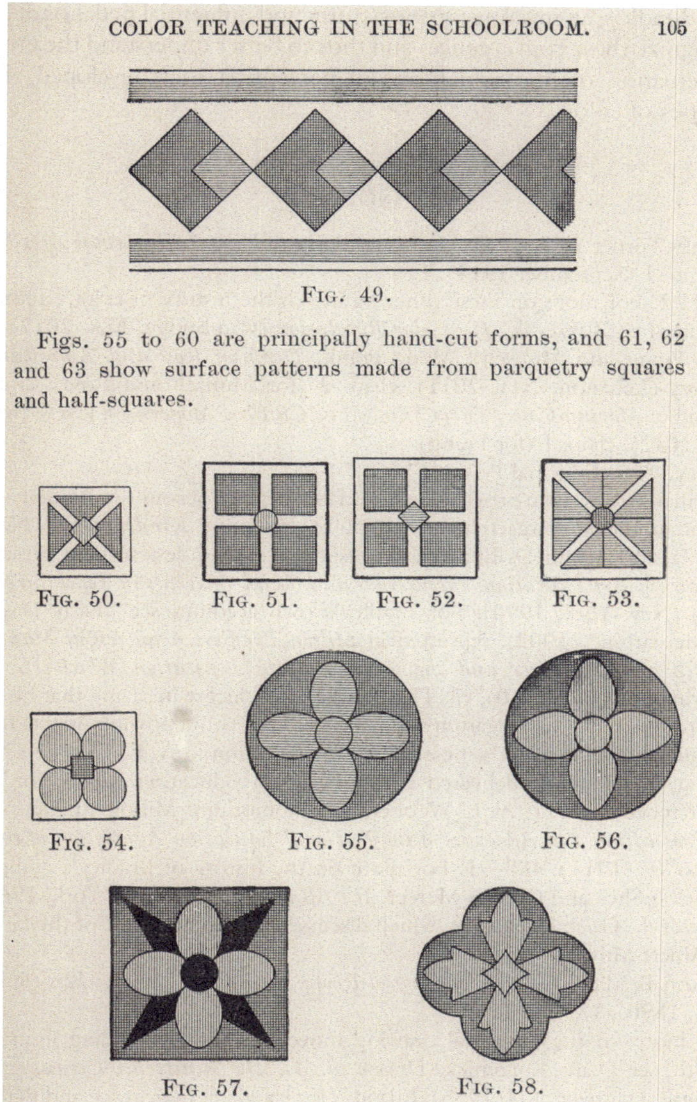
COLOR TEACHING IN THE SCHOOLROOM. 105

FIG. 49.

Figs. 55 to 60 are principally hand-cut forms, and 61, 62 and 63 show surface patterns made from parquetry squares and half-squares.

FIG. 50. FIG. 51. FIG. 52. FIG. 53.

FIG. 54. FIG. 55. FIG. 56.

FIG. 57. FIG. 58.

Fig. 3.4 Students taking the Bradley color course practiced color harmonies and contrasts by creating chromatic patterns in paper and parquetry based on these forms

Source: Milton Bradley, *Elementary Color*, rev. ed. (Springfield, MA: Milton Bradley Co., 1895), 105, RB 603471, The Huntington Library, San Marino, California.

culture, the perceptual modes fostered by these activities display an affinity with the visual demands of the department store, the advertisement, and the other familiar objects of the history of turn-of-the-century consumption.[55] The career of Milton Bradley, an inventive manufacturer and influential pedagogue, enables us to recognize these convergences and thus to better understand the emergence and perpetuation of historical forms of perception that developed alongside material uses of color.

Notes

1. Henry Turner Bailey, "The Editorial Point of View," *The School Arts Magazine* 14, no. 1 (September 1914): 1.
2. Ibid., 2. For more on these other figures in the history of color education, see Regina Lee Blaszczyk, *The Color Revolution* (Cambridge, MA, 2012), chap. 2 (for Prang and Munsell); Marie Frank, *Denman Ross and American Design Theory* (Lebanon, NH, 2011), chap. 2 (for Munsell and Ross); and Joshua Yumibe, *Moving Color: Early Film, Mass Culture, Modernism* (New Brunswick, NJ, 2012), chap. 1 (for Prang).
3. Bailey, "The Editorial Point of View," 2.
4. Norman Brosterman provides an especially skeptical account of Bradley's involvement in the kindergarten movement in *Inventing Kindergarten* (New York, 1997), and Arthur D. Efland takes a similar, though less strident position in *A History of Art Education: Intellectual and Social Currents in Teaching the Visual Arts* (New York, 1990). For Bradley's own account, see "Early Days of the Kindergarten" (1902), reprinted in *Milton Bradley: A Successful Man: A Brief Sketch of His Career and the Growth of the Institution Which He Founded* (Springfield, MA, 1910), vii. That Bradley was sincere in saying that he "became interested in the kindergarten as a man, before it could possibly appeal to me as a manufacturer" receives a measure of corroboration in A. L. Webber's memorial eulogy for Bradley, delivered at the National Education Association's annual conference in 1911. A. L. Webber, "In Memorium: Milton Bradley," *Journal of Proceedings and Addresses of the National Education Association of the United States* 49 (1911): 488–91. For more on the history of Bradley's company, see James J. Shea and Charles Mercer, *It's All in the Game* (New York, 1960).
5. Blaszczyk, *Color Revolution*, which discusses Bradley—as part of the larger story of Albert Munsell—in chap. 2.
6. Milton Bradley, *Color in the School-Room: A Manual for Teachers* (Springfield, MA, 1890), 13.
7. For more on the industrial drawing movement and its leading figure, Walter Smith, see Diana Korzenick, *Drawn to Art: The Nineteenth-Century American Dream* (Hanover, NH, 1985); Efland, *History of Art Education*; and Peter Smith, *The History of American Art Education: Learning about Art in American Schools* (Westport, CT, 1996).
8. Bradley, "Early Days of the Kindergarten," 33.
9. Milton Bradley, *Color in the Kindergarten: A Manual of the Theory of Color and the Practical Use of Color Material in the Kindergarten* (Springfield, MA, 1893), 4.
10. Milton Bradley, *Elementary Color* (Springfield, MA, 1895), 15.
11. Bradley, *Color in the Kindergarten,* 3.
12. See James Mark Baldwin, *The Mental Development of the Child and the Race* (New York, 1895); William T. Preyer, *The Mind of the Child* (New York, 1888); Milicent Washburn Shinn, *Notes on the Development of a Child* (Berkeley, CA,

1893–1899); and James Sully, "The New Study of Children," *Littell's Living Age,* December 7, 1895, 579–89.

13. Bradley, *Color in the School-Room,* 14; see also Bradley, *Color in the Kindergarten,* 3, and Bradley, *Elementary Color,* 6.
14. "New Wool Goods," *New York Times*, February 9, 1890. I would like to thank Michael Rossi, whose paper for the GHI conference on "Bright Modernity" introduced me to this article.
15. "New Wool Goods."
16. Bradley, *Color in the Kindergarten,* 23.
17. For a discussion of how Ridgway, Pillsbury, Bradley, and the philosopher Christine Ladd-Franklin all addressed this confusion by developing scientific ways of accounting for color, see Michael Paul Rossi, "The Rules of Perception: American Color Science, 1831–1931," (PhD diss., Massachusetts Institute of Technology, 2011), chap. 4.
18. Editors' note following a letter from Louis Prang, *Nature*, November 21, 1895, 56.
19. J. H. Pillsbury, "A Scheme of Colour Standards," *Nature,* August 22, 1895, 390, 392.
20. Bradley, *Elementary Color,* 43.
21. Ibid., 15.
22. See Bradley, *Color in the Kindergarten,* 6.
23. Bradley, *Elementary Color,* 11–12.
24. Ibid., 17. For the curious, the results (in "ten millionths of a millimeter") are as follows: "Red, 6571; Orange, 6085; Yellow, 5793; Green, 5164; Blue, 4695; violet, 4210."
25. Bradley, *Elementary Color,* 8 (see also 79–80).
26. Pillsbury, "A Scheme of Colour Standards," 390. It is not clear how Bradley and Pillsbury produced this giant spectrum.
27. Bradley, *Color in the Kindergarten,* 11.
28. Bradley, *Elementary Color,* 20.
29. The persistent attempts in the nineteenth century to achieve a science of color, rather than a hodgepodge of color sciences, makes for a fascinating study in the powers and limitations of scientific reason, not least because these attempts repeatedly failed to bring color to order. In this light, one of the important lessons of Blaszczyk's *Color Revolution* is that color was only successfully "managed" once color engineers mustered all the tools of corporate capitalism to bring it under practical, if not theoretical, control.
30. Bradley, *Elementary Color,* 17.
31. The disks were named after the British physicist James Clerk Maxwell, who had devised a method of combining the circles by "cutting a radial slit in each disk from circumference to center," but the colors they bore were those of the Bradley Colored Papers. Bradley, *Color in the Kindergarten,* 11.
32. Bradley, *Color in the Kindergarten,* 23. Bradley and Pillsbury introduced and defended this system in the pages of *Science* and *Nature* as well as in Bradley's own books. Besides those articles already cited, see J. H. Pillsbury, "A New Color Scheme," *Science* 19 (February 26, 1892): 114; Pillsbury, "The Standard Color Scheme," *Science* 21 (June 9, 1893): 310–11; and Pillsbury, "Spectrum Color Standards," *Science,* n.s. 6 (July 16, 1897): 88–91.
33. Milton Bradley, "The Color Question Again," *Science* 19 (March 25, 1892): 176. Bradley included a similar passage about "telephoning colors" in *Color in the*

Kindergarten, 18. It is unclear how many companies—besides Bradley's own—adopted his particular system. In "A New Color Scheme," 114, Pillsbury reported, "One manufacturing firm proposes to use the wheel and disks in connection with the coloring of textile fabrics," and he vaguely observed that "architects and artisans find the scheme convenient in studying the effect of adjacent colors," but he did not name names. Bradley made a similarly general comment in reference to the "color top," a miniature version of the color wheel, informing readers that "practical applications of the color top are already being made, as for example, in the selection of house furnishings." Bradley, *Elementary Color,* 112.

34. Rossi, "The Rules of Perception," 247.
35. Later color standardizers, such as the Textile Color Card Association discussed in Chapter 9 of the present volume, created "cable numbers" for use in describing hues in cable and telegraph communications.
36. See Albert H. Munsell, "A Measured Training of the Color Sense," *Education* 29, no. 6 (February 1909): 360–80; and *A Color Notation: A Measured Color System, Based on the Three Qualities Hue, Value, and Chroma with Illustrative Models, Charts, and a Course of Study Arranged for Teachers*, 2nd ed. (Boston, 1907).
37. See Louis Prang, Mary Dana Hicks, and John S. Clark, *Color Instruction: Suggestions for a Course of Instruction in Color for Public Schools* (New York, 1893).
38. Bradley, *Elementary Color,* 79.
39. Bradley, *Color in the Kindergarten,* 34.
40. Bradley, *Elementary Color,* 84.
41. Bradley, *Color in the Kindergarten,* 35.
42. Bradley, *Elementary Color,* 88–89, 97; Bradley, *Color in the Kindergarten,* 40.
43. Bradley, *Color in the Kindergarten,* 40.
44. Ibid., 32.
45. Bradley, *Elementary Color,* 6.
46. Katherine M. Ball, "The Development of the Color Sense," *Journal of Proceedings and Addresses of the National Education Association of the United States* 49 (1911): 486.
47. See William Leach, *The Land of Desire: Merchants, Power, and the Rise of a New American Culture* (New York, 1993); and Blaszczyk, *Color Revolution.*
48. L. Frank Baum, *The Art of Decorating Dry Goods Windows and Interiors: A Complete Manual of Window Trimming, Designed as an Educator in all the Details of the Art, According to the Best Accepted Methods, and Treating Fully Every Important Subject* (Chicago, 1900), 27.
49. Ibid., 35.
50. Bradley, *Color in the School-Room,* 13.
51. Ibid.
52. Bradley, *Elementary Color,* 99.
53. Bradley, *Color in the Kindergarten,* 20.
54. See Foster Wygant, *School Art in American Culture, 1820–1970* (Cincinnati, OH, 1993), 61–62, and Mary Ann Stankiewicz, *Roots of Art Educational Practice* (Worchester, MA, 2001), 36, for accounts of how the systematic color instruction programs of Bradley, Prang, and Munsell gave way to methods that privileged "free expression" over the laws of color harmony.

55. For other attempts to understand the historical intersections between education and consumerism in terms of sensory training and the immersive qualities of play, see Gillian Brown, "Child's Play," *differences: A Journal of Feminist Cultural Studies* 11, no. 3 (Fall 1999): 76–106; Joshua Yumibe, "On the Education of the Senses: Synesthetic Perception from the 'Democratic Art' of Chromolithography to Modernism," *New Review of Film and Television Studies* 7, no. 3 (September 2009): 257–74.

PART II

Gender and Color

CHAPTER 4

"Real Men Wear Pink"? A Gender History of Color

Dominique Grisard

The first thing that happens to a newborn baby today is that it is color-coded—pink if a girl, blue if a boy. For girls, in particular, this is just the beginning of an extensive color-coded gendering process. At two months, a pink sparkly headband adorns a girl's hairless head. At age one, her little bed has been taken over by pink cuddly things. By the time she is two or three, this girl will likely be the proud owner of a pink empire populated by Disney Princess, Barbie, Hello Kitty and Princess Lillifee paraphernalia. The anthropologist Christine Yano has coined the term "pink globalization" to refer to this transnational phenomenon, the pinkification of girl culture and the particular femininity that it recycles and circulates around the globe[1] (Fig 4.1).

Since the early 2000s, however, more and more girl advocates have openly criticized pink's seductive pull on little girls. They are sure that pink incites girls to act in artificial and superficial ways, instead of letting them develop authentic feminine selves. To give these voices credit, it does seem as if the desire to be pretty sticks like an affective glue to the pink princess dresses worn by little girls the world over. On the other hand, when in June 2014 Prince George, the one-year-old son of British royals Prince William and Kate Middleton, the Duke and Duchess of Cambridge, was spotted wearing pink dungarees at his father's polo match, no one seemed to fear that he was falling prey to little-girl princess culture. Instead, mass media stepped in to affirm the little boy's masculinity and agency: "Real men wear pink," proclaimed the free daily newspaper *Metro* cheekily. In fact, little George's pink dungarees were presented to the public as a "real" man's choice for getting in touch with his "feminine side."[2]

D. Grisard (✉)
Center for Gender Studies, University of Basel, Basel, Switzerland

R.L. Blaszczyk, U. Spiekermann (eds.), *Bright Modernity*, Worlds of Consumption, DOI 10.1007/978-3-319-50745-3_4

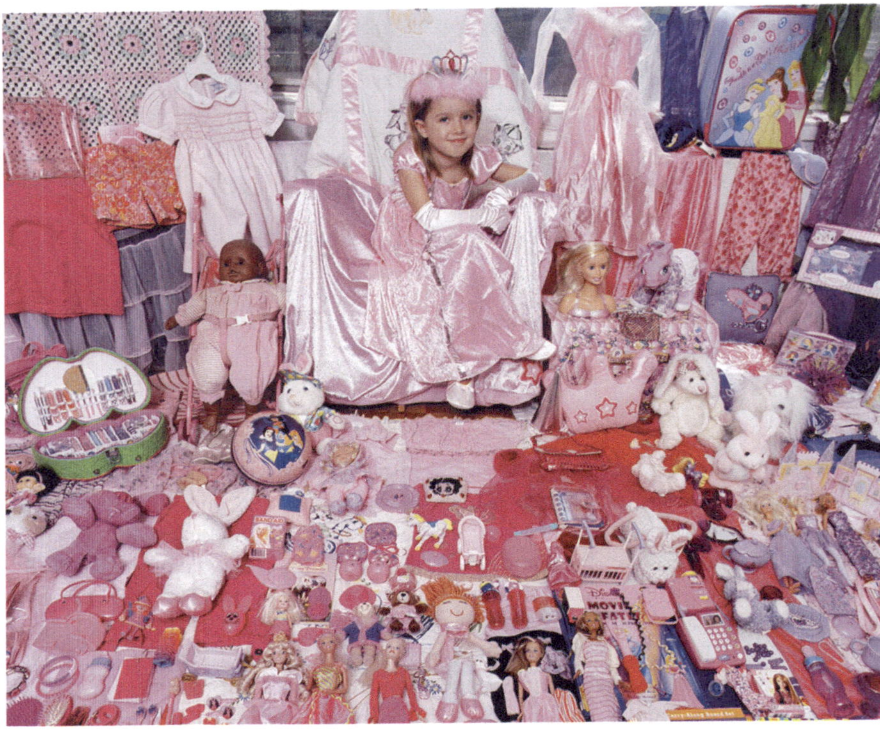

Fig. 4.1 One artist's rendering of transnational pink girl culture: *The Pink Project—Tess and Her Pink and Purple Things*, Lightjet print, 2006, by JeongMee Yoon

Source: Copyright © JeongMee Yoon, 2006, and used with the artist's permission. For more on her Pink and Blue Project, see http://www.jeongmeeyoon.com/aw_pinkblue.htm.

One way of making sense of the different reactions to girls and boys in pink is to look at the relationship between gender and color historically. Tracing the metonymic relationship between color and femininity in the Western history of art, fashion, and marketing helps contextualize current anxieties about pink's feminizing abilities. It will become apparent that the global circulation of color theories and actual paints and dyes since the sixteenth century, on the one hand, and the "color revolution" in marketing and fashion of the early-to-mid twentieth century, on the other hand, paved the way for today's global "affective economy" of pink.[3] Historicizing the current "pinkification" of girl culture will also shed light on the tension between the notion that pink is merely a color, on the surface, and thus superficial, and the anxiety that pink might impact the psyche after all, affecting core gender and sexual attributes. What can past and present preoccupations with pink—and color more generally—tell us about gender and desire?

The first section of this chapter touches on the gendering of color and painting by Italian and French art critics in the sixteenth and nineteenth centuries. It identifies artificiality, superficiality, seduction, and femininity as dominant themes in the history of color. The second section discusses the coloring of gender in nineteenth- and mostly twentieth-century fashion and marketing. It explores the deeply seductive power attributed to color. Whoever fell prey to the allure of color was deemed weak-willed and emotional, personality traits commonly attributed to women. The third section hones in on the gender history of the color pink and explains how in the 1950s pink became attached to a new feminine beauty ideal. In light of this history, the fourth section returns to the gendered ways in which color organizes current Western child culture and the stamp of artificiality, superficiality, and seduction that sticks to pink femininity today.

The Gendering of Color: Sixteenth- and Nineteenth-Century European Art Criticism

In the Italian Renaissance art controversy commonly termed the *paragone*, color was pitted against rational, masculine *disegno*—design or form. To the proponents of *disegno,* line and drawing were the essential and primary features of a painting, whereas color was deemed secondary if not superfluous. Indeed, these sixteenth-century art critics devalued color as superficial by comparing it to women.[4] Two distinct, if related metaphors were invoked. Much like women supposedly used cosmetics to disguise their real selves and seduce men, an artist was believed to use color to enchant and trick the observer. In this logic, color distracted the viewer from appreciating a painting's form, thereby cheating him of direct access to the painting's essence. Thus, the artist's use of color was deemed a form of artistic prostitution.[5] A second metaphor suggested that being transfixed by color was like falling prey to feminine seduction, for artists and viewers alike. Developing too close a relationship to color, like becoming too intimate with one's muse, was believed to have detrimental effects on a painter's genius. It was perceived as a show of excessive emotional involvement, and it revealed a lack of distance to one's art, the end of artistic mastery.[6] By contrast, a good painting, similar to an honest woman's true (read: inner) beauty, was unadorned and natural.[7]

Similar comparisons of color to women can be found in mid- to late-nineteenth-century French art criticism, though this time color and form were seen not as adversaries but as complementary forces. Charles Blanc, head of the French Department for the Visual Arts at the Ministry of the Interior and director of the École des Beaux-Arts, claimed that "the union of design and color is necessary to beget painting, just as is the union of man and woman to beget mankind, but design must maintain its preponderance over color. Otherwise painting speeds to its ruin: it will fall through color just as mankind fell through Eve."[8] All the same, despite conceding the importance of both form and color, Blanc, like his Renaissance predecessors, asserted the dominance of the former over the latter. Employing a gendered metaphor of domesticity, he naturalized the hierarchical relationship of form and color by comparing it to that of men and women.

Thus far, I have highlighted the gendering of color in European art criticism, which entailed a pronounced feminization of color. This coding of color as feminine went hand in hand with the marked feminization of those who let themselves be swayed by color. Unsurprisingly, Charles Blanc dedicated the greater part of his 1875 treatise on ornamentation and dress exclusively to women, equating color with feeling and feeling with women.[9] In his view, rational bourgeois men knew how to control their attraction to color. A human being in his or her "primitive" state, however, was fully controlled by his or her affects and emotions and so would fall prey to color.[10] In line with colonial thinking of the time, not just European women fell into his category of the "primitive"; Blanc also included children and "savages." Of the latter's aesthetic sensibilities, he declared, "the Moor, the Negro, the Arab, and the Indian deck themselves with staring hues."[11]

As the nineteenth century progressed, bright colors became a signifier of bourgeois women, children, and "exotic" Others.[12] Yet as the next section will show, white bourgeois women could set themselves apart from women of other classes, races, and nations by following certain color rules. In the back of male commentators' minds, however, even the most rule-observing bourgeois woman could at any moment fall prey to the affective and emotional pull of color again, which is why male color experts of the fashion and advertising industry made it their goal to attract female consumers.

The Coloring of Gender: Nineteenth- and Twentieth-Century Fashion and Advertising

The innovations in dye technologies in the mid- to late nineteenth century, described by Alexander Engel in Chapter 2, made colorful fabrics available and affordable to the European middle classes.[13] Soon, women's dresses were being made up in the wildest colors imaginable.[14] A discrete children's fashion also emerged, first in England, with other European countries following suit.[15] Bourgeois men, on the other hand, were dressing in dark suits by this time.[16] This practice set them apart from the brightly colored apparel of their middle-class wives and children, the flamboyantly dressed aristocracy, the dingily dressed working class, and the unfamiliar world of the colonial Other (Fig. 4.2).

Still, despite the availability of hundreds of different colors and shades, fashion dictated that bourgeois women exercise restraint.[17] The color of a woman's dress had to harmonize with her complexion and hair color, as prescribed by the prominent French color theorist, Michel-Eugène Chevreul. Soft pinks supposedly suited blondes best, and only the most fair-skinned

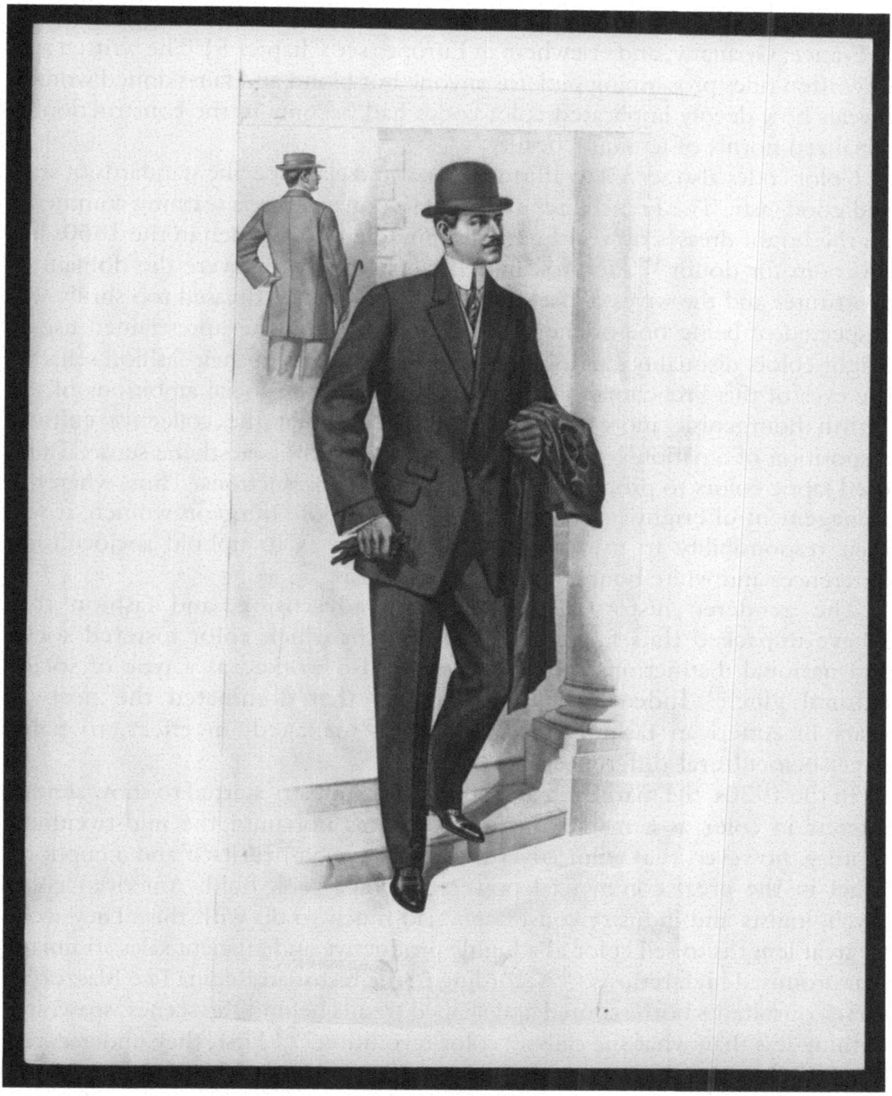

Fig. 4.2 Example of masculine bourgeois fashion at the turn of the century—the dark suit

Source: 1896–1913, Plate 009, Fashion Plates, Men's 1880–1939, Costume Institute Fashion Plates, Metropolitan Museum of Art, New York, NY.

women were believed to be able to pull off certain color combinations without risking ridicule.[18] This performance of restraint was firmly rooted in class, racial, and national biases, all of which were buttressed by fashion periodicals such as *Godey's Lady's Book and Magazine* in the United States, the

Englishwoman's Domestic Magazine in Great Britain, and similar publications in France, Germany, and elsewhere in Europe (see Chapter 5). The written and unwritten rules proscribing pink for anyone but blond and fair-skinned women reveals how deeply implicated color codes had become in the construction of racialized norms of feminine beauty.

Color codes also served to affirm national and class-specific standards of style and good taste. The French literary critic Hippolyte Taine's scathing comments on the bright dresses of wealthy English middle-class women in the 1860s left no room for doubt.[19] He proclaimed that bright colors were the domain of prostitutes and the wives of parvenus. Any woman who dressed too shrilly was suspected of being one or the other.[20] Not only did the unrestrained use of bright colors disqualify English middle-class women and their fashion sense in the eyes of this Frenchman but it also invalidated the social ambitions of the British bourgeoisie more generally. By arguing that the collective cultural disposition of a nation's middle class correlated with its aesthetic sense, Taine used fabric colors to propagate class and national distinctions. Thus, when the management of bright colors became the domain of bourgeois women, it was their responsibility to use colors responsibly so as to uphold sociocultural differences and white bourgeois beauty standards.

The gendered history of art criticism, advertising, and fashion that I have unpacked thus far stresses the ways in which color fostered social and national distinctions. However, color also worked as a type of sociocultural glue.[21] Indeed, the bright colors that dominated the postwar years in American fashion and advertising managed, in effect, to paint over sociocultural differences.

In the 1920s, the marketing and advertising industry started to show serious interest in color as a marketing tool.[22] It was not until the mid-twentieth century, however, that color advertising fully established itself and a euphoric belief in the great commercial powers of color took hold. American color psychologists and industry consultants had much to do with this. They went to great lengths to sell color as a highly productive and efficient sales stimulant that promised high returns.[23] According to the historian Regina Lee Blaszczyk, these consultants both scouted and shaped trends behind the scenes, spawning nothing less than what she calls a "color revolution."[24] First, they underscored how color garnered consumers' attention. In the words of one contemporary advertising expert, color possessed a "pulling power." Consultants emphasized color's "attention and illustrative value" to advertisers and clothing manufacturers and, more importantly, the ways in which color influenced consumers, whether they wanted it or not.[25] According to the eminent color consultants Faber Birren and Eric P. Danger (who are discussed at length in Chapter 10), color affected human beings on a base, "primitive," and "subconscious" level.[26] Color appealed to emotion, not reason, they concurred, and feeling was "likely to dominate reason."[27] Danger reasoned that this was why babies (ostensibly) responded earlier and more strongly to color than they did to form.[28]

Numerous color experts opposed the common perception that color just added superficial allure to a product. Instead they maintained that color affected mood and temperament, even to the point of provoking physical sensations in people.[29] Indeed, these experts declared that color produced desires and a need to act on them.[30] Howard Ketcham, one of the most influential corporate advertising psychologists, was confident that the U.S. advertising industry knew how to use color to "create... demand."[31] The close attention that he paid to female role models in film and theater suggested that he envisioned consumers as women: "It's a full-time job keeping tabs on color influence ranging from *My Fair Lady* to *Cinderella*," Ketcham stressed.[32] Indeed, advertising consultants generally presupposed female consumers, and they assumed that these consumers were "more sensitive to color than men."[33] Similarly to the art critics before them, these professionals explained women's color preferences with their ostensibly more emotional and gentle natures.[34]

Thus were the industrial color consultants able to inscribe themselves into a century-old tradition of depicting consumption as a feminine, irrational, and excessive activity—the opposite of production conceived as the domain of white rational man.[35] It was not long, however, before the advertising and fashion industries began encouraging bourgeois men to dress more colorfully as well. The 1950s saw the establishment of men's leisurewear, which brightened the color scheme of men's wardrobes considerably. Early male adopters of the Ivy League look that came to be called "preppy" could now be seen wearing pink dress shirts, although it is likely that their wives or mothers bought them these colorful items.[36]

This circumstance notwithstanding, industrial color consultants such as Faber Birren continued to emphasize the importance of paying attention to gendered color preferences, asserting, for example, that "blue is useful in appealing to men, rose and pink in appealing to women."[37] Louis Cheskin even took the color-coded bourgeois gender difference a step further. This self-made color expert insisted that women who liked colors normally preferred by men exhibited other masculine characteristics, whereas "men who prefer delicate or 'feminine' tints show other effeminate traits."[38] Cheskin never earned the respect of his colleagues.[39] Yet his claim that a person's color preference could reveal his or her true gender identity was only the logical next step in the argument that color consultants had made all along, namely, that color's impact on human beings was profound, that specific colors appealed to men and others to women, whereby women were more sensitive to the emotions, desires, and behaviors triggered by colorful things. The advertising industry and their consultants thus tapped into feminine popular culture to produce emotional and affective attachments to brightly colored Cinderella fantasies. Feminine hues were applied to all types of consumer goods, even the mundane electric light bulb (Chapter 8). These businesses and experts were convinced that they had mastered the female mentality and therefore consumer demand.[40]

The chromophilia of U.S. advertising from the mid-twentieth century on can be read as a symptom of the feminization of consumer culture more generally. For starters, American women were decisive in both the buying and selling of consumer goods. While white middle-class Mrs. Consumers were in charge of family spending, perfectly styled, ever-attentive "shopgirls" were trained to sell them a particular image and emotion with each product. Male commentators claimed that saleswomen played to their customers' vanity, effectively enchanting them with their brightly colored goods and the "gushy feelings" they represented.[41] Women thus came to embody what the historian Victoria de Grazia has called the "irresistible empire," the mid-twentieth-century American model of consumer capitalism that extended across the globe.[42] That said, the colorful "vain and silly feminine world" of consumption was geared to "seducing" everyone—women, men, and children alike.[43]

The Gender History of the Color Pink

Right around the time when men were incited to wear brighter colors, one color began to be singled out as the most feminine of all: pink. The color pink had long been a favorite in children's fashion.[44] If infants and toddlers from middle-class families were not dressed in white, they would be seen in pretty pastel shades of pink, blue, or yellow. (Fig. 4.3) The association of pink with girls and blue with boys was not dominant until the 1950s or later.[45] In fact, the textile historian Jo Paoletti cites American women's magazines and fashion catalogs of the 1920s and 1930s that declared pink as the "more decided and stronger" color and thus more suitable for boys.[46] Similarly, Catholic regions throughout Europe were known to associate light blue with girls, a tradition attributed to Christian iconography, in which the Virgin Mary was frequently depicted wearing a blue cloak.[47] Mostly, though, pink and blue were used interchangeably as baby colors. Thus, pink did not become synonymous with girlie femininity overnight, especially not in Central Europe, where the gendered blue–pink color-coding seems to have taken hold later than in the United States and where there remain substantial class, religious, and regional differences.[48]

Pink's popularity in the 1950s was not due to girls' princess culture—even though pink's biggest fan, Mamie Eisenhower, was a princess of sorts. The First Lady cultivated the image of the girl. Not only did she dislike the "old lady" look but—like any other girl—she loved to shop.[49] Instead of having her clothes tailor-made, like the First Ladies before her, she claimed to buy her outfits off the rack. She thus came to be the poster child for American mass consumption in the 1950s. Her love of pink seemed to know no bounds. She wore a pink Nettie Rosenstein gown for her husband's inaugural ball, which she had embroidered with over 2,000 gemstones in various pink tones.[50] She also decorated her boudoir in the family section of the White House in assorted pink shades, from the tops of her cosmetic jars

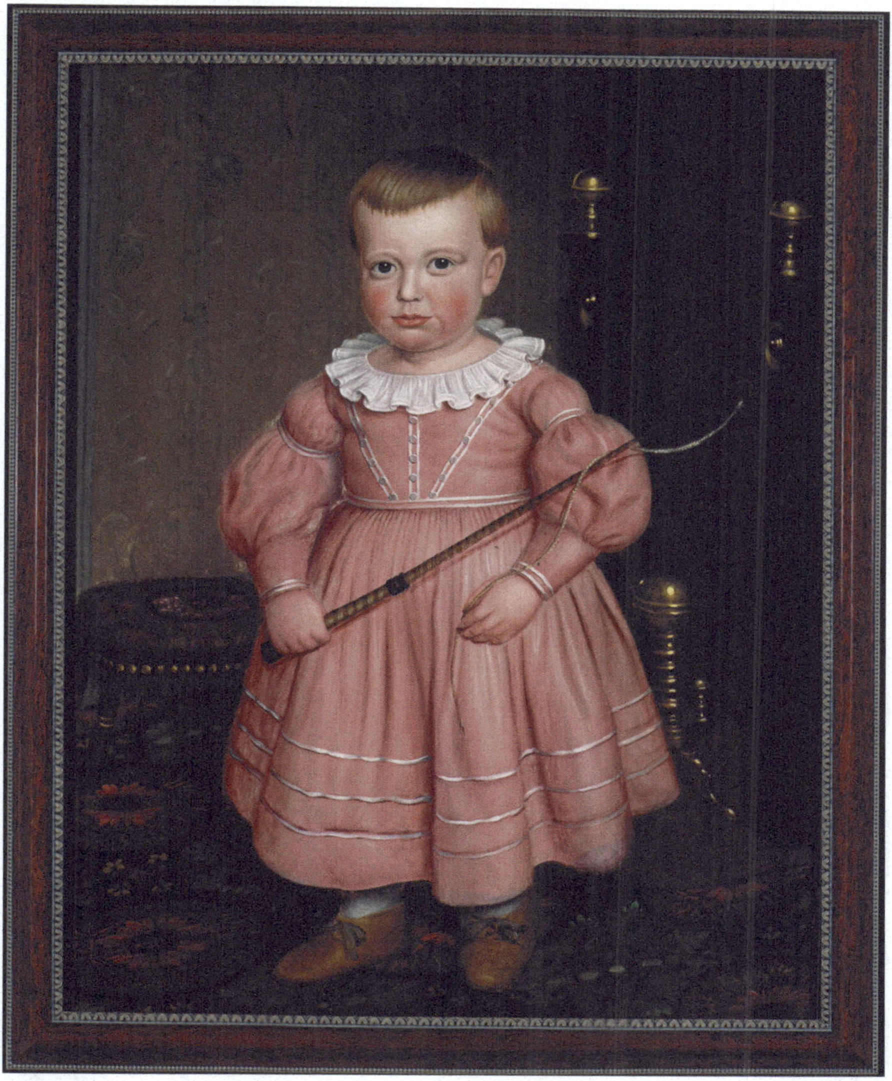

Fig. 4.3 Example of a boy in pink in the early nineteenth century: *Young Boy with Whip*, anonymous, American School, ca. 1840, oil on canvas

Source: Honolulu Museum of Art, bequest of John Gregg Allerton, 1993 (7440.1).

and the headboard of her bed to the fluffy bath mat in her bathroom.[51] If that were not enough, Mamie's Cabin, the vacation home of the presidential couple, and Mamie's Dream House, the couple's post-presidency home, were devoted to the color (Fig. 4.4).

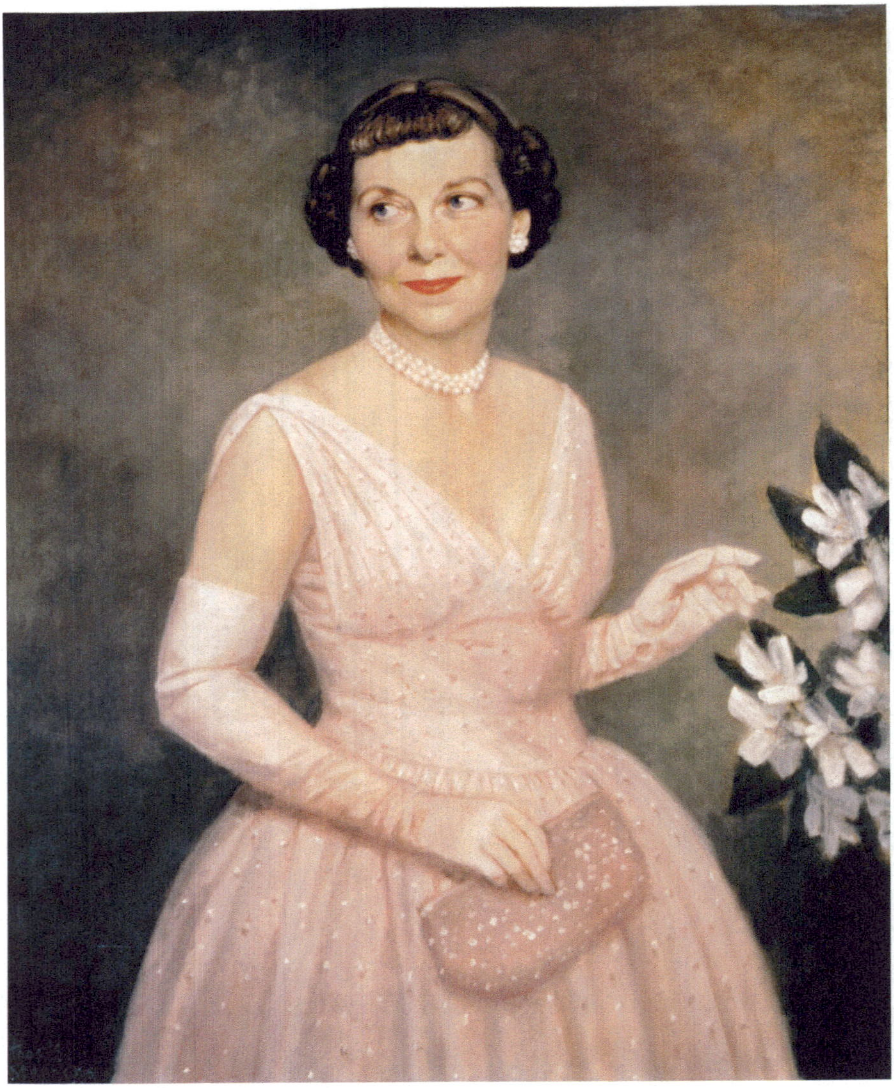

Fig. 4.4 Mamie Eisenhower in her favorite color, oil on canvas by Thomas Edgar Stevens, 1959

Source: White House Collection/White House Historical Association.

It did not take long for middle-class women to catch on. In the United States in the mid-1950s, such women started buying clothes and hats in the pink shade favored by Mamie Eisenhower, one subsequently dubbed Mamie Pink or First Lady Pink.[52] Mamie Pink was a watered down, soft kind of pink that showed little resemblance to the much stronger shocking pink that the Italian fashion designer Elsa Schiaparelli had promoted since the late 1930s.[53]

If Mamie Eisenhower's love of pink contributed to the feminization of the color, it was pink's strong connection to childhood that made it exude youth and an innocent kind of sexiness.[54] The color pink came to be associated with the light-hearted feeling and appealing innocence of rosy-cheeked girls. Teenage girls of the baby-boomer generation embraced pink, which in turn became emblematic of their conspicuous consumption. Indeed, the popularity of the color pink in the 1950s, the cultural historian Karal Ann Marling argues, signaled a fundamental change in fashion, consumption, and femininity. A new focus on the teenage girl supplanted the beauty ideal of the forever thirty-five-year-old woman. A younger generation became the main target of the advertising and fashion industries. New fashion and beauty standards fetishized the adolescent, not fully grown girl's body. Predictably, women's dress sizes began to shrink.[55] Thus, pink's soaring popularity among women in the mid 1950s and early 1960s went hand in hand with increased attention to the girl as a consumer target group and fashion symbol. The latter trend, in turn, promoted the infantilization of adult women's fashion, on the one hand, and the heteronormative feminization and sexualization of the girl child, on the other.

This development raises the question of how the tropes identified in this and the previous sections of this essay—the superficiality and artificiality of color, the power of color to produce desire as well as express core gender differences, and the rise of pink and adolescent girlhood as markers of heteronormative femininity—inform public debate over pink princess culture today. How do the gendering of color, the coloring of gender, and the pinkification of girl femininity play out in children's culture today?

Girls' and Boys' Love of Pink Princess Culture

A 2006 article by Sandy Chiu et al. in the psychology journal *Sex Roles* discusses how parents of boys diagnosed with Gender Identity Disorder "report that their sons are 'obsessed' with the colors pink and purple and that their drawings are often replete with these colors."[56] Indeed, today the connection between pink and girlie femininity is so pervasive that a boy child's preference for the color is quickly read as an indication of homosexuality or a transgender identity. A 2011 *New York Times* article features parents sharing strategies on how to raise boys who love to dress up in what a New York University study terms "PFD" or "Pink Frilly Dresses."[57] These progressive parents negotiate their children's love of so-called pink frilly dresses by letting them dress, act, and feel "pink" around the house.[58] Indeed, there is a growing "intimate consumer public" expressing support of pink boys.[59] An array of self-help books and blogs encourage parents to love their children's gender nonconformity.[60] One prime example is the nonfiction picture book *My Princess Boy*. Its author, Cheryl Kilodavis, tells the story of her "4-year-old boy who happily expresses his authentic self by enjoying 'traditional girl' things like jewelry, sparkles or anything pink."[61] Kilodavis describes when her son Dyson seems truly happy: whenever he is shopping with his mom for pretty pink bags and sparkly pink dresses.

In light of the psychological discourse that construes "sex-dimorphic color preference in children" as an indication of Gender Identity Disorder or Gender Dysphoria, these parents' acceptance is exemplary.[62] The right to an authentic self—to the coherence of one's inner feelings, identity, and outer appearance—seems to be the impetus behind this parental support for the unconventional gender presentation of these children.[63] The parents are invested in their children's authenticity. Indeed, they buy material goods—ballet shoes, nail polish, and pink dresses—to help their children discover their ostensibly true feminine selves.[64] Consumer goods seem to be the magic key to their children's happiness and to the parents' own happiness, too. Literally and figuratively, authenticity comes at a price. For these parents seem to believe that their children can only express their authentic feminine selves with the help of what some might consider artificial, superficial, and expensive consumer goods.

Yet if some boys' predilections for pink has made the news in recent months and years, most interventions about the color pink focus on girls and on how the media and marketing affect girls' self-esteem, aspirations, and body image. One prominent example is the campaign and website *Pinkstinks,* launched by London twins Abi Moore and Emma Moore. These mothers of two sons and two daughters, respectively, "challenge ... the culture of pink which invades every aspect of girls' lives."[65] In addition, *Pinkstinks* educates readers on who reaps the benefits of pink girl culture. In 2010, *Disney* marketed 25,000 different *Princess* merchandising items for total revenue of four billion U.S. dollars (Fig. 4.5).

Since the late 1990s, there has been growing interest in the ways in which girls are affected by pink femininity. Three main positions dominate public debate. Sue Palmer, author of *Toxic Childhood*, espouses what may be called a colors-are-seductive perspective: She is convinced that overexposure to pink stunts girls' personalities. "It's under their skin from a very early age and severely limits choices, and decisions."[66] In an article in the *Daily Mail* with the catchy title "Why Pink Makes Me See Red," Palmer expresses her fear that girls exposed to pink are not "old enough to make rational choices. Their brains simply aren't sufficiently developed for the application of reason. So when marketers turn their big guns on young children, they're not so much entertaining and informing as brainwashing them." The author of *Toxic Childhood* explains that because children "operate mainly on emotion," the "deep emotional attachments made in the first six or seven years are likely to influence the way they behave for the rest of their lives."[67]

Michael Gurian, a therapist and author of *Nurture the Nature*, disagrees.[68] He is a proponent of what might be termed a color-is-superficial view. Too much pink does not have a profoundly negative effect, according to him. "Scientists all argue the same thing—you cannot have a biological organism without having an

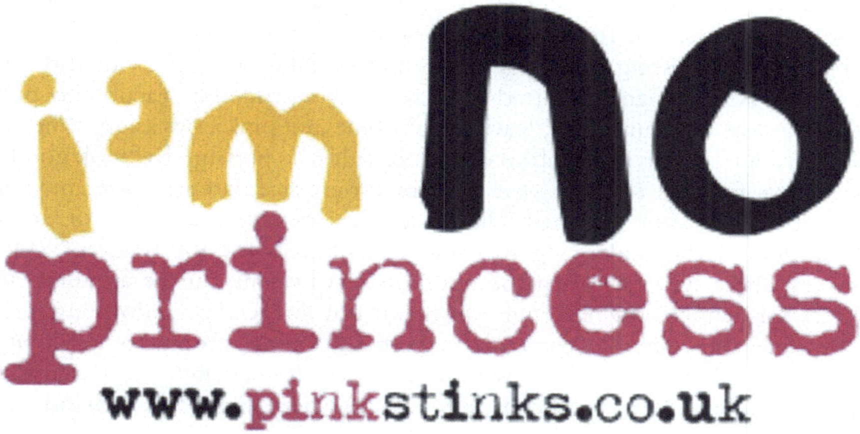

Fig. 4.5 Countering feminized pink consumer culture: "There is more than one way to be a girl . . . "

Source: Pinkstinks, http://www.pinkstinks.co.uk, and used by permission.

environment for it to exist in, but that environment does not change the very basic make-up of that organism."[69] Gurian believes that the effects of exposure to pink or any other color are temporary and inconsequential.

The third position combines the first two views but looks more closely at how pink affects femininity. For Peggy Orenstein, the author of *Cinderella Ate My Daughter*, pink femininity is artificial and superficial, yet it affects girls' core identities. Essentially, Orenstein criticizes how "the all-pervasive media machine aimed at our daughters—and at us—from womb to tomb . . . presents femininity as performance, sexuality as performance, identity as performance, and each of those traits as available for a price."[70] Drawing on the developmental psychologist Deborah L. Tolman's work, Orenstein argues that the commercialization of pink femininity results in girls not knowing how they feel about their true feminine selves anymore: "I have to remind them that looking good is *not* a feeling."[71] In addition, she warns that girls send out sexual vibes before they are emotionally mature enough to understand them. Orenstein posits that the color pink forms part of a shallow type of femininity that is obsessed with appearance. She then contrasts pink femininity with authentic femininity, which is not about superficial looks but deep feelings and healthy autonomy.

Significantly, these three dominant positions in the contemporary debate about the impact of ubiquitous pink marketing on girls reproduce the two contradictions that I have traced historically above. On the one hand, color has been viewed since early modern art criticism as superficial and deceptive, just as the twentieth-century advertising industry promoting attire in gendered colors has been perceived as a vehicle of mere appearance. On the other hand, scholars, parents, and the media focus on color's role in generating core sex differences, suggesting that color deeply affects children's gender identity and sexuality. An analogous contradiction is today's gendered reaction to pink color choices by young girls, leaving both blue and pink boys aside. Whereas pink girls are seen to succumb to consumer culture's pressure to "look good," boys' love for pink (or blue)—at least for progressive parents—is deemed an authentic expression of their child's gender identity, sexuality, or both. Regardless of the underlying psychological motives for the toddlers' color choices, these two views beg the question of why pink can be an authentic choice for gender-nonconforming boys but not for gender-conforming girls. Why does the stain of fakery and superficiality adhere only to girls' pink femininity? Moreover, since newborn babies are immediately immersed in a color-coded, gendered child culture, what and where might this authentic self even be?

In light of these questions, I contend that we need to develop further Ruth Barnes and Joanne B. Eicher's observation that "dress is one of the most significant markers of gender identity."[72] For attire and its color do not just express one's identity to other people but also help form the very fabric of one's identity. As the aphorism goes, "clothes make the man"—and the woman. In other words, the act of buying, wearing, and being seen in pink frilly dresses is central to how today's girls and boys construct their gender and sexuality. To add yet another idiom to the mix, the expression "wearing the pants" underscores how seemingly innocuous fashion trends are intimately bound up with the material and symbolic gender order.[73] Thus, when parents, child advocates, and feminists challenge the growing pinkification of girl culture, they both support and challenge the power of color and dress in the struggle against gender and child commodification.

Conclusion

The two contradictions unpacked in this chapter—the notion that color is superficial but capable of altering core gender differences and the presumption that pink girls have been seduced by outside influences whereas pink boys are merely expressing their true gender identities or sexual selves—are metonymically connected. In the case of gender-conforming girls, color is superficial, the superficial is deceptive, deception is a form of masquerade, masquerade is femininity, femininity is consumerism, consumerism is advertising, and advertising is pink. Boys' choices, by contrast, appear authentic, even those of toddlers in pink dungarees, and the position of boys appears homologous to the subject position of producers. Operating through a discourse that devalues women's collective consumption as irrational but elevates the choice of the masculine individual as rational and authentic, a child's love of pink consumer goods is thus doubly gendered.

Far from arguing that feeling blue is the real deal while happy pink femininity is mere delusion, my intention has been to historicize today's color-coded child consumer culture.[74] Pitting authenticity against pink artificial femininity—feeling good against looking good—does not shed light on the workings of girl culture and feminine identifications. Analyzing these gendered oppositions historically, however, help us to understand how gender and desire are constructed in today's color-coded child consumer culture. For one, the fact that girls' desires are constructed as coming from the outside but boys' desires from the inside reveals how incoherent common understandings of desire and sexual identity really are. Furthermore, today's color-coded child culture reflects a shift in the ways in which gender and sexuality are produced and reaffirmed in contemporary Western societies. There is a growing consensus that gender differences are eroding; the phenomenon of girls surpassing boys in school is often cited as evidence. One glance at the pinkification of girl culture is enough to call this commonly held belief into question. Gender differences may have declined in the legal, political, or educational arenas, but they have become more pronounced in child consumer culture.

Color codes teach girls and boys gendered consumer practices from the moment they are born. If we subscribe to color psychologists' and consultants' belief in color's power to affect the body and the mind in ways beyond the control of those deemed uncivilized or pre-civilized, then pink is the glue that sticks to pink frilly dresses and forms an affective bond among those girls and boys who share pink toys, clothes, and shoes as well as tales of princesses, fairies and unicorns—a cultural imaginary priming pink children for a dreamy prince and the disappointment that ensues when he turns out to be a toad or a regular human being after all. If investment in the authentic self undergirds progressive parents' support of pink boys, it is gendered notions of seduction and disappointment that inform their critique of girls' pink femininity.[75] To borrow Sara Ahmed's term, the "affective economy" of pink draws on a repository of feelings, looks, and ideas about girlie femininity.[76] Indeed, the color pink allows these feelings to be recycled and to circulate globally, establishing an affective bond with pink consumer goods. Despite the fact that the affective economy of pink is undergirded by a long tradition of equating color with femininity and femininity with color, the way in which gender and sexuality is produced and dramatized through color in early childhood today is unprecedented.

Notes

1. See Christine R. Yano, *Pink Globalization: Hello Kitty's Trek Across the Pacific* (Durham, NC, 2013).
2. Alison Lynch, "Prince George Shows Real Men Wear Pink as He Takes Charge at the Polo," *Metro,* June 16, 2014, http://metro.co.uk/2014/06/16/prince-george-shows-real-men-wear-pink-as-he-takes-charge-at-the-polo-4763056/. See also Rebecca Pocklington, "Real Men Wear Pink! After Prince George Wears Pink Dungarees, More Celebrity Men Looking Rosy," *Mirror*, June 15, 2014,

http://www.mirror.co.uk/3am/celebrity-news/real-men-wear-pink-after-3700351; Sara Barns, "Pretty in Pink! Prince George Looks Adorable in Dungarees at the Polo," *Express*, June 16, 2014, http://www.express.co.uk/life-style/style/482782/Prince-George-pink-dungarees.

3. Regina Lee Blaszczyk, *The Color Revolution* (Cambridge, MA, 2012). I am drawing on the concept of "affective economy" as developed by Sara Ahmed, "Affective Economies," *Social Text* 22, no. 2 (2004): 121–39.
4. David Batchelor, *Chromophobia* (London, 2000); Claire Bates, "Should We Not Dress Girls in Pink?," *BBC News Magazine*, January 8, 2009, http://news.bbc.co.uk/2/hi/uk_news/magazine/7817496.stm; Daniela Bohde, *Haut, Fleisch und Farbe—Körperlichkeit und Materialität in den Gemälde Tizians* (Emsdetten, 2002); Jacqueline Lichtenstein, "Making Up Representation: The Risks of Femininity," *Representations* 20 (1987): 77–87; Jacqueline Lichtenstein, *The Eloquence of Color: Rhetoric and Painting in the French Classical Age* (Berkeley, CA, 1993).
5. Lichtenstein, "Making Up Representation," 79.
6. Ibid., 80.
7. Ibid., 78.
8. Charles Blanc, *Grammaire des arts du dessin: Architecture, sculpture, peinture* (Paris, 1867), 23; also Misook Song, *Art Theories of Charles Blanc* (Ann Arbor, 1984), 61–62.
9. Charles Blanc, *L'Art dans la parure et dans le vêtement* (Paris, 1875); English translation: Charles Blanc, *Art in Ornament and Dress* (New York, 1877).
10. Blanc, *Art in Ornament and Dress,* 67; Blanc, *L'Art dans la parure et dans le vêtement*, 90.
11. Blanc, *Art in Ornament and Dress,* 67. On the infantilization and exotization of color, see also Michael Taussig, *What Color Is the Sacred?* (Chicago IL, 2009), 4.
12. Blanc, *Art in Ornament and Dress,* 71.
13. Anthony S. Travis, *The Rainbow Makers: The Origins of the Synthetic Dyestuffs Industry in Western Europe* (Bethlehem, PA, 1993).
14. Blaszczyk, *Color Revolution*, 42.
15. Ingeborg Weber-Kellermann, *Die Kindheit* (Frankfurt am Main, 1997); see also Weber-Kellermann, *Der Kinder neue Kleider: 200 Jahre deutsche Kindermoden in ihrer sozialen Zeichensetzung* (Frankfurt am Main, 1985).
16. John Harvey, *Men in Black* (Chicago, IL, 1995); see also Anja Meyerrose, *Herren im Anzug: Eine transatlantische Geschichte von Klassengesellschaften im Langen 19. Jahrhundert* (Cologne, 2016).
17. Robert Finlay, "Weaving the Rainbow: Visions of Color in World History," *Journal of World History* 18, no. 4 (2007): 383–431.
18. Philippe Perrot, *Fashioning the Bourgeoisie: A History of Clothing in the Nineteenth Century* (Princeton, NJ, 1994), 102.
19. Hippolyte Taine, *Notes on England* (New York, 1872), 23.
20. Ibid., 42.
21. Victoria de Grazia, *Irresistible Empire: America's Advance Through Twentieth-Century Europe* (Cambridge, MA, 2005), 10–11.
22. For example, *Pittford's Manual for Advertisers* (Chicago, 1924), 153 and 124.
23. Ibid., 124.
24. Blaszczyk, *Color Revolution.*
25. Daniel Starch, *Principles of Advertising* (Chicago, 1926), 579.

26. Birren believed that color affected the most "primitive" level of human existence, while Danger focused on color's influence on the "subconscious." Both addressed some kind of base instincts, however. Faber Birren, *Selling Color to People* (New York, 1956), 159; Eric P. Danger, *How to Use Color to Sell: A Cahners Management Guidebook* (Boston, MA, 1968), 5; also Louis Cheskin, *Business Without Gambling: How Successful Marketers Use Scientific Methods* (New York, 1963), 245.
27. Birren, *Selling Color to People*, 159. On Birren, see Wolfgang Saxon, "Obituary: Faber Birren, 88, Expert on Color," *New York Times*, December 31, 1988, See also Blaszczyk, *Color Revolution*, 237.
28. Danger, *How to Use Color to Sell.*
29. Louis Cheskin, *Color Guide for Marketing Media* (New York, 1954), 15.
30. *Pittsford's Manual for Advertisers* (Chicago, 1924), 125.
31. Howard Ketcham, *Color Planning for Business and Industry* (New York, 1958), 203. On Ketcham, see Blaszczyk, *Color Revolution* (Boston, 2012), 242–46.
32. Ketcham, *Color Planning for Business and Industry*, 203; Cheskin, *Color Guide for Marketing Media*, 20; Alfred E. Clark, "Obituary: Louis Cheskin, 72, Studied Motivations and Effects of Color," *New York Times*, October 10, 1981. See also Blaszczyk, *Color Revolution*, 236.
33. W. O. Woodward and George A. Frederick, *Selling Service with the Goods: An Analysis and Synthesis on the Planning, Designing, Construction and Installation of Window Displays* (New York, 1921), 34.
34. Birren, *New Horizons in Color* (New York, 1955), 116.
35. Advertisements portrayed the consumer as an irrational "creature of suggestion" who was easily hypnotized by advertising; Ludy T. Benjamin, *A Brief History of Modern Psychology* (Malden, MA, 2007), 100–101. Excellent histories of the gender of consumption are Kathy Peiss, *Hope in a Jar: The Making of America's Beauty Culture* (New York, 1999); De Grazia, *Irresistible Empire*; Eva Illouz, *Consuming the Romantic Utopia: Love and the Cultural Contradictions of Capitalism* (Berkeley CA, 1997).
36. Karal Ann Marling, *As Seen on TV: The Visual Culture of Everyday Life in the 1950s* (Cambridge, MA, 1994), 40. Brooks Brothers, for example, had been selling pink shirts for "Ivy League Men or Women" since 1949. See Marling, *As Seen on TV*, 173.
37. Birren, *New Horizons in Color*, 127.
38. Cheskin, *Color Guide for Marketing Media*, 20.
39. Blaszczyk, *Color Revolution*, 236.
40. Birren, *Selling Color to People*, 15.
41. De Grazia, *Irresistible Empire*, 430.
42. Ibid., 26.
43. Brent Shannon, *The Cut of His Coat* (Athens OH, 2006), 44.
44. Jo B. Paoletti, *Pink and Blue: Telling the Boys from the Girls in America* (Bloomington, IN, 2012), 88.
45. Jo B. Paoletti, "Dressing for Sexes," n.d., at Midwife Archives, http://www.gentlebirth.org/archives/pinkblue.html; Jo B. Paoletti, "The Gendering of Infants' and Toddlers' Clothing in America," in *The Material Culture of Gender / The Gender of Material Culture*, ed. Katharine Martinez and Kenneth L. Ames (Winterthur, 1997); Jo B. Paoletti, "Clothing and Gender in America: Children's Fashions 1890–1920," *Signs* 13, no. 1 (1987): 136–43. See also

Diane N. Ruble et al., "Pink Frilly Dresses (PFD) and Early Gender Identity" *Princeton Report on Knowledge: Pink* 2, no. 2 (2010), http://www.princeton.edu/prok/issues/2-2/pink_frilly.xml; Jeanne Maglaty, "When Did Girls Start Wearing Pink? Every Generation Brings a New Definition of Masculinity and Femininity that Manifests Itself in Children's Dress," Smithsonian.com, April 7, 2011, http://www.smithsonianmag.com/arts-culture/when-did-girls-start-wearing-pink-1370097/.

46. Paoletti, *Pink and Blue*, 85.
47. Ibid., 89; Eva Heller, *Wie Farben wirken: Farbpsychologie, Farbsymbolik, Kreative Farbgestaltung* (Reinbek bei Hamburg, 1999), 118; see also Ernest Biggs, *Colour in Advertising* (London, 1956).
48. Dominique Grisard, "Rosige Haut, Blaues Blut, Pinkes Tutu: Eine Prinzessinnengeschichte in Farbe," in *"Als habe es die Frauen nicht gegeben": Beiträge zur Frauen- und Geschlechtergeschichte*, ed. Sabine Braunschweig (Zurich, 2014), 101–13; Grisard, "Rosarot und Himmelblau: Die Farbe süsser Beeren und des Himmels bei prächtigem Jagdwetter: Warum Mädchen Rosa lieben," in *Ich Mann: Du Frau: Feste Rollen seit Urzeiten?*, ed. Brigitte Röder (Freiburg, 2014), 54–67.
49. Marling, *As Seen on TV*, 24.
50. Ibid., 34.
51. Ibid., 38.
52. Gay Pauley, "Originator of First Lady Pink Also Standardizes Our Colors," *Wilmington Sunday Star*, August 30, 1953, 16; see also Marling, *As Seen on TV*, 38–40.
53. Blaszczyk, *Color Revolution*, 276. Mamie Pink also contrasted starkly with the black-pink color combination popular with the 1950s youth subcultures that professed to emulate African-American and working-class fashion styles. See William Graebner, *Coming of Age in Buffalo: Youth and Authority in the Postwar Era* (Philadelphia, 1990), 57. See also Lucy Rollin, *Twentieth-Century Teen Culture by the Decades: A Reference Guide* (Westport, CT, 1999), 74.
54. Marling, *As Seen on TV*, 40.
55. Ibid., 43.
56. The article concedes that these observations by parents have not been backed up by empirical research. Sandy W. Chiu. et al., "Sex-Dimorphic Color Preference in Children with Gender Identity Disorder: A Comparison to Clinical and Community Controls," *Sex Roles* 55 (2006): 387.
57. Jan Hoffman, "Boys Will be Boys? Not in These Families," *New York Times*, June 11, 2011; Ruble et al., "Pink Frilly Dresses."
58. I by no means want to suggest that all parents embrace gender nonconforming boys. In fact, the sociologist Emily W. Kane's research indicates that there are next to no worries about girls who act in ways that are perceived to be gender nonconforming, whereas many parents and particularly fathers tend to react negatively to boys liking pink frilly clothing, nail polish, make-up, and Barbie. They also discourage exhibiting "excessive emotionality," which in their perception goes hand in hand with these material goods. Emily W. Kane, "'No Way My Boys Are Going to Be like That!' Parents' Responses to Children's Gender Nonconformity," *Gender and Society* 20, no. 2 (April 2006), 160; Hoffman, "Boys Will be Boys?"

59. On intimate publics, see Lauren Berlant, *The Female Complaint: The Unfinished Business of Sentimentality in American Culture* (Durham, NC, 2008), 10.
60. To name but three: Diane Ehrensaft, *Gender Born, Gender Made: Raising Healthy Gender-Nonconforming Children* (New York, 2011); Lori Duron, *Raising My Rainbow: Adventures in Raising a Slightly Effeminate, Possibly Gay, Totally Fabulous Son* (New York, 2013), as well as blogs such as *Pink is For Boys*, https://pinkisforboys.wordpress.com.
61. Cheryl Kilodavis, *My Princess Boy* (New York, London, and Toronto, 2009).
62. In 2013, the American Psychiatric Association introduced the term "Gender Dysphoria" in the *Diagnostic and Statistical Manual of Mental Disorders: DSM-5* (Washington, DC, 2013) to replace the diagnostic name Gender Identity Disorder (GID). Gender Dysphoria refers to the clinically significant distress associated with gender nonconformity, which is the marked difference between the individual's expressed and experienced gender and the gender others would assign him or her.
63. Hoffman, "Boys Will be Boys?"
64. As Sahar Sadjadi suggests, parents and their prepubescent children increasingly seek hormone and other medical treatments to align the sex assigned at birth with the child's gender identity and gender presentation; Sahar Sadjadi, "The Endocrinologist's Office—Puberty Suppression: Saving Children from a Natural Disaster?," *Journal of Medical Humanities* 34, no. 2 (2013): 255–60.
65. Abbi Moore and Emma Moore, "Pinkstinks Mission Statement," n.d., http://www.pinkstinks.co.uk.
66. Sue Palmer, *Toxic Childhood: How The Modern World is Damaging Our Children and What We Can Do about It* (London, 2006), 233.
67. Sue Palmer, "Why Pink Makes Me See Red," *Daily Mail* (2009), text available at http://www.suepalmer.co.uk/modern_childhood_articles_why_pink.php.
68. Michael Gurian, *Nurture the Nature: Understanding and Supporting Your Child's Unique Core Personality* (New York, 2007).
69. Claire Bates, "Should We Not Dress Girls in Pink?," *BBC News Magazine*, January 8, 2009, http://news.bbc.co.uk/2/hi/uk_news/magazine/7817496.stm.
70. Peggy Orenstein, *Cinderella Ate My Daughter: Dispatches from the Frontlines of the New Girlie-Girl Culture* (New York, 2011), 184.
71. It seems worth noting that while all authors in question worry about girls and their commodification, they focus on different age groups—Gurian on all ages, but especially 4-to-7-year-olds, Palmer on 3-to-8-year-old girls, and Orenstein on preteens and young adolescents. Orenstein, *Cinderella Ate My Daughter*, 7. See also Deborah L. Tolman et al., "Looking Good, Sounding Good: Femininity Ideology and Adolescent Girls' Mental Health," *Psychology of Women Quarterly* 30 (2006): 85–95; Deborah L. Tolman et al., "Girls' Relationship Authenticity and Self-Esteem Across Adolescence," *Development Psychology* 44, no. 3 (2008): 722–33.
72. Ruth Barnes and Joanne B. Eicher, *Dress and Gender: Making and Meaning in Cultural Contexts* (New York, 1992), 1.
73. Trousers in particular have long been associated with masculinity and mobility. The change from breeches to trousers symbolized a boy child's rite of passage from a mama's boy to a little man. Jo Paoletti, *Pink and Blue*, 42.

74. After all, the dictum "seeing life through rose-colored glasses" implies a deception inherent in a rose-colored filter.
75. On women's culture of disappointment, see Lauren Berlant with Jay Prosser, "Life Writings and Intimate Publics: A Conversation with Lauren Berlant," *Biography* 34, no. 1 (Winter 2011): 183.
76. Ahmed, "Affective Economies"; see also Sara Ahmed, *The Cultural Politics of Emotion* (New York, 2004).

CHAPTER 5

New Words and Fanciful Names: Dyes, Color, and Fashion in the Mid-Nineteenth Century

Charlotte Nicklas

In December 1871, a reader wrote to the *Englishwoman's Domestic Magazine*, observing that "chemical science has given to the world bright hues in scarlet, and blue, and green . . . enhancing the natural beauty of woman."[1] This color enthusiast was alluding to the exciting advances in the dye chemistry of the preceding decades, which included the development of synthetic aniline textile dyes made from coal tar. These substances allowed the production of dress textiles in vivid colors, which acquired names like "mauve," "magenta," "azuline," and "violine." Such references to color filled the fashion reports of magazines aimed at middle-class women in Great Britain and the United States in the mid-nineteenth century, demonstrating the enthusiasm with which fashion journalists and many female consumers greeted the variety of colorful dress textiles.

Male colorists—dye chemists who worked for textile manufacturers developing and testing dyes—constituted an important group of customers for these new dye products. Dye manufacturers employed a language of color in their promotional literature that included many of the same terms used by fashion writers. Both colorists and manufacturers were very much aware of the market for bright, preferably long-lasting color in fashion textiles. Recent work on the history of dyes in the nineteenth century acknowledges the central importance of consumer demand, especially that by women, as a spur to dye development.[2] This chapter expands this argument by examining the transatlantic language shared by female domestic consumers and male business customers to discuss the new dyes and the colors they produced. In doing so, it makes new connections between these

C. Nicklas (✉)
College of Arts and Humanities, University of Brighton, Brighton, United Kingdom

R.L. Blaszczyk, U. Spiekermann (eds.), *Bright Modernity*, Worlds of Consumption, DOI 10.1007/978-3-319-50745-3_5

communities across a traditional gender divide, arguing that these groups adopted similar strategies to navigate a novel world of color.

As the dress of many fashionable women became brighter in the mid-nineteenth century due to the development of synthetic textile dyes, male dress remained, by comparison, darker, indeed often black.[3] Social roles, as well as clothing, were highly differentiated according to gender during this period, [4] as highlighted by Dominique Grisard in Chapter 4. Businesses and advertisers increasingly positioned and represented women as consumers, especially because opportunities for promotion and consumption were growing in the second half of the century.[5] The male colorists discussed in this chapter, however, were also pursued by manufacturers hoping to secure their business.

To examine the words, practices, and materials shared by these male customers and female consumers, this chapter uses two main sources: women's magazines and colorists' notebooks. The women's magazines with the largest circulations in the mid-nineteenth century, *Godey's Lady's Book and Magazine* (1830–1898) in the United States and the *Englishwoman's Domestic Magazine* (1852–1877) in Great Britain, both targeted middle-class readers. Their monthly issues contained a mixture of content that helped them succeed, including fiction, poetry, essays, and practical domestic advice, as well as fashion news reports and illustrations.[6] Colorists often kept notebooks documenting their experiments with dyeing and printing.[7] Some of these records, primarily from printed cotton cloth (calico) manufacturers, have been saved in archives in northwest England, along with ledgers noting manufacturers' production.[8] These periodicals and colorists' notebooks show how particular dye materials and color words appeared and disappeared in domestic and professional contexts.

This chapter begins by introducing the aniline dyes of the 1850s and 1860s and the new color terms that emerged to refer to the colors created from these dyes. It then discusses the range of "fanciful names" applied to fashionable colors, along with the importance of being able to distinguish colors from one another.[9] The chapter concludes by examining the increasing accessibility of branded dye products during this period. Both the language of fashionable color and the variety of new dye products available linked the worlds of male colorists and female consumers. Both groups had a hand in the "color revolution" that began to transform Western visual and material culture in the mid-nineteenth century.

New Dyes and New Words

In 1856, the young English chemistry student William Henry Perkin accidentally made a colorfast purple dye from coal tar aniline. By late 1858, after many months of work to develop the dye for the commercial market, dyers and colorists could purchase aniline purple from the recently established G. F. Perkin and Sons, as well as from French dye manufacturers such as

Monnet and Dury.[10] Colorists began to experiment with aniline dyes, but synthetic dyes did not replace natural dyes immediately. As Alexander Engel explains in Chapter 2, natural and synthetic dyestuff use overlapped substantially.[11] The fashion press discussed these dyes mostly in terms of the colors they produced, words that were also used by colorists in their records, showing their orientation to the fashion market. Reflecting their novel materials and methods of manufacture, many of these aniline dyes and the colors they made acquired new color names.

An emphasis on novelty and continual change is the defining aspect of fashion and consumer society in the modern era.[12] Color was the great enabler that permitted many industries to generate endless novelty, introducing ever-greater visual excitement into the fashion cycle. In the mid-nineteenth century, fashion writers narrated this change in colors for female dress using a large variety of terms, with references in fashionable color names ranging from the natural world to current fashion leaders. Authors used a number of descriptive strategies that ranged from straightforward announcements of fashionable colors to the characterization of colors as "favourite," "desirable," or "in vogue."[13] Novelty in color was thus an important element of fashionability, with writers frequently indicating the prominence of a different shade or tint of a color compared to those fashionable in previous seasons or years. Other ostensibly new colors seem to have been novel in name only, underscoring the inventiveness and commercial awareness of fashion writers and perhaps manufacturers and shops. Some references, however, alluded to novelty resulting from developments in dye chemistry that made certain colors possible. Women's magazines disseminated the names of new colors and sometimes their origins. Acquiring this knowledge was part of keeping up with fashion for the middle-class female consumer.

Shades of purple made from the precursors to British and German aniline dyes were fashionable in the mid to late 1850s, which encouraged Perkin to develop his accidental discovery into a marketable textile dye.[14] Perkin advertised and sold his dye as "aniline purple" or even "Tyrian Purple," consciously alluding to the valuable purple dye of antiquity.[15] The French word *mauve*, however, quickly became the popular name for this new color, as the pages of fashion reports and colorists' notebooks reveal. A new color word in English, "mauve" reflected the chic denoted by French in the language of fashion, acknowledged by both male business customers and female household consumers.[16] The unfamiliarity of "mauve" was clear in its initial appearances. The first mention in the *Lady's Book*, in April 1858, used words taken directly from the *Illustrated London News*, in which the report of Princess Alexandra's wedding described Queen Victoria's dress of "rich mauve (lilac) velvet."[17] Two months later, a fashion news report in the same periodical mentioned, "mauve, or queen's lilac, a rich shade of purple," also helpfully defining the word for readers.[18] In colorists' records, varied spellings, frequent capitalization, and other kinds of demarcation, such as inverted commas and underlining, signaled the novelty of the word. These early references clearly show how the word entered the contemporary vocabulary of fashion for dye customers and textile consumers.

Records from the Langley Printworks and the Chadkirk Printworks, both in Cheshire in northwest England, contained references to "mauve" beginning in 1860, showing how this fashionable word made its way into manufacturers' practice.[19] The references to mauve in fashion reports had appeared 2 years earlier, so fashion led the way for these colorists. John Lightfoot, the accomplished colorist at Broad Oak Printworks, undertook "Trials on Imitation of aniline 'Mauve purple' with mixture of 'Fuchshine' and Ultramarine" in 1860.[20] The 1868–79 notebook of Abel Wimpenny (who worked for a textile printer in the Midlands) held a recipe for "Mauve Pink Stand[ard]" that included no aniline or synthetic product.[21] The colorists' attempts to create "imitation" mauve, probably using substances less expensive than those available from Perkin, indicated the desirability of the new dye, its name, and the new color it produced.

In his experiments, Lightfoot used what he called "The new Red color . . . called 'Fuchshine.'"[22] He was referring to aniline red, developed by French dye chemist François-Emmanuel Verguin in 1858 and early 1859. This dye produced bright pinkish-red colored textiles. Although initially called "fuchsine" after the fuchsia flower, the color became popularly known as "magenta," another new color word. Magenta was a town in northern Italy where the French defeated the Austrian army in June 1859, so the name reflected the contemporaneity of the dye. Retailers also called the color "Solferino," another French victory from the same month.[23] In the early 1860s, shortly after aniline red appeared on the market, colorists at printworks throughout England recorded tests of "magenta" and "solferino."[24] The word "magenta" also appeared in fashion reporting soon after the dye's patenting. In July 1860, the *Englishwoman's Domestic Magazine* declared that the "favourite colors" for fashionable evening dress were "the new shades of pink, called Solferino and Magenta."[25] Lightfoot, who left the most detailed notes of all these British colorists, documented many tests of "Magenta" and (ever thrifty) even recorded an attempt to make "Fuchshine Pink" from the older dye murexide.[26] The women's magazines were soon encouraging consumers to concoct their own dyes in some of the new fashionable hues, showing consumers how to "make do" with ingredients that were available for household recipes. In August 1868, the *Lady's Book* published reader-submitted dyeing instructions that called for "red dye powder," but the recipe's title, "To Color Magenta," used the newer color word.[27] It is impossible to know what color would have been produced with this recipe, but its publication indicated consumer desire for magenta or approximations of the color. The market primed by mauve, both colorists and fashion journalists reacted enthusiastically to this second aniline dye.

Aniline red led to a proliferation of aniline dyes. The French chemists Ernest Girard and Georges Ernest Camille de Laire patented a procedure to make aniline blue in July 1860.[28] In his 1874 dyeing manual, the dye chemist

William Crookes listed many of the trade names for aniline blue, including one manufactured by Girard and de Laire called "Lyons Blue." This dye name referred to the city of Lyon, the center of the French dyeing industry.[29] Crookes also noted "Azuline" and "Azurine" as names for aniline blues, newly invented color words that combined the fashionable term "azure" with the suffix in "aniline." Colorists experimented with "azuline" in the early 1860s, as these aniline blues became available.[30] Fashion writers adopted the word as well, with the *Englishwoman's Domestic Magazine* pronouncing in December 1861, "The most fashionable colour in silks is the azuline blue," and the September 1861 *Lady's Book* noting "decidedly new" colors in autumn ribbons, one of which was "*Azurline.*"[31]

A similar new color word, "Violine," emerged to describe aniline purple dyes that became available in the mid-1860s. In 1863, the German chemist August Wilhelm Hofmann outdid his former student, William Henry Perkin, by patenting a range of aniline purple dyes that were less expensive and easier to use than Perkin's mauve.[32] Although this color term did not appear in colorists' notebooks, fashion journalists adopted it. The *Lady's Book* noted in August 1864 that "the new purples are of the reddish cast" and included "Violine," which it considered among "the prettiest" of these new colors.[33] In April 1870, a fashion report in the *Englishwoman's Domestic Magazine* commented on "the pure and beautiful tone" of currently available faille silks, among them "violine—a beautiful mauve," thus allying the new color to the earlier one created from a synthetic dye.[34] Unlike "mauve" and "magenta," "violine" and "azuline" did not survive as color words, but their circulation among colorists' records and the fashion press registered the excitement in both communities over the colors produced by the new aniline dyes.

Naming and Distinguishing Fashionable Colors

Female dye consumers and male dye customers showed their interest in color in a number of ways, particularly by using a range of fashionable color terms and by carefully distinguishing colors from one another. The fashionable language of color in the mid-nineteenth century drew on traditional as well as modern sources. Many color names alluded to natural referents, such as fruit, flowers, or bodies of water. For example, in March 1873 the *Englishwoman's Domestic Magazine* referred to fashionable light blues "of very light tones—water blue, and *ciel* [sky]."[35] A more imaginative reference to the sky (or rather the heavens) appeared in the *Lady's Book* in December 1867, when the fashion writer described a silk for an evening dress in "the lovely shade of blue known as *Céleste.*"[36] Dye manufacturers and colorists also seem to have been familiar with this allusion, as Thomas Royle at Swaisland Printworks tested a bright blue dye called "Celestine" in February 1863.[37]

Newly available synthetic dyes provided an excellent opportunity to develop this creative color language, as the earlier discussion of "mauve" and "magenta" demonstrated. Purple dyes and the colors they produced inspired particularly inventive names, probably due to the historical importance and value of the color. In his handbook, William Crookes observed, "The aniline violets include a formidable list of colours," some of which were "mauve," "parma," "dahlia," "violine," "Violet Imperial," and "Regina purple." He then noted a further "series of aniline violets, sold under a number of fanciful names," including Hofmann's violet and G. F. Perkin and Sons' "Britannia violet" (not to be confused with the company's earlier mauve).[38]

Many of these "fanciful names" appeared in colorists' notebooks. Advertising material from 1873 by the dye manufacturer Brooke, Simpson and Spiller in a notebook by Wilkinson and Co. promoted "Regina Purple" and "Imperial Violets," and Royle noted trials of "Imperial Violet" at the Swaisland works in September 1861.[39] The colorist at Wilkinson tested "Britannia violet"—supplied by Perkin and Sons—along with two of the Hofmann violets in 1867.[40] In their evocations of power, these terms all continued the tradition of classical and royal allusions of Perkin's "Tyrian Purple," allying it with contemporary British imperial power as the color became available to a growing number of consumers.

Variations of these names also appeared in women's magazines, highlighting the overlap between the worlds of fashion and chemistry. In February 1867, the *Englishwoman's Domestic Magazine* described a ball dress, noting that "the violet colour in this beautiful toilet is of a light bright tint, more inclining to red than blue. This lovely tint is called the Regina violet, and is very fashionable this year for ball toilets."[41] In January 1868, the fashion news report in the *Lady's Book* included among the fashionable colors "Regina, which is pink lilac."[42] At least in the pages of the *Lady's Book*, the precise color of Regina was not always described consistently. In December 1868, a fashion reporter for the magazine asserted, "Regine purple is, like blue flame, the most intense purple, a deep, magnificent color"; and eleven months later, the fashion news report noted that the color "is darker than mauve."[43] The earlier descriptions' references to a lighter, redder purple underscores the unstable equivalences of name and color, especially as a new color term was making its way into the language of fashion. "Regina," however, was clearly a popular term for purple, probably because of its reference to royalty (the name means "Queen") and, in its language, classical antiquity. Although these dyes were the products of cutting-edge research in chemistry, historical color associations appeared in their names, highlighting the continued presence of tradition in modern fashion.

The enthusiasm about the colors produced with aniline dyes also manifested itself in careful discrimination between different shades of these colors, evident in language used by—and directed at—male colorists and female fashion consumers alike. Long before the advent of aniline purple, the fashion press had differentiated between purples, as, for example, in a January 1847 short story in the *Lady's Book*. There, in an upscale Philadelphia dry-goods store called Levy's, Mrs. Whately summons her courage to speak to the fashionable Englishwoman Mrs. Howard, whom she asks, "Pray, ma'am, which of these shades of purple silk do you think the most stylish—the blue purple or the red purple?"[44] Brooke, Simpson and Spiller, the primary British manufacturer of the Hofmann violets, continued this distinction by labeling its dyes from reddest (R.R.R.) to bluest (B.B.B.).[45] The Wilkinson colorist acquired samples from this firm, testing "B Hoffman," "BB Hoffman," and "R Hoffman" in 1867. By 1869, the company was selling an even bluer violet, called "Soluble Violet B B B B (Extra Blue)" (Fig. 5.1).[46]

In a similar way, many colorists were discriminating between shades of mauve soon after its arrival on the market, as was the fashion press. The Wilkinson colorist wrote out separate recipes for "Dark Mauve" and "Pale Mauve" in December 1860, and John Lightfoot and Abel Wimpenny also recorded recipes for light and dark mauves in their notebooks.[47] A particularly splendid example of this distinction appeared in a fashion plate in the July 1864 issue of the *Englishwoman's Domestic Magazine* in a description of the Patti Dress, named after Adelina Patti, the renowned Italian-French opera singer. The dress, placed in the center of the image, was "of mauve-coloured silk in two shades, the dark above the light silk.... The upper part of the bodice is of the lightest shade, the lower part in the darkest silk"[48] (Fig.5.2). The reference to the famous performer and the fashionable color made this dress very much

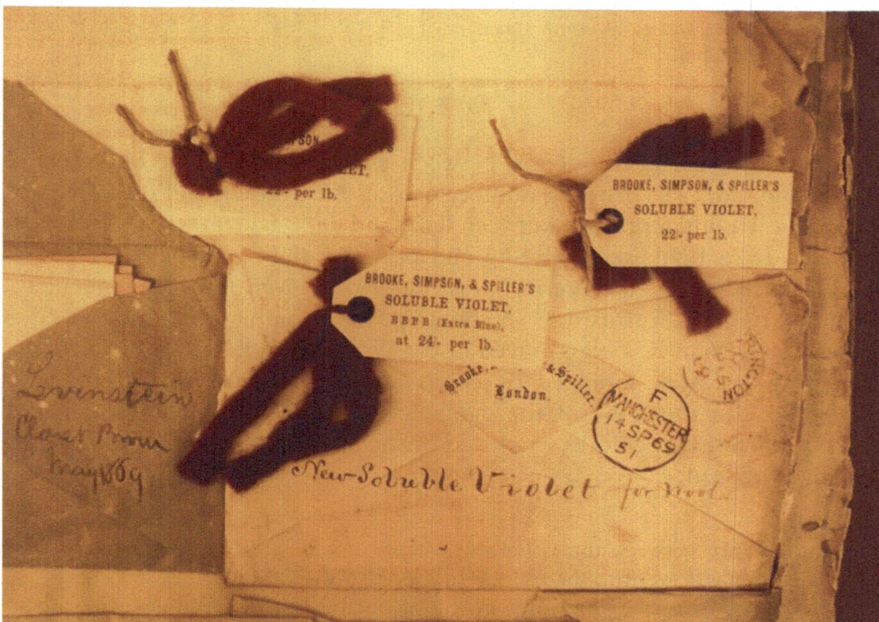

Fig. 5.1 Page (detail) from notebook kept by colorist at John Wilkinson and Co

Source: John Wilkinson and Co. (Oakenshaw Printworks), England (Oakenshaw, near Blackburn, Lancashire), 1856–60, 1867–74. Manchester Archives M75/Historical Collection 104 [Green 1301]. Courtesy of Coats.

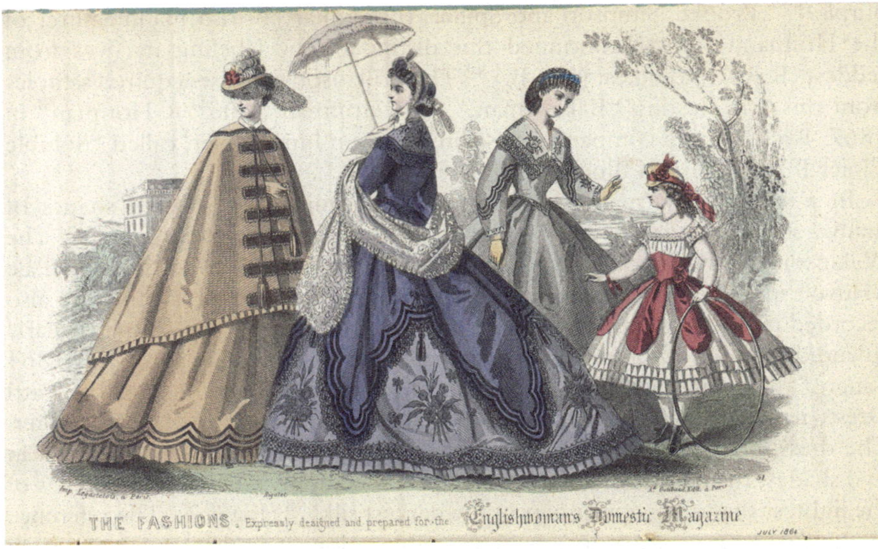

Fig. 5.2 Fashion plate from 1864 showing the Patti Dress

Source: "The Fashions. Expressly designed and prepared for the Englishwoman's Domestic Magazine," ***Englishwoman's Domestic Magazine,*** n.s. 9, July 1864. General Research Division, New York Public Library.

of the moment. The distinction between shades of the color underscored excitement about the growing number of available purples, and it echoed the colorists' own differentiation between light and dark mauve.

In his 1876 book about dyeing and printing, the dye chemist Frederick Crace-Calvert noted that "cerise" was the "name given to a color manufactured by Knosp, of Stuttgard."[49] A contemporary pamphlet from the Swiss dye manufacturer John R. Geigy—saved in the Wilkinson notebook—advertised a great range of dyes, arranged by color and often accompanied by dyeing instructions. In this copy of the pamphlet, "cerise" was underlined in red pen, presumably by a colorist employed by the manufacturer. The text describing the color read,

> The difference between this color and Magenta is simply, that the first dyes a considerably yellower tint than the second.—With *Cerise* you can easily produce shades of brown, which otherwise can only be obtained, with difficulty, by mixing different dyes, such as: Orchil, extract of Orchil or Cudbear, and Brazil wood.[50]

Red ink also underlined the phrase "shades of brown," suggesting one of the ways in which the Wilkinson colorist planned to use this product. The Geigy pamphlet clearly distinguished between two synthetically produced colors, educating potential customers in the company's color language. The circulation of these fashionable color terms in texts written, read, or otherwise used by dye manufacturers and their colorist customers—and by fashion journalists and consumers—evinced the importance of careful differentiation in the bright new world of synthetic color.

Branding Dye Products

Before the introduction of synthetic textile dyes in the late 1850s, both colorists employed by textile manufacturers and dyers working in the domestic sphere relied mainly on natural dyestuffs. Dye recipes included in the *Lady's Book* and the *Englishwoman's Domestic Magazine* included many of the ingredients that colorists commonly recorded in their notebooks, such as fustic, logwood, and copperas.[51] As commercially manufactured branded dyes and dyeing materials, particularly aniline dyes, became available to colorists during the 1860s and 1870s, similar products for home use also appeared on the market. While the domestic market was much smaller than the commercial market comprised of dye manufacturers, the common materials and language further demonstrated a shared culture of color and dye chemistry.

During the second half of the nineteenth century, goods were increasingly becoming associated with the names of their manufacturers as the modern system of branding developed. Gradually, manufacturers began to package their products, and retailers moved away from measuring out goods for individual customers.[52] Evidence of this process appeared in both colorists' notebooks and women's magazines, as materials such as logwood and copperas were replaced more and more by the names of ready-made dye products. Dye manufacturers became increasingly sophisticated in marketing their products.[53] Colorists, of course, still possessed specialized dyeing skills and many still experimented with their own dyes, but branded dye products appeared with increasing frequency as the century progressed.

Colorists were using some branded dye materials even before aniline dyes became available, particularly dyewood extracts. In 1841, for example, a member of the Lightfoot family of dyers recorded trials with Bury's logwood extract, as did the Wilkinson colorist in 1858.[54] Christian Simon highlights the growing industrialization and standardization of the dye industry in the second half of the nineteenth century, processes which caused "the origins of the colours, whether from nature or from the synthetic processes created by chemists, [to become] less important" than their consistent quality.[55] Dyes such as aniline red and Hofmann's violets, however, could only be produced in factories, not in small batches by colorists, because they required large-scale manufacture with specialized equipment and substances.[56] Many of the branded dye products available to both colorists and domestic dyers were synthetic dyes.

Dye manufacturers often distinguished their products through the use of proper names, usually of the inventor or company owner(s), often one and the same. In their working records, colorists generally recorded the names of the companies from which they acquired new dyes. Perkin, as the inventor and manufacturer of the first aniline dye, appeared in several colorists' notebooks. In 1861, John Lightfoot tested "Perkins Tyrian Purple 'Mauve,'" recording both the trade name ("Tyrian Purple") and the fashionable name ("Mauve") of this dye.[57] Thomas Royle, at Swaisland Printworks, noted two trials of "Perkin's Purple" on silk in March 1862.[58] Unlike Lightfoot, Royle did not use the trade or fashion name in his notes. A light-hearted celebration of Perkin's invention in the popular magazine *Household Words* in 1859, however, was titled "Perkins Purple."[59] Colorists' naming of Perkin was thus rooted in professional esteem, discussion in the popular press, and recognition of his recently formed company, G. F. Perkin and Sons. Similarly, the colorist at Wilkinson experimented with a dye called "Nicholson's Blue." The dye was named for the chemist Edward Nicholson, who developed a soluble aniline blue as an owner of the company that preceded Brooke, Simpson and Spiller, the firm from which the dye was obtained.[60] In 1868, the Wilkinson colorist made notes comparing Nicholson's Blue to "Blue No. 2," a sample received from an agent. Nicholson's Blue was more expensive, but provided a better color in this colorist's opinion.[61] During this period, adulteration, along with other questionable business practices, was common in many industries, including dye manufacturing, so some companies used proper names to try to guarantee the quality of their products.[62]

Dye manufacturers signaled the origins of their products through other naming conventions as well. John Lightfoot noted tests of dyes called "French No. 1 Mauve" and "French No. 2 Mauve" from the French suppliers E. Coez in 1861.[63] In March 1870, the Wilkinson colorist received a letter and printed samples from Poirrier, the Paris-based manufacturer of Paris Violet. The letter claimed, "This Violet can be had in all the known shades and when used in the same manner as Hofmann's is fully as fast and stands the light equally as well ... In addition to the superior beauty, the Paris Violet, in point of cost, will stand comparison with the cheapest on the market."[64] This letter highlights the international rivalry among dye manufacturers for clients wanting new, viable, inexpensive dyes.[65] The Poirriers even traveled to Manchester in 1867 to promote their violet dye.[66] In these dye names, "French" and "Paris" referred to the locations of their manufacturers, reflecting the traditional association of products with the place they originated.[67] These names, however, also signaled France's importance in the world of fashion to colorists aware of female consumers' desire for fashionable colors.

One brand targeting the domestic market, Judson's Dyes, began to appear in the *Englishwoman's Domestic Magazine* in the early 1870s, as advertisements were becoming increasingly acceptable in middle-class periodicals.[68] In May 1875, one article suggested, "As a spring investment we ought all to lay in a supply of Judson's dyes, those invaluable aids to economy." The writer went on to underscore "what an exceedingly simple process these dyes make the formerly elaborate task" of dyeing.[69] Two years earlier the magazine had claimed,

"Dyeing small articles is by no means a difficult or a dirty process, if Judson's dyes be employed.... Feathers and silks, whether ribbon or piece silk, also dye admirably.... We may remark that nearly all the new tints are to be had in the sixpenny bottles, which may be obtained of chemists."[70] In September 1874, the magazine's fashion writer included detailed instructions for readers about how to dye items with the same brand-named product. She concluded, "The colours of Judson's Dyes are very beautiful, and the most fashionable colours can always be had."[71] All of these examples presented this company's product as an easy and inexpensive way for a woman to add color to her wardrobe, especially in trimmings.

The brand was mentioned so frequently in the *Englishwoman's Domestic Magazine* that it seems likely the fashion editor was receiving free samples of the dyes, or some other benefit. The company advertised widely, appearing in many other contemporary textual sources.[72] The second volume of George Eliot's novel *Middlemarch*, published in 1871–72, included another advertisement, featuring testimonials about "Judson's Simple Dyes" from *The Family Herald, The Mechanics' Magazine*, and *Cassell's Household Guide.*[73] The *Household Guide* quotation asserted, "The thing would be worth trying from motives of economy; and much more real amusement would result from it than from many of the melancholy recreations to which young ladies of the present day are condemned."[74] Advice and fictional examples in contemporary women's magazines acknowledged the difficulty of dyeing full garments; home dyeing recommendations were, as noted above, usually confined to dyeing "small articles."[75] These advertisements, along with periodical advice, positioned this kind of domestic dyeing as a kind of useful entertainment to occupy women readers.

Judson's Dyes promotional material often placed "mauve" and "magenta" first in the list of available colors, associating their products with colors that many readers would have known to be industrially produced. One advertisement even suggested that "the Magenta and Mauve Dye mixed together make a beautiful shade of colour."[76] The appearance of Judson's Dyes in women's magazines echoes the growing numbers of branded dye products in male colorists' records, revealing another important development in the language of the consumption of color. In both professional and domestic dyeing contexts, clever, informed consumption was becoming more important than technical expertise.

Conclusion

The aniline dyes of the mid-nineteenth century garnered attention from professional colorists and the fashion press, for the novelty of their manufacture and for the brightness of the colors they produced. New words, such as "mauve" and "magenta," emerged to describe these colors and were quickly adopted by male colorist customers and female fashion consumers, indicating a shared culture of color across the contemporary separation of genders. Traditional conventions of naming fashion colors survived as well, such as the use of words containing references to royal power. Colorists and fashion journalists distinguished carefully among individual shades of these new colors, thereby displaying their subtle powers of discernment. These new products did not immediately supplant established dyes, and colorists continued to use the natural dyes that they had relied on in the past. As commercially branded dye products became available, however, both colorists' notebooks and women's magazines recorded their increasing use.

The uneven transition from natural to synthetic dyes and from handmade to ready-made dyes and the long coexistence of all these products was mirrored in a language that included old and new color terms. By employing new color words, differentiating among shades, and learning to consume new branded colors, both groups—the male dye-house colorists and the female fashion consumers—demonstrated their deep interest in color and their strategies for negotiating a new, sometimes overwhelming world of color.

Notes

1. "The Englishwoman's Conversazione," *Englishwoman's Domestic Magazine*, n.s. 2, 11 (1871): 377.
2. Anthony S. Travis, *The Rainbow Makers: The Origins of the Synthetic Dyestuffs Industry in Western Europe* (Bethlehem, PA, 1993), 37, 51, 56; Christian Simon, "The Transition from Natural Dyestuffs to Synthetic Dyestuffs: The Case of Basel, 1850–1940," in *Natural Dyestuffs and Industrial Culture in Europe, 1750–1880*, ed. Robert Fox and Agustí Nieto-Galan (Canton, MA, 1999), 322; Agustí Nieto-Galan, *Colouring Textiles: A History of Natural Dyestuffs in Industrial Europe* (Dordrecht, 2001), 168; Regina Lee Blaszczyk, *The Color Revolution* (Cambridge, MA, 2012), 27.
3. John Harvey, *Men in Black* (Chicago, IL, 1995), 23–39.
4. Mary Poovey, *Uneven Developments: The Ideological Work of Gender in Mid-Victorian England* (Chicago, 1989); Leonore Davidoff and Catherine Hall, *Family Fortunes: Men and Women of the English Middle Class, 1780–1850*, 2nd ed. (London, 2002).
5. Lori Anne Loeb, *Consuming Angels: Advertising and Victorian Women* (Oxford, 1994).
6. Margaret Beetham, *A Magazine of Her Own? Domesticity and Desire in the Woman's Magazine, 1800–1914* (London, 1996), 59–81; John William Tebbel and Mary Ellen Zuckerman, *The Magazine in America, 1741–1990* (New York, 1991), 32–36.
7. Philip Sykas, *The Secret Life of Textiles: Six Pattern Book Archives in North West England* (Bolton, UK, 2005), 96–97.
8. Materials were consulted in the following archives: Manchester Archives (MA), Macclesfield Silk Museum (MSM), and Manchester Metropolitan University (MMU). For each notebook or ledger referenced, the colorist's name (if known) and the document's date (if known) are noted.
9. Quotation from William Crookes, *A Practical Handbook of Dyeing and Calico Printing* (London, 1874), 191.
10. Travis, *Rainbow Makers*, 36, 46–51.

11. Nieto-Galan, *Colouring Textiles*, 190; Simon, "The Transition," 313.
12. Elizabeth Wilson, *Adorned in Dreams: Fashion and Modernity*, 2nd ed. (London, 2005), 3; Lars Svendsen, *Fashion: A Philosophy*, trans. John Irons (London, 2006), 24–27.
13. For examples, see "The Fashions and Practical Dress Instructor," *Englishwoman's Domestic Magazine* 7 (1858): 159; "Chitchat upon New York and Philadelphia Fashions for November," *Godey's Lady's Book* 75 (1867): 460.
14. Travis, *Rainbow Makers*, 46, 49; Blaszczyk, *Color Revolution*, 22–23.
15. Anthony S. Travis, "Perkin's Mauve: Ancestor of the Organic Chemical Industry," *Technology and Culture* 31, no. 1 (January 1990): 80.
16. Travis, *Rainbow Makers*, 46.
17. "Princess Royal's Wedding," *Godey's Lady's Book* 56 (1858): 381. In *The Rainbow Makers*, Travis cites the description of Queen Victoria's costume from the April 3, 1858, edition of the *Illustrated London News*. He notes that the fabric for the queen's dress was most likely *not* dyed with the new aniline dye, because it was probably made in France, where mauve would not yet have been in use in early 1858. The color of the queen's dress would have been achieved with a non-aniline purple dye, probably murexide or French purple. As Travis asserts, however, the light purple color, however achieved, was growing more and more popular and "mauve" was the word that the public had begun to use for the color associated with Perkin's discovery (49).
18. "Chitchat upon New York and Philadelphia Fashions for August," *Godey's Lady's Book* 57 (1858): 96.
19. Langley Printworks (near Macclesfield, Cheshire), ledger, February 1859–April 1861, PA 9735–14993, MSM; Sydall Brothers, Chadkirk Printworks (Cheshire), notebook, after 1858, 75/Historical Collection 114 [Green 1329], MA.
20. John Lightfoot, Jr., Broad Oak Printworks (Accrington, Lancashire), notebook, 1859–1865, M75/Historical Collection 22 [Green 1307], MA.
21. Abel Buckley Wimpenny, Hayfield Printing Company (Derbyshire), notebook, 1868–1876, M75/ Historical Collection 88 [Green 1318], MA.
22. Lightfoot, notebook, 1859–1865, M75/22, MA.
23. Travis, *Rainbow Makers*, 67–71.
24. Sydall, notebook, after 1858, M75/114, MA; Langley Printworks, ledger, February 1859–April 1861, PA 9735–14993, MSM; Thomas Royle, Swaisland Printworks (Crayford, Kent), notebook, 1850s–1860s, MMU; John Wilkinson and Co., Oakenshaw Printworks (near Blackburn, Lancashire), notebook, 1856–1860, 1867–1874, M75/Historical Collection 104 [Green 1301], MA; Hayfield Printing Company, notebook, 1861, M75/ Historical Collection 92 [Green 1301], MA.
25. "The Fashions," *Englishwoman's Domestic Magazine,* n.s., 1 (1860): 141.
26. John Lightfoot, Jr., Broad Oak Printworks (Accrington, Lancashire), notebook, 1861, M75/Historical Collection 25 [Green 1307], MA; Lightfoot, notebook, 1859–1865, M75/22, MA.
27. "To Color Magenta," *Godey's Lady's Book* 77 (1868): 171.
28. Travis, *Rainbow Makers*, 72.
29. William Crookes, *A Practical Handbook of Dyeing and Calico Printing* (London, 1874) 195; Travis, *Rainbow Makers*, 67.
30. Lightfoot, notebook, 1861, M75/25, MA; Langley Printworks (near Macclesfield, Cheshire), ledger, May 1863–September 1865, PA 18965–19155 and B1-4055, MSM.

31. "The Fashions," *Englishwoman's Domestic Magazine,* n.s., 4 (1861): 91; "Chitchat upon New York and Philadelphia Fashions for September," *Godey's Lady's Book* 63 (1861): 263.
32. Willem J. Hornix, "From Process to Plant: Innovation in the Early Artificial Dye Industry," *British Journal for the History of Science* 25, no. 1 (1992): 75.
33. "Chitchat upon New York and Philadelphia Fashions for August," *Godey's Lady's Book* 69 (1864): 185.
34. "The April Fashions," *Englishwoman's Domestic Magazine,* n.s. 2, 8 (1870): 225.
35. "Spinnings in Town," *Englishwoman's Domestic Magazine,* n.s. 2, 14 (1873): 150.
36. "Chitchat upon New York and Philadelphia Fashions for December," *Godey's Lady's Book* 75 (1867): 553.
37. Royle, notebook, 1850s–1860s, MMU.
38. Crookes, *A Practical Handbook*, 187, 190–94.
39. Wilkinson and Co., notebook, 1856–1860, 1867–1874, M75/104, MA; Royle, notebook, 1850s–1860s, MMU.
40. Wilkinson and Co., notebook, 1856–1860, 1867–1874, M75/104, MA.
41. "The Fashions," *Englishwoman's Domestic Magazine,* n.s. 2, 3 (1867): 89.
42. "Chitchat upon New York and Philadelphia Fashions for January," *Godey's Lady's Book* 76 (1868): 107.
43. "Chitchat on Fashions for December," *Godey's Lady's Book* 77 (1868): 556; "Chitchat on Fashions for November," *Godey's Lady's Book* 79 (1869): 463.
44. "The Lady her own Housekeeper," *Godey's Lady's Book* 34 (1847): 39.
45. Crookes, *A Practical Handbook*, 192.
46. Wilkinson and Co., notebook, 1856–1860, 1867–1874, M75/104, MA.
47. Ibid.; John Lightfoot, Jr., Broad Oak Printworks (Accrington, Lancashire), notebook, 1857–1861, M75/Historical Collection 19 [Green 1306], MA; Wimpenny, notebook, 1868–1876, M75/88, MA.
48. "Our Coloured Fashion Plate," *Englishwoman's Domestic Magazine* 9 (1864):143.
49. Frederick Crace-Calvert, *Dyeing and Calico Printing* (London, 1876), 382.
50. Wilkinson and Co., notebook, 1856–1860, 1867–1874, M75/104, MA.
51. For examples from women's magazines, see: "Things Worth Knowing," *Englishwoman's Domestic Magazine* 4 (1855): 63; "Receipts, &c." *Godey's Lady's Book* 47 (1853): 93; and "Receipts, &c. Miscellaneous," *Godey's Lady's Book* 51 (1855): 464. These ingredients appear throughout colorists' notebooks, but for representative examples, see: MA, Joseph Lawton Sydall, Chadkirk Printworks (Cheshire), notebook, 1843–1859, M75/Historical Collection 113 [Green 1329] (fustic), MA; Wimpenny, notebook, 1868–1876, M75/88 (logwood), MA; Sydall Brothers, notebook, after 1858, M75/ 114 (copperas), MA.
52. Jane Pavitt, "In Goods We Trust?," in *Brand New*, ed. Jane Pavitt (London, 2000), 33.
53. Blaszczyk, *Color Revolution*, 31.
54. John Emanuel Lightfoot or Thomas Lightfoot, notebook, 1840–1844, M75/Historical Collection 29 [Green 1308], MA; Wilkinson and Co., notebook, 1856–1860, 1867–1874, M75/104, MA.
55. Simon, "The Transition," 322. Simon discusses the case of the Swiss company Geigy and Co., which marketed dyes and extracts to British dyers and colorists, demonstrated by the preservation of English-language advertising material from Geigy and Co. in the John Wilkinson and Co. notebook (Wilkinson and Co., notebook, 1856–1860, 1867–1874, M75/104, MA).

56. Hornix, "From Process to Plant," 65.
57. Lightfoot, notebook, 1861, M75/25, MA.
58. Royle, notebook, 1850s–1860s, MMU.
59. "Perkins' [*sic*] Purple," *Household Words*, April 30, 1859.
60. Simpson, Maule and Nicholson, established in 1853 by three Royal College of Chemistry graduates, was a London-based company that manufactured chemicals. Nicholson retired in 1868 and the firm became Brooke, Simpson and Spiller (Travis, *Rainbow Makers* 53–54, 135).
61. Wilkinson and Co., notebook, 1856–1860, 1867–1874, M75/104, MA.
62. Loeb, *Consuming Angels*, 111–14; Travis, *Rainbow Makers*, 148.
63. Lightfoot, notebook, 1861, M75/25, MA.
64. Wilkinson and Co., notebook, 1856–1860, 1867–1874, M75/104, MA.
65. This fierce competition resulted in German dye companies controlling the synthetic dye industry by the mid-1870s. See Travis, *Rainbow Makers*, 237–39; Blaszczyk, *Color Revolution*, 29.
66. Travis, *Rainbow Makers*, 142.
67. Pavitt, "In Goods We Trust?" 33.
68. Loeb, *Consuming Angels*, 5. The first reference to Judson's Dyes appeared in "The Englishwoman's Conversazione," *Englishwoman's Domestic Magazine*, n.s. 2, 12 (1872): 255.
69. "Flittings," *Englishwoman's Domestic Magazine*, n.s. 2, 18 (1875): 262.
70. "Simple, Effective Dyes," *Englishwoman's Domestic Magazine*, n.s. 2, 14 (1873): 391.
71. "Spinnings in Town," *Englishwoman's Domestic Magazine*, n.s. 2, 17 (1874): 154–55.
72. See, for example, Edward McDermott, *The Popular Guide to the International Exhibition of 1862*, (London: W. H. Smith and Son, [1862]), ix.
73. Judson's Simple Dyes, advertisement, in George Eliot, *Middlemarch*, vol. 2 (Edinburgh: William Blackwood, 1871–72), 16. Many thanks to Leslie Eckel for bringing this advertisement to my attention.
74. Eliot, *Middlemarch*, 16 [advertisements].
75. See, for example, "Fanny Parkinson, or, My Brother's Funeral," *Ladies' Cabinet* 3 (1840): 79–80; "To Correspondents," *Godey's Lady's Book* 49 (1854): 475; and "The Englishwoman's Conversazione," *Englishwoman's Domestic Magazine*, n.s. 2, 15 (1873): 224.
76. McDermott, *Popular Guide*, ix.

CHAPTER 6

Let's Go Color Shopping with Charles Sanders Peirce: Color Scientists as Consumers of Color

Michael Rossi

In July 1889, Ogden N. Rood, a physics professor at Columbia College (the precursor to Columbia University) in New York City, made a foray from his home on East 58th Street to a department store on lower Broadway in order to answer a question for his friend, the philosopher and mathematician Charles Sanders Peirce. Both Rood and Peirce were researchers in what was then the new field of color science—a polyglot endeavor comprising the physics, physiology, psychology, and sometimes neurology and anthropology of human color vision. Rood had earned a measure of renown as the author of *Modern Chromatics* (1879), a survey of the state of the art in nineteenth-century color science that found a wide readership among scientists and medical doctors as well as painters and architects.[1] Peirce—a brilliant but prickly personality at the best of times—had recently been dismissed from his post as a lecturer in logic at Johns Hopkins University and was working on several projects, including performing measurements and calculations on gravity for the United States Coastal Survey (a position he had held for many years) and writing definitions on numerous topics, including color, for the *Century Dictionary*.[2] The two men had met in New York in the late 1870s at the Century Club—a "facility for social intercourse among gentlemen of cultivated and liberal pursuits," as one of the club's historians put it—and formed a friendship based on their mutual interest in the sciences of sensation.[3]

Peirce's question for Rood was simple. Had he ever heard of a color called "Isabel," and if so, what did it look like? Rood had no immediate answer, having neither seen nor heard of the color, but—as he explained in a letter mailed in reply—he made every effort to ferret out the wished-for data. First,

M. Rossi (✉)
Department of History, The University of Chicago, Chicago, IL, USA

R.L. Blaszczyk, U. Spiekermann (eds.), *Bright Modernity*, Worlds of Consumption, DOI 10.1007/978-3-319-50745-3_6

Rood asked "several ladies" if they knew what color Isabel was, but he had no luck. His interlocutors did not know. Then he journeyed to A. T. Stewart's store, a mammoth retail establishment on lower Broadway famous for its kaleidoscopic overabundance of consumer goods. As the *New York Times* put it, "a better selection of the known and unknown articles appertaining to a lady's dress can be made in [A. T. Stewart's] than was formerly possible by a trip half round the world."[4] This unparalleled selection, noted another *Times* article, included "moiré and lace stripe silks in blue, pink, cream, and white . . . Spanish lace, colored artemisians, olive, and light to dark red"—an unsurpassed "richness of color and material and elegance of design."[5] If "Isabel" were to be found, it would be in A. T. Stewart's. Nevertheless, as Rood explained to Peirce, "The people there had not heard of [Isabel color] and then I examined the pattern books with 'shades' of color and names, many of which were quite new to me, but the term 'Isabel' did not make its appearance."[6] Rood's expedition was a failure.

But although he did not manage to secure the desired Isabel, this deceptively banal incident—a man goes to the store for his friend and comes up empty-handed—nevertheless opens a window onto an important and deep-seated tension between the efflorescence of commercial colors in nineteenth-century America and the emergence and scope of the novel field of color science. Rood's note to Peirce was more than just an apology for not finding the wished-for information. It served to reiterate the precise nature of the relationship between color science and the commercial manufacture of colored goods. On the one hand, Rood's note verified that he had checked on the identity of Isabel color with some of the most knowledgeable sources on unusual or novel colors at his disposal—women of social standing and clerks in extravagant retail stores. On the other hand, in carefully delineating the provenance of his research, Rood simultaneously established beyond doubt that he himself—although a scientist known around the world as an expert on color—knew little about the names of commercial colors. Thus Rood carved out a tenuous, if clearly defined space for the science of color against the bustle of commerce in color. Color, as it was accessible to everyday consumers, was a matter for ladies and shopkeepers; color as a scientific matter, on the other hand, was a different category of thing entirely.

This tension, moreover, was by no means limited to the epistemologies of Peirce and Rood. In its most general formulation, the "color question" (as the game-maker and color researcher Milton Bradley termed it in an article in *Science* in 1892) concerned how properly to understand the formal relationship between color as a property of objects and color as a phenomenon manifested primarily in the minds of observers. Christine Ladd-Franklin, a psychologist who had been Peirce's student at Johns Hopkins University, drew a sharp distinction between knowledge of color gained through "introspection"—that is, through the disciplined examination of one's own color sense, for example, as practiced by a professional scientist such as herself—and the more or less arbitrary knowledge of color gained through trade in "certain easily accessible dye-stuffs or paint-stuffs."[7] It was not that viewing color in relation to objects was wrong, but there was a clear moral hierarchy in scientific practice, which held the understanding of color-as-sensation to be superior to the understanding of color as represented in "stuffs." To put it another way, color science in the nineteenth century was not, strictly speaking, a matter of studying things but rather of studying abstract perceptions. The absolute essence of color, insisted the most serious students of nineteenth century color science, was antecedent to the human ability to manifest color in commercial goods.

By way of contrast, this essay presents scientists such as Rood, Peirce, Ladd-Franklin, and their peers as active, if ambivalent, consumers of color. In spite of the sharp epistemological boundaries that they drew between the production of knowledge about color perceptions and the consumption of colorful goods, the work of nineteenth-century color scientists did not transcend the hustle of everyday commerce. Rather, their work was intimately tied not only to the material but to the moral orders of nineteenth-century consumer culture. The point here is not to invert the order of hierarchy of color science from one that asserts the primacy of abstract purity to one that insists upon the apotheosis of definite matter. Nor is it to simply make the rather trivial observation that knowledge of color has historically tended to derive from observers' subjective experiences of objects-in-the-world instead of from some sort of notionally pure introspection. Rather, it is to point out that the forceful distinction made by Rood and his peers between knowledge of color sensations and consumption of colorful matter belied the deep entanglements between the subjects of scientific research on color, consumers of colored goods, and those colored goods themselves. Indeed, color scientists were, in many instances, the primary subjects of their own investigations. And as much as they attempted to posit a formal order of subjective color perception that placed the ambit of commercial manufacture outside (or beneath, or subject to) the ambit of science, their research fundamentally drew from and referred to values common to science and commerce alike. The efforts that Rood, Peirce, and their peers in color research made to position color as a pure object of science—while simultaneously embracing and ignoring its commercial aspects—suggest in microcosm the ways in which emerging consumer culture was concerned not simply with the manufacture of goods but also with the manufacture of individuals—consumers, workers, scientists—with sensory and cognitive capacities to understand their visual world as a product of modern, industrial society.

***

In writing on the conjoined histories of textiles and colors in 1857, the Irish historian A. Hume remarked that "the term 'Isabella-coloured,' is unknown among the peasantry and operatives [laborers], but is familiar to the readers of our older literature." For Hume, the second group comprised members of the educated upper-classes in the British Isles—those with the means and education to appreciate that the pale, yellowish gray color that graced fashionable laces and silks was named in honor of Isabella I of Castile, the wife of Ferdinand II of Aragon, who had vowed not to change her white "innermost garment" whilst her husband laid siege to Grenada during the final years of the *Reconquista*. The siege lasted longer than Isabella had expected, and by the time Ferdinand was victorious, the princess's snowy undergarment "had assumed," in Hume's words, "the peculiar hue known as "whitey-brown."[8] Later commentators cast doubt on the term's apocryphal origins, proposing that Isabella was probably an adulteration of the Italian term *zibellino*, which referred to the buff-colored summer coat of the sable, a popular accessory among noblewomen in sixteenth-century Europe. Nonetheless, Hume's main point about elites' usage of the term remained intact.[9]

Isabella (or Isabel) remained an obscure, specialist term in the late-nineteenth-century United States.[10] Perhaps ironically, however—considering the judiciousness with which Peirce and his contemporaries distinguished science and commerce—its users were principally those audiences most concerned with science, on the one hand, and retail commerce, on the other.

For scientific researchers, Isabel found particular use in chemistry and mineralogy. In a notice on recent chemical findings, for instance, the *American Journal of Science* reported in 1860 that salts of the element ruthenium have an "Isabel yellow color."[11] When applied to a particular chemical reaction, noted another source, "stannous chloride . . . produces an isabel yellow precipitate."[12] In what would later be called geosciences, Karl Reichenbach, a German polymath versed in chemistry, geology, and natural philosophy, discovered flecks of an "Isabel-yellow colored" mineral in an iron meteor.[13] And a Boston geologist remarked that, "under the microscope," a sample from a mass of stratified rock was "seen to be composed of an isabel yellow and dirty white base holding . . . feldspar crystals."[14] Minerals aside, and although more common in Britain than in the United States as a descriptor for flora and fauna, "Isabel" found some use among American naturalists for describing parts of living and nonliving things. The thorax of a new species of crane fly, noted one entomologist, was "almost isabel-yellow, with three brown stripes,"[15] while the *Pseudohelotium isabellinum* mushroom described by the Botanical Survey of Nebraska bore eponymous witness to its own "isabel-colored" underside.[16]

At the same time, "Isabel" also served nineteenth-century American writers on fashion and textiles as a descriptor standing not just for pale grayish yellow but also for lushness and consumer availability. An item in *Harper's Bazaar* in March 1876, for instance, announced the season's "shades for evening silks" as "ceil, glacé, which is a very lustrous shimmering blue, *sourire* (a smile), rosy-tinted lavender, sea-foam green, and every shade that has a yellow hue, such as cream, *paille* or straw-color, *chair* or flesh, Isabel, buff, canary, etc." The following year, *Harper's* again described Isabel as a "new" color in New York fashion, testifying both to Isabel's continued presence as a staple of nineteenth-century textile color names and to a perceived need for continuous novelty in color selections. In 1883, the attentive shopper could find her stylish bonnet trimmed with "a great bunch of wall-flowers, shaded from dark mandarin to pale Isabel yellow, with leaves and long stems" as one writer explained.[17] In 1887, meanwhile, the *New York Post* extolled "the latest novelties in society," which included dresses sporting "elegant and expensive" stripes of velvet on silk, such as one of "corn yellow" and "cream-white satin, brocaded with clusters of Isabella roses and foliage in antique brocatelle."[18] Underneath such a dress, in 1891, one could wear a girdle of "Isabel" lace over "rose de chine" silk.[19]

Considering the judiciousness with which Peirce and his contemporaries policed the bounds of science and commerce, the dominant use of "Isabel" in describing scientific and commercial objects was perhaps ironic, but not unexpected. "Isabel" and a host of other new color names spoke to values such as precision, accuracy, and discernment, which were common to scientific and commercial practices alike in the nineteenth century. Moreover, terms such as these did not just indicate aesthetic or moral discrimination but were themselves discriminatory—helpful in defining the distinct mentalité of the truly modern observer. As the Canadian science writer Grant Allen put it in *The Colour Sense: Its Origins and Development* (1895), "if a naturalist discovers for the first time a new animal—say an argus pheasant—he will minutely characterize its shape, size, colour, external appearance, and internal structure, detailing all these points in extremely abstract language; whereas a countryman who goes to the Zoological Gardens will simply describe it as 'between a peacock and a guinea-hen'"—and as with birds, so with colors.[20] Just as one could not expect "peasants and operators" to use a term like "Isabel" to describe fabric, one could not expect a scientific description from "countrymen" ill-versed in scientific regimens of thought. For those with sufficient sophistication and capacity for abstract thought, therefore, a fly's thorax, an evening silk, a mineral deposit, a fake flower on a hat, and a salt precipitated in a solution were not simply to be understood as "whitey brown." They were "Isabel," a term whose use captured not just the physical properties of the material world but the moral and psychological properties of its observers.

This said, as an elite and abstract practice, scientific observation aimed to scrutinize natural phenomena and to describe the universal laws that underpinned them, whether the field was chemistry, physiology, zoology, or psychology. In contrast, capitalism and consumer culture were predicated on the practice of recycling and reinventing ideas and images, an endeavor that was the polar opposite of scientific observation. Just as Isabel might be a "new" color, year after year, other consumer colors shifted their identities in strange ways, slipping free of the tight correspondence between terms for things and things themselves that (ideally) defined scientific work. An 1882 article on fashion in *Harper's Bazaar*, for instance, called attention to a profusion of new colors that took their names from the natural world: "a new dark green is called elder green, another shade is sycamore, and the olive greens are called lichen green; a purple-red like scabieuse is marked petunia…[and] the Turc and Sicily reds are brighter shades than the dull garnet so long worn and are similar to carnation red."[21] Here was refinement and discrimination, but also confusion and instability—olive green was called lichen green; scabieuse was called petunia; carnation red was relabeled Turc or Sicily red, and none according to any obvious law or rule.

Of course, these were abstract terms—who could say whether a particular green was *actually* "elder" or "olive"?— but then, in this sense their abstraction seemed to derive not from a structural understanding of the natural world but from a whimsy that bordered on absurdity. As Robert Ridgway, an ornithologist at the Smithsonian Institution with a sideline in color study, complained in 1886, "the popular nomenclature of colors has of late years, especially since the introduction of aniline dyes and pigments, become involved in almost chaotic confusion through the coinage of a multitude of new names, many of them synonymous, and still more of them vague or variable in their meaning." He criticized color names such as "Zulu," "Crushed Strawberry," and "Elephant's Breath" as hollow terms "invented at the caprice of the dyer" and unsuitable for any sort of "practical utility."[22] Colors, for Ridgway, ought to have been understood as absolute properties—though how, precisely, to extricate the absolute essence of color from its bond with colored items was not easy to articulate.

***

Peirce's work with the *Century Dictionary* gives some sense of the difficulty faced by color scientists in drawing the line between colored things and colored sensations. The *Dictionary* was an eight-volume behemoth. Its mandate, among other things, was to provide a "general dictionary of the English language…serviceable for every literary and practical use," including a "very complete presentation of the present status of human knowledge of [the physical] sciences." Color study was an explicit part of this knowledge.[23] For his entries in this publication, Peirce elected to describe particular colors in both qualitative and quantitative terms. Thus "green" he defined as "the color of ordinary foliage; the color seen in the solar spectrum between wavelengths 0.511 and 0.543 microns."[24] Similarly, he described "yellow" as "the color of gold, butter, the neutral chromates of lead, potassa, etc. and of light of wavelength about 0.581 microns."[25]

In his precise definition of color itself, however, Peirce drew a sharp line between color sensations and colored things. In an early draft of his definition of "color" for the *Century Dictionary* he proposed that "the color sensations are the peculiar sensations *of which we become conscious* when the optic nerves are excited. Color, on the other hand, is that property of a body" that gives color sensations.[26] In other words, for Peirce, color as experienced by humans could only be properly understood as a product of human consciousness—not of things in the world. Indeed, given the project at hand—a dictionary of "the present status of human knowledge"—Peirce's insistence on linguistically distinguishing objective and subjective color should be seen as an assertion of both the novelty of this idea and the seriousness with which he took it.

Rood in large part shared Peirce's epistemological outlook. In 1879, D. Appleton and Company published Rood's *Modern Chromatics: With Applications to Art and Industry*, a comprehensive survey of the state of the art of color science up to that point. Rood chose his title specifically as a counterpoint to British artist George Field's popular color theory manual, *Chromatics, or An Essay on the Analogy and Harmony of Colors* (1817), explaining that whereas Field had endeavored to define affinities between colors in terms of speculative theories of musical harmony, Rood relied on empirical science.

In explaining what he took to be the true science of color, Rood was particularly indebted to the physiological theories of the German physicist Hermann von Helmholtz, who, in his 1867 *Handbuch der physiologischen Optik* (Handbook of Physiological Optics), posited that all color sensations came from three types of "nerve" in the retinas of normal observers. These nerves were keyed to respond to "vibrations" from long, medium, and short wavelengths of electromagnetic radiation (light), and these wavelengths corresponded to red, green, and blue color sensations, respectively. Thus, when light of long wavelength impacted the retina, the red-sensitive nerves would respond (but not the green- and blue-sensitive ones), and the observer would experience sensations of red. The same went for green and blue sensations; each corresponded to particular wavelengths of light hitting the retina of the observer. When light caused more than one type of nerve to respond, the result was a mixed color. Purple, for instance, was the result of light of particular wavelengths causing red- and blue-sensitive nerves to respond simultaneously. Sensations of reddish-purple were caused by a greater response by red-sensitive than blue-sensitive nerves; bluish purple was caused by a greater response by blue-sensitive than red-sensitive nerves. The sensation of white was caused by proportional amounts of stimulus from all three kinds of nerves—or, to put it another way, sensations of white were, in reality, a mix of all three fundamental colors. Black, for its part, was indicative of no input from any nerve.[27]

The point was that any of the millions of colors that an observer could experience was understood by Helmholtz as the result of different amounts of response from three basic types of nerve. Nonetheless, not all sensations of color could be said to be equally applicable to "arts and industry." In his notes on the vibrant colors produced by polarized light, Rood paused to lament that "the purity of the hues and the audacious character of their combinations cause their gayety to appear strange and unnatural to eyes accustomed to the far more somber hues appropriate to a world in which labour and trouble are such important and ever present elements."[28] Rood was not so much bemoaning the sobriety of the world of lived experience as suggesting that the laboratory of the color scientist was of a piece with—but phenomenally different from—the everyday world that the reader was likely to experience (Fig. 6.1).

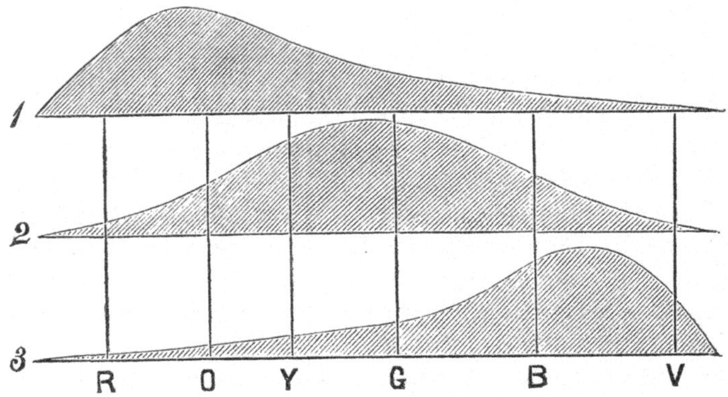

FIG. 43.—Curves showing the Action of the Different Colours of the Spectrum on the Three Sets of Nerve Fibrils. (Helmholtz.)

Fig. 6.1 Helmholtz's diagram indicating the responsiveness of different nerve "fibrils" in the retina to red (1), green (2), and blue (3) light

Source: Ogden Rood, *Modern Chromatics* (1879; New York: D. Appleton and Company, 1881), 114. Reproduction courtesy of the Chemical Heritage Foundation collections.

Indeed, in Peirce's review of *Modern Chromatics* in the *Nation* (1879), Peirce took Rood's suggestion a step further, beginning with the assertion that "the utility and significance of visual perceptions distract attention from the mere sensuous delight of color and light." "Yet," Peirce continued, "few elementary pleasures are more sensational." This was because, for Peirce, color was best understood as a class of mental phenomenon, "as near to the first impression of sense, as any perception which it is in our power to extricate from the complexus [or embrace] of consciousness."[29] As such, the purpose of color science—what Peirce and Rood both called "chromatics," was "to be distinguished from several other sciences which touch the same ground." Peirce clarified, writing that color science "is not chemistry, nor the art of treating pigments, nor optics (which deals with light as an undulation, or, at least, as an external reality); nor is it a branch of physiology, which might study the various ways of exciting the sensation of color, as by direct sensation, contrast, fatigue, hallucination, etc.; nor is it the account of the development of the color sense." Rather, "chromatics"—the science of color perception—was to take as its ultimate subject the structure of the mind itself through the formal mapping of its most fundamental operation, the perception of color.[30]

***

But if "chromatics"—color science—was neither more nor less than the exploration of a particularly pure strain of mental phenomena, then how ought the conscientious scientist go about accessing these phenomena as separate from "chemistry," "pigments," or even "optics"? This was an especially vexing question since so much color science depended on the scientist's own use of manufactured colored goods such as mass-produced pigments, papers, and textiles. In order to wrest color from the complexus of consciousness, color scientists had to submit to the complexus of consumer culture—a balancing act that required constant care.

One key way in which researchers queried the color sense was a method called "introspection." That is, a trained scientist might simply trust in his or her own powers of cerebration as he or she analyzed the structures and qualities of his or her own perceptions of color—typically while gazing upon colored goods such as ribbons or colored papers. Thus, for instance, in an undated note marked "*a faire*" (to do), Ladd-Franklin described an experiment to compare two sets of color gradients: "get a long good bk–wh series, + by its side a long, good bk–gr series. Sit down before them and by introspection see if they are or are not similar series."[31] Were gradations between black and grey similar to or different from gradations between black and white? The way to find out was to set out a series of sequentially arranged pieces of colored paper, look at them, and evaluate how one felt. Ladd-Franklin kept sample books of commercial colors for just such reference. In a similar way, Peirce attempted to sort a series of ribbons by degrees of brightness (rather than hue), using only his own consciousness of the effects of the ribbons on his mental state.

This method yielded important qualitative data about the nature of color sensations, but it could only go so far. Indeed, as William James—Pierce's close friend, a Harvard psychologist and America's champion of introspection—pointed out, through introspection it was possible to "have an evenly gradated order of luminosities from white to black; of tints from yellow, through green, to blue; of loudnesses, of all intensities, of good and evil, and so on; but the position of any item in these orders, although it may be metaphorically expressed on a spatial scale, is not directly intuited by the mind as objectively existing in such a scale."[32]

A quantitatively more robust way for the scientists to experimentally transform material colors into their sensorial ideals was to use the "Maxwell disk"—the same device used by art supply manufacturer Milton Bradley to study color mixtures by the eye (Chapter 3). An invention of the British scientist James Clerk Maxwell, the Maxwell disk (or "color wheel" or simply "rotating disk") was a wooden circle mounted on a stand and set up to spin rapidly around a central axis. The central axis typically extended a centimeter or so beyond the surface of the wheel, allowing its users to affix circles of colored paper that were cut to allow them to overlap. Although any color of paper could, in principle, be used on the color wheel, the paper segments were typically painted with red, green, and blue-violet pigments to correspond with the optimum response frequency of the retinal "nerves" proposed by Helmholtz.

When the experimenter spun the disk rapidly, the colored segments blurred, mimicking the combinatory action of the mind in bringing different "nerve" impulses to bear on specific colors. (This phenomenon is familiar to anyone who has seen the spokes on a rapidly spinning bicycle wheel blur into a more-or-less solid grayish color.) For instance, a disk showing red, green, and blue-violet segments in the correct proportions ought to appear white (or light gray) when spun rapidly because red, green, and blue-violet were optical primaries, which when combined formed white. Just so, a researcher could adjust the proportions of the segments of a disk such that when it was set in motion, the combined appearance of the blurred segments would match a sample of a given colored object, such as a swatch of colored fabric. Thus, by ascertaining the percentages of the visible portions of the colored segments in the spinning disk that best matched the solid sample, it was possible to render a quantitative accounting of otherwise qualitative colors. For example, Peirce analyzed several popular commercial colors using disks he had made and found the popular color called "crushed strawberry" to be composed of 49 percent red, 10 percent green, 15 percent blue-violet, and 26 percent black.[33] "Hair Brown," meanwhile, was 29 percent red, 13 percent green, 3 percent blue-violet, 55 percent black; and "Burnt Sienna" was 29 percent red, 7 percent green, 4 percent blue-violet, and 60 percent black[34](Fig. 6.2).

Beyond simply providing a sort of rough and ready way of analyzing colors quantitatively, the Maxwell disk provided a glimpse of the underlying structure of color phenomena. As described by Maxwell in 1857, it was possible to use readings from the disk to plot specific colors as coordinates on a ternary diagram with red, green, and blue-violet at each corner. This "color triangle" thereby enforced a sort of structural order on otherwise chaotic color sensations, or, as Rood put it in *Modern Chromatics,* the color triangle "enables us to express our ideas about colour in a geometrical form and with a certain degree of precision."[35] Peirce put the matter more bluntly to Rood in a letter penned around 1878, writing that the color triangle presented "light in its purely subjective form."[36](Fig. 6.3)

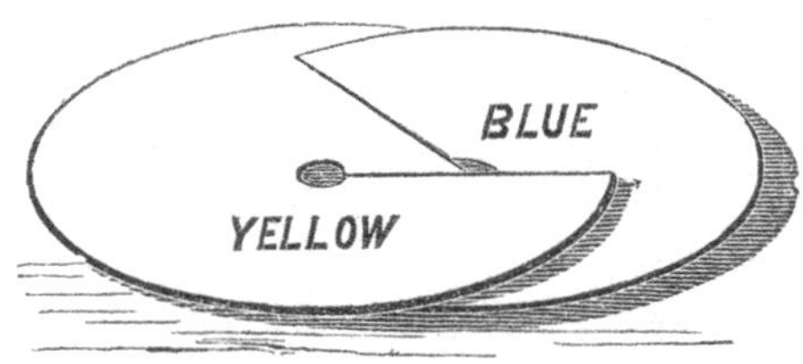

FIG. 37.—Maxwell's Disks. Blue and Yellow Disks in the Act of being combined.

Fig. 6.2 Illustration depicting the design and arrangement of colored-paper disks for measuring color sensation

Source: Ogden Rood, *Modern Chromatics* (1879; New York: D. Appleton and Company, 1881), 109. Reproduction courtesy of the Chemical Heritage Foundation collections.

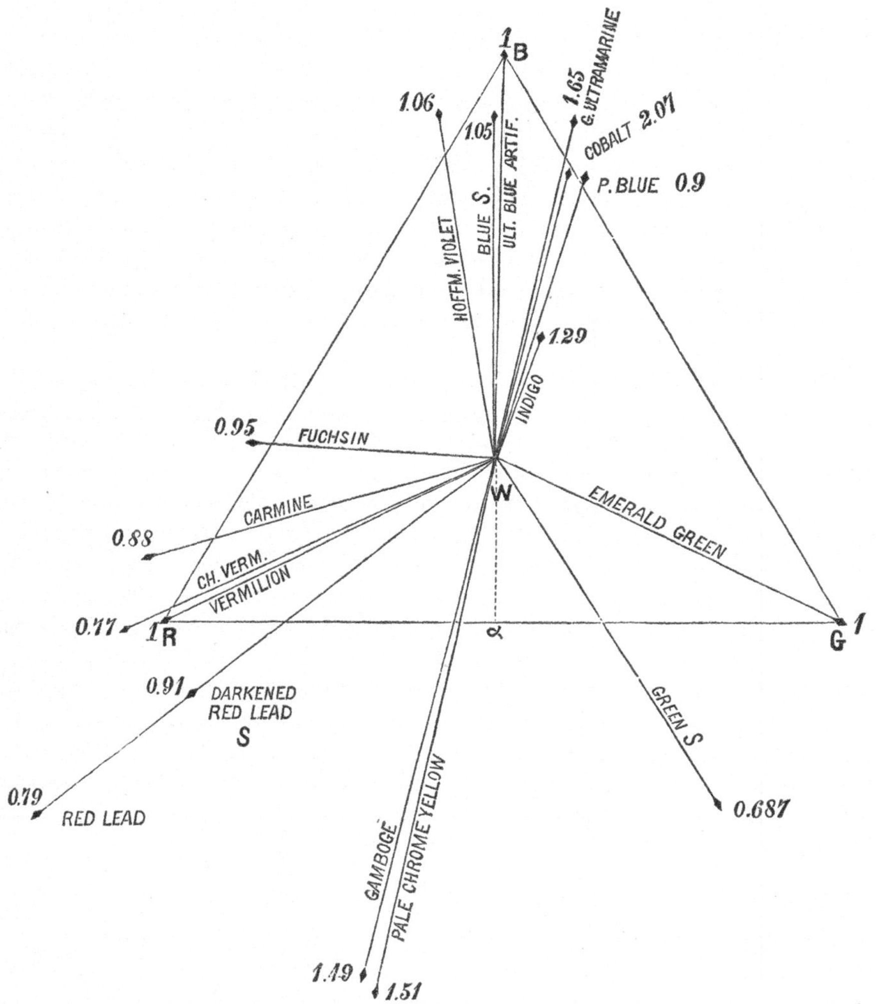

Fig. 103.—Maxwell's Colour-Diagram as constructed by O. N. R.

Fig. 6.3 Rood's ternary diagram depicting the relative positions of color mixtures based on red, green, and blue primaries

Source: Ogden Rood, *Modern Chromatics* (1879; New York: D. Appleton and Company, 1881), 228. Reproduction courtesy of the Chemical Heritage Foundation collections.

The pure subjectivity of the triangle notwithstanding, producing ideal realizations of color nevertheless required a significant amount of technical facility with commercially available colorants and coloring processes. Rood, for instance, was a serious amateur watercolorist, maintaining an active membership in the American Watercolor Society from 1867 to 1877. During this time, he kept notes on how he produced the pigments for his color wheels. This knowledge, in turn, made its way to his friend Peirce. A page from one of the latter's 1877 notebooks on color, for instance, records that Peirce had used "Rood's fundamental Blue Violet Apr 1875 made with Hoffmann's violet BB and artif. Ultramarine" and "Rood's 'Staats' Emerald Green" to conduct his own color analyses. In other words, Rood's records of the commercial colors he had used in making his color wheels guided Peirce.[37] Milton Bradley similarly came upon his scientific understanding of color in no small part through work in color commerce. He had made his fortune as a printer, and dedicated large portions of his later life to mixing colors in his factory as he searched for ways to produce ideal color standards.[38]

Furthermore, when personal facility in color technique was lacking, color scientists could turn to a ready supply of commercial printers and colorists for assistance. Ladd-Franklin turned to a printer named C. Snyder in Germany for help in formulating charts to describe her color theory (the printer wrote back to say that although he was very interested in her ideas, he could not understand the full system from the charts that she had sent).[39] The Boston ophthalmologist Benjamin Joy Jeffries, meanwhile, worked closely with Sylvester Kohler, a technical manager at the Louis Prang printing company in Boston, in an attempt to devise tests for color blindness using Maxwell disks.[40] (And in another corner of the color universe, Louis Prang vied with Milton Bradley for control of the market of color supplies for art instruction.[41]) As for Peirce, in addition to using Rood's formulas, he benefited in another way from his friend's interventions. On June 10, 1886, Peirce noted, "In the evening Rood sent two sets of beautiful measuring disks."[42] He set immediately to work using the disks to research aspects of the color triangle.

***

What distinguished modern chromatics from former color systems, then, was not the material substrate of the system—that is, the pigments themselves—but rather what the material stood for. In *Modern Chromatics,* Rood explained that color systems were nothing new. German and French natural philosophers had long experimented with them. Rood cited works by Jacob Cristoph Le Blon (1735), Tobias Mayer (1758), and Johann Heinrich Lambert (1772) as examples constructed "by mingling weighed portions of the fundamental pigments and of lamp-black in such a manner as to obtain as great a variety of tints as possible, which were then arranged in an orderly series." Michel-Eugène Chevreul's color system, explained in his 1830 treatise, *Leçons de chimie appliquée à la teinture,* was of a similar character. This French chemist-turned-textile-expert had taken red, blue, and yellow (not green) as his primaries, matching the hues of pigments as closely as possible with "certain portions of the prismatic spectrum [that he had] selected as standards."[43] Both ways of understanding color—as weighed pigments and as locations on the solar spectrum—were insufficient, according to Rood, "not only in the main arbitrary, but also vague." Neither could be regarded as "a true step toward a philosophical classification of color."[44]

This was not simply a problem of the benighted past. Confusion as to the limits of materiality in color science could beset even respectable researchers. In his 1886 *Nomenclature of Colors for Naturalists and Compendium of Useful Knowledge for Ornithologists*, the Smithsonian Institution scientist Robert Ridgway presented his readers with 166 tiny rectangles of painted paper, painstakingly categorized into like hues, pasted (mostly by Ridgway's wife) into rows and columns on tipped-in plates, and labeled with evocative names. The point was to overcome what Ridgway saw as the chaos of commercial color names with a rationally systematized set of colors.

To organize his system, Ridgway explained, he had initially set out to base his color system in the state of the art of color science (following, Helmholtz and Maxwell, for example). But since it was impossible to optically mix physical pigments on a page in the same way that one would mix sensations of light using a color wheel, Ridgway—who, like Rood, was a serious watercolorist—decided instead to base his system on 36 commercially available watercolors, half of which, Ridgway explained, were selected from his personal collection of three hundred "quality" watercolors "for convenience, rather than because they are necessary."[45] Instead of coordinates on the color triangle or percentages of optical color mixes, therefore, Ridgway provided his readers with recipes for the particular colors on his page. On plate VII, for instance, which was devoted to orangey-red colors, item number 17, "Salmon Color," could be recreated with a combination of "scarlet vermilion + cadmium orange + white." Item number 9, "Poppy Red," was equivalent simply to the French pigment maker "Bourgeois's 'laque ponceau.'"[46] This approach was not so different in process from the recipes that Rood had provided to Peirce. But whereas Rood had simply treated pigment as an aspect of a higher order of color, Ridgway made commercial pigments the basis of his system.

Violating the rules of epistemological hygiene that separated thoughts and things earned Ridgway the ridicule of his peers in color science. In her notes on Ridgway's book, Ladd-Franklin voiced astonishment that Ridgway had abandoned the properly scientific color scheme provided by color science in favor of pigments—"if he only had the color triangle before him!!!" she jeered.[47] It was not, of course, the fact that Ridgway placed such a high value on his collection of commercially available watercolors. After all, Ladd-Franklin herself cultivated an extensive collection of colored goods of her own, from swatch books of cosmetic colors to samples of commercial colored papers like those made by the Milton Bradley Company and the Prang Educational Company. She found Bradley's Spectrum Standard papers particularly favorable, "on account of their greater saturation than that of any other colors available." Indeed, she thought common blotter paper provided one of the closest approximations to the sensations of the "green" nerve of any sort of commercially manufactured material.[48] But whereas Ridgway's system stopped at the colors of goods, Ladd-Franklin felt that consumer goods were simply the tip of a much larger structural iceberg.

The structure that Rood, Peirce, Ladd-Franklin, and even Ridgway (however dimly his peers regarded his efforts) sought to expose amounted to a meticulous rethinking of what it meant to see colors as an observer in a modern, consumer society. This was the heart of modern color science writ large—a program that Rood proclaimed when he announced in the introduction to *Modern Chromatics* that the book was written specifically to "prevent ordinary persons, critics, and even painters, from talking and writing about colour in a loose, inaccurate and not always rational manner."[49] That is, understanding color as a function of mental space, as a coordinate on the color triangle, and as a matter of nerves and curves entailed relearning those mental processes that were "near to the first impression of sense." To understand "modern" chromatics, color scientists—and, by extension, the laypeople who would read their books, attend their lectures, and refer to the definitions that they wrote for popular dictionaries—had to simultaneously embrace and deny color sensations as a function of the consumption of material goods. Being a "modern" observer meant understanding color not as a product of consumer objects, but of the mind—even when the focus of the mind was precisely geared towards understanding those objects.

This, then, was the thicket of entwined social, cultural, and scientific meanings into which Rood stepped when he visited A. T. Stewart's store in the summer of 1889. As he looked for "Isabel" among swatch books and textiles, querying ladies and clerks, he undertook a project of epistemological triage. On the one hand, he was there in Stewart's, in the name of science, to find a color for a colleague who was engaged in a scientific endeavor. At the same time, in his reports to this colleague, he made serious efforts to distinguish the knowledge held by a color scientist from the knowledge of colorful materials for sale in a store. Science was not commerce. Colorful things were not colorful perceptions that disavowed the material origins of color sensations, even as Rood reinforced the strict ideology of color science. Thus, in spite of the deep connection between colored stuffs and the construction of a powerful tool for understanding color perception—and, indeed, the human mind—Rood did not see colors at Stewart's, only colored things. In shopping for a definition of "Isabel," he and Peirce were also shopping for a definition of color science.

As for "Isabel," in his final definition for the *Century Dictionary*—printed in 1891—Peirce defined the color as "a yellowish-gray or grayish buff color; a kind of drab." Another way of thinking about it, continued the entry, was as "a mixture [produced] by rotating disks of ¾ black, 1/6 bright chrome yellow, and 1/12 white, [which] gives an Isabel-yellow."[50] Gone were the dirty underclothes, mushrooms, minerals, and evening silks—replaced by a fantasy portrait of the mental life of the modern observer, constituted by the operations of color science. Peirce had found what he was shopping for.

Notes

1. Rood is today particularly well known as one of the scientists who most influenced French Impressionism and Post-Impressionism. For a short synopsis of his influence in this respect, see Martin Kemp, "The Impressionists' Bible," *Nature,* May 1, 2008, 37. See also Phoebe Pool, *Impressionism* (New York, 1967), 243–44. Rood also had a noteworthy influence on architecture; see, for example, Lauren S. Weingarden, "The Colors of Nature: Louis Sullivan's Architectural Polychromy and Nineteenth-Century Color Theory," *Winterthur Portfolio* 20, no. 4 (Winter 1985): 243–60; and William W. Braham, "Solidity of the Mask: Color Contrasts in Modern Architecture," *RES: Anthropology and Aesthetics* 39 (Spring 2001): 192–214. As an example of Rood's usefulness to philologists, see Edward W. Hopkins, "Words for Color in the Rig Veda," *American Journal of Philology* 4, no. 2 (April 1, 1883) 179. For biographical information on Rood, consult W. LeConte Stevens, "Ogden Rood," *Science,* n.s., 15 (December 5, 1902): 881–84. Faber Birren also offers a short biography of Rood in his introduction to *Modern Chromatics* (New York, 1973), 11–18; on Rood's early years, see Michael Rossi, *From Physics to Landscape Painting and Back Again* (forthcoming).
2. Upon meeting Peirce for the first time in 1861, William James famously described him as "a very 'smart' fellow with a great deal of character" but "pretty independent & violentsa"; see *The Correspondence of William James,* ed. Ignas K. Skrupskelis and Elizabeth M. Berkeley (Charlottesville, 1992), 4:43. James would prove one of Peirce's only enduring friends. Rood was not so lucky—his friendship with Peirce soured in 1894 (Ogden Rood to Charles Peirce, March 14, 1894, Charles S. Peirce papers, MS Am 1632, Houghton Library, Harvard University). An excellent short analysis of Peirce's life vis-à-vis the development of pragmatism can be found in Louis Menand, *The Metaphysical Club* (New York, 2001), 151–201. For a short overview of Peirce's color work, see Thomas C. Cadwallader, "Charles S. Perice (1839–1914): The First American Experimental Psychologist," *Journal of the History of the Behavioral Sciences* 10, no. 3 (July 1974): 291–98. The question of whether it is possible to retrospectively call Rood and Peirce's practice "experimental psychology" is an open one, though certainly some of Peirce's students at Johns Hopkins University (such as Christine Ladd Franklin and Joseph Jastrow) became psychologists as the discipline emerged and credited Peirce with a measure of influence.
3. John Hamilton Gourlie, *The Origin and History of "The Century"* (New York, 1856), 5.
4. "Exposition of Textile Fabric and A. T. Stewart's Store—A Magnificent Display," *New York Times,* February 9, 1871.
5. "Fall Opening at A. T. Stewart's: An Extensive Display of Attractive Novelties," *New York Times,* October 4, 1881.
6. Ogden Rood to Charles Peirce, July 31, 1889, Charles S. Peirce Papers, MS Am 1632 (L 382) Houghton Library, Harvard University.
7. Christine Ladd-Franklin, "Color-Introspection on the Part of the Eskimo," *Psychological Review* 8, no. 4 (July 1901): 399.
8. A. Hume, "Spinning and Weaving: Their Influence on Popular Language and Literature," *Ulster Journal of Archaeology* 5 (1857): 93–110. Hume only identifies the siege of a "Moorish" town. In other etymologies of the color Isabel, the

princess is identified as Isabella Clara Eugenia, whose husband, Archduke Albert of Austria, besieged Ostend from 1601 to 1604.

9. "Isabelline as a Colour," *Notes and Queries* (September 24, 1904): 253.
10. Writers throughout the nineteenth century used "Isabel" and "Isabella" interchangeably—often with a clarifying modifier ("Isabel yellow," for example)—to name the color. In this chapter I do not correct the orthography and usage of individual commentators, insofar as it is clear that all refer to the same color.
11. "Scientific Intelligence: Constitution of the Chemistry of Platinum Metals," *American Journal of Science* 79, no. 87 (May 1860): 426
12. Andrew Ure, *Dictionary of Arts, Manufactures, and Mines Containing a Clear Exposition of their Principles and Practice* (New York, 1863), 839.
13. Oliver Cummings Farrington, "Catalogue of the Meteorites of North America," *Memoirs of the National Academy of Sciences* 13 (1866): 141.
14. M. E. Wadsworth, "On the Trachyte of Marblehead Neck, Massachusetts," *Proceedings of the Boston Society of Natural History* 21 (1883): 290.
15. Baron R. Osten Sacken, "Description of Some New Genera and Species of North American Limnobina," *Proceedings of the Entomological Society of Philadelphia* 4 (1865): 232.
16. *Botanical Survey of Nebraska: Report on Collections Made in 1892* (Lincoln, NE, 1892), 15.
17. "New York Fashions: Spring Millinery. Pokes, Small Bonnets, Etc. Round Hats. The Greuze Capote. Materials For Trimming. Stylish Colors, Etc. Manner Of Trimming. Varieties," *Harper's Bazar*, March 3, 1883, 131.
18. "The Fashions," *New York Evening Post,* February 5, 1885.
19. Emmiline Raymond, "Paris Fashions," *Harper's Bazaar,* April 4, 1891, 252.
20. Grant Allen, *The Colour-Sense: Its Origin and Development* (London, 1892), 251.
21. "New Fashions," *Harper's Bazaar,* February 18, 1882, 99.
22. Robert Ridgway, *A Nomenclature of Colors for Naturalists and Compendium of Useful Knowledge for Ornithologists,* (Boston, 1886), 26.
23. "Preface," *Century Dictionary,* (New York, 1891), i, xiii–xiv.
24. *Century Dictionary,* (New York, 1891), s.v. "Green," by Charles S. Peirce.
25. Ibid., s.v. "Yellow," by Charles S. Peirce.
26. Notes on Color Words and Words about Luminosity, Charles S. Peirce papers, MS Am 1632 (1154) Houghton Library, Harvard University; italics added.
27. Hermann von Helmholtz, *Handbuch der physiologischen Optik* (Leipzig, 1867), esp. 290–92.
28. Ogden Rood, *Modern Chromatics* (New York, 1879), 48.
29. Charles Peirce and Russell Sturgis, review of *Modern Chromatics* by Ogden Rood, *Nation,* October 16, 1879, 260.
30. Ibid.
31. Christine Ladd-Franklin, undated notes, box 50, folder: Experiment to do re: vision, MS Coll Franklin, Christine Ladd-Franklin and Fabian Franklin Papers, Library of Rare Books and Special Collections, Columbia University.
32. William James, "The Spatial Quale," *Journal of Speculative Philosophy* 13, no. 1 (January 1879): 67. To be clear, this article concerns the perception of space—not color. But James's point was apposite to the case at hand, insofar as it concerned the limits of true introspection. For James, the arrangement of color in space—as proposed, for example, by Albert H. Munsell—was anathema because it did not truly represent mental phenomena.

33. Experimenters using the wheel for color matching frequently found it necessary to include black in addition to the three optical primaries, in part in order to mimic the differential reflectance of material objects.
34. Color Experiment, Charles S. Peirce Papers, MS Am 1632 (1019) Houghton Library, Harvard University.
35. Rood, *Modern Chromatics,* 221.
36. Charles Peirce to Ogden Rood, n.d. (probably 1878), Charles S. Peirce Papers, MS Am 1632 (1018) Houghton Library, Harvard University
37. Notebook, February 1877, Charles S. Peirce Papers, MS Am 1632 (1018) Houghton Library, Harvard University.
38. For remembrances of Bradley and the early days of the Milton Bradley Company by friends and executives of the corporation, as well as for some material by Bradley himself, see the commemorative publication by the Milton Bradley Company on the occasion of the company's fiftieth anniversary: *Milton Bradley, a Successful Man* (New York, 1910). James J. Shea's *It's All in the Game* (New York, 1960) is a longer and more extensively researched account of Bradley's life, authored by the mid-twentieth-century president of the corporation to celebrate the company's centennial.
39. Christine Ladd-Franklin, box 50, folder: Charts, Christine Ladd-Franklin and Fabian Franklin papers.
40. Benjamin Joy Jeffries to Sylvester Rosa Koehler, March 11, 1877, in "Benjamin Joy Jeffries, Correspondence, 1877–1891," Crerar Ms 202, Special Collections Research Center, University of Chicago.
41. Regina Lee Blaszczyk, *The Color Revolution* (Cambridge, MA, 2012), 46–50.
42. "Notebook entitled "Color Miscellaneous," June 10, 1886, Charles S. Peirce Papers, MS Am 1632 (1016) Houghton Library, Harvard University.
43. Rood, *Modern Chromatics,* 222.
44. Ibid., 222–23.
45. Ridgway, *A Nomenclature of Color for Naturalists,* 27.
46. Ibid., 34.
47. Christine Ladd-Franklin, box 58, folder: R. Ridgway, Christine Ladd-Franklin and Fabian Franklin Papers.
48. Christine Ladd-Franklin, box 53, folder: TS of PP7-8 of Journal paper by CLF of color experiment, Christine Ladd-Franklin and Fabian Franklin Papers.
49. Rood, *Modern Chromatics,* v–vi.
50. *Century Dictionary,* (New York, 1891), s.v. "Isabel," by Charles S. Peirce.

PART III

Ringmasters to the Rainbow: Color Inventions and Visual Culture

CHAPTER 7

Movies Meet the Rainbow

Joyce Bedi

"Technicolor is . . . the next big thing in pictures, *the* coming revolution in the cinema world—maybe."[1] Color had seeped into most segments of American life by 1930, from cars to appliances to fashion, so color in motion pictures seemed inevitable.[2] *Fortune's* 1934 pronouncement nevertheless showed a healthy amount of skepticism. Color movies and Technicolor specifically had been tried and found wanting before. Still, profound technological change was not foreign to the motion picture industry.

In a few short decades, moviemaking had matured rapidly from the production of short, silent, black-and-white films made in and around New York City at the dawn of the industry in the early 1900s. By 1930, feature-length films had become the norm and the studio system had solidified in Hollywood. The movie business was increasingly controlled by the vertically integrated studios—Paramount, Loew's (the parent company of MGM), Fox, RKO, and Warner Brothers—that not only made films but also owned the theaters in which they were shown.[3] Meanwhile, behind the scenes, the motion picture industry had become a finely tuned technological system. An array of inventions—including cameras, lighting, makeup, sets, and more, all overseen by a community of technical professionals—had to work together seamlessly. That system had continued to expand and become more complex as the industry as a whole initially fought and then embraced sound, the first important disruptive technology of the studio era. Although the industry was now about to repeat the process for color, an invention that would change

J. Bedi (✉)
Lemelson Center for the Study of Invention and Innovation, Smithsonian Institution, Washington, DC, USA

R.L. Blaszczyk, U. Spiekermann (eds.), *Bright Modernity*, Worlds of Consumption, DOI 10.1007/978-3-319-50745-3_7

the look of movies forever, *Fortune's* tepid prediction in 1934 made it clear that the outcome was still undecided.

Techniques for introducing color to movies, however, were nearly as old as motion pictures themselves. In addition to hand-coloring, two of the most common methods were tinting and toning, used alone or together. Tinting added color to the light parts of a film, giving an overall color wash. Toning colored only the dark parts of the frame, leaving the highlights untouched. Trailblazing filmmaker D. W. Griffith, whose work influenced the migration of the industry from the East Coast to the West Coast as well as the direction in which Hollywood and the studio system would develop, dabbled in color, tinting some scenes in his landmark film *The Birth of a Nation* (1915).[4] Equally noteworthy was Abel Gance's epic *Napoleon* (1927), in which tinting was only one of many innovative techniques used.

The history of technology chronicles numerous instances of "simultaneous" invention, when a new idea seems to drive the community of inventors.[5] This was true of the quest to bring natural color to the big screen, resulting in a number of competing systems.[6] These encompassed, as film historian Sarah Street describes them, "tinting alternate film frames red and green; putting rotating coloured filters on projectors; using light-splitting prisms with cameras and sensitising film stock."[7] Kinemacolor was the most successful process commercially and the best known worldwide. A two-color additive technique "developed between 1902 and 1906 by British film pioneer George Albert Smith under the patronage of American film producer Charles Urban," Kinemacolor made its public debut in 1909.[8] Such additive processes, in which color was "added" back to the film at the time of projection by various means, suffered from a number of problems. Because each scene was captured twice—typically, one exposure was made to record the green light and a second for the red—there was a very slight time lag between each frame. When recombined, people and objects in motion tended to blur around the edges because the time difference caused the colors to shift out of registration in a phenomenon called "fringing." This was one of the greatest weaknesses of Kinemacolor, but in the end it was patent infringement litigation that resulted in the revocation of Smith's patent in 1914. Kinemacolor production ceased soon after.[9]

A vast array of other two-color and three-color, additive and subtractive processes were developed in the early 1900s; Prizmacolor, Magnacolor, Natural Colour, Chronochrome, Multicolor, Vitacolor, and Cinecolor were some of the groundbreakers in the field.[10] All of these processes were relatively short-lived, but one company persevered and proved that it was completely dedicated to color by experimenting, prototyping, and tweaking all aspects of its product—and then convincing the industry to adopt it.[11] That company was Technicolor.

Like many inventions, Technicolor went through a number of iterations before it became an industry standard. The first version was the work of Massachusetts Institute of Technology graduates Herbert Kalmus and Daniel Comstock and technician W. Burton Wescott (the "Tech" in Technicolor was a nod to Kalmus and Comstock's alma mater).[12] Comstock and Wescott started an eponymous industrial research and development consulting firm in 1912; Kalmus joined them in 1913, and the name was changed to Kalmus, Comstock & Wescott; the Technicolor Motion Picture Corporation was incorporated as a spin-off in 1915.[13] In 1938, Kalmus spoke about the beginnings of Technicolor to the Society of Motion Picture Engineers:

> The earliest Technicolor laboratory was built within a railway car [Fig. 7.1]. This car was completely equipped with a photochemical laboratory, darkrooms, fire-proof safes, power plant, offices, and all the machinery and apparatus necessary for continuously carrying on the following processes on a small commercial scale; sensitizing, testing, perforating, developing, washing, fixing and drying negative; printing, developing, washing, fixing, and drying positive; washing and conditioning air; filtering and cooling wash water; examining and splicing film; and making control measurements and tests. In 1917 the car was rolled over the railway tracks from Boston, Massachusetts, where it was equipped, to Jacksonville, Florida, where the first Technicolor adventure in feature motion picture production was to take place.[14]

That film, *The Gulf Between* (1917), demonstrated the earliest version of Technicolor, known as Technicolor Process Number One. It was a two-color, additive method that used a camera designed by Wescott. Inside the camera, an arrangement of prisms split the image and sent it through separate green and red filters, recording each color record onto separate

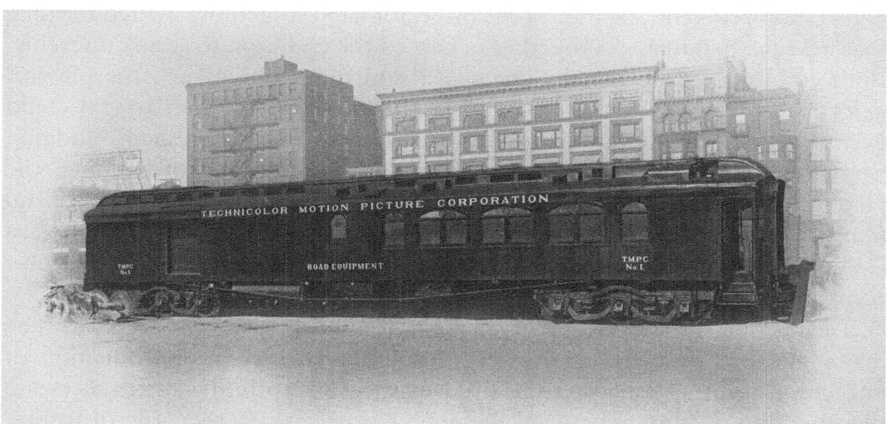

Fig. 7.1 The railroad car that housed the first Technicolor lab

Source: Courtesy of National Museum of American History, Smithsonian Institution.

frames of standard black-and-white motion picture negative film.[15] As an additive process, the color had to be recreated when the film was projected, using a custom-built projector designed by Comstock and equipped with a prism, filters, two lenses, and optical reflecting plates to fine tune the registration of the images. Consequently, if the projectionist did not have everything perfectly adjusted, the projected image displayed considerable fringing.[16] Kalmus himself noted that the "special attachments on the projector required an operator who was a cross between a college professor and an acrobat."[17] *The Gulf Between* was hardly a commercial success, but it served to introduce the movie industry to the possibilities of color, even if those possibilities were flawed at first.

Comstock realized that the next iteration could not rely solely on a special projector. Technicolor Process Number Two was two-color and subtractive, which meant that primary colors were absorbed or "subtracted" to reveal their opposites; in two-color Technicolor, red-orange was "minus green," and blue-green was "minus red." The color was contained in the finished film itself and the film could be screened using a standard projector.

The newly designed camera, invented by Comstock's former student J. Arthur Ball, still split the image and sent it through green and red filters, but in this instance the green record was stacked upside down below the red record on the negative. The biggest change in Process Number Two, however, was the introduction of dyes. The camera negative was exposed onto a special film stock called a matrix which, when developed, left a raised relief image on the stock, similar to the relief on an engraved printing plate or lithographer's stone. The matrices were dyed with their complementary colors—blue-green for red and red-orange for green—with the areas of thicker relief representing darker areas in the filmed scene and taking up more of the dye. The strips were then cemented together to produce the projection print. Although this solved the registration problem, the heat of the projector lamp sometimes melted the glue that held the two matrices together or caused the emulsion to shrink unevenly. Both conditions distorted the image.[18] "And the cupping [i.e., the physical deformation caused by the separation or buckling of the film layers] could occur in either direction, more or less at random," Kalmus recalled. "Judging from the complaints, at each such change in the direction of cupping, the picture would jump out of focus."[19] Still, a number of reasonably successful films were made with Process Number Two, including *The Toll of the Sea* (1922), which was shot in Hollywood and earned the fledgling Technicolor company its first profit.[20]

Technicolor Process Number Three was similar to its predecessor. The major changes were the addition of a soundtrack and the introduction of imbibition printing, or using the dyed matrices like printing plates to create the final film. Without the need to cement matrices together, the distortion problems caused by the heat inside the projector were solved.[21] Still, Technicolor in 1930 was more an experiment than a profit-maker, most commonly used for short subjects and segments of a movie rather than for complete feature-length films.[22] *Fortune* noted,

> Certainly the time has not yet arrived [for color movies]; it is probably several years and perhaps a decade away. Simply put, the reason comes down to this: to the degree that we are aware of the imperfection of color it is a distraction and consequently hinders rather than promotes dramatic action. To cease to be a distraction, color must be so perfect as to be *unnoticeable* except by contrast with absence of color.[23]

These not-quite-perfected early Technicolor processes are often referred to as "two-strip color," although each iteration originated from a single strip of black-and-white negative motion picture film in the camera. That was about to change, however. By 1930, Comstock and Kalmus had dissolved their partnership.[24] Kalmus had been the business head of Technicolor from the start, responsible for securing funding for ongoing research and for promoting the latest technical process to studio heads, and he continued in that capacity until he retired in 1960. His effectiveness was captured by *Fortune* in 1934 with the quip, "Businessmen regard Dr. Kalmus as a scientist and scientists regard him as a businessman, which gives him rather an edge with both. For he is always an expert in one field in which the other man is a novice."[25] The company had also opened its first plant in Hollywood in 1924, and it expanded into two additional buildings at the end of the decade.[26] In the split, J. Arthur Ball chose to stay with Technicolor. He became the lead inventor of the new three-strip camera, a crucial component in the next iteration of the technology.

Full color came to the screen with Technicolor Process Number Four. Moving beyond the two-color processes that had produced movies primarily in shades of bluish green and reddish orange, Process Number Four made possible the saturated palette for which Technicolor is still known. It fulfilled "the ultimate goal of workers in the field of color cinematography," according to Ball, to "add a full scale of color reproduction to the existing black-and-white product without subtracting from any of its desirable qualities, without imposing any complications upon theater projection conditions, and with a minimum of added burden in the cost of photography and in the cost of prints."[27]

Ball's new camera was the heart of the system. In it, three strips of black-and-white negative motion picture film were exposed simultaneously by light coming through the lens. The light was divided by two prisms and a mirror and directed through two separate openings. Behind one opening, light passed through a green filter and the green record was captured on one strip of film. Behind the other opening, light passed through a magenta filter to expose two strips of film spooled together with their emulsions touching. The front strip received the blue record and served as a blue filter, allowing the red light to pass through to the back layer of film (Fig. 7.2). When the three negative film strips were developed, their silver densities correlated to the filtered colors, just as they had in the two-color processes. The three negatives were exposed onto matrices and each matrix was dyed and contact-printed, in succession and under pressure, onto special film stock—called the "blank"—that was treated

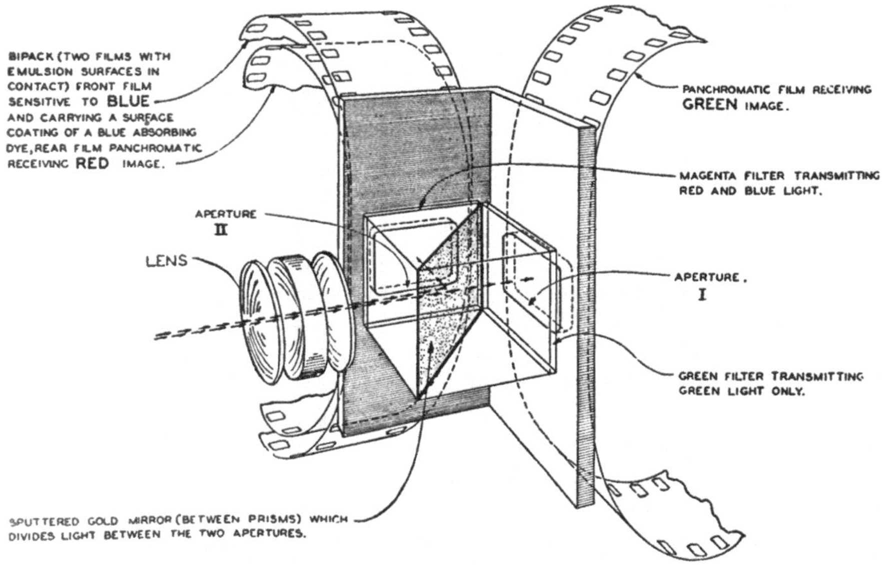

Fig. 7.2 Arrangement of optical system and films in J. Arthur Ball's three-color camera

Source: Joseph A. Ball, "The Technicolor Process of Three-Color Cinematography," *Journal of the Society of Motion Picture Engineers* 25, no. 2 (August 1935), 130.

with chemicals known as mordants to hold the dyes. The blank also carried the soundtrack, frame borders, and a "key," which was a 50 percent gray positive image of each frame that made the shadows richer and improved contrast. This final dyed and printed film was then shown in theaters.[28]

The Technicolor camera was an unwieldy beast, later described by filmmaker Richard Haines as "a huge and cumbersome machine usually bolted to a crane or dolly on wheels (Fig. 7.3). The noisy machine was encased in a 'Blimp' (outer covering) to quiet it."[29] It was also a rare piece of moviemaking apparatus. An article published in 1944 cited only thirty cameras in existence, and four of those were in use by Technicolor's branch in England.[30] Operating the camera took special training, so studios had to hire Technicolor technicians to oversee shooting. Haines explains, "Generally speaking, the cameraman had to take a crash course with the lab to learn the ins and outs of color photography as dictated by Kalmus and staff. Since Technicolor supplied the equipment and handled all aspects of the process from negative developing through release printing, the terms were tough."[31]

The technical, financial, and creative demands outlined by Haines made it difficult for Herbert Kalmus to convince studios to adopt Technicolor. He astutely assessed the situation: "With Technicolor Process Number Four, we were at a familiar starting gate: we had a new product to promote to the

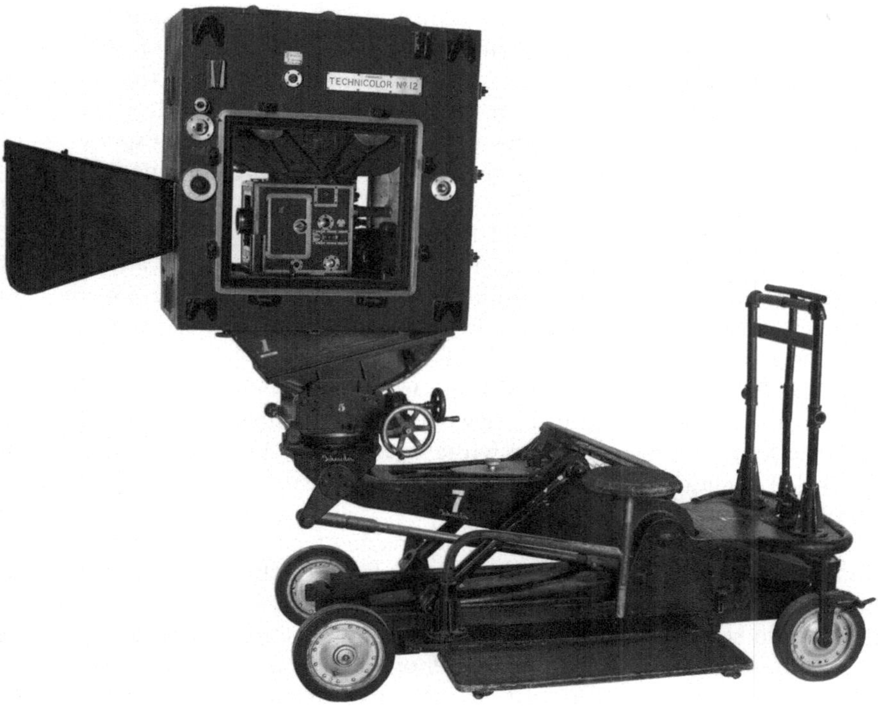

Fig. 7.3 Technicolor camera encased in a sound-dampening blimp, used in the filming of *The Wizard of Oz*

Source: Photograph by Richard Strauss, 2016. Courtesy of National Museum of American History, Smithsonian Institution.

usual customers—Hollywood's cost-conscious producers."[32] There were, however, two exceptions among the usual customers—Jack L. Warner and Walt Disney.

This was not the first time that the Warner brothers were at the forefront of incorporating a new technology into their business. Samuel Warner had been a leading proponent of the possibilities of adding sound to motion pictures and was the founding president of Vitaphone, the system that synced a sound recording on disc with a film; its most famous application was in *The Jazz Singer* (1927).[33] "After the introduction of the 'talkies,'" the *Literary Digest* noted in 1935, "Warner Brothers looked elsewhere, and Jack Warner saw something in color which he first used in the sequences in 'The Desert Song [1929],' and, later, in the first all-color, all-'talkie,' 'On With the Show [1929].'"[34] Later characterized as "the stereotype of the crude, rough, all-powerful movie mogul," Warner's primary motivation for experimenting with color seemed to be profit, and for a short time, that strategy worked.[35] "Just as the Warner experiment with sound led the other producers into the noisy cinema, so *On With the Show* resulted in a color vogue," *Fortune* reported.[36] The weaknesses inherent in the two-color Technicolor process used in that film, combined with the drop in movie attendance as the Great Depression took hold and the inexperience of filmmakers with the technology meant that color's initial vogue was short-lived. "Everybody on the sets," *Fortune* pointed out, "had grown up in a black and white universe and did things in a black and white way."[37] The technical staff at Technicolor steadily improved the process and Herbert Kalmus continued to recruit studios, convincing them to take a chance on color. It was a cartoon maker, however, who brought Technicolor the broader exposure that Kalmus craved.

In 1923 Walt Disney left a lackluster career in commercial art and animation in Kansas City and headed to Hollywood.[38] His acclimation to California did not take long. In June 1924, he wrote to his friend and fellow animator Ub Iwerks, "I wouldn't live in K.C. now if you gave me the place—yep—you bet—Hooray for Hollywood!!"[39]

Disney was quick to embrace new filmmaking technologies that would give his cartoons an edge in theaters, later remarking that by 1930, "cartoons had become the shabby Cinderella of the picture industry."[40] He was among the first to add sound, for example, using a sound-on-film system called Powers Cinephone (based on Lee DeForest's Phonofilm system) to add music, sound effects, and voice to a series of four cartoons that included *Steamboat Willie* (1928) starring Mickey Mouse.[41] Disney and his colleagues William E. Garrity and Wilfred Jackson also invented a method to accurately synchronize sound with animated films. For standard motion pictures, the soundtrack was recorded at the same speed as the action, but cartoons were filmed one frame at a time, offering unique challenges to synchronization. Disney, Garrity, and Jackson received U.S. Patent 1,941,341 for their "Method and Apparatus for Synchronizing Photoplays" in 1933.[42]

When Herbert Kalmus approached Disney about using the three-color Technicolor process for cartoons, Disney was more than receptive. Kalmus recalled their meeting: "I invited Walt Disney to come by for a private view of the new process. He had been intrigued with the idea of adding color to his cartoons for years... He was enchanted with the effects we were getting, and decided to scrap a cartoon he was making for his *Silly Symphony* series and remake it in full color."[43] Walt Disney's brother Roy Disney, who ran the business end of the studio, was skeptical. The extra expense of starting over, and starting over in color, seemed ill-advised to him. "You'll ruin us," he reportedly predicted.[44] Walt prevailed, later asserting that "A black-and-white print looked as drab alongside *Flowers and Trees*, as a gray day alongside a rainbow."[45] Kalmus and Disney came to an agreement that gave Disney a two-year exclusive on using the three-color process for cartoons. All other cartoon makers would be limited to earlier versions of Technicolor or other inferior color processes.[46]

Flowers and Trees debuted at Grauman's Chinese Theater on Hollywood Boulevard late in 1932. It won the Academy Award for Best Cartoon of 1931–32 (Technicolor received a Certificate of Honorable Mention) and was followed by other Disney cartoons filmed in Technicolor, including *The Three Little Pigs* (1933; winner of the Oscar for Best Cartoon, 1934) and *Snow White and the Seven Dwarfs* (1937, the first Disney animated feature in Technicolor). The Academy of Motion Picture Arts and Sciences presented Disney with a special award for *Snow White*, citing it as "a significant screen innovation which has charmed millions and pioneered a great new entertainment field for the motion picture cartoon." The award consisted of a normal-size Oscar statuette and seven smaller versions, presented by actress Shirley Temple.[47]

While Disney worked on cartoons, Kalmus and financier John Hay "Jock" Whitney signed a deal to produce live-action Technicolor films. The first was a two-reel short subject titled *La Cucaracha*, released in 1934. It, too, won an Academy Award, for Best Short Subject.[48] With these successes in hand, production of the first full-color, live-action Technicolor feature film began. *Becky Sharp*, directed by Rouben Mamoulian and starring Miriam Hopkins, was released in 1935.[49]

Still, the industry's transition to Technicolor was complicated. *The Literary Digest* summarized the challenges: "The early color-pictures failed since the methods used—in make-up, sets, lighting—were those employed in the black and white film."[50] Herbert Kalmus was certainly aware of the hurdles his company faced, recalling director William Wellman's comments during the filming of *A Star Is Born* in 1936:

> Technicolor cameras are more cumbersome than black and white; they are hard to handle, and slow down the work. The camera requires three strips of negative instead of one, and takes longer to thread between takes. It demands more light, which means more arc lamps, more carpenters, more electricians, more current, and more time—not to mention all the problems of color composition, lighting, and makeup.[51]

While numerous inventions, including improved lighting and faster film emulsions, addressed some of these problems, perhaps the solution with the greatest impact on and off the set was the makeup created for Technicolor by one of the best-known names in cosmetics—Max Factor.

Born in Poland, Max Factor (originally Max Faktor) learned his trade as an apprentice to a respected cosmetician and wig maker in Lódź. His gift for enhancing beauty became so well-known that he was ordered into compulsory service as the cosmetician to both Czar Nicholas II's uncle and the Imperial Russian Grand Opera. Seeking independence, he and his wife and children escaped to the United States in 1904, emigrating to St. Louis. He opened a barbershop, but the lure of plying his craft in the budding motion picture business induced him to move the family to Los Angeles in 1908.[52]

Customers who visited Factor's wig and theatrical makeup shop on South Central Avenue were his introduction to the film industry. According to Factor's biographer Fred E. Basten, "From the 1920s to the 1970s, all the wigs and hairpieces seen in motion pictures were made by the Max Factor hair department, with sales and rental rivaling, often surpassing, those of the company's cosmetics."[53] In his small lab at the back of the shop, Factor developed a new makeup that gave screen actors a more natural appearance than the heavy greasepaint stage makeup that tended to crack when an actor moved his or her face.[54] In addition, he also developed his theory of "color harmony," which paired shades of makeup with particular hair, complexion, and eye colors.[55]

The makeup that Factor had developed for black-and-white movies, however, did not work with Technicolor. Its slight sheen tended to reflect the color of whatever an actor was near onto his or her face. Factor's son Frank (who changed his name legally to Max Factor, Jr., after his father's death in 1938) took the lead in developing a new formulation. Together, they introduced "Pan-Cake" makeup, which was more porous and less reflective. The new makeup was used in *Vogues of 1938,* a Technicolor film released in September 1937.[56]

Given the importance of Max Factor's work to Technicolor, it is not surprising that he crossed paths with someone equally crucial to the company's success—Herbert Kalmus' ex-wife Natalie (née Dunphy).[57] She had been an art student when she met Herbert, who was then an MIT undergraduate. The couple married in 1902.[58] Natalie Kalmus was involved in the development of Technicolor from its beginning, often acting as a test model for color experiments. She worked on the set of *The Gulf Between* and even went behind the camera a few times.[59]

When Natalie and Herbert divorced in 1921, Natalie continued to play a role as Technicolor's chief color consultant, and her name appeared on the credits of Technicolor films throughout the 1940s.[60] As head of the Technicolor Color Advisory Service, she and her fellow consultants were the color authorities on the set, making decisions about makeup, costumes, sets, and lighting. "The design and colors of sets, costumes, drapes, and furnishings," she wrote, "must be planned and selected just as an artist would choose the colors from his palette."[61]

Natalie Kalmus and the other consultants read the scripts and created color schemes for each production; developed a schedule and budget with the producers; and coordinated the work of the costumes, art, and props departments to ensure that everything on the set was in harmony.[62] She described the process:

> In the preparation of a picture we read the script and prepare a color chart for the entire production, each scene, sequence, set, and character being considered.... [T]his chart must be in absolute accord with the story action. Again, it must consider the art, principles of unity, color harmony, and contrast. Again, it must consider the practical limitations of motion picture production and

> photography.... We carefully analyze each sequence and scene to ascertain what dominant mood or emotion is to be expressed.... We plan the colors of the actor's costumes with especial care. Whenever possible, we prefer to clothe the actor in colors that build up his or her screen personality.[63]

Clearly, Natalie Kalmus had very strict ideas about the proper use of color, which may seem surprising in the context of the sometimes flamboyant rendering of Technicolor. In a talk presented to the Technicians Branch of the Academy of Motion Picture Arts and Sciences in 1935, she asserted that "a superabundance of color is unnatural.... We must constantly practice color restraint."[64] Though she once described her work as "playing ringmaster to the rainbow," Kalmus thought color should have a supporting role in a movie, not the lead.[65] She advocated for the use of color as an emotional storytelling tool, for subdued and neutral color schemes, and for avoiding any jarring contrasts of color that would distract movie viewers from the narrative.[66]

Directors, cinematographers, set designers, and costume designers often resented her uncompromising vision. Rouben Mamoulian, who directed *Becky Sharp*, reportedly laid down an ultimatum: "Look, tomorrow, either she is not there or I am not there."[67] Henri Jaffa, who served as the primary color consultant on *The Wizard of Oz* (and received second billing for that role in the film's credits), recalled, "'Mrs. Kalmus came out to *The Wizard of Oz* one day.... She'd appear at odd intervals on my pictures and ride the camera boom and take it all over. Mervyn LeRoy [the film's producer] just said, 'Look Natalie, we're not having any trouble on this film, so why don't you go to the set around the corner?'"[68] Natalie Kalmus, however, saw herself as the ultimate mediator between the lab and the silver screen, unwavering in her commitment to make Technicolor shine.

By the end of the 1930s, an originally tight-knit group of players, all connected through their association with the Massachusetts Institute of Technology, had dispelled the doubts that *Fortune* voiced about Technicolor in 1934. Daniel Comstock and J. Arthur Ball were especially important to its technical development. Herbert Kalmus had been instrumental in convincing studios that color was worth the extra cost—and in ramping up Technicolor's production capacity to meet demand. Natalie Kalmus helped define the parameters for the use of color, advising moviemakers who had always worked in black-and-white on the new potential of color.

The complex Technicolor process was only part of a finely tuned technological system that required ancillary inventions like lighting, makeup, and set design to function at its peak. "Like a motion picture, which results from the collaborative work of writer, director, actor, cinematographer, and so many, many more," Herbert Kalmus noted, "Technicolor was not the result of one invention, one patent or one process. It was the result of progressive development, one step at a time.... We had to invent and build new machines, new processes, new lights, new dyes, and new techniques as we went along."[69] A community of increasingly specialized professionals grew alongside the community of technologies that came together on the soundstages of the motion picture industry. This collaboration among invention, business, and art culminated in the landmark films of the period: *The Wizard of Oz* (1939), *Gone with the Wind* (1939), and Walt Disney's breakthrough animated feature, *Fantasia* (1940).

"To the stormy decade from 1929 to 1939," film historian John Baxter wrote some thirty years later, "we owe all that is good in American cinema and much that is great in film at large."[70] At the close of the 1930s, Hollywood was thriving. The studios had a firm grip on all aspects of filmmaking, from production to distribution. Sound-on-film had won as the system of choice for adding not just sound effects but full dialogue to motion pictures. In 1941, reflecting on his career, Walt Disney captured the zeitgeist of the movie industry in the thirties: "That's what I like about this business, the certainty that there is always something bigger and more exciting just around the bend; and the uncertainty of everything else."[71]

Technicolor embodied that cycle of promise and failure, finally emerging triumphant from decades of experimentation and proof-of-concept testing. When Dorothy stepped into Oz, she led moviegoers out of the grays and browns of Kansas, and beckoned filmmakers to follow her into a new world of rainbow hues. "So far," Rouben Mamoulian offered somewhat lyrically, "the screen has been using a pencil; now it is given a palette with paints."[72]

Notes

1. "What? Color in the Movies Again?," *Fortune*, October 1934, 92; emphasis in original.
2. For the best exploration of color in all parts of contemporary society, see Regina Lee Blaszczyk, *The Color Revolution* (Cambridge, MA, 2012).
3. Although still influential, the smaller studios—Universal, Columbia, and United Artists—wielded somewhat less power. Fox and 20th Century Pictures merged in 1935 to form 20th Century-Fox; see Aubrey Solomon, *Twentieth Century-Fox: A Corporate and Financial History* (Metuchen, NJ, 1988), 22.
4. Martin Williams, *Griffith: First Artist of the Movies* (New York, 1980), 65; Aljean Harmetz, *The Making of the Wizard of Oz* (1977; Chicago, IL, 2013), 219.
5. Multiple inventors have laid claim to inventions as diverse as the automobile, the incandescent light bulb, the telephone, radio, and television, for example.
6. For a discussion of early color motion picture processes, see Sarah Street, *Colour Films in Britain: The Negotiation of Innovation 1900–55* (London, 2012), esp. the "Technical Appendix" prepared by Simon Brown. Also informative is Adrian Cornwell-Clyne, *Colour Cinematography,* 3rd ed. (London, 1951).
7. *Street, Colour Films in Britain*, 12.
8. Ibid., 275.
9. Ibid., 13. For more on the invention and demise of Kinemacolor, see James Layton and David Pierce, *The Dawn of Technicolor, 1915–1935* (Rochester, NY, 2015), 32–36.
10. See Cornwell-Clyne, *Colour Cinematography,* 3–37; Street, *Colour Films in Britain,* 9–36, 259–87.

11. Layton and Pierce point out, "Like Kinemacolor, Prizma and Multicolor had all of the same capabilities as Technicolor, with patents, technical experience, and funding, but lacked the visionary management and patient investors to persist through repeated disappointments" (*Dawn of Technicolor,* 20). Interestingly, Burton Wescott had seen Kinemacolor projected during a trip to London and "acquired a segment of a Kinemacolor print" to show Comstock (ibid., 32). For another example of how technology is only part of the story, with management and marketing counting for a great deal, see Chapter 2 of the present volume by Alexander Engel.
12. From its founding in 1861 until its move from Boston's Back Bay neighborhood to Cambridge in 1916, MIT was familiarly known as "Boston Tech"; see Samuel C. Prescott, *When M. I. T. was "Boston Tech," 1861–1916* (Cambridge, MA, 1954). Kalmus himself later reported,

    A heavy volume . . . lay on the desk . . . On the cover was the title "Technique 1904." It was the annual year book of the Massachusetts Institute of Technology of the year of my graduation. I found myself fingering the leaves of this book, reflecting on the life of a "Tech" man. . . . I still needed a name . . . for a company that would own, control and embrace all we had done so far in our endeavor to put color into motion pictures . . . [T]he word "technique" sank into my mind and into my emotions. It struck me as a perfect word . . . its meaning was made to order for my purpose. . . . I suddenly added "color" to the word in my head. . . . I had it! I knew I had it!

    Herbert T. Kalmus with Eleanore King Kalmus, *Mr. Technicolor* (Absecon, NJ, 1993), 10–11.
13. Layton and Pierce, *Dawn of Technicolor*, 29; Richard Haines, *Technicolor Movies: The History of Dye Transfer Printing* (Jefferson, NC, 1993), 1–2; H. T. Kalmus with E.K. Kalmus, *Mr. Technicolor*, 44.
14. Herbert T. Kalmus, "Technicolor Adventures in Cinemaland," *Journal of the Society of Motion Picture Engineers* 31 (December 1938): 564–85, here 565. Burton Wescott designed the configuration of the rolling lab; see Layton and Pierce, *Dawn of Technicolor*, 46.
15. William Burton Wescott, Motion-picture camera, US Patent 1,383,357, filed September 11, 1916, and issued July 5, 1921.
16. Haines, *Technicolor Movies,* 2–3; Layton and Pierce, *Dawn of Technicolor*, 36–39; American Widescreen Museum, *Technicolor*, p. 1, last modified 2003, http://www.widescreenmuseum.com/oldcolor/technicolor1.htm.
17. H. T. Kalmus, "Technicolor Adventures," 566.
18. Haines, *Technicolor Movies,* 4–13; Layton and Pierce, *Dawn of Technicolor*, 69–75.
19. H. T. Kalmus, "Technicolor Adventures," 570–71.
20. Haines, *Technicolor Movies,* 5–6; American Widescreen Museum, *Technicolor,* p. 2, last modified 2003, http://www.widescreenmuseum.com/oldcolor/technicolor2.htm; H. T. Kalmus with E. K. Kalmus. *Mr. Technicolor,* 42–44.
21. Haines, *Technicolor Movies,* 8–13; American Widescreen Museum, *Technicolor,* p.3, last modified 2003, http://www.widescreenmuseum.com/oldcolor/technicolor3.htm

22. A notable exception was Douglas Fairbanks's film, *The Black Pirate* (1926), shot entirely in Technicolor; see Layton and Pierce, *Dawn of Technicolor*, 126–33.
23. "Color and Sound on Film," *Fortune*, October, 1930, 124; emphasis in original.
24. "Dr. Comstock has not been actively associated with the Technicolor Company or its development since late in the year 1925," unsent draft of a letter from Herbert Kalmus to the Editor of the *Boston Herald*, April 12, 1930, Herbert T. Kalmus Papers, 1916–1963 (bulk 1927–1963), MSS28175, Manuscript Division, Library of Congress, Washington, DC, box 58, folder "HTK Publicity 1930–1939." For more detail on the breakup, see Layton and Pierce, *Dawn of Technicolor,* 146–48. The core problem: "Comstock and Wescott wanted to divest themselves of [Kalmus, Comstock & Wescott's] commitment to Technicolor in order to pursue other avenues of business. They no longer wanted to be treated as employees in a company they co-owned" (147).
25. "What? Color in the Movies Again?," 166.
26. Layton and Pierce, *Dawn of Technicolor*, 110, 215, 245. Blueprints for plant no. 4, completed in 1930, are in the Lockwood Greene Records, AC1113, Archives Center, National Museum of American History, Smithsonian Institution, map case 4, folders 1378 and 1382.
27. Joseph A. Ball, "The Technicolor Process of Three-Color Cinematography," *Journal of the Society of Motion Picture Engineers* 25, no. 2 (August 1935): 127.
28. Layton and Pierce, *Dawn of Technicolor*, 252–53; Adrian Hope, "Video Timebomb in the Film Industry," *New Scientist*, December 30, 1971, 283; Haines, *Technicolor Movies*, 7–24; Joseph A. Ball, Three-color cinematographic camera, US Patent 1,871,649, filed June 7, 1929, and issued August 16, 1932; Joseph A. Ball, Cinematographic camera, US Patent 2,072,091, filed August 20, 1931, and issued March 2, 1937.
29. Haines, *Technicolor Movies*, 21.
30. Frank J. Taylor, "King and Queen of Technicolor," *Reader's Digest*, August 1944, 62.
31. Haines, *Technicolor Movies*, 24.
32. H. T. Kalmus with E. K. Kalmus, *Mr. Technicolor*, 93.
33. Edward W. Kellogg, "History of Sound Motion Pictures: First Installment," *Journal of the Society of Motion Picture and Television Engineers* 64 (June 1955): 297; Richard Koszarski, *Hollywood on the Hudson: Film and Television in New York from Griffith to Sarnoff* (New Brunswick, NJ, 2008), 148–49; Layton and Pierce, *Dawn of Technicolor*, 211.
34. "Technicolor May Revolutionize the Screen," *The Literary Digest*, June 8, 1935, 24.
35. Douglas Gomery, *The Hollywood Studio System* (New York, 1986), 104–8, quote 112; Koszarski, *Hollywood on the Hudson*, 149.
36. "What? Color in the Movies Again?," 95.
37. Ibid., 96.
38. Richard Schickel, *The Disney Version: The Life, Times, Art and Commerce of Walt Disney* (1968; New York, 1985), 85.
39. Profiles in History, *Hollywood Auction 44* [catalog] (Calabasas Hills, CA, 2011), 105.
40. Walt Disney, "Growing Pains," *Journal of the Society of Motion Picture Engineers* 36 (January 1941): 33.
41. Donald Crafton, *The Talkies: American Cinema's Transition to Sound, 1926–1931* (New York, 1997), 390–93; J. P. Tellotte, *The Mouse Machine: Disney and Technology* (Urbana, IL, 2008), 46.

42. Walter E. Disney, Wilfred E. Jackson, and William E. Garrity, Method and apparatus for synchronizing photoplays, US Patent 1,941,341, filed April 2, 1931, and issued December 26, 1933.
43. H. T. Kalmus with E. K. Kalmus, *Mr. Technicolor*, 93–94. Layton and Pierce note that both black-and-white and color versions of *Flowers and Trees* were produced, but United Artists, who distributed Disney cartoons, decided to release it in color only. They quote former Disney cameraman William Cottrell recalling that "after the black & white version was photographed, 'they took all the [original] cells and carefully washed all the reverse side,' leaving the original ink and paint outline on the front, 'then repainted them in color on the back'" (*Dawn of Technicolor*, 270–71).
44. H. T. Kalmus with E. K. Kalmus, *Mr. Technicolor*, 94.
45. Disney, "Growing Pains," 35.
46. H. T. Kalmus with E. K. Kalmus, *Mr. Technicolor*, 94; Layton and Pierce, *Dawn of Technicolor*, 274; Telotte, *The Mouse Machine*, 47–48.
47. *The Official Academy Awards Database*, http://awardsdatabase.oscars.org. Disney remained loyal to Technicolor for all of his animated films until Technicolor's Hollywood plant closed in 1975; see Haines, *Technicolor Movies*, 18–19.
48. *Official Academy Awards Database*.
49. Miriam Hopkins was nominated for a Best Actress Oscar but did not win; *Official Academy Awards Database*.
50. "Technicolor May Revolutionize the Screen," 24. On the transition in makeup necessitated by the move from theater to films in the first place, see Michael R. Müller and Anne Sonnenmoser, "Medial Beauty: Three Sociological Theses on Late Modern Body Aesthetics," in *Globalizing Beauty: Consumerism and Body Aesthetics in the Twentieth Century*, ed. Hartmut Berghoff and Thomas Kühne (New York, 2013), 64–65.
51. Quoted in H. T. Kalmus with E. K. Kalmus, *Mr. Technicolor*, 103.
52. Fred E. Basten, *Max Factor: The Man Who Changed the Faces of the World* (New York, 2008), 1–20.
53. Ibid., 95.
54. Anne Massey, *Hollywood Beyond the Screen: Design and Material Culture* (New York, 2000), 78.
55. Fred E. Basten with Robert Salvatore and Paul A. Kaufman, *Max Factor's Hollywood: Glamour, Movies, Make-Up* (Los Angeles, 1995), 41.
56. Basten, *Max Factor*, 109–112; Basten et al., *Max Factor's Hollywood*, 139–47. See also Chapter 8 of the present volume, in which Margaret Maile Petty discusses Factor as a spokesman for modernity who linked a pleasing appearance to the culture of personality.
57. Her birth name was Nettie Mabelle Dunphy and she changed her first name to Natalie around 1910; see Layton and Pierce, *Dawn of Technicolor*, 191.
58. Haines, *Technicolor Movies*, 1.
59. "Natalie M. Kalmus Dies at 87; A Co-Developer of Technicolor," *New York Times*, November 18, 1965, 47.
60. "Natalie was dropped by the company [in 1949], when she sued her former husband over their 1922 alimony agreement." Layton and Pierce, *Dawn of Technicolor*, 293.
61. Natalie M. Kalmus, "Color Consciousness," *Journal of the Society of Motion Picture Engineers* 25 (August 1935): 140.

62. Scott Higgins, *Harnessing the Technicolor Rainbow: Color Design in the 1930s* (Austin, TX, 2007), 41.
63. N. M. Kalmus, "Color Consciousness," 145.
64. Ibid., 142, 147. To be clear, the idea of "color restraint" did not originate with Natalie Kalmus. Sarah Street points out that "a 'shift towards restraint' in the discussion of colour is perceptible around 1907–08 in the USA..." (*Colour Films in Britain*, 11). Robert Edmond Jones, who designed the color for *La Cucaracha* and *Becky Sharp*, had similar thoughts on the use of color in films. According to Layton and Pierce, "Jones was the country's leading theatrical designer.... His theories of designing for the stage informed his view of cinema: 'A good stage setting is not necessarily a 'stage picture,' not a pictorial background against which players move. It is a shell of light and color, so arranged as to express and intensify the playwright's vision'" (*Dawn of Technicolor*, 281). In 1938, Jones expressed some frustration with filmmakers' reticence to embrace color, writing "Black-and-white thinking still dominates the screen"; Robert Edmond Jones, "The Problem of Color," *New York Times*, February 27, 1938.
65. "Natalie M. Kalmus Dies at 87," 47.
66. Higgins, *Harnessing the Technicolor Rainbow*, 16–19.
67. Quoted in ibid., 49. The film's original director, Lowell Sherman, had died during production; see Layton and Pierce, *Dawn of Technicolor*, 293.
68. Aljean Harmetz, *The Making of the Wizard of Oz* (Chicago, 1977, 2013), 227.
69. H. T. Kalmus with E. K. Kalmus, *Mr. Technicolor*, 1.
70. John Baxter, *Hollywood in the Thirties* (London, 1968), 153.
71. Disney, "Growing Pains," 40.
72. Rouben Mamoulian, "Some Problems in Directing Color Pictures," *Journal of the Society of Motion Picture Engineers* 25 (August 1935), 149.

CHAPTER 8

Glamour Pink: The Marketing of Residential Electric Lighting in the Age of Color, 1920s–1950s

Margaret Maile Petty

Urging retailers to carry its new line of Coloramic incandescent light bulbs, General Electric proclaimed its message for the 1956–57 selling season to be "color, color, color!"[1] This was just one example of the nationwide, pan-industry fascination with the environmental, psychological, economic, and aesthetic potential of color, as the postwar era witnessed a rich chromatic invasion of the consumer landscape. From jewel tones to soft buttery pastel hues, in the postwar period color signaled a fashionable, glamorous chic and represented a broadening palette of consumer choice. This was due in no small part to the perceived role of color in motivating consumer product sales.[2] Such attitudes led electrical manufacturers—including General Electric, Westinghouse, and Sylvania—to begin production of a range of "decorator" light bulbs for the residential market in the mid-1950s. Coated in pastel-colored ceramic, the new bulbs were promoted as an easy means of enriching colors in textiles, adding luster to polished wood surfaces, harmonizing furniture groupings, and creating attractive new "looks" affordably for the home. Attributing to the new product the power to instantly glamorize all that it illuminated, the marketing of these bulbs emphasized the flattering quality of the colored light for the complexion of the homemaker and the appearance of her home.[3]

However, while the color fever of the mid-1950s was without doubt a key driver in the development of these specialty incandescent bulbs, it was but one factor in their marketing. In addition to the standard rhetoric emphasizing personal choice and fashionable accessorizing through color selection, marketing

M.M. Petty (✉)
School of Design, Creative Industries Faculty, Queensland University of Technology, Brisbane, Queensland, Australia

R.L. Blaszczyk, U. Spiekermann (eds.), *Bright Modernity*, Worlds of Consumption, DOI 10.1007/978-3-319-50745-3_8

and promotional materials for the new colored bulbs also drew on a complex array of deeply entrenched cultural beliefs and practices informing feminine identity and the role of the homemaker within the domestic environment. Employing such commonly held notions of feminine beauty, personality, and agency, the industry's marketing strategies situated these products within the twin discourses of home decoration and feminine beauty, positioning electric light within familiar, well rehearsed beliefs and practices.[4]

More than a one-off novelty or marketing gimmick, the pastel-hued bulbs of the mid-1950s occupied an important position in the material and cultural history of electric lighting in the United States. Such electric lighting applications targeted the increasing economic and cultural influence of female consumers in the first half of the twentieth century.[5] These products and the narratives employed in their marketing represented a specific iteration of evolving beliefs regarding the composition and enhancement of feminine beauty. Guidelines for feminine beauty in the latter nineteenth century and throughout the first half of the twentieth century encouraged the harmonizing of a number of elements, including individual temperament or type, personal complexion and coloration, and even interior decoration. With the popular adoption of electric light around the turn of the century, the necessity of addressing artificial lighting conditions was added to the realm of female responsibilities.[6]

Through such tactics (and others) the electric industry was relentless in its efforts to domesticate electric light, offering it as a powerful tool for the capable homemaker. This chapter explores the ways in which industry marketing transformed the popular image of electric light from a utility to an expression of personality and lifestyle. It contains three main themes: the synthesis of marketing rhetoric within gendered beliefs and practices, widespread educational outreach addressing appropriate residential lighting applications, and the situating of new, simplified products within the contemporary discourse of consumer choice and color conditioning.

Personality, Beauty, and Feminine Identity

In the popular discourse on feminine beauty and social roles during the first two decades of the twentieth century, "personality" supplanted the nineteenth century's "character" as the primary mode of American self-expression. This transformation was representative of a larger shift in the United States from a broad cultural belief in personal character as the basis of a moral and sound society to one largely organized around the secular and individualistic identification with personality that came to prominence in the twentieth century.[7] The historian Warren Susman attributes this shift to the nation's transition from a producer-based to a consumer-oriented society, identifying the emergence of a "new modal psychological type" within the American middle class as a response to the nation's newfound "culture of abundance."[8] For women, especially, this new, more fluid and adaptable psychological outlook became more pronounced in the first decades of the twentieth century, as popular culture increasingly celebrated well-known personalities as models of feminine beauty. The cultivation of the right "look" was equated with the ability to make the right "impression," to get the right job, or to capture the attention of the right man. In the twentieth century, such associations increased as beauty became a central means for American women to access social acceptance, popularity, and admiration. Sarah Berry, a historian of Hollywood's star culture, has identified the emergence of a "democratic" concept of beauty in the United States that aligns with Susman's culture of abundance. Berry argues that this new model of beauty was predicated upon the logic of a consumer economy, particularly in its proposition that that any woman could appear beautiful with "good grooming and makeup." Berry proposes that beauty held a recognized value for women within the nation's growing capitalist and service economy and as such was understood as a legitimate form of social capital. She writes, "Women's cosmetic self-maintenance came to be seen as one of the requirements of feminine social values, rather than an unethical preoccupation with personal vanity."[9]

Such notions were evident in the pronouncements of leading voices in the articulation of modern beauty standards in the United States from the 1920s onwards. Max Factor, a prominent makeup artist during Hollywood's golden age and a founding figure in the modern cosmetics industry, claimed in an interview from 1929, "Beauty is more than skin deep when observed by the onlooker. It is everything. It creates the first impression. It may be the key to happiness and success, the open door through which a girl finds access to those things most desired. Nature's work is often incomplete. Beauty is naturalness—idealized."[10] The foundation of this naturalness for Max Factor was associated with a woman's personality, not her character. Factor instructed women to look long in the mirror, studying the face to determine the personality belonging to the reflected image.[11] His insistence on women's recognizing their own personality through the 'look,' which suggested a form of externalized self-scrutiny, was very much in keeping with the popular discourse of the day, particularly in regard to the expression and embodiment of personality as something uniquely recognizable to others. As Factor argued, "There is a mental, guiding psychology about the decoration of one's face. The girl who is sprightly, vivacious, colorful in personality and disposition may wear a more colorful make-up and not have it appear unnatural. But there is the more siren-like, the more languorous type of beauty who must resort to more subdued tones."[12] Factor correlated appropriate makeup choices not with a woman's complexion type, as was typical in the nineteenth century, but rather with her personality.[13] Such instruction appeared across women's advice literature and the promotional materials marketed to women consumers. The frequent message was that attending to one's grooming, color palette, and general aesthetic coordination offered women a means to exercise personal agency.

There was an additional benefit for industry in shifting emphasis to personality—unlike character or complexion, personality could be altered or exchanged easily through makeup or the color selection and coordination of one's attire. Personality, as a fluid form of identity, could be determined by the individual woman to suit her mood or objectives.[14] Such attitudes were heavily promoted in Hollywood's fan literature in the 1920s and 1930s.[15] The popular Hollywood star Joan Blondell, for example, advised readers of the fan magazine *Photoplay* in 1939, "The whole secret of beauty is change . . . A girl who neglects changing her personality gets stale mentally as well as physically. So I'm going to vary my hair style, my type of make-up, nail-polish, perfume."[16] This emphasis on adapting one's personality, a message offered in a Hollywood fan magazine and therefore in relation to the beauty standards demonstrated by the movie stars, also informed industry marketing campaigns during the period. For example, a Lady Pepperell advertisement series ran in *Photoplay* and cast popular actresses such as Joan Crawford in "Personality" bedrooms with linens color coordinated to their screen personas.[17]

Such accounts of the role of personality in the feminine performance of identity were common in beauty advice literature in the United States throughout the 1930s and 1940s. The *New York Times* beauty columnist Martha Parker wrote in 1943 of a range of facial "lighting effects" possible with a new cosmetic powder that would allow a woman "to change her skin tone to the color of her costume almost as easily as an electrician switches a stage set from rose to gold." According to Parker, the luminous new powder would allow any woman to "wear any dress shade at all, becomingly."[18] Here, as in other similar examples from the period, one may find the correlation of the transformative powers of electric illumination with that of cosmetics and other feminine beauty aids. Certainly, in the latter 1930s and 1940s there was increasing popular interest in electric lighting—particularly in scenic or theatrical lighting in this instance—as an accessible and adaptable agent of transformation. In the popular press, such self-styling actualized through new lipstick hues, facial powders, or other cosmetic fashions was associated with personal pleasure and empowerment, particularly, as Berry argues, the "pleasure of potentiality."[19]

Personality and Color in the Domestic Interior

The growing emphasis on personality as a mechanism for both expressing one's individuality and navigating an increasingly complex landscape of consumer choice in the beauty industry soon began to appear as a common theme in advice literature addressing the domestic interior and women's roles in making these spaces. Indeed, establishing and maintaining personality within the domestic environment became a mainstay of the popular literature of the period. The well-known women's advice columnist and author Emily Post played an important role in applying a spatialized concept of personality to the domestic environment.[20] In her 1930 publication, *The Personality of a House,* Post set out a refinement of gendered nineteenth-century notions that closely linked the appearance and psychological spirit of the interior with that of the female head of household. In Post's account, this symbiotic connection was both expressed and realized through personality. [21] Advising homemakers to approach the domestic environment as a personalized "backdrop" for daily life, she instructed that it be precisely tailored to the woman that it framed. Post outlined a number of ways in which a woman might create a charming and enchanting home that embodied her own unique personality. In Post's taxonomy, color was a primary consideration in establishing a "room of charm" because "the first thing the average person notices on entering a room is color."[22] Others in the period similarly ranked color as highly important to the physical manifestation of personality. In general, color was broadly considered a primary mode through which to express or modify one's personality.

Such discourse uniting color choice with the expression of personality in the home and for the woman herself also carried over to new lighting applications. In 1932, for example, the *Los Angeles Times* reported on a demonstration of new electric lighting techniques given by George M. Rankin, director of lighting for the Southern California Edison Company, who showed how colored lights were used in retail window displays to "enhance the richness of drapes and gowns."[23] Proposing that these same techniques could be equally effective in the home, Rankin used a wax figure to demonstrate how various combinations of colored light could "change the color of the hair and complexion, as well as the contours of a person's face."[24]

The promise of such lighting applications for the domestic environment and the homemaker's personal beauty largely were put on hold during World War II. Wartime restrictions and the disruption of typical family life in the United States shifted popular discourse away from such concerns and focused instead on personal restraint and contribution to the war effort.

Electric Light: A "Background for Living"

In the decade following the war, however, the leading electrical manufacturers took direct and purposeful actions to expand the domestic consumer market for electric lighting.[25] The competitive pressure on even the biggest of American companies to establish and maintain market share was significant, as General Electric's president, Charles E. Wilson, candidly described in 1947 for *The Wall Street Journal:* "We're not kidding ourselves. The fight for business in the period ahead will be more rugged than anything we've been in up to now." He further suggested that the company's production of consumer items would be greatly expanded in order to "bring into balance for the first time G.E.'s consumer and industrial business."[26] In the hopes of gaining advantage in the booming postwar consumer goods market, Westinghouse, Sylvania, and G.E. focused on the all-important American way of life, positioning electric lighting as an essential condition of modern living.

While the major electrical manufacturers by and large had employed some variation of the "Better Light—Better Sight" marketing campaign prior to the war, in the postwar period emphasis was shifted to the lifestyle benefits of a diversity of domestic lighting applications. With the right lighting, one could achieve increased familial harmony and psychological wellbeing, more attractive and personalized interiors, the beautification of objects and inhabitants alike, as well as improved seeing for the efficient performance of daily domestic tasks.[27] Such eclectic light–enabled lifestyle makeovers were also marketed in the "light-conditioning" campaigns of the mid-1950s. As G.E. advocated in its corporate promotional literature, "Light-conditioning offers a better way of living and of enjoying our homes. It gives you Light for Living."[28]

The new focus was quickly absorbed and disseminated through popular media. Homemakers were advised that lighting simply for utility and function was old-fashioned, that improving the overall quality of light was essential for the modern interior.[29] In particular, indirect, shadowless illumination was broadly promoted as the most flattering and all-around pleasing kind of light. However, indirect lighting alone was not sufficient, and homemakers were instructed that is should be understood as a foundation upon which to build a more sophisticated luminous environment through the combination of a variety of general, direct, and indirect applications. By employing a layered lighting composition, it was suggested, one could easily enhance or adjust the appearance of any room along with its contents and inhabitants. A variety of sources—including popular home and garden literature, lighting spokeswomen (who typically worked for manufacturers), residential lighting demonstrations, and how-to booklets—inundated homemakers with information and advice about how to best integrate electric lighting into their interior décor to create luminous "backgrounds for living."[30] As G.E claimed, "We are no longer just selling light bulbs; we are selling luminous environment."[31]

A Light Bulb That Flatters

One of the more commonly cited problems in selling modern lighting to postwar consumers was the complexity of applications and the many elements necessary to realize a complete interior illumination scheme. While it was a something of a straightforward marketing task to sell electric washing machines, dryers, dishwashers, and other domestic appliances, electric lighting was a complicated system of parts that could not be easily wrapped up and sold as a self-contained unit to American consumers. This problem was amplified further by the increasing emphasis on indirect lighting as the most flattering backdrop for modern living because this approach required the integration of lighting fixtures into architectural elements or the use of other masking and reflecting devices. Furthermore, indirect lighting did not obviate the need for localized task and accent lighting, and there remained the issue of control systems, including dimmers and switches. For example, a typical feature appearing in *The American Home* in 1949 entitled "New Life with New Light!" encouraged readers to transform their living spaces and lifestyles with modern electric lighting.[32] The article suggested a number of applications, including recessed lighting in bookshelves, accent lighting for the china display cabinet, niche lighting for a shadow box that was adjustable with dimmers, and recessed cove lighting along a room's cornice (Fig. 8.1). Choosing and implementing the right products for these purposes would certainly have proved a daunting challenge for many homemakers with limited knowledge of the standards and requirements of such varied and complicated lighting installations. And this was just one example. As *The Washington Post* observed in 1956, "it is obviously impossible to arrive at a single lighting formula that can be applied to all situations."[33]

Addressing this issue, the electrical industry consolidated its efforts in the early 1950s to simplify the message to consumers. Lighting manufacturers and regional utility providers joined forces on a variety of educational marketing campaigns to communicate simplified guidelines for residential lighting to consumers.[34] These programs typically suggested a limited range of solutions to the most common lighting challenges in the home, often presenting illumination guidelines as "recipes," invoking familiar tasks for the homemaker and thereby further naturalizing the technology of electric light and its integration into daily domestic life.[35] By and large, this material did little to simplify domestic lighting, however. For example, the thirty-eight-page General Electric booklet *See Your Home in a New Light,* distributed to over fourteen million readers by 1955, included a dizzying range of specialized and detailed recommendations (Fig. 8.2).[36]

Perhaps more appropriate given the issue at hand, the industry also was developing much more simplified lifestyle lighting products in this period that promised a host of benefits in a single application. The actress and beauty columnist Arlene Dahl eagerly announced just such a rumored product in her syndicated column "Let's be Beautiful" in 1955.[37] Warning readers that lighting "can do a lot toward making or breaking a beauty reputation," Dahl breathlessly described the flattering effects of a new pink-toned light bulb: "It's amazing how your complexion—and indeed your whole room—gets a beauty boost when you use these bulbs instead of ordinary white ones."[38] Dahl, perhaps mimicking the era's gossip columnists, did not name the manufacturer of the new pink bulbs, indicating only that a "major electric company" had developed them. Despite the hushed tone, these new pink bulbs and other pastel colored bulbs like them were hardly a secret and indeed would garner much attention in the media during the second half of 1955. Importantly, these bulbs united popular beliefs and aspirations regarding feminine beauty, the decoration of the domestic interior, and obtaining a modern lifestyle for maximum marketing appeal.[39]

One of the first of these products was the Softlight incandescent bulb, introduced by Sylvania Electric in early 1955 and promoted as specially designed to "flatter home furnishings and occupants."[40] Coated with a "pearl-pink" ceramic finish, the bulb produced a softer light than conventional frosted types, which warmed the appearance of colors within its luminous reach. The Softlight made yellow appear orange, blue register as soft gray,

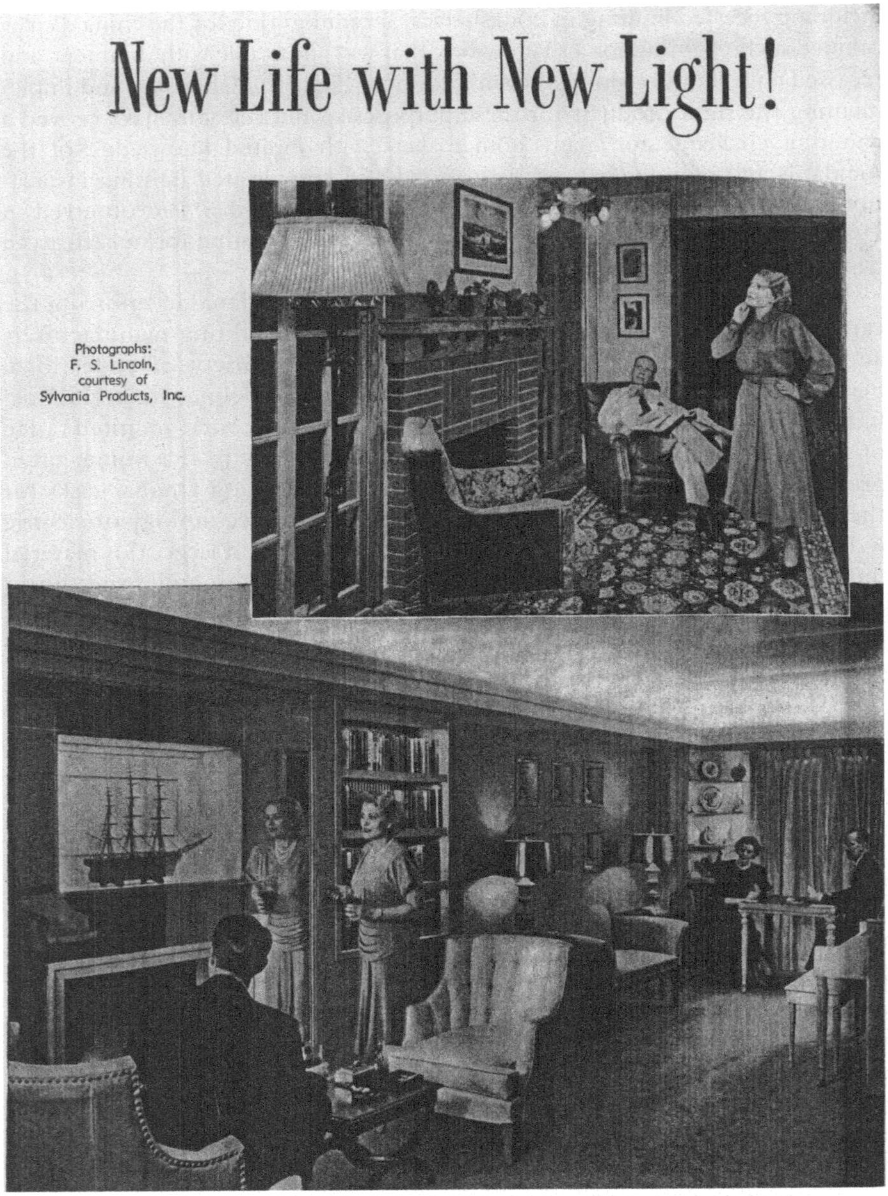

Fig. 8.1 Gendered before-and-after illustrations of the new lighting possibilities promoted in popular and trade media

Note how each image features the normative middle-class female homemaker-as-consumer standing in her living room. One is in a housedress pondering what might be done about the lighting and the other is dressed smartly for the evening and her guests, who can enjoy an elaborate configuration of modern lighting applications, including one that creates a reflection of their hostess.

Source: "New Life with New Light!," The American Home, May 1949, 98, author's collection.

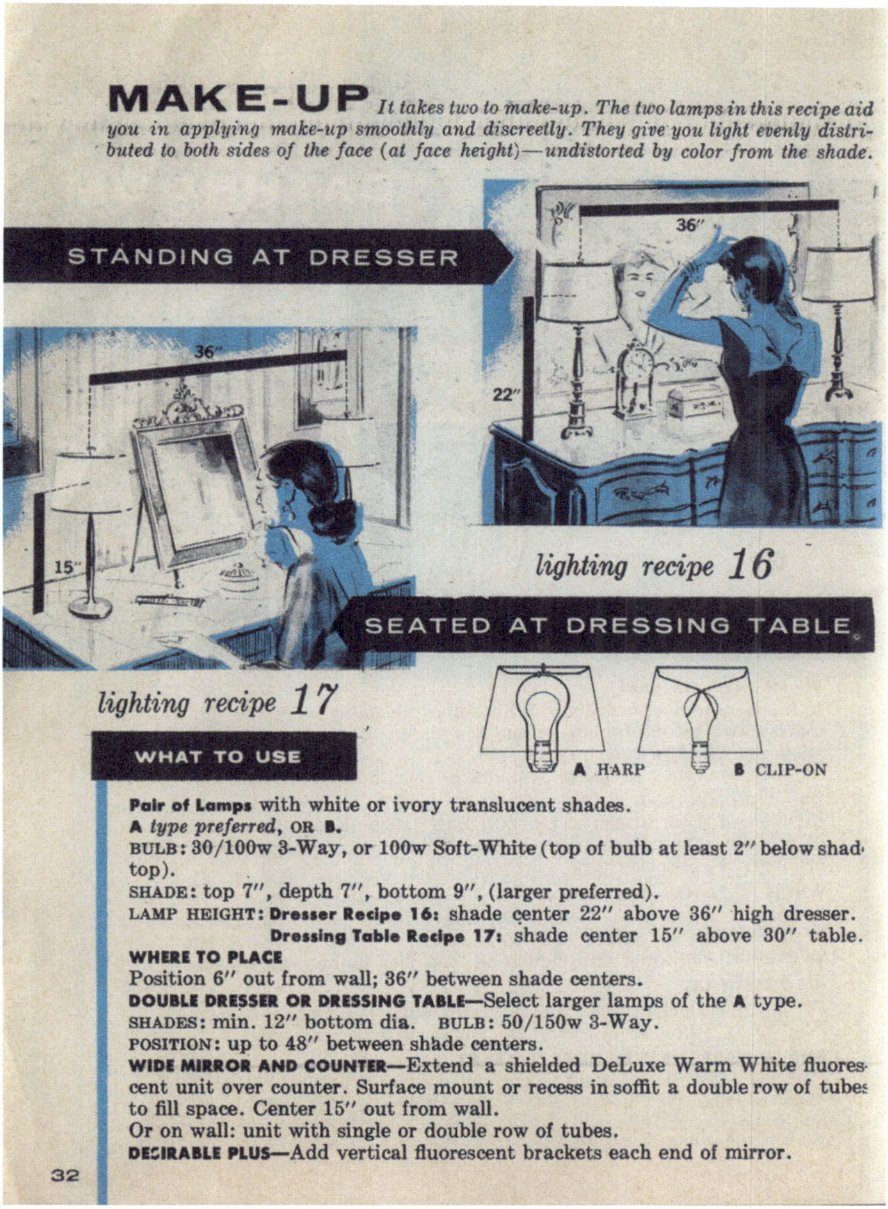

Fig. 8.2 Sample pages from G.E. promotional materials featuring lighting recommendations for women's and men's grooming rituals

The straightforward language and illustrations were intended to educate the consumer on the requirements necessary for each task-specific application. On these pages, that consumer was a woman.

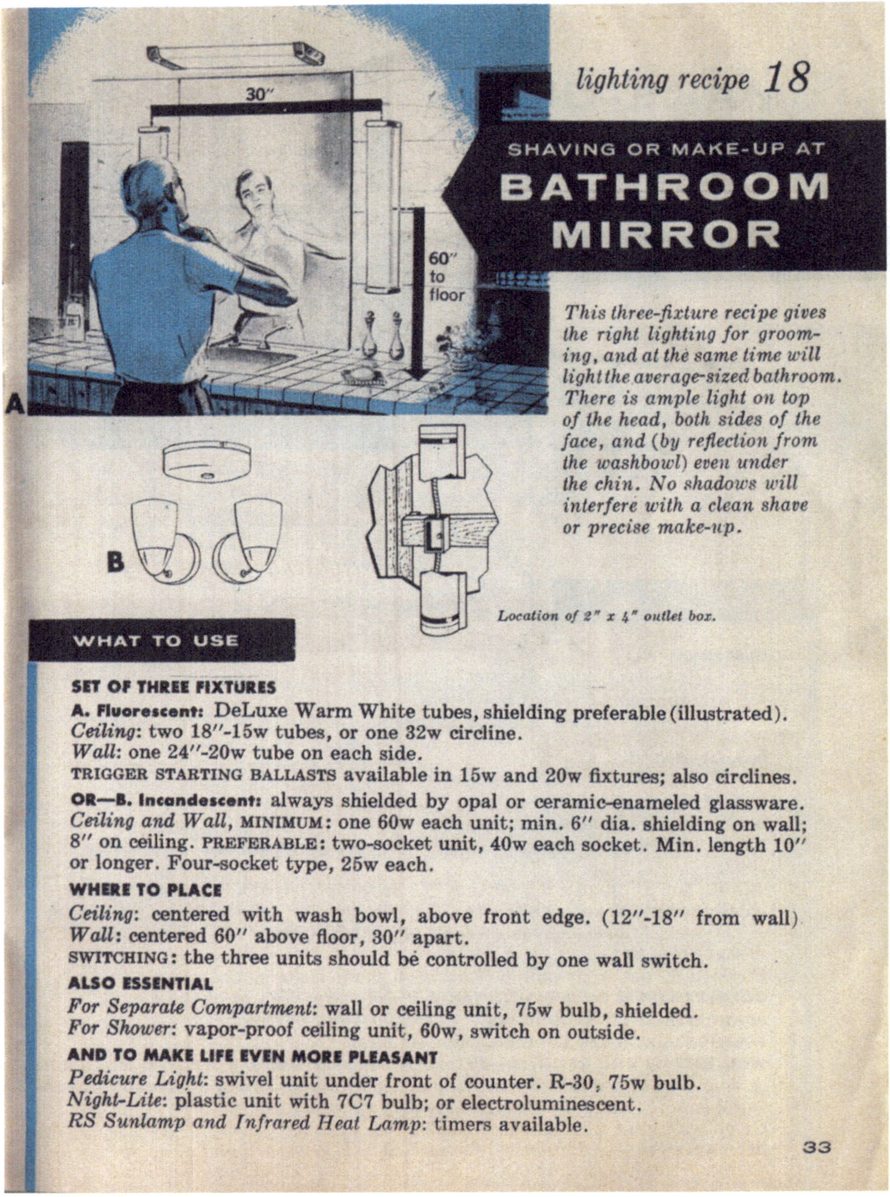

lighting recipe 18

SHAVING OR MAKE-UP AT

BATHROOM MIRROR

30″

60″ to floor

A

B

This three-fixture recipe gives the right lighting for grooming, and at the same time will light the average-sized bathroom. There is ample light on top of the head, both sides of the face, and (by reflection from the washbowl) even under the chin. No shadows will interfere with a clean shave or precise make-up.

Location of 2″ x 4″ outlet box.

WHAT TO USE

SET OF THREE FIXTURES

A. Fluorescent: DeLuxe Warm White tubes, shielding preferable (illustrated).
Ceiling: two 18″-15w tubes, or one 32w circline.
Wall: one 24″-20w tube on each side.
TRIGGER STARTING BALLASTS available in 15w and 20w fixtures; also circlines.

OR—B. Incandescent: always shielded by opal or ceramic-enameled glassware.
Ceiling and Wall, MINIMUM: one 60w each unit; min. 6″ dia. shielding on wall; 8″ on ceiling. PREFERABLE: two-socket unit, 40w each socket. Min. length 10″ or longer. Four-socket type, 25w each.

WHERE TO PLACE

Ceiling: centered with wash bowl, above front edge. (12″-18″ from wall)
Wall: centered 60″ above floor, 30″ apart.
SWITCHING: the three units should be controlled by one wall switch.

ALSO ESSENTIAL

For Separate Compartment: wall or ceiling unit, 75w bulb, shielded.
For Shower: vapor-proof ceiling unit, 60w, switch on outside.

AND TO MAKE LIFE EVEN MORE PLEASANT

Pedicure Light: swivel unit under front of counter. R-30, 75w bulb.
Night-Lite: plastic unit with 7C7 bulb; or electroluminescent.
RS Sunlamp and Infrared Heat Lamp: timers available.

33

Fig. 8.2 (continued)

The text on the left began with a play on words about romantic relationships and then addressed the female homemaker directly: "It takes two to make-up. The two lamps in this recipe aid you in applying make-up smoothly and directly. . . . "

Source: General Electric Company, Lamp Division, See Your Home in a New Light: Tested Light-Conditioning Recipes that Create Light for Living, 1955, author's collection.

and gave a "warmer, deeper tone to orange and beige colors."[41] Flattering "complexions, wood grains of furniture and colors of fabrics," the Softlight bulbs also provided "indirect lighting without special fixtures."[42] Directly on the heels of Sylvania, General Electric released its Glamour Pink bulb in September 1955. Promoting it nationwide, G.E. utilized much of the same marketing rhetoric as Sylvania had for its Softlight product, emphasizing the ways in which the pink enamel coated bulb could enrich warm colors and the luster of polished furniture. G.E.'s most striking claim, though, was that the glamour pink bulb would "do more for a woman's complexion than any lighting device since the candle."[43]

In August of the following year, Westinghouse Electric introduced the Beauty Tone family of pastel tinted light bulbs. Like Sylvania's Softlight and G.E.'s Glamour bulb, this new product line was promoted for its decorative and beauty-enhancing effects.[44] Building on the "phenomenal" acceptance of the previous year's pink-tinted light bulbs, Westinghouse offered its own version and introduced two additional colors. The Candlelight Beauty Tone amplified yellows, yellow-reds, and yellow-greens, and the Aqua Beauty Tone provided "an atmosphere of coolness" and complimented blues and blue greens. The general manager of Westinghouse's lamp division, F. M. Sloan, reported to the *Tribune*: "The various tinted light bulbs can be used to cool or warm a room or a corner, to express taste and personality, to create a special atmosphere for an evening or a season, or to recast a color scheme to accommodate new purchases or a change in furniture arrangement."[45]

One month after Westinghouse released its line of colored bulbs, General Electric introduced the Coloramic family in four shades: Dawn Pink, Sky Blue, Sun Gold, and Spring Green. G.E. advertised its new product line in fashionable, full-color, full-page layouts in popular, nationally distributed magazines as well as in television commercials aired during primetime.[46] An advertisement appearing in *Life* magazine in 1957 was typical of the new marketing campaign (Fig. 8.3). Enticing readers to "Give your home four 'new looks,' " the advertisement featured a photograph of a stylish modern living room divided into four sections, each corresponding in hue to one of the Coloramic bulbs to illustrate the dramatic effects of their colored light on the décor. Summarizing the properties and benefits of the new pastel bulbs, the advertisement described the range of desirable and lively atmospheres they produced. Carrying the "Live Better Electrically" logo, the advertisement also situated the new G.E. products within the industry's larger lifestyle campaign.[47]

The marketing of colored incandescent light bulbs, in addition to appealing to such traditional home decoration concerns, capitalized on the intense interest in color as a consumer lifestyle choice in the postwar period.[48] Color had long been a focal point of interest and concern for women in terms of beauty, interior decoration, and personal expression. In the United States, moreover, from the 1930s onwards color—particularly "color conditioning"—became a primary concern across a spectrum of industries as a means of enhancing a host of human activities involving vision, safety, worker satisfaction, and consumer

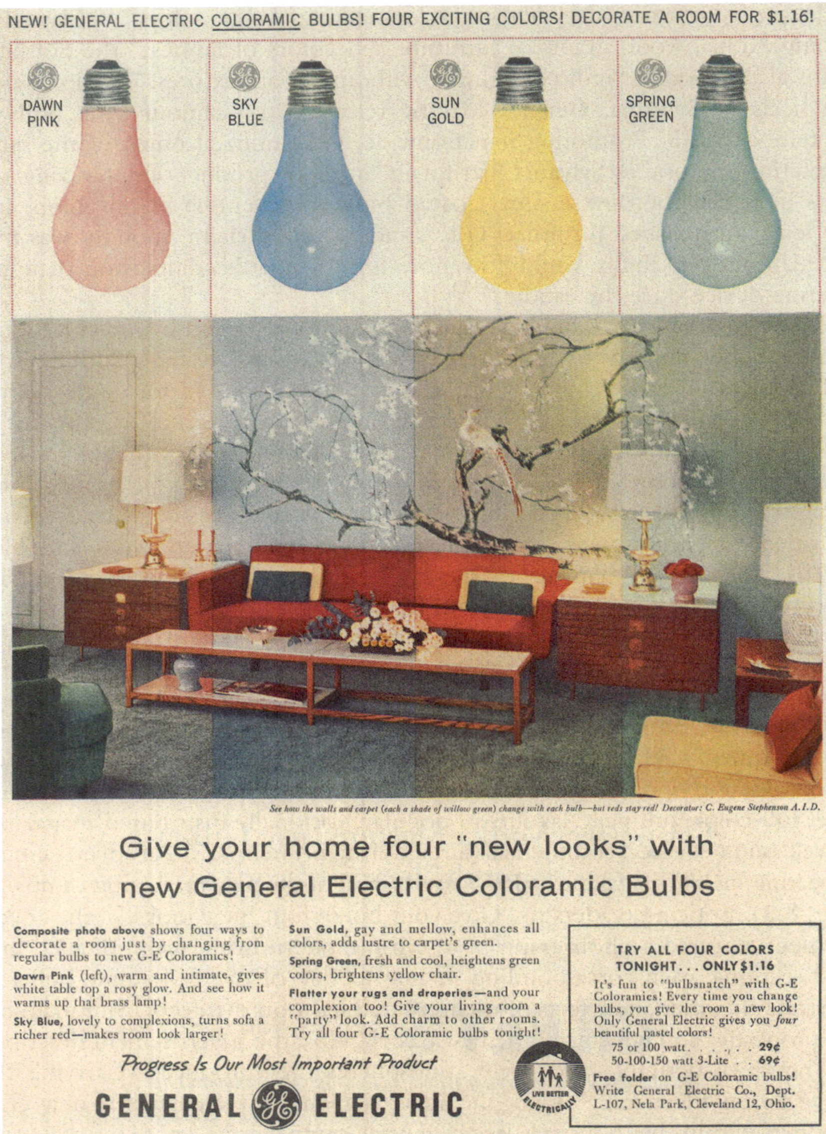

Fig. 8.3 Advertisement for Coloramic light bulbs by General Electric, 1957

The focus on the living room and interior decoration presupposed a female audience, as did the language. The "Dawn Pink" bulb is "warm and intimate," lending the "white table top a rosy glow"; "Sky Blue" is "lovely to the complexion" and, claims the ad, "makes the room look larger" (a clear theme in Fig. 7.1 as well). After describing the decorative effects of the other two bulbs, the text returns to the homemaker's appearance: "Flatter your rugs and draperies—and your complexion too!"

Source: Life, October 28, 1957, 147, collection of Regina Lee Blaszczyk.

interest.[49] In the postwar period, however, the fascination with color as a mechanism for fueling the consumer market reached unprecedented levels. An article appearing in *The Washington Post* in 1951 called attention to the rising swell of support for color across industry and the consuming public as the decade opened.[50] Interviewing Faber Birren, one of nation's leading industrial color consultants, the author described Birren's belief in the benefits of color for the home and the workplace, but ultimately and most importantly for sales: "We buy food when it looks appetizing, clothes when they are becoming, and we insist that our homes be attractive and livable. Color is often the determining factor in what we select and what we reject."[51] Similarly, in 1953 the *New York Times*, covering recent marketing and advertising news, reported: "The [color] trend is expected to be accelerated in the consumer goods field as the country moves into an expanding buyers' market."[52] The *Times* also interviewed the color consultant Howard Ketcham, who argued that the introduction of color television was a major factor in the use of color in the marketing of products, particularly in the decorating, apparel, and home furnishing sectors. As Ketcham explained, marketers in these areas were "planning to present their products in full color on the screen." As a means of further differentiating consumer products, colors were selected for products according to their gender appropriateness. Cosmetics were to be packaged in "soft feminine colors," while razor blades would be packaged in "more masculine hues."[53]

It made sense then that General Electric first approached the market with its colored incandescent bulbs in Glamour Pink or that Westinghouse responded with Candlelight and Aqua. The research of color consultants like Birren and Ketcham suggested that manufacturers could reasonably expect that women would identify with these distinctly feminine colors. Furthermore, the pastel light bulbs enabled women to easily and affordably exchange one fashionable hue for another, thus engaging with the rhetoric of personality and the need to be able to adjust or change its expression at will. The ability to quickly transform a look with color, whether addressing personal beauty or a home interior, had been a primary means of expressing personality since at least the 1930s. Thus, the ease with which a woman could switch a light bulb and change the entire color palette of her environment was an obvious advantage and lamp manufacturers were careful to emphasize this feature. General Electric's Coloramic advertisements boldly proclaimed that for a little over a dollar a homemaker could "decorate a room." If color trends changed with the seasons, a woman could keep pace with fashions by simply "bulbsnatching"—an act facilitated by purchasing Coloramic bulbs in a convenient four-pack carton.[54] While this was a particularly accessible price point for such stylish impulses, the same consumer logic of color was applied across a wide range of domestic products—from phones and clocks to washing machines and refrigerators. As Regina Blaszczyk summarizes in *The Color Revolution*, "the manufacturers' challenge was to turn a utilitarian product into a fashion accessory."[55]

Clearly indicative of the major electrical manufacturers' desire to stake out the largest possible share of the residential lighting sector, the marketing of these products incorporated the principle decorative responsibilities of the modern homemaker and provided a simple solution coalesced within a single pastel-tinted light bulb. For at least half a century women had been instructed through etiquette manuals, home decoration guidebooks, advice columns, and other popular literature to embody and express their personality through their attire and interiors, to color coordinate and harmonize their interiors and themselves within these spaces, to select cosmetics that would flatter their complexions, and to determine the right light in which they should be seen. With the introduction of colored incandescent light bulbs, women were placed at the center of a cultural and technological trajectory that gathered together these broad themes and developments within a solitary colored light bulb. The soft-hued light of these bulbs was associated with transformative and harmonizing abilities that could enrich and glamourize textiles and furnishings, provide atmosphere and charm, and beautify the homemaker and her guests.[56] Although evidence of the effectiveness of this message on its target audience remains elusive, certainly such notions played an important role in the lighting industry's efforts to expand the market for domestic lighting products in the postwar period. In this respect, the industry was successful, with over one billion incandescent bulbs sold to the residential market in 1955.[57]

Conclusion

The postwar American consumer market was a heady environment, redolent in the promise of a more improved way of life than anyone had ever seen—more of everything, and everything better, bigger, brighter, and more colorful. With women in command of much of the household purchasing, American industry tailored key products and messages to the female consumer. Color was, perhaps more than ever, a primary factor in gendered marketing efforts as well as in broader industry aims to encourage the color-conditioning of the American consumer environment.[58] The postwar marketing of electric lighting, particularly as evidenced in the pastel-coated light bulbs of the mid-1950s, was exemplary of the character of America's postwar consumer culture and its widespread embrace of color. The electrical industry framed its marketing campaigns of select products to engage female consumers with long-held notions of home and domestic space, particularly that of the creation and nurturing of this environment as an extension of themselves. Furthermore, finding and using the "right" light was correlated with personal beauty and pitched as an ephemeral, but powerful modern beauty aid. In the postwar period, electric light, especially colored light, was sold as an agent of glamour—flattering and beautifying textiles, furniture, and people. The vibrant, multihued interiors featured in G.E.'s Coloramic advertisements represented the fashionable potential of electric light in the postwar era.

In countless advertisements, promotional items, and advice pieces, electric light was described as a uniquely adaptable and effective aid in the management and decoration of the home. In these accounts, not only did electric light facilitate the performance of daily tasks—sewing, cooking, reading, dressing, and so on—but it also promised to make everyone within the household feel and look better.[59] Such messages were surely difficult to ignore and would seem to have proved effective for the lighting industry. By 1961 half of all electric light bulbs sold in the United States were for residential use; and by 1965 over three billion light bulbs were being sold each year.[60] As the electrical industry had hoped at the outset of the postwar period, by the close of the 1950s they had successfully sold electric lighting as a vital ingredient in the "American way of life," as a powerful tool in the arsenal of the homemaker, as an easily accessible means of personalizing the domestic environment.

Notes

1. General Electric marketing flyer, "Look What's Behind Coloramic Bulbs," ca. September 1956.
2. See Regina Lee Blaszczyk, *The Color Revolution* (Cambridge, MA, 2012); and Penny Sparke, *As Long as it's Pink: The Sexual Politics of Taste* (London, 1995), 194–295.
3. "A Light Bulb that Flatters," *Wall Street Journal*, January 27, 1955; "Firms Develop Light Bulb in 'Glamor' Pink," *Chicago Daily Tribune*, September 4, 1955; "Pastel Tints are Developed in Light Bulbs," *Chicago Daily Tribune*, August 19, 1956.
4. This was, however, a white middle-class identity, silently, but unquestionably, grounded in the privileged position of white culture in pre–civil rights America. See Richard Dyer, *White* (New York, 1997).
5. Much excellent scholarship exists on the intimate relationship between feminine identity, consumer culture, and the domestic interior, including Judy Attfield and Pat Kirkham, *A View from the Interior: Feminism, Women, and Design* (London, 1989); Sparke, *As Long as It's Pink*; Jennifer Scanlon, *Inarticulate Longings: The Ladies Home Journal, Gender, and the Promises of Consumer Culture* (New York, 1995); Victoria de Grazia, ed., *The Sex of Things: Gender and Consumption in Historical Perspective* (Berkeley, CA, 1996); Beverly Gordon, "Women's Domestic Body: The Conceptual Conflation of Women and Interiors in the Industrial Age," *Winterthur Portfolio* 31, no. 4 (Winter 1996): 281–301; Regina Lee Blaszczyk, *Imagining Consumers: Design and Innovation from Wedgwood to Corning* (Johns Hopkins University Press, 2000).
6. See, for example, Antoinette Donnelly, "Good Lighting is Half the Trick in Applying Makeup," *Chicago Daily Tribune* August 5, 1926, 27; "Begone, Ye Paint, Powder! Make-up by Light Has Come," *Los Angeles Times*, June 12, 1927, 28; Rosalind Shaffer, "Makeup Expert Able to Paint Personality on Faces," *Chicago Daily Tribune*, August 25, 1935.
7. Simon J. Bronner, ed., *Consuming Vision: Accumulation and Display of Goods in America*, 1880–1920 (New York, 1989), 4.
8. Warren Susman, *Culture as History: The Transformation of American Society in the Twentieth Century* (New York, 1972), xix–xxi, see also 271–90.

9. Sarah Berry, "Hollywood Exoticism: Cosmetics and Color in the 1930s," in *Hollywood Goes Shopping*, edited by David Dresser and Garth S. Jowett (Minneapolis, MN, 2000), 108–38, quote 111.
10. Peak, "Hollywood's Master of Make-Up."
11. "Six Original Designs for that Wise Form of Vanity, the Dressing Table," Vogue, November 15, 1924, 42–43. General Electric advertisement, "Can You Light Your Bedroom Correctly," *Better Homes and Gardens*, April 1, 1931, inside front cover.
12. Peak, "Hollywood's Master of Make-Up."
13. See Peiss, "Making Up, Making Over," 312.
14. Antoinette Donnelly, "Theater has Makeup Tips for Amateurs," *Chicago Daily Tribune*, May 10, 1940, 26.
15. Rosalind Shaffer, "Makeup Expert Able to Paint Personality on Faces: Features of a Subject Serve as a Canvas," *Chicago Daily Tribune*, August 25, 1935.
16. Carolyn van Wyck, "Photoplay's Own Beauty Shop," *Photoplay,* January 1939, 66, quoted in Berry, "Hollywood Exoticism," 116.
17. See, for example, the advertisement "Lady Pepperell Colored Sheets," featuring Joan Crawford, published in *Photoplay* (October 1929).
18. Martha Parker, "Powder for Beauty," *New York Times*, August 1, 1943.
19. Berry, "Hollywood Exoticism," 116; Peiss, *Hope in a Jar,* 200–201.
20. "Emily Post is Dead at 86: Ruled Etiquette Scene for Four Decades," *Chicago Daily Tribune*, September 27, 1960; Marion Rodgers, "The Woman Behind the Manners," *Washington Times*, November 2, 2008.
21. Emily Post, *Etiquette in Society, in Business, in Politics, and at Home* (New York, 1922). On the discursive construction of personality in Post's *Personality of a House,* see Karen Halttunen, "From Parlor to Living Room: Domestic Space, Interior Decoration, and the Culture of Personality," in *Consuming Visions: Accumulation and Display of Goods in America 1880–1920*, ed. Simon J. Bronner (New York, 1989): 157–90, especially pages 178–87.
22. Post, *Personality of a House,* 8.
23. Myra Nye, "Club Notes," *Los Angeles Times*, February 17, 1932; and obituary, "George M. Rankin, Utility Chief, Dies," *Los Angeles Times*, November 10, 1949.
24. Nye, "Club Notes."
25. On corporate-led efforts to encourage and promote American consumer culture during and after World War II, see Cynthia Lee Henthorn, *From Submarines to Suburbs: Selling a Better America, 1939–1959* (Athens, OH, 2006).
26. Joseph Guilfoyle, "General Electric Co., Is Six Industries in One; Makes 200,000 Products," *The Wall Street Journal*, April 14, 1947.
27. For example, see Claire Winslow, "'Better Light, Better Sight,' is New Slogan," *Chicago Daily Tribune*, September 29, 1935; "Eyesight Aids for Building More Popular: Painting and Decorating Stressed as Important to Lighting," *The Washington Post*, September 8, 1935; and David A. Loehwing, "Bright Prospects: The Makers of Lighting Fixtures Look for Continued Growth," *Barron's National Business and Financial Weekly*, February 10, 1958.
28. General Electric Company, Lamp Division, *See Your Home in a New Light: Tested Light-Conditioning Recipes that Create Light for Living*, 4th edition (Cleveland, OH, 1955).
29. See for example, Mary Roche, "Lighting to Accent Line and Color," *New York Times*, December 2, 1945.

30. Roche, "Lighting to Accent line and Color."
31. David Loehwing, "Spreading Light: The Electrical Industry Finds Rewards in Vanquishing Darkness," *Barron's National Business and Financial Weekly*, June 11, 1956, 3; quote from Donald L. Millham, General Manager, Lamp Division of General Electric.
32. "New Life with New Light!" *The American Home*, May 1949, 98.
33. "These Recipes are Different," *The Washington Post*, September 8, 1956.
34. David Loehwing, "Spreading Light," 3.
35. "These Recipes are Different"; and General Electric Company, Lamp Division, *See Your Home in a New Light: Tested Light-Conditioning Recipes that Create Light for Living*, 4th ed. (Cleveland, OH, 1955).
36. General Electric Company, *See Your Home in a New Light.*
37. Arlene Dahl, "Simple Tricks of Lighting in Home Will Help to Enhance Your Beauty," *Chicago Daily Tribune*, August 3, 1955.
38. Dahl, "Simple Tricks of Lighting."
39. On pink and femininity, see Dominique Grisard's discussion in Chapter 4 of this volume, especially regarding Mamie Eisenhower as First Lady.
40. "A Bulb that Flatters," 7.
41. "Lamps Light at the Touch of a Finger," *New York Times*, August 18, 1955.
42. Ibid.
43. Photo Standalone 20, no title, *The Hartford Courant*, September 11, 1955.
44. "Pastel Tints are Developed in Light Bulbs," *Chicago Daily Tribune*, August 19, 1956.
45. Ibid.
46. General Electric marketing materials, "Look What's Behind Coloramic Bulbs," ca. September 1956.
47. A subset of the Live Better Electrically campaign, the Light for Living program, introduced by the Edison Electric Institute's National Electric Living Program, was developed to "sell better lighting for the home" and aimed to "light condition" half of the houses in the United States over a ten-year period. In the second half of the 1950s, this campaign was further unified under the "Medallion Home Program," which awarded new homes a special medallion for meeting specified standards of "electrical excellence." The desired features included "full house power," all major electrical appliances, electrical heating, and "light for living." Sam H. Schurr, *Energy in the American Economy, 1850–1975: An Economic Study of Its History and Prospects*, (Baltimore, MD, 1960), 623–24; Building Research Institute, ed., *Building Illumination: The Effect of New Light Levels*, pub. 744 of the National Academy of Sciences–National Research Council (Washington, DC, 1959), 5–7; "These Recipes are Different," *The Washington Post*, September 8, 1956; "Country-Wide Support Given to New Program," *Los Angeles Times*, June 1, 1958; "Homes on Display: Top 1958 Lighting Standards," *The Hartford Courant*, September 21, 1958.
48. Howard Ketcham, *Color Planning for Business and Industry* (New York, 1958), 2. For the continued role of color in home decoration, particularly in relation to enhancing feminine beauty, see Frances Lee, "When You Choose Your Living Room Palette, Make Sure the Colors Merge into a Flattering Background for You," *The Washington Post*, November 11, 1956.
49. See Blaszczyk, *The Color Revolution*, esp. 215–40 on "Mood Conditioning."

50. Kay Barrington, "Color Can, and Does, Change Your Life," *The Washington Post*, July 22, 1951.
51. Ibid.
52. James Nagle, "News of the Advertising and Marking Fields," *New York Times*, August 23, 1953.
53. Nagle, "News of the Advertising and Marking Fields."
54. "Bulbsnatching" was a term employed in General Electric advertisements throughout the 1950s to encourage the frequent swapping out of light bulbs to achieve varied effects and, of course, to sell more light bulbs. For example, see the General Electric advertisement "Give Your Home Four New Looks," *Look*, October 29, 1957, 72.
55. Blaszczyk, *The Color Revolution*, 256.
56. Beulah Rodgers, "Lighting Plays New Roles in Today's Homes: Adds Decorator Effects, Glamorizes Rooms," *Chicago Daily Tribune*, August 12, 1956. Other typical examples: "Lighting Steps Forward with Modern Décor," *Chicago Daily Tribune*, April 14, 1957; and "More to a Light than Meets Eye," *Chicago Daily Tribune*, September 22, 1957.
57. Loehwing, "Spreading Light," 3.
58. See Blaszczyk, *The Color Revolution*, 244–45, 256–57.
59. Alison Bisgood, "The Light Changes," *Vogue*, January 1957, 137–39.
60. "Bulb Sales," *The Hartford Courant*, December 16, 1961, 23; and "Record Bulb Sales," *Chicago Tribune*, January 27, 1966.

CHAPTER 9

Life in Color: *Life* Magazine and the Color Reproduction of Works of Art

Melissa Renn

> *If there was one important influence in my life as far as art went, it was Life magazine because for the first time there were good reproductions of American paintings.*
>
> —Robert Indiana, artist, 2009[1]

> Life *[is] the most significant single force in the appreciation of art in America.*
>
> —C. Powell Minnigerode, director of Corcoran Gallery of Art, 1940[2]

Although *Life* magazine has most often been associated with the publication of powerful black-and-white photographs, it played a pioneering role in the history of color reproduction and color photography.[3] *Life*'s "large scale experiment in color printing" was due to the editorial staff's desire, from the

Research for this chapter was made possible by two generous grants: a Robert L. Platzman Memorial Fellowship at the University of Chicago Special Collections Research Center, and a Harry Ransom Center Research Fellowship supported by the Fleur Cowles Endowment Fund at the University of Texas at Austin. Thank you to Daniel Meyer, Alice Schreyer, Barbara Gilbert, Julia Gardner, Leah Richardson, Christine Colburn, Thomas F. Staley, Steven Hoelscher, Roy Flukinger, Linda Briscoe Meyers, Dorothy Seiberling, James Moske, Tara Craig, Heather Clewell, Gael Newton, and Michael Komanecky for their help with my research. Thank you also to Regina Lee Blaszczyk, Uwe Spiekerman, Joyce Bedi, Mark Stoneman, Alex J. Taylor, and Nancy Renn for their comments on earlier versions of this essay.

M. Renn (✉)
Harvard Business School, Boston, Massachusetts, USA

R.L. Blaszczyk, U. Spiekermann (eds.), *Bright Modernity*, Worlds of Consumption, DOI 10.1007/978-3-319-50745-3_9

outset, to print works of art in color for its readers.[4] As editor Henry Robinson Luce articulated in the magazine's 1936 prospectus, readers would not only "see life" and "see the world" but also "see man's work—his paintings, towers, and discoveries."[5] And they would see much of it in color.

Since the magazine was founded during the broader color revolution of the 1930s, *Life*'s editors—including Luce, John Shaw Billings, and Daniel Longwell—were keen on using color in a range of ways in their new publication, from advertisements to stories on art and other subjects.[6] Printing art in color, in particular, was central both to the magazine's mission and to Luce's larger vision of an "American Century." In that now famous essay of 1941, Luce argued that the United States should not only abandon its isolationist stance and spread democracy abroad but also export its culture and technology. Indeed, he asked his readers to envision "an America which will send out through the world its technical and artistic skills."[7]

R. R. Donnelly and Color Reproduction Technology

Life's ability to print color reproductions of art for a mass audience was made possible by key advances in printing processes in 1934 by R. R. Donnelley and Sons, the Chicago-based firm that also printed Luce's *Time* magazine.[8] By combining a rotary press with smaller printing cylinders, building a gas heater right into the printing press, and developing a heat-set process for instantly drying ink, Donnelley could print both sides of coated paper simultaneously and thus increase production from six thousand to fifteen thousand impressions an hour. This quick, efficient, and cost-saving four-color printing process meant that Donnelley could mass-produce color images in a periodical format at a low cost.

Time tested these methods in an experimental color insert on the American painters Thomas Hart Benton, John Steuart Curry, Grant Wood, and others for their December 24, 1934, issue, which featured Benton on the cover. Due in part to the success of this insert, the editors discussed forming a picture magazine, one that would not only print the best photographs but also regularly include color spreads on art. According to Daniel Longwell, "the real start of the whole art program [at *Life*] was this little four-page experiment in TIME. It gave us a hint of the popularity of the paintings and gave us our theme for the first few years."[9]

Not long after, Luce contracted Donnelley to print his new magazine, *Life*. The inaugural issue, published on November 23, 1936, and best remembered for Margaret Bourke-White's now-iconic black-and-white photograph of the Fort Peck Dam on its cover, contained a four-page, full-color feature on the art of John Steuart Curry.[10] *Life* followed this story with a piece on art nearly every week thereafter, alternating between articles on European masters and contemporary American artists.[11]

In 1937, *Life* explained the revolutionary color printing process that made such colorful spreads possible in a "Speaking of Pictures" article entitled "How a Four-Color Letterpress Page is Printed." On the left side of the opening spread, in black and white, were photographs and a detailed diagram illustrating the process of how an advertisement was printed for the magazine. The caption below the images touted the new technology's incredible productivity: "This press prints 3,200 to 4,000 color sheets, with as many as 18 LIFE pages on one side of the sheet, in an hour."[12] On the right side of the spread, *Life* printed at the top of the page—in color—the four color swatches used in standard letterpress printing. Below was a step-by-step explanation, using an image of a tree as an example, of how "varying colors are achieved not by printing dots of color on top of each other but by printing dots so closely together that, to the naked eye, they seem to merge."[13] While many "Speaking of Pictures" articles were printed in black and white, this one, significantly, used color to show precisely how the process worked.

Donnelley likewise celebrated its printing innovations in its own advertisements, such as one entitled "Exploding Ink!" Below a colorful image showing printers at work, the text recounted the origins of Donnelley's pioneering printing process, which made it possible to produce a high-quality magazine, such as *Life,* for what was then a low newsstand price of ten cents. The advertisement explained,

> In 1936 one of our clients wanted to publish a new magazine—LIFE—a magazine to combine 50¢ magazine quality with news speed. They wanted to take photographs one day and ship finished magazines the next. Furthermore they wanted their pictures printed with all the snap and brilliance possible—and lots of contrast.
>
> Fortunately, for six months we had been experimenting with a new combination of methods and materials: new ink, new papers, and a new gadget on a rotary press—a blast furnace on a small scale. The new ink was made not with the traditional linseed oil, but with something very like naphtha. The instant after ink met paper, the printed paper, traveling hundreds of feet a minute, flashed through the flames, and right there—at 2100 °F, or so—the 'something' went up in smoke, exploded right out of the ink, leaving the pigment hard and dry.... LIFElike pictures at high speed.[14]

Praise for Color in *Life*

Donnelley's innovations made color printing so fast and cost-effective that *Life* could publish reproductions of art in color in its pages on a weekly basis, not to mention advertisements and other features. (See, for example, Fig. 8.3). *Life*'s readers wrote in frequently, commending the magazine for its accomplishments in color printing. One reader stated that the art reproductions were "the best feature in LIFE, and the editors should have at least one art subject each week," while another commented that "here at last is a magazine, that will bring to the eyes of the public, American works of art."[15]

Life wanted not only the public's approval, however, but also that of the art establishment. In late 1937, a *Life* staff member, David Scherman, wrote the director of The Metropolitan Museum of Art, Herbert E. Winlock, with a request for him to evaluate the content of the magazine's recent articles on art as well as the quality of the color reproductions. Scherman sent Winlock a copy of the December 6, 1937, issue, which featured a story on historic Japanese prints, and asked for his expert opinion:

> As you may perhaps have noticed, LIFE has, since its beginning a year ago, made classical and contemporary art an integral part of its weekly editorial presentations. To find out what degree of success LIFE has enjoyed in this field, we can only turn to those who know... [Y]ou would be doing LIFE an invaluable service by letting us have your reactions to what we have been trying to do this past year—for, after all, it is only through the critical comment of experts that future editorial policies can be intelligently guided.[16]

That December also saw the publication of one of *Life*'s first large-scale color art stories, which the magazine created in collaboration with the staff of the Frick Collection in New York. Published as the cover story for the Christmas issue, the article contained a portfolio of the Frick's greatest works, including Piero della Francesca's *St. John* and Giovanni Bellini's *St. Francis in the Desert*.[17]

Life's feature on the Frick Collection was the first of many Christmas issues that reproduced art in color for special cover stories. Beginning with its December 28, 1942, issue—which printed Raphael's *Alba Madonna* in color on the cover—the editors regularly highlighted art in its Christmas annual.[18] Of the thirty-six Christmas issues *Life* produced during its years of weekly publication, sixteen were centered on art, and fourteen of those featured canonical Christian art from the Renaissance.[19]

Besides publishing art at the Christmas holiday, *Life* also produced other series on European art. In 1938, for example, it announced plans for a group of articles focused on "America's Great Collections" in order to bring its readers "outstanding art treasures from all schools and all centuries... in full rich color reproductions."[20] It began with a piece on "England's Greatest Portraitists in America," and followed with surveys of Italian, Spanish, German, Flemish, and French paintings in American collections.[21] Letters again poured in from readers with appreciation for the color spreads of art in *Life*. For example, Morris Graves, Kenneth Callahan, and the ten other members of the Seattle-based artists' association Group of Twelve, along with three other artists practicing in the Pacific Northwest (Louis Demott Bunce, Malcolm Roberts, and Andrew McD. Vincent), wrote, "We wish to express our profound appreciation of your contribution to American culture by the reproduction of masterpieces of painting, both old and modern. Your choice of pictures and the technique of reproduction are of the highest order."[22]

Life's series on European paintings in American collections not only made such art more accessible to the American public, it also portrayed the United States as the heart of the art world by emphasizing European art in specifically American collections. These articles both anticipated and contributed to the postwar shift in the art world from Paris to New York. Through the series "Great Paintings in American Collections," the magazine presented the United States as a site where art collecting flourished and where one could experience great masterpieces. Although the decision to do such stories was due, in part, to *Life*'s difficulty in getting "color cameras into Italy or Germany or France" to photograph art at sites and in collections abroad before and during World War II, the magazine's editors also aimed to show the United States as a key player in the global art scene.[23] As Daniel Longwell later reflected, while the "war shut us off from the great museums of the world[,] . . . it made us realize that many of the art treasures of the world were in American museums and American collectors' hands."[24]

Life not only covered historical art in American collections but also the work of contemporary American artists, producing stories on Charles Burchfield, Georgia O'Keeffe, and Charles Sheeler, among many others.[25] In 1940, the magazine further expanded its reach by publishing its first book on art, *Modern American Painting*. For this project, the editors enlisted the critic Peyton Boswell, Jr., of *Art Digest*, to write a book on "America's new school of native painting."[26] Drawn largely from *Life*'s articles on American art, the book featured eighty-nine full-color reproductions of works by American artists ranging from Benjamin West and John Trumbull to George Bellows and Edward Hopper (all but one of the works had been previously published in the magazine). For the contemporary section, Boswell—and *Life*—selected predominantly American Scene and realist painters, artists they viewed as quintessentially American both in subject and style. With the exception of Georgia O'Keeffe, no other artists from Alfred Stieglitz's circle were included, nor were American modernists working in a cubist or abstract idiom (the work they included by O'Keeffe was her 1932 representational painting *White Barn*).[27]

Many of the living artists selected for inclusion in *Modern American Painting* appreciated the publicity and recognized what *Life* was doing for American art with the book, and more broadly. Shortly after the book's release, Thomas Hart Benton wrote to one of the editors:

> Although I follow painting pretty closely the book was a revelation to me. I don't think I had ever realized the extent and strength of our American movement. This book brings out conclusively the existence of a great American school, varied, interesting and alive. I am glad to be a part of that school and as a part of it glad also to say that this first pictorial survey of its effect which *Life*, Dodd-Mead, and Peyton Boswell have organized is going to be of inestimable benefit in setting up closer relationships between the American public and the art which belongs to it.[28]

Grant Wood also congratulated *Life* on the publication: "Frankly, the thing that impressed me most was seeing all those beautiful reproductions brought together and realizing fully for the first time what a tremendous thing you folks of LIFE have done for American art."[29]

In his introduction to *Modern American Painting*, Boswell likewise credited *Life* for the "growth of American art appreciation" and for "sagaciously recognizing the presence of an authentic American School even before it became the vital movement it is today."[30] He then argued: "America today is developing a School of Painting which promises to be the most important movement in the world of art since the days of the Italian Renaissance."[31] Boswell continued,

> A major difference between [Winslow] Homer, [Albert Pinkham] Ryder and [Thomas] Eakins and such present-day painters as [Edward] Hopper, [Henry Ellis] Mattson and [Alexander] Brook is that the contemporaries have the good fortune to live in an age that wants to understand them. America now, mature and flushed with the pride of national strength, demands an art of her own. It was not thus when Copley traded his honest Yankee birthright for the frills of George III's London, or the lonely Ryder painted his gems in a dirty New York garret. Our painters have discovered America. And America has discovered her painters. Today America need no longer dwell in Europe's house and live with Europe's art. America, in art, as in material progress, has a native spirit.... Only when our artists began to explore the highways and byways of their own land did their art take on the earthy fragrance of their native soil. Grant Wood is one of those artists who came home to learn.[32]

In this book, Boswell and *Life* presented the United States as the heir of Western civilization, and as its very future, a sentiment that *Life*, and Luce, frequently expressed. As the magazine stated in an advertisement that opened the January 30, 1939 issue, "LIFE firmly and sincerely believes that the great future of the world's Art lies in America, rather than in war-torn Europe." Boswell's nationalism clearly resonated with the American public, and the book sold in record numbers. Significantly, it was also one of the first publications to reproduce so many works of contemporary American art in color.[33]

The War in Color

During World War II, *Life* continued to produce stories on art, covering historical art in American collections as well as contemporary American art. In 1941, the magazine also began commissioning artists to document the war in color.[34] Between 1941 and 1945, *Life* sent its artist-correspondents worldwide to sketch, paint, and record every aspect of the war, from preparations at home to battles abroad to the experiences of civilians during wartime.[35] The editors viewed these commissions as an essential supplement to the magazine's photographic reporting. As an early 1943 advertisement stated, the purpose of the program was to "get a series of pictures that will make *Life* readers feel they have actually eye-witnessed the great events taking place at the front."[36] One of *Life*'s artist-correspondents, Fletcher Martin, likewise argued that painters could not only document events but also convey the emotional experience of war:

> The painter can make a more personal statement than the camera. His record can be stronger than the camera's because he can eliminate unnecessary detail and concentrate on the significant. Some of my work that digressed frankly from actuality met the approval of the fighting men themselves. They responded to it and said I'd got the feel of the action. That was the acid test.[37]

Technical limitations of cameras at the time also led to the editors' decision to hire artists to paint the war. Even though more portable and faster cameras had been developed by the 1940s, the technology had not advanced enough to shoot all aspects of war. As editor Daniel Longwell described, "One of the things to remember about the war artists was that Eastman had not yet developed fast color film and the color film procedure was too slow to report the war in action."[38]

Of course, when it could, *Life* published color photographs of the war in its pages. One especially notable example was a 1944 article entitled "War Ravages Italy's Art: Allies Try to Save the Great Relics," which included color photographs by staff photographer George Silk.[39] Clearly there was a demand to see the war in color. As Longwell noted, "Probably the single article in LIFE that caused the most talk and interest in the past month were the color pictures of ruined churches and their Medieval art that appeared in the July 24 issue."[40]

For *Life*'s editors, the combination of paintings, drawings, photographs, and text could give a more complete picture of the war, and with the color reproduction technology already in place, the magazine could easily print reproductions of war art for its readers. It published the work of its artist-correspondents both as part of its regular war reports and in special features. In 1943, for its Christmas issue, it published, in color, Fletcher Martin's painting of a nurse tending to a wounded soldier lying in a tent in North Africa. The flaps of the tent open to reveal a single bright star shining in a dark night sky over ruins in the distance, the composition evoking the Nativity. Inside the issue was a thirty-six-page color portfolio of war paintings by six of the war artists, with a commentary by John Hersey.[41] Two years later, in the April 30, 1945 issue, *Life* published another twenty-five-page full-color article highlighting the work of its artist-correspondents. As editor Edward K. Thompson later reflected, "[other publications] didn't have the graphic approach which put our readers *right at the ringside*... You've heard scores of people say that LIFE outdid the newspapers in reporting the war."[42]

The World in Color

After the war, *Life* expanded its art program even further, sending its staff to every corner of the world to photograph historic works of art and architecture, many of which had been previously inaccessible. In 1945, for its annual

Christmas issue, the magazine did a feature on the Benozzo Gozzoli frescoes in Florence and included a color foldout of Fernand Bourges's photographs of the frescoes in the Chapel of the Magi in the Palazzo Medici.[43] In 1948, the Christmas issue highlighted Giotto's frescoes in the Scrovegni Chapel in Padua, and featured twenty-three pages of color photographs.[44]

The following year, in 1949, *Life* produced a twenty-two-page cover story on the Sistine Chapel, publishing the first color photographs of Michelangelo's frescoes, along with a three-page foldout of the ceiling. The special issue broke all sales records.[45] According to Daniel Longwell, "it was the only art feature I ever knew of that sold out an issue completely... [T]he copies all but disappeared from the New York newsstands on the day of publication."[46] Many in the art world wrote the editors with their praise. René d'Harnoncourt, the director of the Museum of Modern Art, for example, commended *Life* for the "beautiful reproductions of the Sistine Ceiling," acknowledging that he never "believed it possible that so much of its monumental strength could be conveyed through the pages of a magazine."[47]

Capitalizing on the story's success, *Life* also issued reprints of the Sistine Ceiling foldout for museums to sell. This experience led the editors to consider, two years later, creating a "Print of the Month Club" modeled after the Book of the Month Club's stamp program. The project would have produced —for potential sale at museums nationwide—miniature reproductions of great works of art on stamps, which collectors could paste into scrapbooks.[48] Although this specific plan never materialized, it revealed *Life*'s continual interest in expanding its art enterprise.

In the postwar period, *Life* increasingly covered non-Western art. In 1946, for example, the magazine produced a lavish cover story on the art and architecture of Beijing. The article showcased striking color photographs of the city's "timeless treasures" by staff photographer Dmitri Kessel.[49] Such reports on China were not uncommon in *Life*, as Luce had a lifelong fascination with the East. Born in China in 1898, Luce was passionate about Chinese culture, history, and politics. His early years in China shaped his view on the role of the United States in the world, and often influenced the editorial content of *Life*, infusing the magazine with a global cultural perspective.[50]

In 1947, *Life*'s editors inaugurated their most ambitious educational effort to date. Realizing that they had yet to publish a complete survey of Western art, they produced a ten-part series, much of it illustrated in color, on the history of Western culture. Although similar surveys were also published during this period, no contemporaneous publications on the topic printed as many color images as *Life* did.[51] The series opened with the "Renaissance Man" in Italy, in order "to give Americans a perspective on history... so that they can determine their future."[52] Four years later, the articles were assembled into a single book, to which was added a final chapter devoted solely to the United States. In both structure and viewpoint, the book echoed George Berkeley's 1726 poem "Westward the Course of Empire" and Frederick Jackson Turner's 1893 "The Significance of the Frontier in American History."[53] *Life's Picture*

History of Western Man was an immediate bestseller. In 1951 alone, sales reached two hundred thousand.[54]

America in Color

Life followed its successful history of Western culture with an eight-part survey of American art, architecture, and design from the colonial period to the present entitled "America's Arts and Skills." Launched in 1955, the series was initially proposed by Charles F. Montgomery, the director of the Winterthur Museum in Delaware. Two years earlier, in 1953, Montgomery wrote a *Life* staff member,

> Long before I came to Winterthur I was deeply interested in American antiques as cultural history. My belief has always been that as a part of American history they are infinitely more important than as collectors' items or isolated objects of art... Having been a reader of LIFE since the first issue, I have watched closely the marvelous coverage which you have had of European arts and the great series on both them and the History of Western Man. Occasionally and, I hastily add, more often than any other national magazine, you have carried material on American arts. However, as I look back on it, it seems to me that the coverage has been in the nature of bits and pieces.... Sometime I hope it will be feasible for LIFE to do a survey of American culture in a continuing series of articles.[55]

In that same letter, Montgomery invited the magazine's staff to "spend a day or two" in Delaware to experience the museum's collection and its newly founded Winterthur Program in Early American Culture.[56] Alves quickly replied with enthusiasm. Agreeing with him that such a story would "undoubtedly make a fine contribution to our cultural independence," she swiftly passed his proposal on to the art department.[57]

Montgomery's suggestion fell on receptive ears; certainly a project focused on America's contributions to civilization logically followed the Western culture survey. In another letter, Montgomery outlined his vision for the series—how it would trace "the development of a distinct American cultural tradition as represented by the things our people have used in the business of daily living" from "their trestle tables, Philadelphia highboys, Murphy beds,... butter churns and automatic dishwashers" to their "harpsichords and television sets; their salt box houses and garden apartments; their prairie schooners and family trailers."[58]

Montgomery, as director of the first graduate program in the United States devoted to the interdisciplinary study of material culture and the decorative arts, explained his rationale for selecting such everyday objects to the editors: "America's strongest esthetic impulse has been until recent years in the direction of the utilitarian arts," and such objects were the "very essence of our national culture."[59] Montgomery's proposal appealed to them, and the project advanced.

Life then hosted two conferences, first at Winterthur, and then in New York, bringing together experts to determine the scope and content of the series. The first conference, held on December 6, 1954, was called the "Winterthur Conference on the Place of Objects and Ideas in Early American History."[60] *Life* followed it with an event four days later at Rockefeller Center entitled "Series on American Culture in Perspective." For this occasion, some of the scholars from the earlier Winterthur conference—including Roger Butterfield, Marshall Davidson, and Howard Mumford Jones—came to New York to share their ideas with *Life*'s staff. Afterward, the editors sent the magazine's best photographers—including Eliot Elisofon, Arnold Newman, Andreas Feininger, and Gjon Mili—nationwide with detailed shooting scripts.[61]

Published in 1955–1956, *Life*'s "America's Arts and Skills" series was promoted nationwide through museums, events, and even on television, such as a short film on the making of a traditional New England boiled dinner at Sturbridge Village.[62] The pioneering series presented American culture, in color, with an emphasis on American innovations and ingenuity. It began with the "The Practical World of the Colonists" and progressed chronologically to cover the "Look of Liberty in Craftsmanship," "The Age of Homespun," "The Magnificent Greek Revival," "The Fabulous Frontier," "The Timeless Southwest," and "An Age of Gilded Opulence," and concluded with an article on the invention of mass production and a celebration of the beauty of industry.[63]

Historians and curators worldwide congratulated *Life*'s staff on the series. For example, John Cummings, curator at the Bucks County Historical Society, wrote Eliot Elisofon, complimenting him on his photography, and added, "Articles such as these are an extremely valuable contribution to American culture and the perpetuation of our American heritage."[64] The series likewise received positive reviews abroad, as Daniel Longwell related to his fellow editors:

> The biggest item of prestige for LIFE I heard about in Europe was your Americana series.... Editors, Museum Directors and so forth abroad all spoke about it. It was a curious feeling to have the assistant director of the Museum of Modern Art in Paris tell me ... that what she would like to see from America were some of the things LIFE was printing on the early arts and crafts. She was fascinated by the development of American architecture from wooden houses. In a dumb way I suddenly realized that they haven't had wood to build with in France or Italy for a thousand years or more and naturally their architecture developed from stone.[65]

Given the great response to the articles, *Life,* as it had previously done with other successful series, compiled the individual stories and published them in 1957 as a full-length survey entitled *America's Arts and Skills,* which included an introduction by Charles F. Montgomery.[66] The lavishly illustrated book was published almost entirely in color, which was notable for its time.[67] Indeed, if not for *Life*'s early advances in the field of color reproductions, such a volume would not have been possible. In his review of the book for the *New York Times*, Francis Henry Taylor, director of the Worcester Art Museum, thanked the magazine for using its "vast and almost limitless photographic resources" and for the "editorial ingenuity of its writers."[68] Not since the Index of American Design during the Works Progress Administration in the 1930s, had a group of artists, photographers, curators, and scholars come together to document, in color, the artistic and material culture of the United States.[69]

The Color Spectacle

The "America's Arts and Skills" series was but one manifestation of *Life's* innovations during the 1950s in the use of color in both its stories and on its covers. In 1953, it published a pioneering twenty-four-page spread of color photographs of New York, which it had commissioned from the Austrian-born photographer Ernst Haas.[70] Throughout the decade, *Life* frequently featured color photographs by staff photographer Eliot Elisofon, who had a passion for color, as he emphatically stated in 1966: "Color to me has perhaps been the dominating factor of my creative life . . . whether it has been as a painter or as a photographer or as a participant in motion pictures."[71] In 1955, besides working on the "America's Arts and Skills" series, Elisofon also did a special cover story for *Life* on the South Pacific.[72] The bright and colorful cover featured his striking photograph of a young Tahitian girl, surrounded by lush green tropical plants, wearing pink flowers in her hair and bathing in a pool of water. The article, "Voyages to Paradise," combined Elisofon's evocative color photographs of the South Seas with literary passages selected by the novelist James Michener, including quotations from Joseph Conrad, Jack London, Mark Twain, and Robert Louis Stevenson.

In 1961, the magazine again broke new ground in color photography and printing with a new feature, the "color spectacle." Rather than consisting of a series of images spread over multiple pages, as was the case in the magazine's traditional photo-essay format, the color spectacles showcased single color photographs, printed across two pages, with little accompanying text. *Life*'s creation of this feature was undoubtedly influenced by periodicals such as *National Geographic*, which had been publishing color images of exotic locales in its pages since the early twentieth century, printing, for example, early color photographs of the North Pole in 1926. As Gael Newton has shown, the monthly *National Geographic* was an important precedent for *Life* (along with other early illustrated magazines such as *VU*, *The Illustrated London News*, and the *Berliner Illustrirte Zeitung*).[73] *National Geographic* was also likely shaped by *Life*. It began using color photographs on its covers in July 1959, perhaps to compete with *Life*, which had 5.8 million subscribers in 1956, double that of *National Geographic*.[74]

The first "color spectacle" focused on African art and culture.[75] This was not *Life*'s first article on the subject, however. Nearly a decade earlier, the magazine published an article, in black and white, with Elisofon's photographs of African art, entitled "Mystic Art of Tribal Africa," that explored the "phenomenal influence" of "Negro sculpture" on modern artists such as Paul Klee and Pablo Picasso.[76] For the 1961 color spectacle, *Life* published Elisofon's photographs of African art and culture, this time, in vibrant color spreads coupled with short texts drawn from great works of literature. The story was announced in an advertisement in the *New York Times*:

> Africa in the news today most often means revolution, bitterness, prejudice, death. But in LIFE this week, the other side of Africa is seen—the side that has inspired poet and story-teller. Witch doctors, warriors and waterfalls—native girls, glowing butterflies, leopards, and elephants. 22 pages of incredible full-color photographs by Eliot Elisofon, who journeyed 20,000 miles to capture the many moods of Africa on film. His pictures are captioned not by LIFE but with excerpts from the works of the world's greatest writers on Africa—Conrad, Kipling, Churchill, Teddy Roosevelt and many others.... "The Storied World of Africa," in this week's LIFE, is an intermingling of rare visual beauty and literary imagery that you could find only in LIFE. Today, more than ever, LIFE is a great magazine of adventure, of beauty, of human experience.[77]

Such features were clearly part of the magazine's effort to retain readers and advertisers and to attract new ones in the face of rising competition from a new visual medium, television. Although *Life* remained America's most popular magazine until its end as a weekly periodical in 1972 (with a circulation of eight million in 1970), the rise of television eventually led to the magazine's demise. As the historian Juliann Sivulka explained,

> When network television attracted large audiences that large periodicals previously enjoyed, the advertising revenues for mass-circulation magazines were no longer sufficient to subsidize rising production and distribution costs. Publishers tried offering cut-rate subscriptions... [O]thers even limited readership. But nothing worked. Dozens of magazines folded, including *Collier's* and *Women's Home Companion* in 1957, the *Saturday Evening Post* in 1969, *Look* in 1971, and *Life* in 1972.[78]

Increasing competition, especially from television, pushed *Life* to find innovative ways to present art and other subject matter to its readers, such as through the dynamic color spectacle.

Color Reproductions as Resource

During its years as a weekly publication, from 1936 to 1972, and through its continual investment in color reproduction and color photography, *Life* brought art and culture from around the world to its readers, stimulating both the novice and the professional artist. As one artist, Robert Indiana, stated in a 1963 interview, "I don't recall ever visiting [the Indianapolis] Museum until I was in . . . high school . . . Probably my first exposure to art besides the chromos in my mother's house was . . . *Life* magazine and the . . . color reproductions of American regional painting which was very much in domination at that time."[79]

Life was a place where some readers first encountered art. For others, it was a rich resource used for a range of purposes. As the poet Carl Sandburg recalled, "I have subscribed for LIFE each year since its first number . . . [and] I have mutilated copies of LIFE, for sake of convenience tearing out precious art reproductions."[80] The accessible, affordable, large-format color reproductions in *Life* made it particularly apt for use and re-use by artists. Sidney Friedman, a magazine dealer in New York City, for example, was quoted in a 1953 *Life* advertisement on how the magazine's back issues were among his bestselling and most sought after items, primarily because people had "a specific need for color pictures that have appeared nowhere else." His clientele included artists, who "often need pictures of historical costumes and period furniture." According to Friedman, he specifically got "lots of calls for *Life*'s 1947 article, 'The Golden Age of Furniture.'" [81]

Many American artists—from Joseph Cornell to James Rosenquist—clipped images from *Life*'s pages for use in their art, or to decorate their studios. Cornell, for example, incorporated photographs from the magazine into his boxed constructions, such as his 1945–46 *Penny Arcade Portrait of Lauren Bacall.* Robert Motherwell, moved by Ralph Morse's groundbreaking color photographs of the caves near Montignac, France, which were published in *Life* in 1947, began a series of works inspired by the prehistoric paintings. As the art historian Robert Mattison noted in 1985, "Motherwell still has in his library a February 24, 1947 issue of *Life* magazine which featured extensive color reproductions of the Lascaux caves."[82] In a 1984 interview, the artist Myron Stout recalled how fellow artist Hans Hofmann covered his studio walls in Provincetown, Massachusetts, with clippings, many taken from *Life* magazine, including images from the articles "on the Sistine Chapel . . . [and] the Arena Chapel at Padua of Giotto's." Stout additionally commented on the quality of the reproductions: "[*Life*] didn't do a bad job for a mass magazine."[83]

Robert Rauschenberg regularly mined *Life*, and, while he also appropriated images from the *New York Times, Newsweek, National Geographic, Sports Illustrated*, and other publications, *Life* was the source to which Rauschenberg most frequently returned for his works in the 1960s, in part because of the high quality of the reproductions, which worked especially well for his transfer drawing process.[84] In 1965, he even used images culled from the magazine in a work of art he expressly created for publication in *Life*. The piece, *A Modern Inferno,* was commissioned for *Life* by art editor Dorothy Seiberling as part of a special issue celebrating Dante's 700th birthday.[85]

The artist perhaps best known for appropriating images from *Life* was Andy Warhol, who famously re-used Charles Moore's three photographs of police dogs attacking civil rights protestors in Birmingham, Alabama, for his *Red Race Riot* in 1963.[86] As the art historian Susan Dackerman has recently shown, the artist, nun, and teacher Corita Kent also found the magazine to be a "fertile resource" for both her "teaching and printmaking practices."[87] She not only "hoarded copies of the weekly publication in her classroom, dispensing assignments from its pages" but also appropriated images and texts from the magazine, reworking, for example, the iconic red *Life* logo in her brightly colored 1967 screenprint *life is a complicated business.*[88]

The many color advertisements in *Life* were a rich resource for other Pop artists as well. As James Rosenquist recalled, "I was cutting pages out of *Life* and as I was looking at them I began to say to myself, this stuff is *ridiculous*. Even the cigarette ads were bizarre… You just had to laugh at all this magazine advertising. It was so strange."[89] Rosenquist took the clippings, stapled them to the walls, and collaged them with other newspaper fragments and his own drawings. These collages formed the basis of many of his large billboard-sized paintings, such as his 1961 *I Love You with My Ford.*[90]

Investing in America

In a double-page advertisement that appeared in the April 7, 1958 issue, *Life* celebrated its coverage of art and the technological advances in color printing that had made such stories possible.[91] At the top of this advertisement—above a color photograph by Irving Penn of an unidentified older man with white hair and spectacles, smoking a pipe while seated in a chair reading a copy of the magazine—was the header: "He used to think art was for high-brows." The text continued:

> You'd think when a man got to be my age he'd know it didn't pay to be pigheaded. But it took LIFE to show me how much I was missing.… Oh, sure, I knew about the Mona Lisa's smile, but modern art was just a mess of paint to me. I really had the wrong picture before LIFE. LIFE changed my way of looking at things.… It gets you excited and interested. For instance, the LIFE portfolio on the Sistine Chapel.… LIFE's color pictures were great, too. I'd say it was next best to being there.[92]

Beneath this statement was a color illustration showing printers at Donnelley hard at work making the high-quality color reproductions for which the magazine had become famous. The caption below the illustration proclaimed, "LIFE's art reproductions are masterpieces." Indeed, as the advertisement suggested, through *Life*, readers not only encountered the world's great art, they could also hold it in their hands.

For thirty-six years, *Life* brought historical and contemporary art to its readers while simultaneously creating a marketable, affordable, and popular product—one that was variously read, saved, stored, and even mined for use in future works of art. In fact, the magazine produced so many stories on art that it warranted the creation of an index. In 1959, independently of *Life*, Jane

Clapp published, through Scarecrow Press, an index for the years 1936–56. Six years later, she published another for 1957–65.[93]

Life's and Donnelley's innovations in the field of color reproduction were not only appreciated by the magazine's readers but also by corporations, especially when it came to advertising in the magazine. Such advances made it possible for companies like Upjohn to reproduce art in their own pharmaceutical advertisements. In one notable case, the Upjohn advertisements even became the subject of an art story in *Life*.[94]

Life ventured into cutting-edge color photography and color reproduction technology not merely to increase sales but as part of its investment in America, in line with Luce's vision of "a better nation of better men."[95] A major impetus behind the magazine's early entry into the culture business was Luce's deep desire to see art become a central part of American life. To accomplish this goal, *Life* spared no expense. In a 1952 lecture at the American Federation of Arts, Daniel Longwell disclosed that the magazine "had spent something over 23 million dollars in the last 15 years... photographing and printing reproductions of contemporary art and the art treasures of the great museums and collections."[96] The investment clearly paid off.[97]

What began as a way to introduce contemporary art—in color—to a mainly national audience, quickly became a global enterprise. *Life*'s color reproductions were used for a range of purposes, from education to advertising to international outreach.[98] Through its investments in color technology, *Life* became a leader in the fields of color printing and color photography, delivering art from all ages and nations right to its readers' doorsteps on a weekly basis, and placing the United States at the center of the global art world.

Notes

1. *Conversations with Robert Indiana*, directed by Dale Schierholt (Acadia, ME: Acadia Moving Pictures in Association with the Farnsworth Art Museum, 2009), DVD.
2. Noted in Peyton Boswell, Jr., *Modern American Painting* (New York, 1940), 5.
3. Previous studies of *Life* magazine have predominately focused on how *Life* shaped national identity, most significantly Erika Doss, ed., *Looking at* Life *Magazine* (Washington, DC, 2001), xiii. None of the major studies on *Life*—including Erika Doss, *Benton, Pollock, and the Politics of Modernism: From Regionalism to Abstract Expressionism* (Chicago, IL 1991); Bradford Collins, "*Life* Magazine and the Abstract Expressionists, 1948–51: A Historiographic Study of a Late Bohemian Enterprise." *The Art Bulletin* 73, no. 2 (June 1991): 283–308; and Wendy Kozol, Life*'s America: Family and Nation in Postwar Journalism* (Philadelphia, PA, 1994)—have explored in-depth *Life*'s investment in color reproduction technology or its collaborations with printing firms such as R. R. Donnelley & Sons.
4. Thomas M. Folds, "A Consumer's Guide to Color Prints," *Magazine of Art*, May 1943, 185.

5. "A Prospectus for a New Magazine," 1, subseries 1, folder 2, box 192, R. R. Donnelley & Sons Company Archive, Special Collections Research Center, The University of Chicago (hereafter Donnelley Archive).
6. See Regina Lee Blaszczyk, *The Color Revolution* (Cambridge, MA, 2012). For more on other innovations in color printing at the time, see Michele H. Bogart, *Artists, Advertising, and the Borders of Art* (Chicago and London, 1995), 9; and Neil Harris, *Cultural Excursions: Marketing Appetites and Cultural Tastes in Modern America* (Chicago, 1990), 318–40.
7. Henry R. Luce, "The American Century," *Life*, February 17, 1941, 65.
8. For more, see Kim Coventry, *Printing for the Modern Age: Commerce, Craft, and Culture in the R. R. Donnelley Archive* (Chicago, 2006).
9. Daniel Longwell to *Life* Archives, June 20, 1951, box 14, Daniel Longwell Papers, Rare Book and Manuscript Library, Columbia University (hereafter Longwell Papers).
10. See "Curry of Kansas," *Life*, November 23, 1936, 28–31. Donnelley's Lakeside Press Galleries also organized exhibitions on these artists, with catalogues featuring color reproductions. See *Catalogue of a Loan Exhibition of Drawings and Paintings by Thomas Hart Benton* (Chicago, IL, 1937) and *Catalogue of a Loan Exhibition of Drawings and Paintings by John Steuart Curry* (Chicago, IL, 1938). Copies of these catalogues and the correspondence regarding these exhibitions can be found in series IV, box 309, folders 5–6; box 309, folder 13; and box 310, folders, 1–3, Donnelley Archive.
11. For recent analysis of some of *Life*'s early art stories and its efforts to make art accessible to a popular audience, see Isadora Anderson Helfgott, "Art in *Life*: Fashioning Political Ideology through Visual Culture in Mid-Century America," *American Periodicals: A Journal of History, Criticism, and Bibliography* 20, no. 2 (2010): 269–94.
12. "Speaking of Pictures . . . This is how a Four-Color Letterpress Page is Printed," *Life*, July 26, 1937, 4.
13. Ibid., 5.
14. As reproduced in Coventry, *Printing for the Modern Age*, 17.
15. Harry Shepard and Yacob Pell, respectively, letters to the editors, *Life*, September 13, 1937, 9, and April 12, 1937, 15.
16. David E. Scherman to Herbert E. Winlock, December 2, 1937, folder: *Life* Magazine, 1937–1952, Office of the Secretary Records, The Metropolitan Museum of Art Archives (hereafter MMA Archives).
17. "The Frick Home becomes $40,000,000 Art Museum: First Reproductions in Color," *Life*, December 27, 1937, 30–39.
18. In the rare event that such art was not used on the cover, such as in the December 25, 1939, issue, which instead had a photograph of a young girl making snowballs on its cover, the interior still included art, in this case, a color article with works by artists from Giotto to Gauguin. See "The Nativity in Art," *Life*, December 25, 1939, 24–26.
19. *Life* also printed contemporary art on its Christmas covers from time to time. In 1941, *Life* published an article on a contemporary Chinese art exhibition at New York's American Bible Society. See "The Story of Christ in Chinese Art: Scholars at Peking University Make a Christmas Portfolio for *Life*," *Life*, December 22, 1941, 40–49. The December 25, 1944, issue featured a *Madonna and Child* on the cover that the magazine had commissioned from contemporary American

artist Lauren Ford. And in 1947, to vary the Christmas annual, *Life*, at Luce's request, commissioned a group of contemporary American artists to illustrate Christmas carols for its December 22nd issue. See Daniel Longwell to Henry R. Luce, January 28, 1948, box 29, Longwell Papers. Such Christmas-themed presentations of art were so well received that *Life* also published a compilation of those articles as a book. See Margit Varga, *The Christmas Story* (New York, 1946).

20. Advertisement in *Life*, December 27, 1937, n.p.
21. "England's Greatest Portraitists in America," *Life*, January 24, 1938, 28–35; "Great Primitive Paintings in America," *Life*, February 7, 1938, 27–29; "Italian Renaissance Paintings in America," *Life*, March 21, 1938, 26–31; "Great Flemish Painters in America," *Life*, April 11, 1938, 20–24; "Great Spanish Paintings in America," *Life*, May 16, 1938, 40–45; "Great German Painters in America," *Life*, July 11, 1938, 38–40; "English Landscape Paintings in America," *Life*, September 12, 1938, 42–45; "French 18th Century Paintings in America," *Life*, September 26, 1938, 34–39; and "French Impressionists in America," *Life*, October 10, 1938, 24–29.
22. The Group of Twelve, Louis Demont Bunce et al., letters to the editors, *Life*, June 20, 1938, 6.
23. Daniel Longwell, interview with Celia Sugarman, March 6, 1958, 38, box 26, Longwell Papers.
24. Daniel Longwell to Andrew Heiskell, November 29, 1951, box 28, Longwell Papers.
25. See, for example, "Burchfield's America," *Life*, December 28, 1938, 24–29; "Georgia O'Keeffe Turns Dead Bones to Live Art," *Life*, February 14, 1938, 28–30; and "Sheeler Finds Beauty in the Commonplace," *Life*, August 8, 1938, 42–45.
26. Boswell, *Modern American Painting*, 5.
27. Ibid., 124.
28. Thomas Hart Benton to Daniel Longwell, October 6, 1939, box 1, Longwell Papers.
29. Grant Wood to Daniel Longwell, October 14, 1939, box 7, Longwell Papers.
30. Boswell, *Modern American Painting*, 5.
31. Ibid., 11.
32. Ibid.
33. In terms of sheer volume of color reproductions, I have found no contemporary publication on American art that equals *Modern American Painting*. A contemporary reviewer also acknowledged as much in his review of the book, writing that it was "richly illustrated... The publishers have done an impressive printing job." Robert Jay Wolff, "Is There an American Art?," *The Kenyon Review* 2, no. 3 (Summer 1940): 373–74.
34. *Life* commissioned both art and architecture from its earliest years of publication. For a detailed discussion of *Life*'s patronage, see Melissa Renn, "*Life* in the Art World, 1936–1972" (PhD diss., Boston University, 2011), chap. 2.
35. For more on *Life*'s wartime commissions, see Melissa Renn, "From Life: Tom Lea and the World War II Art of *Life* Magazine," in Adair Margo and Renn, *Tom Lea,* Life *Magazine, and World War II* (El Paso, TX, 2016).
36. As quoted in Loudon Wainwright, *The Great American Magazine: An Inside History of* Life (New York, 1986), 137.

37. Fletcher Martin, press release, folder: War Art Exhibition 1943, Office of the Secretary Records, MMA Archives.
38. Daniel Longwell to Irene Saint, April 24, 1968, 1–2, box 80, Longwell Papers.
39. *Life*, July 24, 1944.
40. Daniel Longwell to John Shaw Billings, August 8, 1944, 1–2, folder: John Shaw Billings, box 27, Longwell Papers.
41. John Hersey, "Experience by Battle," *Life*, December 27, 1945, 48–84.
42. Edward K. Thompson to Daniel Longwell, June 19, 1946, 2, John Shaw Billings, Time-Life-Fortune Collection, South Caroliniana Library, University of South Carolina; emphasis in original.
43. "Medici Chapel: A Great Florentine Art Treasure is Photographed for the First Time in Color," *Life*, December 24, 1945, 43–52.
44. "The Story of Christ: The Noblest Paintings of the Saviour's Life were done by Giotto for a Chapel in Italy," *Life*, December 27, 1948, 34–57.
45. "Michelangelo's Sistine Chapel," *Life*, December 26, 1949, 25–49. *Life* not only invested in color technology for reproducing art in its weekly pages, it also collaborated with museums and companies on groundbreaking photographic exhibitions, most notably its 1956 exhibition *Illuminations*. For more on this exhibition, see Renn, "Within Their Walls: *Life* Magazine's *Illuminations*," *Archives of American Art Journal* 53, nos. 1–2 (2014): 30–51.
46. Daniel Longwell to Andrew Heiskell, November 29, 1951, 2, box 28, Longwell Papers.
47. D'Harnoncourt, letter to the editors, *Life,* January 16, 1950, 6.
48. In 1951, Longwell also suggested to staff, "perhaps we should be issuing LIFE prints" in order to take "full advantage of this public interest," especially since *Life* "did as much as anyone to create that interest." Longwell to Phil Wooten and Oliver Allen, March 13, 1951, box 14, Longwell Papers.
49. "Peiping: China's Ancient Capital is Rich in Art Treasure," *Life*, April 29, 1946, 67–76. *Life* organized, with the American Federation of Arts, a photographic exhibition based on the spread. It opened at The Metropolitan Museum of Art in 1947, and was supplemented with objects from the museum's collection. See folder: Peiping Exhibition, Office of the Secretary Records, MMA Archives.
50. For more on Luce's views on China, see Walter Guzzardi, Jr., *The Henry Luce Foundation: A History, 1936–1986* (Chapel Hill and London, 1988), especially 12–14; Alan Brinkley, *The Publisher: Henry Luce and His American Century* (New York, 2010); Robert R. Herzstein, *Henry R. Luce,* Time, *and the America Crusade in Asia* (New York, 2005); and Patricia Neils, *China Images in the Life and Times of Henry Luce* (Savage, MD, 1990).
51. See, for example, Aline B. Loucheim, *5000 Years of Art in Western Civilization* (New York, 1946). Based on a special issue of *Art News* published for the 75th anniversary of The Metropolitan Museum of Art, the entire book was printed in black-and-white.
52. "The History of Western Culture," *Life*, March 3, 1947, 69. *Life* followed its opening issue on the Renaissance with "The Middle Ages" (April 7, 1947); "Medieval Life" (May 26, 1947); "The Glory of Venice" (August 4, 1947); "The Age of Enlightenment" (September 5, 1947); "The Edwardians" (November 17, 1947); "The Age of Exploration" (March 22, 1948); "The Protestant Reformation" (June 14, 1948); "18th Century England" (September 13, 1948); and closed with a survey of the political, industrial, and

artistic revolutions of the nineteenth century (November 22, 1948). The series' sequence was overall consistent with how Western Civilization was taught by history departments at the time. See, for example, Gilbert Allardyce, "The Rise and Fall of the Western Civilization Course," *The American Historical Review* 87, no. 3 (June 1982): 695–725. *Life,* however, began its "course" with the Renaissance, only briefly touching on the ancient world. The editors explained, "Our Modern Western Civilization, which owes much to classical Greece and Rome, had its roots in the Middle Ages and grew most directly out of the Renaissance." "LIFE Announces a Series of Articles on the History of Western Culture," *Life*, March 3, 1947, 69. *Life* would later do a seven-part series on Greece in 1963, followed by a series on Rome in 1965–66.

53. The editors were keenly aware of both works. In 1935, just prior to the founding of *Life*, Longwell asked his secretary to order him a copy of Turner's thesis. Daniel Longwell to Miss Locke and Miss Bulger, April 11, 1935, box 26, Longwell Papers.
54. David Dempsey, "In and Out of Books," *New York Times Book Review*, December 30, 1951, BR5. *Life* also transformed the series into a filmstrip for classroom education, and many of the spreads from this series were also used in photographic exhibitions.
55. Charles F. Montgomery to Mary Alves, August 5, 1953, box WC106, Winterthur Archives.
56. Ibid.
57. Mary Alves to Charles F. Montgomery, August 6, 1953, box WC106, Winterthur Archives.
58. Charles F. Montgomery to Margit Varga, November 13, 1953, box WC106, Winterthur Archives.
59. Ibid.
60. For a complete list of the conference participants, and a transcript of the proceedings, see box WC106, Winterthur Archives.
61. Examples of such shooting scripts can be found in box 23, folder 23, Eliot Elisofon Papers and Photography Collection, Harry Ransom Center, The University of Texas at Austin (hereafter Elisofon Papers).
62. "*Life* Goes for Boiled Dinner Party in Old Yankee Sturbridge Village," *Gazette*, Barre, MA, April 14, 1955. Original clipping in box 21, folder 19, Elisofon Papers.
63. The eight-part series was published in order in the following issues of *Life*: April 18, 1955; May 30, 1955; July 18, 1955; August 29, 1955; October 17, 1955; November 28, 1955; January 16, 1956; and March 5, 1956.
64. John Cummings to Eliot Elisofon, April 15, 1956, box 21, folder 19, Elisofon Papers.
65. Daniel Longwell to Edward K. Thompson, October 26, 1955. Folder: Edward K. Thompson, box 80, Longwell Papers.
66. *America's Arts and Skills* (New York, 1957).
67. For example, both John Kouwenhoven and Marshall B. Davidson's contemporaneous surveys of American art and culture had far fewer illustrations, and were published solely in black-and-white. See Kouwenhoven, *Made in America: The Arts in Modern Civilization* (Garden City, NY, 1948) and Davidson, *Life in America* (Boston, 1951).
68. Francis Henry Taylor, "Things of Use and Beauty and Our Own," *The New York Times Book Review*, October 27, 1957, 1.

69. While the Federal Art Project's Index of American Design consists of approximately 18,000 watercolor renderings of American decorative arts objects from the colonial period through the nineteenth century, this archive was not as easily accessible to the general public or published in an affordable format.
70. See Haas's photographs in "Images of a Magic City, Part 1," *Life*, September 14, 1953, 108–24 and "Images of a Magic City, Part 2," *Life*, September 21, 1953, 116–26. For more on Haas and color photography, see especially: Ernst Haas and Ruth A. Peltason, *Ernst Haas: Color Photography* (New York, 1989); Gael Newton and Anne O'Hehir, *Colour Concept: International Colour Photography* (Canberra, 2002); and Katherine A. Bussard and Lisa Hostetler, *Color Rush: American Color Photography from Stieglitz to Sherman* (New York and Milwaukee, 2013).
71. Elisofon, "The Meaning of Color" (lecture, June 9, 1966), 4, box 58, folder 42, Elisofon Papers. For more Elisofon and color, see especially Elisofon, *Color Photography* (New York, 1961); and Roy Flukinger, *"To Help the World to See": An Eliot Elisofon Retrospective* (Austin, TX, 2000).
72. "Voyages to Paradise: A Camera in the South Seas, photographed for *Life* by Eliot Elisofon," *Life*, January 24, 1955, 60–77. For more on Elisofon and this series, see box 22, Elisofon Papers.
73. See Newton's lecture, "American *National Geographic* Photographers in the Pacific" for the conference "Broken Images: A Symposium on Early American Photography in the Asia Pacific, 1850–1950," hosted by Griffith University, July 2–4, 2014, at https://itunes.apple.com/us/itunes-u/broken-images-early-american/id908118871.
74. The first color cover was a photograph of an American flag. Since World War II, the magazine had been using an American flag on its July cover, and for the July 1959 issue they photographed the new forty-nine-star banner because Alaska had recently entered the Union. For more on *National Geographic* and color photography, see Stephanie L. Hawkins, *American Iconographic:* National Geographic, *Global Culture, and the Visual Imagination* (Charlottesville, 2010), 48, 171. See also Catherine A. Lutz and Jane L. Collins, *Reading* National Geographic (Chicago, 1993), 31–32.
75. "Storied World of Africa," *Life*, October 13, 1961, 66–86.
76. "Mystic Art of Tribal Africa," *Life*, September 8, 1952, 116–125. Elisofon was also a prominent collector of African art and an expert in the field. See Werner Gillon et al., *Collecting African Art* (New York, 1980) and Elisofon and William Fagg, *The Sculpture of Africa: 405 Photographs* (New York, 1958). Upon his death in 1973, Elisofon's African collection and photographic archives were donated to the Smithsonian Institution; they are in the National Museum of African Art in Washington, DC. See also the 2014 exhibition *Africa ReViewed: The Photographic Legacy of Eliot Elisofon*, http://africa.si.edu/exhibits/africa-reviewed.
77. *New York Times*, October 11, 1961.
78. Sivulka, *Soap: A Cultural History of American Advertising* (Boston, MA, 2012), 269.
79. Robert Indiana, interview with Richard Brown Baker, September 12–November 7, 1963, Archives of American Art, Smithsonian Institution, http://www.aaa.si.edu/collections/oralhistories/transcripts/indian63.htm.

80. Carl Sandburg, "How I feel about *Life*: Life is Like That," advertisement, *Life*, February 20, 1956, 132.
81. Sidney Friedman, "How I feel about *Life: Life* file," advertisement, *Life*, December 14, 1953, 159.
82. Robert Mattison, "The Art of Robert Motherwell during the 1940s," (PhD diss., Princeton University, 1985), 203.
83. Myron Stout, interview with Robert Brown, March 26–October 3, 1984, Archives of American Art, Smithsonian Institution, http://www.aaa.si.edu/collections/oralhistories/transcripts/stout84.htm.
84. For more on his use of images from *Life* and other sources, see Robert S. Mattison, *Rauschenberg: Breaking Boundaries* (New Haven, CT, 2003).
85. For more on this commission, see Renn, "*Life* in the Art World, 1936–1972," chap. 2.
86. See "The Dogs' Attack is Negroes' Reward," *Life*, May 17, 1963, 30–31. See also: Anne Wagner, "Warhol Paints History, or Race in America," *Representations* 55 (Summer 1996): 98–119; Okwui Enwezor, *Archive Fever: Uses of the Document in Contemporary Art* (New York, 2008); and Martin A. Berger, *Seeing through Race: A Reinterpretation of Civil Rights Photography* (Berkeley, CA, 2011).
87. Susan Dackerman, ed., *Corita Kent and the Language of Pop* (New Haven, CT, 2015), 104.
88. Ibid., 104–5.
89. James Rosenquist with David Dalton, *Painting Below Zero: Notes on a Life in Art* (New York, 2009), 80–81.
90. For more on Rosenquist's use of images from *Life*, see Julia Blaut's essay in Walter Hopps and Sarah Bancroft, *James Rosenquist: A Retrospective* (New York, 2003).
91. Two years later, for the twenty-fifth anniversary issue, the magazine did a color feature showing the range of its color reproductions of art over the years, from the Sistine Chapel to paintings by Jackson Pollock; "In a Quarter Century, A Vast Panorama . . . 25,000 Years of Art," *Life*, December 26, 1960, n.p.
92. *Life*, April 7, 1958, 114–15.
93. Jane Clapp, *Art in* Life (New York, 1959) and *Art in* Life*: Supplement* (New York, 1965).
94. "Art in Advertising," *Life*, May 14, 1945, 75–77. For more on Upjohn, the Container Corporation of America, and other companies' use of art reproductions in advertisements, see Bogart, *Artists, Advertising, and the Borders of Art,* especially chap. 6.
95. Henry R. Luce, "The Place of Art in American Life," *Architectural Forum* (January 1956): 132.
96. Lecture, May 28, 1952, American Federation of Arts, box 10, Longwell Papers.
97. From the beginning, *Life* had extraordinary circulation numbers. Its first press run in 1936 of 466,000 sold out immediately, and by 1939 it had a circulation of more than two million. In 1960, its circulation was three times that—approximately six million copies per issue. These statistics, as Erika Doss has noted, do not include its "passalong" rate of four to five people per issue. Factoring that in, "each issue reached as many as forty million people." Erika Doss, "Looking at *Life:* Rethinking America's Favorite Magazine, 1936–1972," in Doss, *Looking at* Life, 1–3. The magazine's numbers remained high throughout the 1950s and

1960s, until, in the 1970s, television outdistanced it. For more on *Life*'s circulation and audience, see also James L. Baughman, "Who Read *Life*? The Circulation of America's Favorite Magazine," in Doss, *Looking at* Life, 41–51.

98. *Life International* and *Life en Español* were also founded in the 1950s to expand *Life*'s market. These magazines were specifically designed for audiences abroad, and often highlighted American accomplishments in technology, art, and society.

PART IV

Predicting the Rainbow

CHAPTER 10

The Color Schemers: American Color Practice in Britain, 1920s–1960s

Regina Lee Blaszczyk

Consumer demand goes against standards.

—Faber Birren, *Design* (London), 1961[1]

In 1966, the distinguished British graphic designer Norbert Dutton, best known for his iconic Cadbury chocolate wrappers, wrote to colleagues at the Council of Industrial Design with concerns about the state of British color practice. The Council of Industrial Design was a quasi-public organization created under the auspices of the Board of Trade in 1944 to help British manufacturers design products that could compete in foreign markets. Since 1963, the Council had sponsored an Advisory Committee on Colour and Industrial Design, and Dutton was helping them create a policy on color coordination for products used in architecture and interior design.[2] Dutton warned against American color imperialism.

During World War II, Dutton had looked favorably on the development of the industrial design profession in the United States, but he was now skeptical of the Americans.[3] On this last point, Dutton quoted his 1962 address to the Society of Industrial Artists (a professional association for British designers founded in 1930 and renamed the Society of Industrial Artists and Designers in 1963), on American consultants:

> Twentyfive [sic] years ago Raymond Loewy opened a branch office in London and virtually monopolised the British market with the proposition

R.L. Blaszczyk (✉)
School of History, University of Leeds, Leeds, United Kingdom

R.L. Blaszczyk, U. Spiekermann (eds.), *Bright Modernity*, Worlds of Consumption, DOI 10.1007/978-3-319-50745-3_10

> that only Americans really understand industrial design. Mr Faber Birren is now attempting the same exploit with colour. Mr Birren, by analysing sales records is able to identify the largest-selling, and hence it is argued, the most popular, colours in any given range of paints or products.... From this information Mr Birren forecasts the trend of future demand, and thus professes to offer advice to manufacturers about their marketing and production plans.[4]

The research-driven methods of Birren, based on the principles of scientific management and a belief in consumer sovereignty, were anathema to British designers, who lived and worked within the framework of the social democratic state. What alternative did they envision? Dutton cited a letter from the architect H. L. "Bill" Gloag, a color specialist at the government's Building Research Station at Garston in Hertfordshire, who also disliked the American way: "The future pattern must inevitably be, I think, a closer alliance between architects, industrial designers, industry and scientific research, all representing aspects of the same problem." Dutton implored the Advisory Committee on Colour and Industrial Design to act decisively. He wanted the committee to set up a plan for color coordination among the professions that would protect the British color scene from American opportunists.[5]

This vignette about British perceptions of American color practice speaks to a larger theme in transatlantic studies. Business historians have long been concerned with the transfer of American expertise to war-torn Western Europe under the Marshall Plan, formally named the European Recovery Program. In her celebrated book *Irresistible Empire*, the cultural historian Victoria de Grazia examined the widespread influence of American consumer culture in Western Europe over the course of the twentieth century. More recently, however, scholars have complicated the picture with discussions of the uneven response to American imports, arguing that Europeans were more receptive to American processes rather than to American products.[6]

The example of color management—a process for selecting, forecasting or predicting, and otherwise rationalizing color choice for fashion, consumer durables, capital goods, interior decoration, and architecture—allows for a nuanced contribution to the Americanization debate. American color management practices were mainly received with warmth in Britain from the 1920s to the early 1950s, but fell under harsh criticism by the late 1950s and 1960s. This chapter explores why the British initially revered and emulated American color practices, and why the tide eventually turned. The rejection of American methods was due to a confluence of factors, the two most important of which were a generational shift within the British design establishment and the growing influence of the welfare state, which extended its collectivist ambitions to the realms of architecture and design in part through the Council of Industrial Design.

The Color Revolution in America: A Snapshot

Between 1915 and 1960, American industry perfected methods for managing color for the mass market.[7] Major turn-of-the-century innovations in dyestuffs, textiles, electrification, and science had generated color anarchy that was befuddling the creative industries. There were too many choices and no reliable methods for organizing the palette for art education, fashion, merchandising, and product design. Appalled by the rampant gaudiness in advertising and consumer goods, the Boston art educator Albert H. Munsell invented a color system in the first decades of the new century to help art teachers educate young students on tasteful color choices. The Munsell Color System was added to the designer's bulging color toolkit, which already included French shade cards with fashion hues, dye marketing handbooks from Germany, popular books on color psychology, fabric cuttings from style services in Europe, color chips from paint companies, and nomenclature guides from the natural sciences. Factory art directors had assemblages of these materials, which they consulted on an ad hoc basis when it was time to plan the next year's product lines. Even with these resources, however, color choice remained intuitive and subjective, and the task of selecting colors produced nothing short of migraines.

Starting in World War I, American industry developed strategies for managing the commercial color chaos. The color revolution, discussed in my eponymous book and in the introduction to this anthology, was born in the modernist moment and was shaped by a confluence of forces. American consumer society had inched forward since the Civil War, but it expanded dramatically from World War I onward. The New York garment industry put fashionable ready-to-wear within reach of ordinary Americans, Detroit automakers created "a car for every purse and purpose," and the chemical industry of the Delaware River valley provided the basic building blocks, such as rayon fibers and quick-drying lacquers. Mass production as developed by the Ford Motor Company was superseded by flexible mass production at the General Motors Corporation, where a decentralized organizational structure went hand in hand with rational information gathering and statistical forecasting. Efficiency experts such as Frederick Winslow Taylor, Herbert Hoover, and Roger W. Babson helped companies streamline production and better digest information. Before long, the efficiency craze spilled over to the creative industries, where a generation of color revolutionaries emerged to codify and rationalize the palette.

The color revolutionaries on the American scene from the 1920s to the 1960s aimed to make commercial color predictable and thereby more profitable. The goal was not to replace the highly subjective process of color choice in design with scientific objectivity or a color dictatorship but rather to temper subjectivity so that color selection would be manageable. It is important to understand that the task of managing the palette for fashion, consumer durables, architecture, and interior design involved seemingly disparate areas such as visual analysis and quantitative market research. The color revolutionaries routinely crossed boundaries to achieve their aims. They often combined visual thinking with market studies. They might spend one day browsing the shop windows to develop a feeling for where ladies' fashion trends were going and the next day at their desk crunching statistical data on how many avocado green refrigerators had been sold in California last year. This qualitative and quantitative research was digested and used to create a range of color resources: sets of standards, seasonal forecasts or predictions, narrative reports and newsletters on trends, paint schemes for particular types of interiors, and palettes for specific types of merchandise.

By occupation, the color revolutionaries could be roughly divided into three categories: forecasters working for trade associations, art directors employed by manufacturing firms, and entrepreneurs who ran their own consulting businesses. Collectively, these commercial colorists shared a commitment to scientific management and the democratization of consumption. They all tackled the knotty problem of subjectivity in their efforts to manage color in their corner of the universe. They sometimes adopted similar ideas and ways of working as information about new color practices flowed freely through American commercial culture.

The most influential color revolutionary of the interwar years was the forecaster Margaret Hayden Rorke, managing director of the Textile Color Card Association of the United States (later called the Color Association of the United States). This trade association was established in 1914 to handle the problem of color choice for the textile, fashion, and retailing trades. For decades, the New York textile and garment industries had copied colors on imported French shade cards, until Rorke transformed the business by introducing a set of color management tools designed to address the specific needs of American industry. She looked to Paris for inspiration, but her major objective was to create a triumvirate of color resources—color standards, seasonal color forecasts, and occasional trend reports—that were specially suited to the growing demand for everyday fashion and the tastes of America's multicultural mass market (Figs. 10.1 and 10.2). Rorke had a lasting impact. Twenty-first-century color services such as Pantone, Inc., Première Vision (the subject of Chapter 12), and the Worth Global Style Network (WGSN) create color standards and predict, or forecast, color trends for the global business environment using techniques that she perfected.

H. Ledyard Towle was the color revolutionary who helped to legitimize color management as a design or marketing function within American manufacturing firms. During the interwar years, major corporations began to acknowledge that color could augment sales, provided companies could figure out how to give consumers the colors they wanted. Creative individuals convinced industry to hire color directors to manage the palette and forecast color trends. The leading light was Towle, a fine-arts painter who had learned camouflage on the Western Front and then adapted its techniques to design practice in American industry. Towle was widely known as the pioneer of "reverse camouflage," a method for manipulating color, light, and shade in ways that enhanced, rather than concealed, the salient features of an object or a

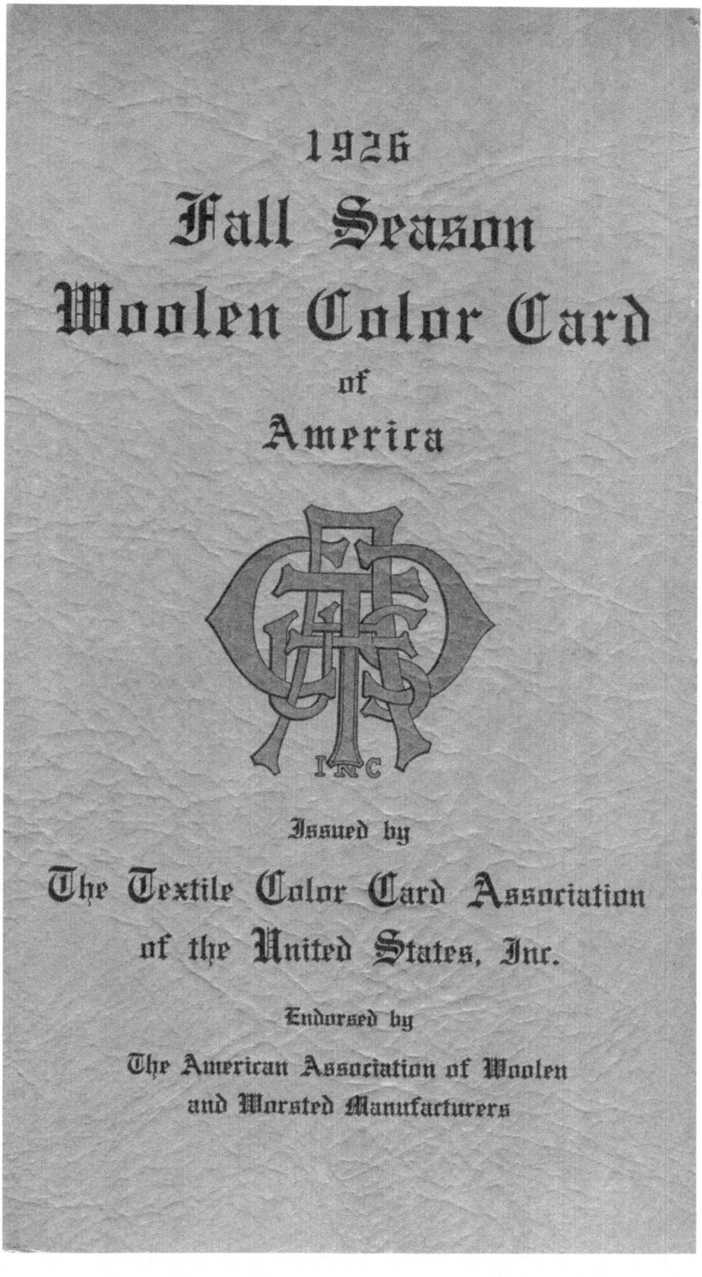

Fig. 10.1 Seasonal color forecast by Margaret Hayden Rorke for U.S. woolen mills, one of many branches of the American fashion trade for which she consulted

Source: Textile Color Card Association, *1926 Fall Season Woolen Color Card of America,* Hagley Museum and Library, Accession 2188, Box 60. Courtesy of Hagley Museum and Library.

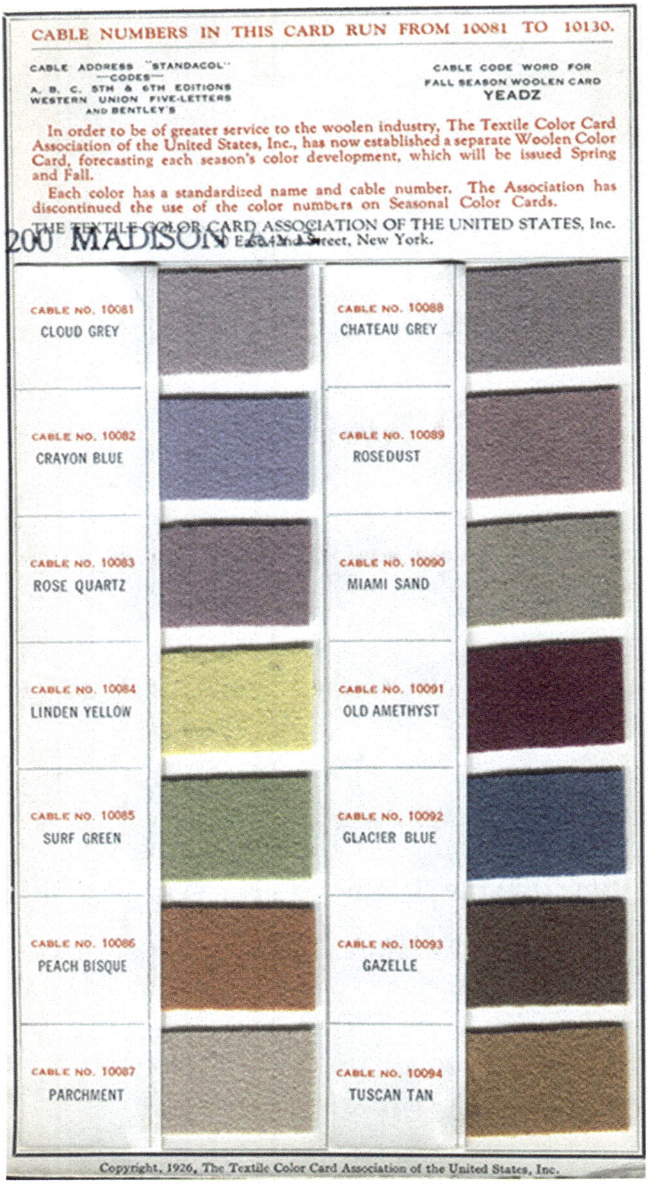

Fig. 10.2 Color card from Rorke's fall 1926 woolens forecast

As a typical color card, this forecast consists of fabric swatches pasted into a cardboard foldout book. Each hue was given a fashionable name such as Chateau Grey or Robinhood Green as a discussion aid for designers, retailers, and marketers, as well as a short cable number for telegraph communications.

Source: Textile Color Card Association, *1926 Fall Season Woolen Color Card of America, Inc.*, Hagley Museum and Library, Accession 2188, Box 60. Courtesy of Hagley Museum and Library.

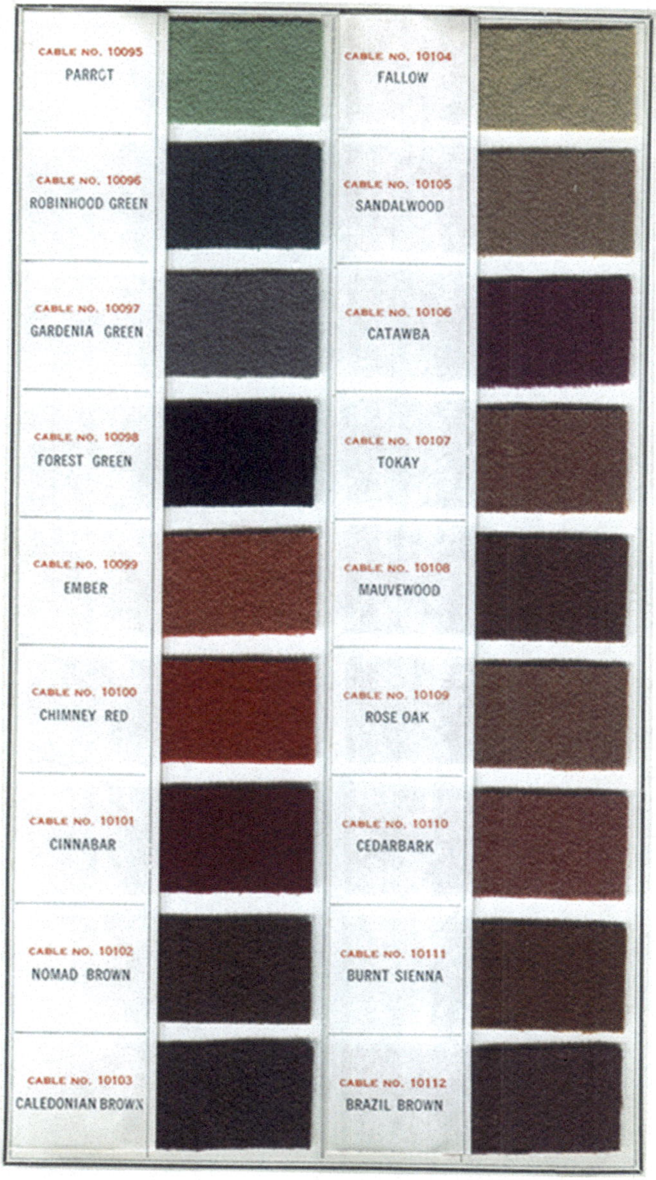

Fig. 10.2 (continued)

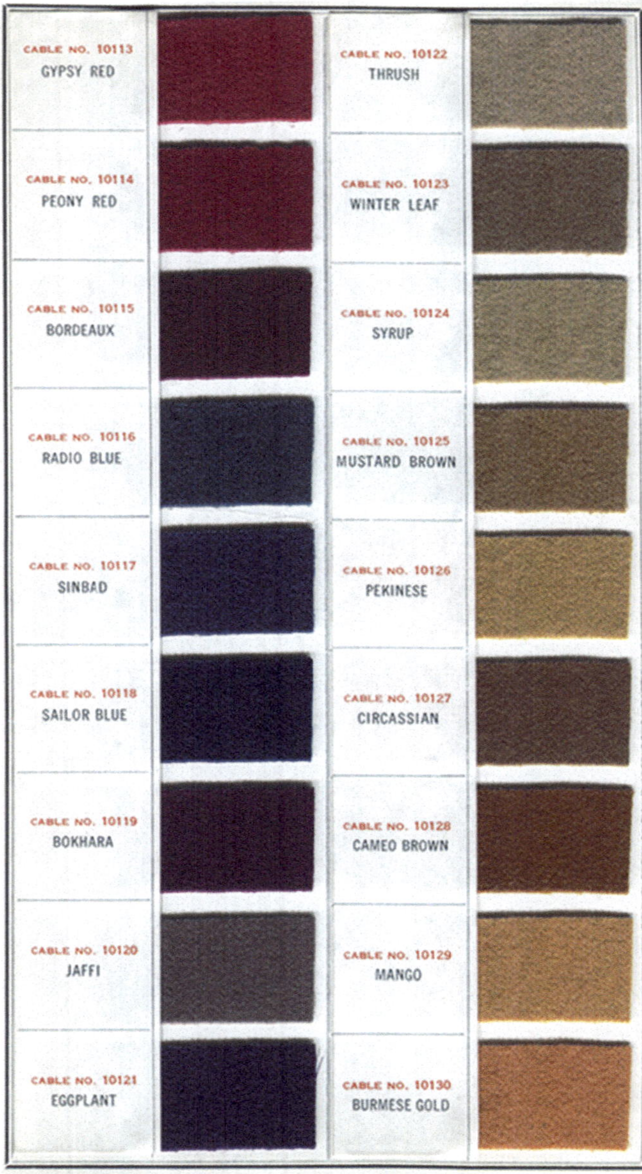

Fig. 10.2 (continued)

space. His career as an industrial colorist included staff positions with the chemical giant E. I. du Pont de Nemours and Company, General Motors, and the Pittsburgh Paint Glass Company (PPG). Towle helped General Motors wrestle the auto market away from Ford with polychrome paint jobs that made boxy cars look streamlined, and he helped PPG sell more interior paint with a promotion called Color Dynamics. This paint-marketing program provided architects, mill owners, and building managers with "reverse camouflage" tips on how to colorize production-line equipment and factory interiors so as to augment vision, reduce accidents, and increase worker productivity.

The color revolutionary Faber Birren (1900–1988) was the leading color consultant in America. After attending art school, Birren decided to pursue industrial art out of admiration for the businessmen whose factories and chain stores provided the masses with everyday comforts.[8] He set up a consultancy in Chicago in response to the 1933 Century of Progress International Exposition, disliking that illuminated, candy-colored spectacle and thinking he could do better (Fig. 10.3). His early clients included the Chicago meat-packers, whose walk-in freezers he repainted in pale blue-green to make the red porterhouse steaks look more appetizing. Relocating to New York in the mid-1930s, Birren steered clear of the cutthroat garment trade to develop a clientele that included major corporations. In 1937, he published *Functional Color*, the first full-length study of how businesses could use color in the work-place to increase morale and productivity. One of his important clients was the DuPont Company, whose engineers had developed Three Dimensional Seeing, a paint program that showed factories how to use "reverse camouflage" techniques to colorize machinery and workstations in ways that reduced eye fatigue. Birren turned Three Dimensional Seeing into the DuPont Safety Color Code for Industry, a set of accident-prevention markers that was eventually adopted as the national standard, and into DuPont Color Conditioning to compete with PPG's paint-marketing program, Color Dynamics. From 1954, Birren consulted for the New York-based Condé Nast publishing empire as the colorist for the *House and Garden* Color Program. Drawing on his meticulous research into color trends, this unique program developed a proprietary palette that was licensed to the home-furnishings industry. Birren used the newest IBM equipment to crunch sales figures obtained from *House and Garden* licensees, analyzing the results to predict next year's best-selling palette. By 1962, some 400 manufacturers and 200 stores offered household products in coordinated *House and Garden* colors.

American color revolutionaries aimed to improve the standard of living by eliminating the inefficiencies in production and distribution. Greater efficiency would translate into lower prices to the consumer. The color revolutionaries operated in the commercial sphere, separate from the scientists, who researched the physical properties of color, matter, and light. However, the search for scientific color "truths" often dominated midcentury professional discussions, much to the irritation of commercial colorists like Birren. "Too much attention has been given to physics, to wave lengths, and a lot of technical things," he

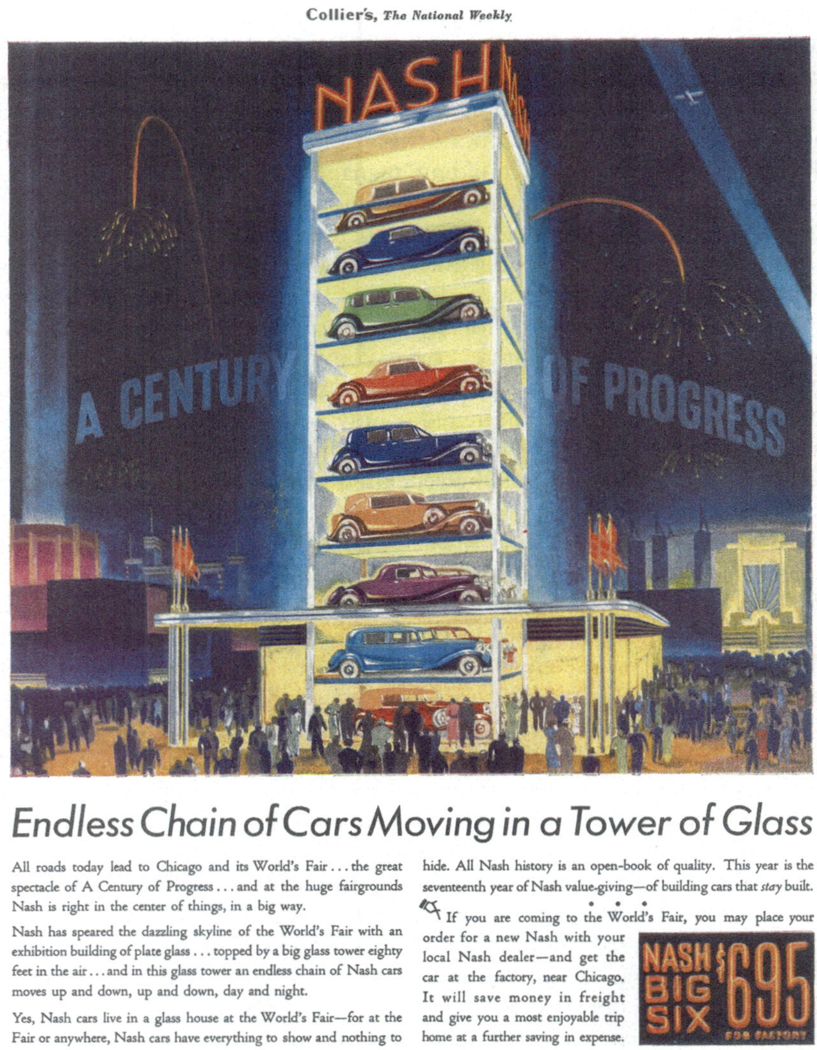

Fig. 10.3 Magazine advertisement for Nash automobiles, 1933, proudly showing the company's brightly lit, varicolored contribution to the Century of Progress International Exhibition in Chicago, the world's fair whose coloring Faber Birren found so garish and in need of ordering

Source: *Collier's, The National Weekly*, July 8, 1933, collection of Regina Lee Blaszczyk.

lamented. "The human nature of color has been neglected for the scientific nature of it."[9] The color revolutionaries tried to overcome this bias with projects to moderate, rather than control, the highly subjective realm of color. They systematically collected information on color trends and used empirical methods to interpret the data. The goal was not to stifle creativity but to harness the human nature of color for the benefit of commerce, culture, and consumers.

The British Colour Council

The British Colour Council was a major effort to rationalize color selection for British industry based on the American trade-association model.[10] The idea for the council dates to around 1926, when Margaret Hayden Rorke visited Manchester, England, to advise a group of industrialists on best practices in color management for the fashion industries. She was well known to British businesses that subscribed to the Textile Color Card Association and received her seasonal color forecasts and trend reports. "If imitation is the highest form of flattery," Rorke told her board in April 1928, "then we should be proud of the fact that our system of standardization and coordination of color between industries, is now being emulated by different industries in several foreign countries."[11] A few months later, the British trade journal *Drapers' Organiser* described a proposal by the Bradford Dyers' Association to form a committee "to consider and prepare ranges of shades for general use." Besides the dyers, representatives from textile manufacturers and merchants in Bradford and Manchester, garment makers and wholesalers, and retailers that sold yard goods and clothing would serve on the committee.[12] In July 1929, the *Yorkshire Post* reported that Rorke, who was traveling from Paris to London on one of her annual visits to the European fashion capitals, had again "been in communication with some of those interested in the project to form a British Colour Council, whose staff would give subscribers early information of world colour tendencies."[13]

Before long, Britain would have its own version of the Textile Color Card Association. In October 1929, representatives from British textile mills, tanneries and shoemakers, dye houses, retailers, and trade associations gathered in London to establish an organization that would "act as a prophet for all the trades allied to textiles... and will indicate each season what colours, and what shades of each colour, are to be fashionable."[14] The women's editor at one British newspaper praised the nascent council for its focus on the "determination, co-ordination, and propagation of colour tendencies for the fashion and allied trades," which would allow Britain to "fall into line with other countries where there is co-operation between the dyeing, weaving, and fashion distributing trades generally." What would this development mean for the British consumer? "When the scheme is fully organised we will have our toilette colours decided for us, season by season," the editor explained. "The Council will say 'Pink,' and pink we will have to wear, for it will be a matter of some difficulty to procure other shades."[15] Whereas some journalists objected to the prospect of being told to think pink, others saw the new organization as a bulwark against the encroachment of bad taste. "Science . . . has given us vivid colours, flamboyant colours, hundreds of exquisite shades of each and every main colour; it has given us scores of subtle gradations from one shade to another," reported another newspaper, "but, alas, it has not been able to give us the capacity to make perfect use of all this modern chemical kaleidoscope. Fashion and good taste have not yet been rationalised." The British Colour Council would apply logic and planning to the chromatic chaos, and the "average person will welcome this long overdue measure of rationalisation."[16]

In August 1930, the British Colour Council Ltd. was incorporated as a subscription service for the textile and fashion industries. Just as the Textile Color Card Association had aimed to create "American Color for the American People" in a nationalistic wartime breakaway from Paris, the British Colour Council blended Taylorist principles with ethnocentric and imperialistic aims. Foremost, the council aimed "to place colour determination for the British Empire in British hands, and thus provide members . . . with early and authoritative information on colour tendencies." Color research would be conducted "in the fashion centres of the world," interpreted for the benefit of British manufacturers, and circulated to them as color cards and trend reports. With this information in hand, member companies could better plan their color choices. Like its American counterpart, the British Colour Council aimed to reduce the risks associated with selecting colors for use in fashion merchandise.[17]

From the start, the London-based British Colour Council had strong ties to manufacturers in West Yorkshire and Lancashire, bridging the famous divide between the industrial north and the cosmopolitan south. Lord Ebury lent the prestige of his peerage to the endeavor through his association with the Army and Navy Co-Operative Society, a retailer established in 1871 to supply military families with household necessities. Founding members from the West Yorkshire woolen and worsted industries included representatives from the Bradford Dyers' Association, the Leeds & District Worsted Dyers' Association, and several textile factories: Prospect Mills in Keighley, Salts Mill in Saltaire, and Lister & Company in Bradford. Founders from the Manchester cotton industry included the directors of the Calico Printers' Association and the British Cotton & Wool Dyers' Association. The London contingent had Martin de Selincourt, an experienced cloth and silk merchant who directed the Drapery Trust; Edward H. Symonds, managing director of the fashion house Reville, dressmakers to Queen Mary and a slew of princesses; and George James Bell, managing director of the rayon giant Courtaulds. An assortment of leather, hosiery, silk, and thread manufacturers and retailers from elsewhere in England and Scotland filled out the ranks.[18]

One observer, in a letter to the *Manchester Guardian*, believed that the British Colour Council would help northern textile mills overcome their "inferiority complex in the fashion world." Since the days of Louis XIV, France had set the pace in fashion, and its leadership position had been solidified with the rise and triumph of Parisian haute couture in the late-nineteenth century. Paris created the new styles for women's wear, and the rest of the world scrambled to keep up. British textile and garment manufacturers tried to emulate French developments, but it was not easy to second-guess fashion trends, including the next season's colors. As in the United States, mismatched colors resulted in wasteful markdowns and financial losses, which could be eradicated through a concerted effort.

> Manufacturers of dress goods, silk stockings, and knitted wear, where the vagaries of fashion dictate to them, have all suffered through the want of coordination in colour. The waste occasioned through the lack of an authoritative lead is appalling; and any efforts to eliminate this waste and material should be strenuously supported. Fashion in colour and design is a fickle jade, and nobody can define where the "lead" begins; but everybody knows that "something different" is the fundamental need. If this "something different" could be authoritatively handled by a representative body . . . it would be a boon to the fashion trades in women's wear.[19]

In 1931, the British Colour Council appointed Robert F. Wilson (1890–1957), a fellow of the Royal Society of Arts, as its first general manager and secretary. By 1934, Wilson was using the title "art director."[20] Trained at the Nottingham School of Art, Wilson had worked as a color instructor at his alma mater until 1915. After the end of World War I, he had resumed his teaching duties with a special emphasis on color in industry.[21] Now Wilson worked at the British Colour Council's office in Piccadilly, in proximity to the wholesale textile and garment showrooms of the West End, the bespoke tailors of Savile Row, and the shops of Regent Street and Oxford Street. In the thick of London commerce, Wilson set about doing business much like Rorke in her Madison Avenue office on the fringes of the New York garment district. Wilson frequently traveled to the Manchester cotton mills and the Macclesfield silk mills to confer with manufacturers.[22] He also established advisory committees to represent different interest groups, such as the silk trade, the fur trade, and the mercers. Wilson met with the committees weekly to discuss fashion trends and plan color predictions.[23] "The council came into being to create colours which would be fashionable in their seasons. Colour is the greatest influence of fashion," he explained. "Before a firm of silk manufacturers would plan their cards for the season, and their shade of, say, 'cerise,' would be different from that of another company, matching this was difficult. . . . America recognised the difficulty, and a council was formed which has had the effect more or less of standardizing shades of any colour. Our aim is similar."[24]

Under Wilson in May 1931, the British Color Council declared British independence from French color cards by issuing its first color forecast, a shade card for autumn.[25] The card of sixty autumnal shades, with expressive names such as Chianti, Crock o' Gold, and Indian Orange, was heralded by Lord Ebury as "a landmark in the fashion industry." No longer would British manufacturers have to depend on French color predictions. "The British Colour Council forecast," he explained, "has been designed to provide reliable information about fashion colours sufficiently in advance of the season to enable buyers to place their orders in good time with the minimum of risk."[26] One radio broadcast explained, "The French fashions before the war were dyed with German dyes, and so French model frocks and hats were produced from French fabrics and German dyes.... Now there has come into being in Great Britain a British Colour Council, which has just issued its first colour card as a guide to the fashionable shades for next autumn, so that we shall no longer be dependent on cards issued by the French interests."[27]

In a backhanded move, the British Colour Council started to lump the Americans and French together as a threat to the British fashion industries. The Textile Color Card Association, which had been the model, was now a rival. "It has been recognized for some time," Wilson explained in June 1931, "by all interests connected with women's fashions, garments and shoes in this country that cooperative effort will be need to combat France and America."[28] In November 1931, when Yorkshire mill owners asked why the first forecast had sixty colors rather than five, Wilson pointed to the color proliferation in France and the United States. The French color card manufacturers had locked horns with the American Textile Color Card Association in a war of hues. The British Colour Council not only had to combat the "idea that any novelty must come from Paris," but it also "had to fight . . . the American textile colour card organization, founded 16 years ago," which some British manufacturers held in the highest esteem. Despite stiff competition from French and American color forecasters, the British Colour Council attracted members.[29] By 1932, the council had 350 subscribers, including members in Australia and New Zealand, and issued four different shade cards for hosiery, silk, wool, and leather twice a year.[30] But nothing about color prediction was straightforward or unidirectional. As with the Textile Color Card Association, the usual information flow between the Continent and the outlier was reversed when the Paris fashion industry began to copy the British forecasts.[31]

There were other ways in which the British Colour Council paralleled the Textile Color Card Association, which it both emulated and envied. Foremost, it created a handbook of basic colors comparable to the Standard Color Card of America. This reference book was helpful to the apparel designer who needed a precision reference tool when matching the colors of thread, buttons, and fabrics. It took Wilson eighteen months to create the first edition. When he solicited color samples, members sent him eighty different sky blues, sixty whites, and forty blacks. Like Rorke, Wilson sifted through the morass and chose the best example of each basic hue. The *British Colour Council Dictionary of Colour Standards*—known simply as the "British standard colour card"—was published in 1934 and issued as a second edition in 1951. The first edition had 220 staple colors, each illustrated with small strips of dyed silk ribbon pasted onto the folded color card and assigned a unique name and number.[32] In concept and layout, the card was virtually identical to its

American equivalent. Following Rorke's example, Wilson also collaborated with external partners on shade cards for special applications. For example, he worked with the London couturier Victor Stiebel and other members of the Fashion Group of Great Britain to create a cobranded color card for ladies' fashions, and he collaborated with the Rayon and Silk Association to produce shade cards for artificial fiber manufacturers such as British Celanese and Courtaulds.[33] By the late 1930s, the British Colour Council, like its American counterpart, was issuing color forecasts for particular segments of the fashion industries, such as the woolen mills and the menswear manufacturers (Figs. 10.4 and 10.5).[34]

How did the transfer of American color management practices shape the actual colors in the British palette? Edward H. Symonds, one of the founders of the British Colour Council, addressed this question by comparing American and British tastes. The American penchant for brassy colors was well known by fashion authorities around the world, while British consumers preferred subtle tones. Symonds attributed British good taste to the British Colour Council. "We pay a great deal of attention to color blending," he told *Women's Wear Daily*. "We solved this problem through cooperation of all fabric, dress and accessory manufacturers in the British Colour Council. Through this organization we have been able to maintain a color alliance.... It saves millions in mark-downs annually to manufacturers and retailers."[35] Here was American scientific management transferred to British industry, digested, adapted, and publicized as being distinctively British in the major American newspaper for the fashion trades.

Functional Color

Wilson also undertook several projects that distinguished the British Colour Council from the Textile Color Card Association. The first of these, dating from 1938, was the creation of a color card for use by horticulturalists. In New York, Rorke kept her eyes fixed on the fashion trades, steering clear of the natural sciences. American researchers in natural history relied on *Color Standards and Color Nomenclature,* published in 1912 by the Smithsonian ornithologist Robert Ridgway.[36] In Britain, the Royal Horticultural Society commissioned the council to have Wilson create a set of botanical color charts based on the *British Colour Council Dictionary of Colour Standards.* Wilson examined 5,000 species of flowers, and "divided the intense spectrum into 64 separate hues, in order that the slightest variation of hue in different flowers was covered."[37] His research was published as *The Wilson Colour Chart* and was adopted as a standard by the International Horticultural Conference in Berlin in 1938.[38]

Another activity that differentiated the British Colour Council from the Textile Color Card Association was the creation of color schemes for the workplace. In the United States, the application of color psychology to factories and offices was the purview of lighting engineers at the General Electric Company, corporate art directors such as Towle at PPG, and consultants such as Birren. Rorke and the Textile Color Card Association, with their emphasis on fashion,

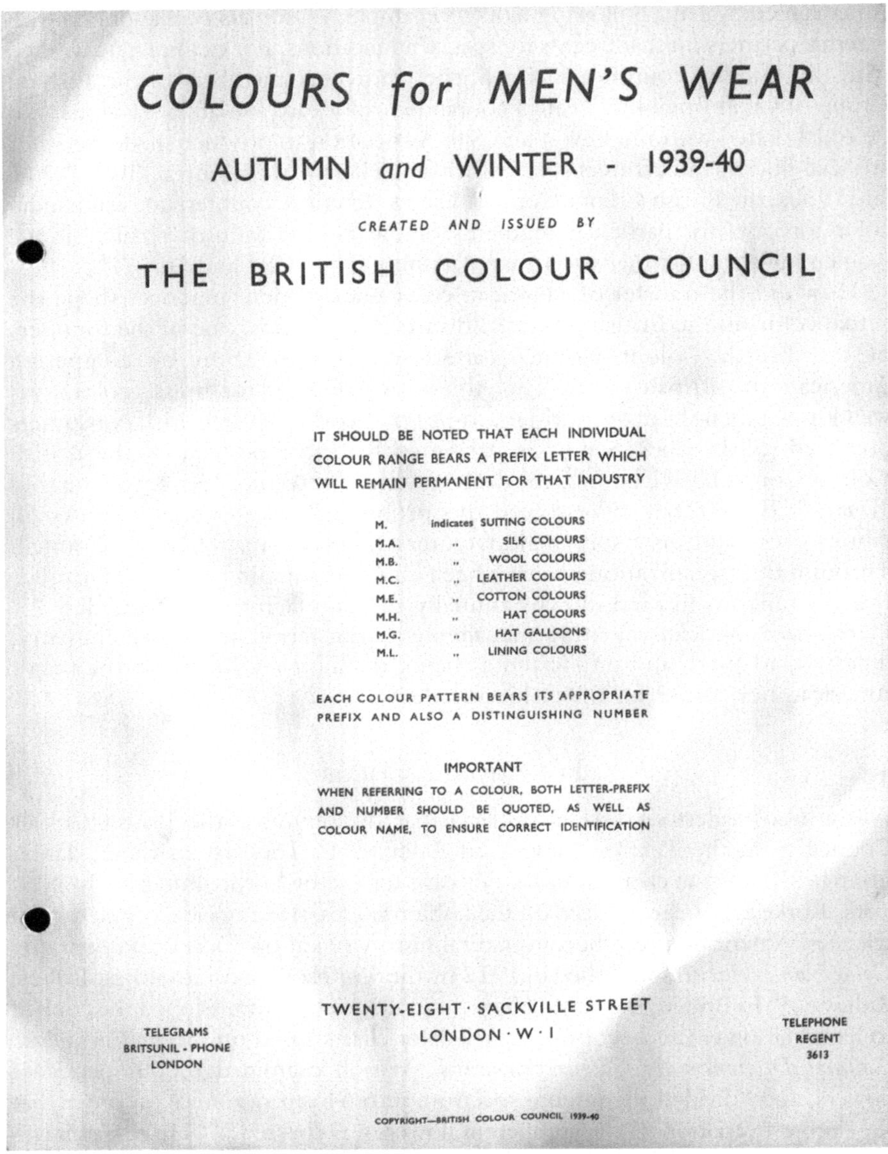

COLOURS for MEN'S WEAR

AUTUMN and WINTER - 1939-40

CREATED AND ISSUED BY

THE BRITISH COLOUR COUNCIL

IT SHOULD BE NOTED THAT EACH INDIVIDUAL COLOUR RANGE BEARS A PREFIX LETTER WHICH WILL REMAIN PERMANENT FOR THAT INDUSTRY

M.	indicates	SUITING COLOURS
M.A.	"	SILK COLOURS
M.B.	"	WOOL COLOURS
M.C.	"	LEATHER COLOURS
M.E.	"	COTTON COLOURS
M.H.	"	HAT COLOURS
M.G.	"	HAT GALLOONS
M.L.	"	LINING COLOURS

EACH COLOUR PATTERN BEARS ITS APPROPRIATE PREFIX AND ALSO A DISTINGUISHING NUMBER

IMPORTANT

WHEN REFERRING TO A COLOUR, BOTH LETTER-PREFIX AND NUMBER SHOULD BE QUOTED, AS WELL AS COLOUR NAME, TO ENSURE CORRECT IDENTIFICATION

TELEGRAMS
BRITSUNIL - PHONE
LONDON

TWENTY-EIGHT · SACKVILLE STREET
LONDON · W · I

TELEPHONE
REGENT
3613

COPYRIGHT—BRITISH COLOUR COUNCIL 1939-40

Fig. 10.4 Seasonal color forecast by The British Color Council, which emulated the Textile Color Card Association's practice

Source: British Colour Council, *Colours for Men's Wear, Autumn and Winter, 1939–40,* Hagley Museum and Library, Accession 2188, Box 233. Courtesy of Hagley Museum and Library.

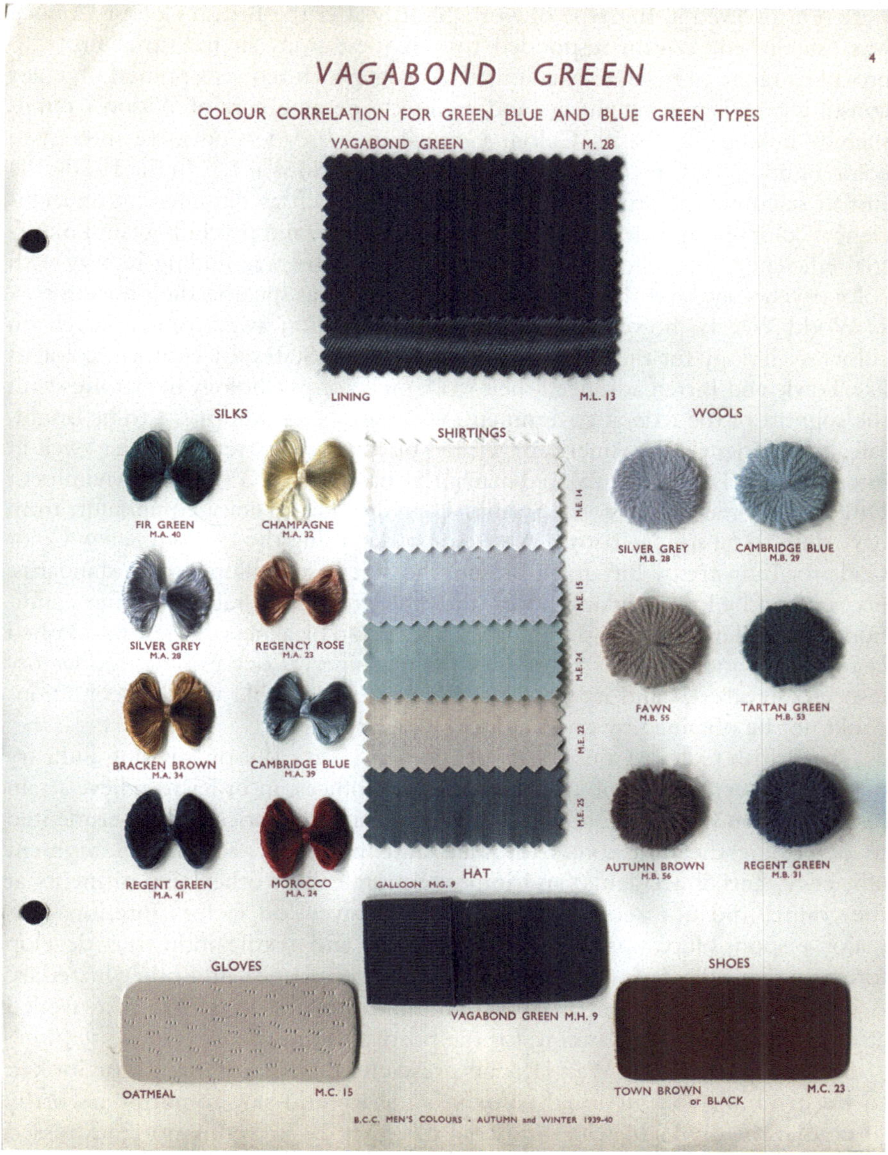

Fig. 10.5 Dressing a man from head to toe

In this page from the menswear forecast for 1939–40, Robert Wilson suggested how British manufacturers, tailors, and retailers could coordinate an entire outfit around the fashionable hue called Vagabond Green.

Source: British Colour Council, *Colours for Men's Wear, Autumn and Winter, 1939–40,* Hagley Museum and Library, Accession 2188, Box 233. Courtesy of Hagley Museum and Library.

were not involved in this type of work. Shortly after the British Colour Council was established, Wilson responded to a request from an industrial firm "to provide a range of machinery colours." As other such requests poured in, color consulting to factory engineers and architects became part of Wilson's remit, thereby linking the British Colour Council to a broader industrial interest in color, lighting, and efficiency that dated back to World War I.[39] In the 1920s, the British scientific literature had addressed topics such as illumination and efficiency, color and health, the psychology of industry, and psychology and industrial efficiency.[40] By the early 1930s, British industry was finding its way with color psychology, and the British Colour Council was spearheading the effort.

World War II, however, diverted British attention away from research on color psychology for the workplace. In the United States, by contrast, colorists like Towle and Birren advanced their work on color psychology in factories with the support of the federal government, which expected war plants to be bright, safe, and efficient. New American factories built with taxpayer dollars had well-lit interiors, pastel walls, and painted machinery based on PPG's Color Dynamics or DuPont's Three-Dimensional Seeing. United States military equipment, from navy ships to oil storage barrels, was color-coded using the DuPont Safety Color Code for Industry by Birren. In Britain, the "increase in illumination standards, necessitated by long working hours, the high production rate and other conditions imposed during the war, emphasised the cold bleakness of the whitewashed factory walls and the drab painting of the machinery," one experienced factory inspector recalled, "and it became apparent that desirable working conditions could not be obtained by good lighting alone."[41]

The British Colour Council stepped forward, with Wilson advising industry on the "correct use of colour in factories and offices, in order to relieve strain resulting from wartime conditions." Wilson visited factories and experimented to determine the best colors for walls and machinery, seeking to augment efficiency, curtail accidents, and improve morale. But other commitments at the council did not allow him to work exclusively on factory interiors. His major responsibility was to help the fashion and textile industries develop forecasts that reflected wartime shortages of dyes, fabrics, and other materials. A color dictionary for interior decoration, conceived in 1938, also needed attention, as did color planning for the postwar home.[42]

Shortly after World War II, one prescient British commentator looked to the triumph of functional color in America and saw something worthy of emulation. In 1946, the industrial designer T. A. Fennemore addressed the Design and Industries Association in London, praising the American chemical companies for advancing the field of functional color. In "this subject of colour application America has been the pioneer," Fennemore said, "and of all the firms in America I think the greatest credit should go to the Dupont Company, who have studied the question most carefully and who have issued some extremely valuable literature on it. The idea of three dimensional seeing, is to use their words, 'to reverse the business of camouflage.'" Although Fennemore did not discuss Birren in connection with DuPont, he acknowledged that the Americans were on to something important with functional color.[43]

In 1946, the British Colour Council made strides with functional color by publishing Wilson's booklet on *Colour and Lighting in Factories and Offices.* In his preface, the architect Wilfred Garrett, who had headed the Factory Inspectorate at the Ministry of Labour during the war, explained that "nearly all workrooms" could be "given internal colour decoration on walls and machines in a way that will provide aesthetic satisfaction and mental invigoration, realised or unrealised, to the persons there at work.... There is much evidence that the demand for colour in factories on the part of workers and employers alike is fast growing to something that may be described as of national significance."[44] As British factories slapped fresh paint on assembly lines in a rush to modernize, there was a repeat of the American experience with the new automotive lacquers in the 1920s. "In too many instances," one factory inspector explained, "the colour schemes applied were haphazard and the effects sometimes bizarre."[45]

To study the best examples of functional color, Wilson went on a whirlwind color tour of the United States and Canada in 1947. In America, he "had the pleasure of meeting Faber Birren, the American specialist on Colour and Lighting." The two colorists exchanged ideas in person, and afterwards, kept "each other informed of the activities in our respective countries." Just outside of Cleveland, Wilson spent three days at Nela Park, the research center for General Electric, where he met the "famous American physicist and authority on Lighting, Matthew Luckiesh."[46] In Boston and Washington, he spoke to researchers at the Massachusetts Institute of Technology and the Bureau of Standards about color science and color standards:

> My talks confirm my opinion that whatever name may be coined—Three Dimensional Seeing, Colour Dynamics, Colour Conditioning—they all really mean the same thing—the use of common sense in colour and lighting in relation to architecture and machinery for the benefit of human beings in a contemporary age.... As I see it now, Britain, through the pioneer work of my Council and those who co-operated with us, can take the initiative on this subject, a subject in which aesthetics and science are partners for the first time since their divorce at the beginning of the industrial era on a recognized large scale.[47]

Wilson saw firsthand how American functional colorists, with their dual emphasis on technology and intuition, created better-illuminated workspaces, and he thus came to believe their methods were worthy of emulation.

After the British Colour Council renewed its commitment to functional color, queries arrived from government and industry around the world. The Australians were new to workplace color, Wilson said, and "their principles and practice followed closely upon that of this country and America." South Africa also "realized the value of this scientific development in social life," sending a delegation to visit the council in London and following up with a large order for *Colour and Lighting in Factories and Offices.* A labor department official from Hong Kong took the booklet back to Asia "in order that factories in that part of the world shall be treated in colour and light according to our principles." Even French style leaders took notice; representatives from the cotton industry of France came knocking.[48]

Building on this momentum, the British Colour Council and the Council of Industrial Design co-sponsored a professional short course on Colour and Lighting in Factories and on Machines, which convened at the Royal Institute of British Architects in London in 1948. Agencies within the British government continued to take an interest in color and the effort to manage it. Along these lines, the Department of Scientific and Industrial Research also participated in the short course, sending representatives from the Building Research Station and the Paint Research Station. In his keynote address, Wilson reflected on the early days of the British Colour Council's involvement with factory colorization and stressed the importance of a methodical approach to architectural color.

> It is now 15 years ago since my Council was first called to advise on colour and lighting in industrial buildings, including the colouring of machinery, and it was brought home to me very forcibly that the mere expression of personal preference was of little value unless backed by scientific reasoning. Since that time I have, on behalf of my Council, advised upon the decoration of new factories and the re-decoration of old ones in many parts of the country.... and it has been a wonderful experience to me to have had the pleasure of working with experts in their own sphere of industry, whose advice was so necessary to the success of my schemes.[49]

Participants in the short course brought different perspectives to bear on the discussion of functional color. The electrical engineer Ralph G. Hopkinson, an illumination expert from the British government's Building Research Station, chided British industry for the slow uptake, but blamed World War II. Having worked at the research laboratories at General Electric from 1934 to 1947, he was a fan of American ingenuity. "The subjective approach to lighting has not had quite the prominence which it deserves in this country. Although the approach which our colleagues in the U.S.A. call 'brightness engineering' received a big impetus here...our preoccupations with the 1939–45 war prevented the development of ideas which were being put forward in the two or three years before the war." The Building Research Station was now on track with illumination studies. "We are conscious of our debt to...the vigorous pioneering efforts of workers in the U.S.A." Like their American counterparts, British illuminating engineers needed to "press hard for the acceptance of the subjective appraisal of a lighting installation" as the only true measure of its success.[50]

Hopkinson credited American innovations in color and lighting as the springboard for experiments underway at the Building Research Station. There, teams of engineers, scientists, and architects worked on practical solutions to illumination challenges, drawing heavily on the research of color scientists in industry, government, and universities. The Building Research Station owed much to "American investigators of the 1915–1930 period," as well as British and European scientists.[51] The architect W. A. Allen, also from the Building Research Station, discussed successful color treatments in factories with reference to "Faber Birren, the American consultant on colour."[52] One specialist on factory interiors explained how machinery could be painted in colors to alleviate eyestrain and serve as a psychological pick-me-up. "The Americans with their usual happy knack of description, have applied the name 'Three Dimensional Seeing' to the principle involved in factory painting, an excellent name which summarises the aim exactly."[53] The proliferation of references to American color pioneers was proof positive that their ideas and practices were making an impact in Britain.

Color Coordination

In the postwar era, major changes to the political economy and to the design profession in Britain expanded the role of public agencies in color management to the detriment of the British Colour Council. Like the Textile Color Card Association, the British Color Council had been established to create and disseminate new knowledge for the benefit of trade, industry, and ultimately, consumers. The impulse that spawned the efficiency movement also gave birth to modern nurturing professions like social work and government agencies for the public welfare. The dramatic wartime expansion of the British government laid the foundation for the birth of the far-reaching welfare state in the postwar years. These transitions affected British color practice.

In the decade after World War II, Wilson spent much of his time expanding the British Colour Council's profile in color psychology and interior decoration. When the council relocated offices from Piccadilly to 13 Portman Square in 1947, one object on prominent display was the mockup for his magnum opus, a large reference book on colors for interior decoration. Wilson had worked on this project since 1938; and in the final push, he was assisted by Betty K. Battersby, the studio director at the council.[54] Battersby conjured up names for colors, taking her inspiration from the world around her—from poetry, flowers, ships, fog, and sunsets.[55] Published in 1949, the *British Colour Council Dictionary of Colours for Interior Decoration* was intended as an investment purchase for art directors in factories that made carpets, curtains, upholstery; pottery, porcelain, enamels, and glassware; stains, paints and varnishes, and wallpaper; and other interior design elements. A companion to the fashion-oriented *British Colour Council Dictionary of Colour Standards*, this hefty three-volume reference set illustrated 378 colors. The council printed 7,500 copies of the first edition of this color "bible," each selling for nearly thirteen pounds.[56]

Wilson also continued his work on functional color. After the publication of *Colour and Lighting in Factories and Offices*, he was the go-to person in Britain for factory engineers and office designers seeking help on color in the workplace. He lectured widely on this subject, warning his audiences that the "lighting and decoration of hospitals as well as factories and schools ... is far too serious a matter to be left in the hands of well-meaning amateurs especially those dear ladies who have been told by some dear friend, or enemy, that they have a 'flair for colour'."[57] Known for his hands-on approach, Wilson never designed a new paint scheme or lighting plan without first visiting the site and standing at the worker's machine or sitting at the desk.[58] Between 1946 and 1956, Wilson prepared more than 500 color and lighting schemes and noticed a definite "change in colour appreciation, brought about by the industrial use of colour." He elaborated: "People working in suitably colourful surroundings in factories and offices are now demanding more colourful surroundings in their homes."[59] In 1953, he published *Colour and Light at Work*, a popular book on color psychology in factories.[60] A further effort to stimulate corporate interest in functional color was an exhibition of Wilson's color schemes for workspaces, including projects for the Shell Research Station at Sittingbourne and for the new Cable & Wireless headquarters at Mercury House in London, at the Portman Square offices.[61]

In 1957, Wilson died at age sixty-eight, and the daily operations of the British Colour Council fell into new hands. This occurred just as the world of color experts was becoming more crowded and competitive. Even before Wilson's passing, observers started to question the usefulness of the British Colour Council. One critic, for example, suggested that the Wilson horticultural chart was too expensive and too complicated for the everyday gardener.[62] While fabric designers in the Yorkshire textile mills still eagerly awaited the seasonal style forecasts of the British Colour Council, a rising tide of independent design thinking was noticeable elsewhere.[63] In many industry segments, art directors and designers—professionals who did not define themselves as color experts per se—increasingly saw color choice as their prerogative.

The new color assertiveness drew sustenance from the growing influence of London authorities on taste and consumption. The British design establishment, represented by the Council of Industrial Design, believed that modernism was the best mechanism for improving the material life of British consumers. Initiatives such as the Britain Can Make It exhibition, organized by the Council of Industrial Design at the Victoria and Albert Museum in 1946, and the larger Festival of Britain on London's South Bank in 1951 celebrated modern design. The positive public response to the strong palette of the Festival of Britain suggested that consumers were game for imaginative color schemes.[64] A new generation of design consultants saw themselves as cultural authorities whose remit was to shape taste. Many of them came to believe that color selection was the responsibility of the creative individual and his or her creative team. This modus operandi differed from the interactive model of colorists like Rorke and Wilson, who solicited input from the members of their organizations and integrated it into the design of color cards, handbooks, and forecasts.

Architects also gained a voice in the new chromatic order through government initiatives to standardize building components, including paint colors. During the 1930s, numerous paint companies each offered twenty to thirty colors, but the defense economy of World War II limited production to the bare essentials for camouflage, government buildings, and factories. In the postwar era, customers wanted more choice, and paint manufacturers and painting contractors found it difficult to cope with the proliferation of hues. Around this time, innovative new schools built by the Hertfordshire county council—buildings with generous windows and fresh coloring—got people excited about colorful architectural interiors. In response, scientists and architects at the Building Research Station undertook the study of color in buildings. In 1952, the British paint industry, the Royal Institute of British Architects, and the British Colour Council exchanged thoughts on the growing public appetite for color in interior decoration and architecture. The whirlwind of activity pointed to the need for national standards in paint colors, as distinct from the fashion and textile colors created by the British Colour Council.

The British government's Department of Industrial and Scientific Research made a major commitment to architectural color through the Building Research Station and the Paint Research Station. Architects at the building station, in particular, saw color as a means for advancing a reform agenda. When the architect W. A. Allen compared American and British approaches to factory design in 1954, he praised the Americans for their ingenious single-story factories with flexible open spaces but was less sanguine when it came to color:

> One curious weakness in American practice is the uncolourful colouring. Here in Britain we are a long way ahead in logic and technique, and the oddness of it lies in the fact that if ever a place needed good colour treatment it is the American near-windowless factory. They just have no conception of using a palette which includes strong, refreshing colours, nor do they have any idea of how to make colour assist visual efficiency of comfort, or how to strike the different character required for, say, a steelworks or a cotton mill.[65]

Allen had attended the 1948 London short course that celebrated Color Dynamics and Three-Dimensional Seeing, so what accounts for his change of heart? Why were British colorists like Allen turning away from American methods for color management? An article in the *Manchester Guardian* helps us to fathom the new attitude among British architects such as Allen:

> One of the most significant developments in colour scheming in this country in recent years has been the advent of the selective scheme; that is, the use of different colours on different walls. It all began 30 years ago in Scandinavia

> when designers tried painting, say, a wall receiving a strong sunlight for most of the day, with a dark tone to reduce glare, while the window wall, being the darkest, was painted brighter to reduce brightness contrast."[66]

As previously, British color practice was influenced by multiple information flows. Aesthetic and technical information from northern Europe now intersected with transatlantic streams, and everything was filtered through the state. British colorists had a deep well from which to draw, and American achievements may have been downplayed in the drive to establish a unique European identity in color practice.

The push for British standards in paint colors came to a head in 1953. That year, the Ministry of Education sponsored Archrome, a set of paint colors for school buildings, calibrated according to the Munsell system. This successful endeavor encouraged the government to consider standardized colors for other types of buildings. In 1955, a collective effort by the paint industry, the Royal Institute of British Architects, the Building Research Station, and the Paint Research Station folded the Archrome colors into a larger palette. The British Standards Institution adopted the new palette of 101 chips as *British Standard 2660: 1955 Colours for Building and Decorative Paints.* Although it had been created by architects, BS 2660 eventually met favor with industrial designers.[67]

Architects at the Building Research Station played a central role in the creation of this national standard. As the architect responsible for the technical work on BS 2660, Gloag was also a critic of the color establishment as embodied by the British Colour Council. A proponent of the top-down modernism of Piet Mondrian, Le Corbusier, and the Council of Industrial Design, Gloag believed that color was too important a topic to relegate to manufacturers and their trade associations. It was the ethical responsibility of British design leaders—the nation's architects and interior designers—to agree on basic colors and collectively work out the requirements of a palette that would meet the nation's needs. For Gloag, BS 2660 demonstrated how scientific collaboration among experts could advance the common good.

In *Design* magazine, the official organ of the Council of Industrial Design, Gloag and his fellow architect Michael Keyte, a former colleague at the Building Research Station, discussed the need for a disciplined approach to color selection.

> In the past, designers had things made to order in special colours; today they usually choose from a wide variety of mass produced articles, each with its own colour, or limited range of colours, pre-determined by the manufacturer. Quite often these ranges are intended to cover sales direct to the public as well as through professional designers, and with so wide and various a market to assess, it is not surprising that manufacturers have trouble in deciding what colours to offer, or that each tends to have different ideas from the next.[68]

The result was a repeat of the color chaos that had plagued the American industry in the first part of the century.

One way to overcome this problem was to design a master palette that worked across a range of consumer products. The only extant proprietary scheme of this type came from the United States: it was the *House and Garden* Color Program coordinated by the consultant Faber Birren. Consumers could buy furnishings, appliances, and household accessories in the matching *House and Garden* proprietary colors, but the British architects Gloag and Keyte were unimpressed. “This kind of uniformity, . . . when based on a small number of colours, puts a very limited interpretation on relationship, and is too inflexible to be workable on a wide scale or to have a lasting appeal to users.”[69] Gloag and Keyte did not explain that the *House and Garden* palette was based on extensive market research into sales trends. Instead, they simply encouraged the widespread adoption of BS 2660 by architects and designers. Gloag and Keyte were showing their cards as tastemakers who saw it as their duty to dictate color choices.

The introduction of BS 2660 was a turning point in color practice for the British creative industries. It shifted chromatic clout from trade associations to architects and government agencies, and pitted British color practice against American achievements. The British standard was the output of technocrats who believed they had the authority to decide colors on behalf of consumers. As such, the new standard color card embodied the ideology of the social welfare state, which took the reshaping of everyday life for the betterment of the people as one of its major responsibilities. Created by technocrats, BS 2660 was a direct challenge to color management in the private sector as embodied by trade associations such as the Textile Color Card Association and the British Colour Council and by color consultants like Birren. It was the first salvo in an ideological color war.

Economic Color Trends

Faber Birren looked to the global economic recovery of the postwar era and recognized unprecedented opportunity to export his methods around the world. European governments were eager to develop overseas trade with the United States to access American dollars. British factories needed to become more efficient to compete in the world of mass production and had to adjust their products to suit American consumption habits. From the late 1950s onward, Birren extended the reach of American Color Trends across the globe. “It should be recognized that while colour preferences may vary from region to region,” he wrote in a promotional booklet on *International Colour Research*, “the same human motivations that rule colour choice are universal in character and will answer to the basic principles of research.” New offices were created to assist clients in Australia, Austria, Belgium, Canada, Denmark, France, Germany, Italy, the Netherlands, New Zealand, Norway, Sweden, Switzerland, South Africa, and the United Kingdom.[70]

In 1959, Birren joined forces with Eric P. Danger, a British marketing specialist who had worked in the export trade, to establish Economic Colour

Trends Ltd., a color and marketing consultancy in London. A few years earlier when a paint company had approached Danger for color advice, the latter found "so little information about colour and marketing that he began a prolonged study of the subject which led to working with Faber Birren." The aim was to adapt the methods and techniques of American Color Trends to the British scene.[71] Years later, Danger went solo as a color consultant using techniques he had learned from Birren: "I am a marketing and market research specialist and I have adapted Birren's methods to British markets and market conditions.... The essential feature of the service that I offer is research. I am not an interior decorator, or designer, and my function is to offer practical advice to management, based on research, and to eliminate guesswork and personal preferences."[72]

By this time, American Color Trends was the leading color consultancy to managers in corporate America. Birren's functional color work for the DuPont Company and his trend forecasts of color for interior design and home furnishings for *House and Garden* magazine were the most sophisticated examples of American color research. His impressive list of American accounts also included General Electric, the Hoover Company, Minnesota Mining & Manufacturing Company (3M), the Monsanto Chemical Company, the National Lead Company, Schick Incorporated, and Sears, Roebuck & Company. Special assignments had been completed for other industry leaders, including the Kelvinator refrigerator division of American Motors, the Chrysler Corporation, Corning Glass Works, Eastman Chemical Products, Firestone Tire & Rubber, Hotpoint, the Radio Corporation of America (RCA), Reynolds Metals, Sheaffer Pen, and Stanley Tools, and for entities of the federal government such as the U.S. Coast Guard and the U.S. Navy.[73]

American Color Trends and Economic Colour Trends were market research organizations that helped manufacturers and retailers extrapolate likely new color directions from the careful analysis of past trends. Birren had perfected a market-driven, bottom-up approach wherein the patterns that emerged from the quantitative data (from sales records, market observations, consumer polls, and retail sales tests) served as a proxy for consumer tastes. In his view, the market, rather than the tastemaker, was in the driver's seat. A promotional booklet, *Colour Research: A Definition*, explained his business philosophy to potential British clients.[74] Birren's research-driven approach differed from the practices of the typical industrial designer, who selected "colour for its aesthetic value; simply to be different; or because of personal preference." He cautioned British companies against the personal approach to color selection, which could be "very dangerous economically especially where mass markets are concerned."[75]

Before too long, Economic Colour Trends had an impressive roster of British clients. Many British managers appreciated Birren's unique blend of quantitative and qualitative analysis on consumer tastes. The dramatic growth of the plastics industry prompted the Shell Chemical Company to seek his advice on colors "having the widest application and greatest demand in household, industrial and functionally thermoplastic mouldings."[76] Lewis Berger, a London paint maker affiliated with the Sherwin-Williams Company of Cleveland, Ohio, asked him to predict "certain colours as winners for 1960."[77] Richards Tiles invited him to address a group of Manchester manufacturers on how the "scientific application of colour in industry had been shown to reduce accidents and absenteeism and had improved production and the quality of work." To this audience, Birren presented a basic lesson on functional color, citing examples from 350 companies that had applied color to the shop floor to eliminate eyestrain, reduce absences, and thereby increase output.[78]

By 1960, Birren was the color darling of the British press. He wrote the foreword to Robert Wilson's book, *Colour in Industry Today: A Practical Book on the Functional Use of Color*, published posthumously.[79] His work on color psychology in household furnishings and ladies' fashions reached British consumers through popular magazines such as *Home*, *Woman*, and *Woman's Illustrated*.[80] One journalist described him as a "gentle, unassuming American whom you might take for a moderately successful economist."[81] With three decades of consulting experience under his belt, Birren was a skilled diplomat who understood the value of compromise. He analyzed data and made suggestions, rather than laying down color mandates. His recommendations were intended as directional tools for management. Managers, in turn, had the prerogative to decide if they would share his color reports with their creative teams.

The success of Economic Colour Trends "raised the hackles" of the new British color establishment, which saw the American free-market approach as a threat to their state-sanctioned authority. In the July 1961 issue of *Design* magazine, the Council of Industrial Design pitted two of its experts, H. L. "Bill" Gloag and the industrial designer F. C. Ashford, against Birren in a color forum. Gloag now directed research on architectural color at the Building Research Station and had just written a new report on *Colouring in Factories*. He also never failed to cite BS 2660 as one of his major achievements. Ashford was a senior industrial designer who had worked in Raymond Loewy's London office before World War II. In 1947, he launched his own design firm, Scott-Ashford Associates, and taught industrial engineering design at the Royal College of Art from 1956 to 1959.[82] The debate in *Design* highlights some of the differences that played out in the turf war between American and British colorists. Birren favored a research-driven approach, while Gloag and Ashford favored top-down expert analysis. Birren, who was concerned with "large volume merchandise sold to average people," sought to "measure the direction" in which color was "going."[83] Gloag and Ashford were tastemakers who were trying to shape consumers' color choices.

Birren told *Design* that his "research organization" was interested in the factors that "motivate" consumers to buy merchandise in certain colors.[84] Over the years, Birren had refined his methods to align with the exciting new field of motivation research. Prominent motivation research consultants, such as Ernest

Dichter of the Institute for Motivational Research in Croton-on-Hudson, New York, sought to understand the psychological reasons why consumers wanted certain things. Dichter studied consumer tastes, gathered specific information from focus groups, analyzed all of this data using psychological theories, and made recommendations about emerging trends to management.[85] Similarly, Birren analyzed his clients' sales records and drew comparisons with similar products to predict the likely color preferences of consumers.

In the *Design* debate, Birren used the example of portable typewriters to illustrate his methods. If a typewriter manufacturer asked him to "find out who buys a portable typewriter," Birren would study their sales records. If his research showed that businessmen bought 40 percent of portable typewriters, Birren would recommend a grey utilitarian palette. If the manufacturer wanted to promote portable typewriters to housewives and their teenage daughters, Birren would explain the use of color in the home, which would be "psychologically quite different."[86] Pink and turquoise would be appropriate colors "regardless of any functional thing, because they'll sell better." The choice of pastel colors had little to do with "visual efficiency" but hinged entirely on the gender dimensions of color (as discussed in Chapter 4 by Dominique Grisard). Western culture had long associated women with pastel colors, including pink, and Birren saw it as his job to translate this cultural predilection into color predictions that would sell more goods to this ostensible group of consumers.[87]

Backed by the authority of the Building Research Station, Gloag scoffed at Birren's "empirical" and "common sense" methods and pressed for the "scientific knowledge of colour itself." He referred to color standards, a subject close to his heart. Weren't the 101 scientifically selected paint colors on the BS 2660 shade card sufficient for the British market? Why were more choices needed?[88]

In keeping with his reputation as a soft-spoken economist, Birren calmly argued for the importance of variety, choice, and change. Shifting consumer preferences were inevitable, and no designer worth their salt would rely on a single set of standard colors. Colorists who understood the fashion system, such as Rorke and Wilson, knew that persistence and change co-existed in the style industries, and color management was all about adjusting to this reality. Basic or standard colors had a lifespan of about seven to ten years, and fashion colors changed with the seasons. The "only permanent thing is change itself," Birren quietly explained. "So you see, when you attempt to set up a line of standards, it frankly would be far short of what creative men will want to work with."[89] Gloag saw this as sacrificing scientific precision "for fashion, for inter-trade competition." Birren had the last word, and set the record straight by returning to the portable typewriter. "No, Mr. Gloag, not at all. We will still make the grey machine, but we will also make the pink and the turquoise. We are forced to do it. We can't evade it, because the manufacturer's primary purpose is not to improve human vision, it's to sell typewriters."[90]

Why Clashes Matter

The Anglo-American turf dispute did not end with the 1961 debate in *Design* magazine. Birren and Danger continued to collaborate for many years, at least until Economic Colour Trends wound up in 1976. Back in the United States, Birren continued to serve as guru for the *House and Garden* Color Program and remained America's leading color consultant into the 1980s. Gloag carried on his crusade within the Council of Industrial Design. Shortly after the Advisory Committee on Colour and Industrial Design issued its first position statement in 1966, Gloag and his compatriots used *Design* as a platform to argue that color was the "missing link in design training" and to advocate for a coordinated approach to color selection for product design and architecture.

> Few designers working in industry have the knowledge and experience required in the manufacture of colour co-ordinated products. Some colour consultants offer advice based on fashion trends, sales results or hunch, and while this may be valuable in certain fields, it has little to do with the functional aims of co-ordination. The CoID will be glad to put manufacturers in touch with the few consultants who possess the requisite skills, but in the meantime the need for training is becoming acute.[91]

We do not know if Birren read these barbed remarks or how he might have reacted to them, but the British Colour Council was not amused. In a 1968 letter to *Design*, executive director Hugh H. Muirhead reproached the Council of Industrial Design and Gloag for overlooking the British Colour Council. By this time, the British Colour Council had 3,000 member firms in a cross section of industry. "The blunt truth is that while colour has become widely accepted as the most important sales factor for an increasing range of products, due largely to the work of the Council and its members, we are still a long way from the situation where the requirements of say, paint, carpets, vitreous ware, vinyl tiles and textiles for a standard range of co-ordinating colours can be met by the issue of a single range." Muirhead lamented the "astonishing dismissal of all existing knowledge and experience on this subject," including the work of the British Colour Council.[92]

Throughout the 1960s, the British Colour Council had continued to advise the textile, fashion, and interior decoration trades, mainly through forecasts and dictionaries. However, the administrative changes of the previous decade, combined with the economic struggles and the decline of its major clientele, the British textile industry, created challenges for the organization. After Wilson's death, functional color had been put on the back burner. The production of large color dictionaries, a tradition established when the textile industry had been desperate for good British reference materials, took precedent. In the 1960s, the British Colour Council undertook to create three new dictionaries—one on interior decoration, another on wool, and a third on cotton and man-made fibers—but the mismanagement of these projects, combined with the troubles of the British textile industry, led to the council's insolvency. In 1970, the British Colour Council sold a mere 743 subscriptions in Britain and 431 subscriptions abroad, which did not produce sufficient income to pay for the dictionaries.[93] After failing to reestablish a sound financial position, the foundering British Colour Council merged with the Council of Industrial Design, which then spent much of the 1970s deliberating the proper place of color practice in British design. The merger was not easy since the British Colour Council mainly focused on fashion forecasting and the scope of the Council of Industrial Design was mainly product design.[94]

As the Council of Industrial Design attempted to find its way with color, tastemakers tried to steer the ship in different directions.[95] Dutton worried about an American invasion; Gloag was concerned to preserve the color authority of the state. A third British perspective—that of Robin Darwin, a great-grandson of the eminent Victorian scientist Charles Darwin—was more sympathetic to the market-driven approach of Birren.[96] This Darwin was a visionary arts administrator who directed the Royal College of Art in South Kensington from 1948 to 1971 and made it into a world-class institution.[97] Like Birren, Darwin was wary of a color technocracy and favored freedom of expression, albeit for his own reasons. As a member of the Council of Industrial Design, he sized up the new Advisory Committee on Colour and Industrial Design, founded at the behest of the Royal Institute of British Architects and the Society of Industrial Artists and Designers, "with a view to the rationalisation and co-ordination of colour in factory made products, such as carpets, tiles, linoleum and vinyl products." In a private letter of 1966, Darwin expressed concern:

> This seems to me on all counts to be very dangerous. With the possible exception of the Swedes, the English have the most underdeveloped sense of colour of any European country and this is primarily due to laziness. If an over-simplified range of colours is brought out by an official body for use by industry, by architects and designers and the like it can only result in encouraging them to think even less. Gone will be all the "clashes" which primarily make the study of colour interesting.[98]

Dutton and Gloag loathed the contrasts and clashes that made color a subjective field. Gloag in particular was keen to create an official box into which color subjectivity could be squeezed. By virtue of their backgrounds from a multiethnic society, American color consultants appreciated the value of variety and difference.[99] A harbinger of the anything-goes future, Birren understood taste as it bubbled up from the street. Darwin capped the debate with a stinging critique of British color preferences and product design, offering a perspective that foreshadowed postmodern color practice. The pioneer color revolutionaries of midcentury—Rorke and Wilson—would have knowingly smiled. No one could limit the use of color and no one could dictate its applications. At best, one could only hope to understand the highly subjective nature of color and to harness its emotional qualities for the benefit of sales—and the delight of consumers.

Notes

1. "Colour Research in Question," Design 151 (July 1961): 59.
2. James Noel White, Deputy Director, Council of Industrial Design, "Statement by the Council of Industrial Design's Advisory Committee on Colour and Industrial Design," January 14, 1966, in folder: Advisory Committee on Colour and Industrial Design, Design Council Archive, Design Archives, University of Brighton, Brighton, UK [hereafter cited as DCA–UB].
3. Michael T. Saler, *The Avant-Garde in Interwar England: Medieval Modernism and the London Underground* (New York, 1999), 166–67.
4. Norbert Dutton to James Noel White, "CoID Colour & Industrial Design Committee: Future Programme," February 5, 1966, in folder: Advisory Committee on Colour and Industrial Design, DCA–UB.
5. Ibid.
6. Victoria de Grazia, *Irresistible Empire: America's Advance through Twentieth-Century Europe* (Cambridge, MA, 2005). On the Americanization literature and the revisionist approach, see Per Lundin and Thomas Kaiserfeld, eds., *The Making of European Consumption: Facing the American Challenge* (New York, 2015), and the various outputs of the German Historical Institute's Transatlantic Perspectives project, including Jan Logemann and Mary Nolan, eds., "More Atlantic Crossings? European Voices and the Postwar Atlantic Community," *Bulletin of the German Historical Institute*, suppl. 10 (2014): 1–182.
7. Unless otherwise noted, the material in this section is drawn from Regina Lee Blaszczyk, *The Color Revolution* (Cambridge, MA, 2012), which offers a comprehensive analysis of color management practices in the American creative industries from 1830 to 1970.
8. Faber Birren, "I Am Weary of Art (An Essay)," 104, in box 2, bound volume: Some More Essays, MssCol 308, Faber Birren Papers, Manuscripts and Archives Division, New York Public Library, New York.
9. Faber Birren, "Color Work Made Easy," *Inland Printer* 95 (May 1935): 62–63.
10. For another discussion of American and British forecasting methods, see Regina Lee Blaszczyk, "The Rise of Color Forecasting in the United States and Great Britain," in *The Fashion Forecasters: A Hidden History of Color and Trend Prediction*, ed. Regina Lee Blaszczyk and Ben Wubs (London, forthcoming 2018).
11. Blaszczyk, *Color Revolution*, 187–88.
12. "The Drapers' Parliament," *Drapers' Organiser* (June 1928): 37.
13. "Colour and Fashions," *Yorkshire Post*, July 2, 1929.
14. "Council of Colour Prophets," *Nottingham Evening Post*, October 3, 1929 (quotation); "Colour Factor in Fashion," *Yorkshire Post*, October 10, 1929.
15. "British Colour Control," *Derby Daily Telegraph*, June 8, 1929.
16. A. E. Tomlinson, "Colours a la Code: The Future of Rationalised Taste," *Devon and Exeter Gazette*, July 31, 1929.
17. Blaszczyk, *Color Revolution*, 78; British Colour Council Ltd., Certificate of Incorporation, No. 250217, August 16, 1930, in folder: British Colour

Council Finance Section, DCA–UB; "Guidance on Colour Questions," *Manchester Guardian*, March 31, 1931 (quotations). Each subscriber to the British Colour Council paid an annual fee of just over £5.

18. Julia Finch, "Army & Navy Brand Consigned to History," *Guardian*, September 29, 2004; British Colour Council, Certificate of Incorporation, 4–8.
19. H. B. Nicolas, Chorltonville, to Editor, "Co-ordination in Colour: Benefits from the New Council," *Manchester Guardian*, October 11, 1929.
20. "Colour Council: Nottingham Artist Appointed General Manager," *Yorkshire Post*, January 27, 1931; "Colour Council: The Appointment of Mr. R. F. Wilson," *Yorkshire Post*, February 3, 1931; "Standardised Colours: Card and 'Dictionary' Issued," *Yorkshire Post*, June 28, 1934.
21. "Colour Council: Nottingham Artist Appointed General Manager"; "Mr. R. F. Wilson," *Journal of the Royal Society of Arts* 105 (March 1, 1957): 302.
22. "Cotton and Colour," *Manchester Guardian*, November 2, 1932.
23. "Autumn Colours," *Yorkshire Post*, March 4, 1931.
24. "Shoe-Soles in Colour: British Fashion Dictator Speaks: Standardising of Shades," *Nottingham Evening Post*, June 19, 1931.
25. "Autumn Colour Schemes: Crock O' Gold and Indian Orange," *Nottingham Evening Post*, May 1, 1931.
26. "Colour Card for Britain: 'Landmark in Fashion Industry': Autumn Forecast," *Yorkshire Post*, May 2, 1931.
27. "Why Not British Dyes? Dr. Levinstein's Talk on Colour and Fashion," *Nottingham Evening Post*, June 11, 1931.
28. "Town and Country Notes," *Northampton Mercury*, June 26, 1931.
29. "Textile Designs and Modern Spirit: Mr. R. F. Wilson on Colour Difficulties," *Yorkshire Post*, November 19, 1931.
30. "The British Colour Council," *Manchester Guardian*, January 6, 1932; "British Colours for Spring," *Manchester Guardian*, January 28, 1932; "British Colours: Widespread Foreign Adoption," *Manchester Guardian*, September 22, 1932.
31. "The Colour Council," *Manchester Guardian*, January 9, 1934.
32. "The British Standard Colour Card," *Journal of the Royal Society of Arts* 82 (December 29, 1933): 200–202; "A Dictionary of Colours," *Manchester Guardian*, July 7, 1934; *The British Colour Council Dictionary of Colour Standards* (London, 1934), item 228, acc. 2188: Papers of the Inter-Society Color Council, Hagley Museum and Library, Wilmington, DE [hereafter cited as ISCC–HML].
33. Clipping, "Eight Colors Selected for British Promotion," *Women's Wear Daily* (New York), May 19, 1938, in AAD/1994/1/8, Scrapbook: American Press Clippings, Victor Stiebel Press Cutting Albums, in Archive of Art and Design, National Art Library, Victoria and Albert Museum, London [hereafter cited as AAD]; "British Agree on Standardization of Knit Rayon Colors," *Women's Wear Daily* (New York), August 24, 1939.
34. British Colour Council, *Wool Card, Spring and Summer 1939* (London, 1939); British Colour Council, *Wool Card, Autumn and Winter 1939–1940* (London, 1939), both in item 232, ISCC–HML; and British Colour Council, *Colours for Men's Wear: Autumn and Winter 1939–40* (London, 1939), item 233, acc. 2188, ISCC–HML.
35. "British-U.S. Interchange of Abilities Urged," *Women's Wear Daily* (New York), June 29. 1936.

36. Robert Ridgway, *Color Standards and Color Nomenclature* (Washington, DC, 1912).
37. Robert F. Wilson, "The Function and Use of Colour," in "Colour and Lighting in Factories and on Machines: Report of Course Held at the Royal Institute of British Architects in November, 1948," 54, in AAD/6/358/1992, Council of Industrial Design Series, Paul Reilly Papers, AAD.
38. *The Wilson Colour Chart* (London, 1938), in Colour Reference Library, Royal College of Art, London [hereafter cited as CRL–RCA].
39. Wilson, "The Function and Use of Colour," 53.
40. "Colour and Lighting in Factories and on Machines," 88.
41. George P. Barnett, "Preface to the Second Edition," in *Colour Schemes for the Interior Decoration of Factories and Offices*, 2nd ed. (London, 1956), 5, CRL–RCA.
42. "Mr. R. F. Wilson," 302.
43. Transcript from meeting of the Design and Industries Association, May 9, 1946, and T. A. Fennemore, ["The Importance of the Use of Colour in Factories"], May 9, 1946, pp. 2–3 (quotation), both in box 4, Collection 3–1983: T. A. Fennemore Papers, AAD.
44. A. W. Garrett, "Preface to the First Edition 1946," in *Colour Schemes for the Interior Decoration of Factories and Offices*, 2nd ed., 7; "Colour for Output," *Yorkshire Post and Leeds Mercury*, January 15, 1946. The first edition of *Colour and Lighting in Factories and Offices* (London, 1946) has been difficult to locate.
45. Blaszczyk, *Color Revolution*, chap. 5; Barnett, "Preface to the Second Edition," 5.
46. Robert F. Wilson, "Introductory Paper," in "Color and Lighting in Factories and on Machines," 3.
47. Ibid.
48. Ibid.
49. Ibid., 2–3.
50. R. G. Hopkinson, "Brightness, Contrast and Glare," in "Colour and Lighting in Factories and on Machines," 38; "Obituary: Professor Ralph Hopkinson," *Independent*, June 27, 1994.
51. Hopkinson, "Brightness, Contrast and Glare," 39.
52. W. A. Allen, "The Development of a Factory Colour Treatment," in "Colour and Lighting in Factories and on Machines," 19.
53. H. Grimshaw, "Colour and Lighting on Machinery," in "Colour and Lighting in Factories and on Machines," 59.
54. "Dictionary of Colour," *Manchester Guardian*, May 1, 1947.
55. "Creating Colours," *Northern Daily Mail,* January 28, 1953.
56. "Dictionary of Colour," *Manchester Guardian*, April 5, 1950; "Colours to Book," *Evening Telegraph* (Dundee), April 8, 1950; *The British Colour Council Dictionary of Colours for Interior Decoration*, 3 vols. (London, 1949), CRL–RCA.
57. See, for example, "Brighter Factories," *Yorkshire Post*, March 29, 1946; "Quiet Colors in Noisy Factories," *Derby Daily Telegraph*, May 11, 1949; "Dear Ladies with Flair for Colour," *Daily Mail* (Hull) April 27, 1950 (quotation).
58. Kathleen A. Battersby [sic], "Common Sense in Industrial Colour Schemes," *Manchester Guardian*, May 29, 1959.
59. Robert F. Wilson, "Introduction," in *Colour Schemes for the Interior Decoration of Factories and Offices*, 2nd ed., 3.

60. Robert F. Wilson, *Colour and Light at Work* (London, 1953).
61. "Colour for Industrialists," *Manchester Guardian*, January 17, 1956.
62. S. J. B., "The R.H.S. Colour Chart," *Manchester Guardian*, February 6, 1954.
63. Arthur J. P. Walsh and Barbara Walsh, interview by author, Burnsall, West Yorkshire, England, May 3, 2014. Arthur Walsh was the managing director at Abraham Moon and Sons, Ltd., a woolen mill in Guiseley, Leeds, from 1953 to 1989.
64. Patrick J. Maguire and Jonathan M. Woodham, eds., *Design and Cultural Politics in Post-war Britain: The "Britain Can Make It" Exhibition of 1946* (London, 1997); Barry Turner, *Beacon for Change: How the 1951 Festival of Britain Shaped the Modern Age* (London, 2011); Cheryl Buckley, *Designing Modern Britain* (London, 2007); Jonathan M. Woodham, *Twentieth Century Design* (New York, 1997); Design Archives, University of Brighton, Designing Britain, 1945–1975: The Visual Experience of Post-War Society, www.vads.ac.uk/learning/designingbritain.
65. W. A. Allen, "Design and Logic in Industrial Buildings: United States Can Teach a Lesson in Adaptability," *Manchester Guardian*, April 5, 1954.
66. John Butterworth, "The Use of Colour in Building," *Manchester Guardian*, September 25, 1956.
67. *Forum 3: Colour: Co-Ordination for Ranges for Buildings* (London, 1961), in folder: Advisory Committee on Colour and Industrial Design, DCA–UB; *British Standard 2660: 1955, Colours for Building and Decorative Paints* (London, [1955]), in folder: The Design Centre, Berger Paint Display Exhibition, DCA–UB; Derek Senior, "Work in Hand at the Building Research Station," *Manchester Guardian*, April 6, 1954.
68. Bill Gloag and Michael Keyte, "Colour Co-Ordination for the Manufacturer and User," *Design* 123 (March 1959): 35.
69. Ibid.
70. *International Colour Research* (New York, n.d.), [11], box 7, series I, Group 1567, Faber Birren Papers, Manuscripts and Archives, Sterling Memorial Library, Yale University, New Haven, CT [hereafter cited as FB–YU].
71. Economic Colour Trends Ltd., *Colour Research, Marketing, Packaging, Evaluation, Services Offered, Facilities Available* (London, n.d.); leaflet, "Using Colour to Sell by Eric P. Danger," [1968], both in folder: The Design Centre, Berger Paint Display Exhibition, DCA–UB.
72. E. P. Danger, "The Use of Colour Research: Packaging Assessment," International Colour Research, London, n.d., file g1739, box 919, British American Tobacco Collection, Truth Tobacco Industry Documents, University of California, San Francisco, CA, https://www.industrydocumentslibrary.ucsf.edu/tobacco.
73. *International Colour Research*, [2, 4].
74. *Colour Research: A Definition* (London, n.d.) has been difficult to locate. It is discussed at length in "Colour Research in Question," *Design* 151 (July 1961): 57–60.
75. "Colour Research in Question," 57.
76. "Shell's New Colour Service for Plastics," *Guardian*, February 6, 1962.
77. Eugenie Fordham, "The Importance of Colour," *Guardian*, May 6, 1960.
78. "Works Accidents Cut by Use of Colour," *Manchester Guardian*, January 13, 1961.

79. Robert F. Wilson, *Colour in Industry Today: A Practical Book on the Functional Use of Colour* (London, 1960).
80. "Find Yourself in Whose Hue," *Home* (London), November 1959; Marjorie Proops, "The Colour in Your Life," *Woman's Illustrated* (London), August 13, 20, and 27, 1960; "Meet Your Colour Mate," *Woman* (London), October 15, 1960; "Which Is the Colour for You?," *Woman*, November 5, 1960, clippings in Group 1567, Series I, Box 3, FB–YU.
81. Fordham, "The Importance of Colour."
82. "Colour Research in Question," 57; H. L. Gloag, *Colouring in Factories*, Factory Building Studies No. 8 (London, 1961).
83. "Colour Research in Question," 58.
84. Ibid.
85. Stefan Schwarzkopf and Rainer Gries, eds., *Ernest Dichter and Motivation Research: New Perspectives on the Making of Post-war Consumer Culture* (New York, 2010).
86. "Colour Research in Question," 58.
87. Ibid., 60.
88. Ibid., 59
89. Ibid.
90. Ibid., 60.
91. "Colour—The Missing Link in Design Training," *Design* 227 (November 1967): 17. See also Susan Forsyth and John E. Blake, "A Co-ordinated Approach to Colour," *Design* 227 (November 1967): 36–38; H. L. Gloag, "Colour Co-ordination Applied to Materials," *Design* 227 (November 1967): 39–42. On the end of Economic Colour Trends, see *London Gazette*, May 21, 1976.
92. Hugh H. Muirhead, "Colour Co-ordination and the BCC," *Design* 231 (March 1968): 65.
93. The demise of the British Colour Council is documented in folder: British Colour Council, Finance Section, DCA–UB. For the number of subscriptions, see "The British Colour Council," [1971], [1].
94. See, for example, "Advisory Committee on Colour and Industrial Design," October 28, 1970 in folder: Advisory Committee on Colour and Industrial Design, DCA–UB; Design Council, Colour Advisory Committee, "Sixth meeting of the committee held on 5 September 1974," in folder: Design Council Advisory Committee on Colour Minutes 1973–74, DCA–UB.
95. For criticisms of the Council of Industrial Design, see Buckley, *Designing Modern Britain* and Woodham, *Twentieth Century Design*.
96. "New Art College Head," *Yorkshire Evening Post*, September 1, 1947.
97. Henrietta Goodden, *Robin Darwin: Visionary Educator and Painter* (London, 2015).
98. Robin Darwin to P. Trevor-Roper, London, January 26, 1966, in folder: Advisory Committee on Colour and Industrial Design, DCA–UB.
99. On the importance of cultural diversity to product design for American consumer society, see Regina Lee Blaszczyk, *Imagining Consumers: Design and Innovation from Wedgwood to Corning* (Baltimore, 2000); and Regina Lee Blaszczyk, *American Consumer Society, 1865–2005: From Hearth to HDTV* (Hoboken, NJ, 2009).

CHAPTER 11

Modeurop: Using Color to Unify the European Shoe and Leather Industry

Ingrid Giertz-Mårtenson

It is a cold day in Zürich, Switzerland, in February 1981. In one of the big meeting rooms of the elegant Hotel Intercontinental, tables with white tablecloths are arranged near the windows. Colorful leather samples, all approximately 20 × 30 cm, are laid out in groups on the tables: dark browns, medium browns, reddish browns, beiges, off whites, navy blues, and the like. On another table, similar leather cuttings are exhibited, but in more lively and vibrant shades: purple-red, dark mauve, forest green, and golden brown. Some fifty people slowly walk around the room, discussing, arguing, pointing at the colors, lifting the samples to get a better view. It seems clear that this meeting is about leather. But what are all these people doing here, who are they, and where did they come from? Why are they discussing colors and shades? And what is the background and the objective of this gathering?

The answers to these questions lie in the history of Modeurop (ME), a European leather industry organization that served for almost forty years (1960–1998) as a base of collaboration for some twenty European countries working together to create influential color forecasts for the European shoe and leather industry. ME was unique in its kind. It was the only organization in Europe for forecasting color and other trends for the shoe and leather industry, and its geographical coverage was extensive. It managed to unite not only the national leather industry associations in Western European countries but also those of Eastern European nations long before the Iron Curtain fell in the wake of the Berlin Wall's collapse in 1989. For several years, ME produced color forecasts that were highly influential on the European market.

I. Giertz-Mårtenson (✉)
Centre for Business History, Stockholm, Sweden

R.L. Blaszczyk, U. Spiekermann (eds.), *Bright Modernity*, Worlds of Consumption, DOI 10.1007/978-3-319-50745-3_11

Unfortunately, very few original business records of Modeurop have been preserved.[1] However, some records concerning ME are available in the archives of Skobranschrådet, the Swedish Shoe Fashion Council or SBR—the organization in which ME's history began and which represented Sweden in ME between 1960 and 1998. To fill out the picture where historical documents were missing, the most important source available has been testimony from former delegates to ME. To obtain this information, I conducted semi-structured oral interviews in Paris, France, and Copenhagen, Denmark, as well as telephone and mail interviews with other ME representatives in Switzerland, Germany, Finland, and Sweden. Documenting the "oral history" of these individuals, some of whom had participated in the ME project for several decades, revealed valuable information about the organization, its objectives, and vision. All the interviews for this study were recorded and transcribed by the author with the permission of these individuals.[2]

The Swedish Shoe Fashion Council: Where It All Began

Sometimes certain ideas and organizations have a fundamental historical impact on the development of an industry, not only in the industry's own country but also in other parts of the world. An examination of the history of collaboration around color trends in the European footwear and leather industry makes clear that SBR in Sweden played just such a critical role.

The origins of SBR lie in World War II. Although Sweden was neutral and managed to avoid being drawn into the conflict that devastated large parts of Europe, six years of war meant that Sweden eventually found itself in a serious economic crisis, as the supply of essential goods and raw materials faced ever greater constraints. Guidelines for the adjustment of domestic production and consumption were drawn up to meet emergency wartime needs. Efforts to steer production and consumption included restrictions on manufacturing and rationing for most consumer goods. Nonetheless, Sweden maintained significant domestic shoe and leather production for civilian consumers. In 1945, there were still 273 shoe factories and forty-seven tanneries at work, and foreign footwear imports were as yet negligible.[3]

In order to steer wartime production, the Swedish government created the Industrial Commission, which regulated production levels, including how many shoes each factory could produce.[4] Regulating the availability of raw materials and production capacity was an absolute necessity. These new rules included, among other things, guidelines for the standardization of colors for shoe uppers. The tanners' upper leather collections, which normally consisted of about 200 colors, were sharply reduced to only a handful, according to rules introduced in August 1941. The standardization of colors also aimed to avoid, if possible, the rationing of shoes by adjusting production to a level that more closely approximated actual consumption needs. The rules were particularly intended to avert a dependence on fashion trends, which would require new shoe models and colors. Thus, the production of ladies' boots was completely prohibited in 1941.[5] Full shoe rationing became necessary by the spring of 1943—every Swede had the right to buy one new pair of shoes a year and to repair one old pair. Rationing was repealed in November 1945, and all remaining price controls and related regulations were lifted in May 1952.[6]

The Swedish footwear and leather industry thus faced a precarious situation after World War II. During the last year of the war, the so-called Shoe Industry Planning Committee met to review opportunities for increased cooperation between producers and retailers in the industry. The result was the Swedish Shoe Fashion Council (SBR), founded on September 11, 1945, whose purpose was to "inform the industry's various branches about shoe trends before every season" and "provide the best possible services to the industry." Special importance was to be given to "forecasts on color and design and general information concerning future trends in shoe fashion."[7]

The initiative for the new council came from the Swedish Shoe Manufacturers' Association with its dynamic chairman, Wilhelm Bahrke, director of Malmö Läderfabriks AB in southern Sweden. Delegates were selected from representatives of manufacturers, retailers, leather tanners, leather importers, and shoe last manufacturers. The council had three subsections, which focused on color, design, and shoe lasts. At the outset, it was also emphasized that the council, "to meet its objectives concerning fashion trends," should initiate cooperation with similar organizations abroad and "establish relations with major cities with a determining role in fashion." Collaboration with the Swedish textile and clothing industries was also considered essential.[8] To coordinate these activities a fashion consultant was to be hired, preferably a woman.... She must have good language skills, sure taste and good judgment... as well as, critically, possess the ability to monitor and interpret changes in fashion."[9]

The eighteen delegates elected to SBRs committees were chief executives of Swedish companies. All were male except one woman, a shoe retailer.[10] The perceived need for the new fashion consultant to be a woman was symptomatic of the prevailing view of fashion at the time. Whereas companies were led by men, women were expected to be more open to fashion and more able to interpret its changes. Aili Pekonen became the first fashion consultant. Pekonen, a well-known artist, illustrator, and designer, had worked as a journalist at several Swedish newspapers and magazines before joining the Shoe Fashion Council. She held the position (except for a brief period during the 1950s) until 1968, when I was appointed to head the SBR. I had had long experience working with French haute couture in Paris, working as a personal assistant to the Head of the House of Givenchy as well as being responsible for PR and Communication at the House of Castillo.'[11]

Paving the Way for a New Council

The activities of the SBR got off to a quick start, with committees meeting several times a season. Soon the first color and fashion forecast was produced and delivered to members—tanneries, shoe manufacturers, shoe retailers, and shoe last manufacturers. Pekonen described her mission for the future in a document dated February 1946: "My most important task abroad is to connect to foreign experts and color organizations. This will be very profitable for the Swedish shoe and leather industry. I will also study color and design both in ready-to-wear and in shoes, in order to regularly update the Swedish shoe manufacturers on the latest trends."[12]

As early as spring 1946, Pekonen made a five-week trip to New York, London, and Paris. In London, she visited the British Color Council (BCC) as well as other trade organizations. Networking and obtaining information from international color groups were seen as crucial to building a color card for Sweden.[13] Other influential color forecasting agencies were also a part of the Swedish network. In the archives of the SBR from 1947, there is a color card from the Textile Color Card Association of the United States (TCCA), together with a copy of that organization's newsletter, *Broadcast*, signed by the TCCA's well-known managing director, Margaret Hayden Rorke. Information is given concerning "Women's shoe and leather colors for spring 1947." A color card for spring/summer of the same year from the British Color Council is also in the archive.[14] In her reports, Pekonen also wrote about the opportunity to inform her new contacts about the work of the SBR. It is therefore likely that the organizations she visited were regularly updated on the ongoing activities and developments in Sweden.

The exchange of information took place every season from 1946 onward. SBR understood early on the importance of staying in tune with international color trends. Working with American and British industrial color groups seems to have been more important than collaborating with organizations in France and Italy. According to reports from visits abroad, fashion and color inspiration from these last two countries came from famous designers and haute couture houses rather than from working with fashion industry associations. Apparently, the leading edge in color forecasting involved the Anglo-American practices pioneered by the TCCA (see Chapter 10).

Contacts with as wide a range of sources as possible were essential. The idea of creating a national Swedish color and fashion look, distinct from international trends, did not exist. On the contrary, the importance of following developments on major foreign markets and interpreting them for the Swedish industry was seen as the main mission. This can be compared to the "patriotic pride" that existed in the United States and the Textile Color Card Association. In *The Color Revolution*, Regina Lee Blaszczyk states that U.S. national pride had to be set aside when French and Italian fashion and color trends grew increasingly influential in the postwar era. "Business realities forced the TCCA to swallow its patriotic pride, put aside color independence, and bow to "the other side."[15] Sweden did not have such problems. It was a small country and early on the Swedish style industries realized the importance of collaboration and the exchange of ideas and inspiration from major actors on the international scene.

There was something else that was new in Pekonen's reports. Unlike most fashion magazines or forecasting reports at the time, which usually covered styles and trends, she also explored the cultural and social significance of the new shoe trends she saw abroad. She referenced the existing social landscape in Sweden and explained why certain styles and trends would not work on the Swedish market while others could become great hits.[16] Pekonen also took a special interest in the psychology of colors in fashion, arguing that routinely not using color in the right way in shoes represented a failure to recognize the importance of the aesthetics of dressing.[17]

Collaboration Across Nordic Borders

The SBR soon inspired the founding of similar councils in the other Nordic countries. Between 1945 and 1948, national organizations for the shoe and leather industry were established in Norway (Skorådet, the Norwegian Shoe Council), Denmark (Dansk Skomoderåd, the Danish Shoe Fashion Council), and Finland (Kenkä- ja Nahka-alan muotineuvosto, the Shoe and Leather Fashion Council). After a few years, in 1949, the four councils decided that it was in their common interest to work more closely together. Coordinating color and fashion trends for leather and shoes on the Nordic market would enhance the commercial success of these sectors in all four countries. Thus, the Nordic Fashion Council (NMR) was founded.

Its establishment was preceded by talks in various groups, and there had already been some collaboration between Nordic tanners and shoe manufacturers. The years after World War II had seen intense activity in the industry, as it sought new business opportunities, trade partners, and markets. In this context, the president of the Finnish Shoe manufacturers, Lauri Kivikäs, wrote a letter to the SBR, dated November 8, 1948, in which he suggested collaboration between the four Nordic countries for their mutual benefit. "I believe that taste directions in the Nordic countries are much the same and also the technical resources."[18]

The inaugural meeting of the NMR was held in Stockholm on November 1, 1949, with subsequent meetings every season in one of the four Nordic capitals—Copenhagen, Helsinki, Oslo, and Stockholm.[19] Denmark became a regular member in 1952.[20] Separate committees handled specific areas, that is, color forecasts, design trends in shoes and accessories, and administration. Members met once or twice every season to discuss the common and identical forecasts to be published every season in each country. Representatives from the respective trade associations of all four nations took part in the meetings. This was a male affair: in the minutes from the NMR meeting in Stockholm on April 26, 1956, a complete list of members of the committees and board of directors indicates that twenty people, all men, were engaged in the various subsections of the council.[21] There were tanners, shoe manufacturers, and shoe retailers as well as shoe last and accessory manufacturers.

On the other hand, fashion expertise was a female affair. All of the fashion consultants appointed to be in charge of the actual color and trend forecasting in the four countries were women. European culture had long deemed fashion a feminine pursuit, for better or worse. This stereotype, which went back to the French Revolution (with certain gendered attitudes about color per se reaching back further, as discussed in Chapter 4), not only influenced patterns of color consumption, but also produced a gender division of labor that relegated women to careers as stylists and fashion advisors. Many entrepreneurial fashionistas took advantage of the opportunities, including Margaret Hayden Rorke. The idea that fashion was connected to femininity, and therefore more suitable for a female consultant, seems to have been an accepted fact in the leather industry.[22]

The Importance of Working Together: Producing a Nordic Fashion Forecast

From the very beginning of the NMR's existence, the four fashion consultants from Denmark, Finland, Norway, and Sweden worked closely together. They made trips to foreign fashion centers in Europe and the United States, mainly New York City. Paris was a "must" for every meeting, with the hegemony of Paris's fashion influence still undisputed in the early 1950s.

The NMR's forecasts, published from 1950 on, are filled with information and exquisite illustrations of new fashion for the coming season—detailed sketches of shoes (women's and men's), of garments, and of handbags combined with information on colors and materials. The color collection from fall 1954 consists of twenty-four shades, most of them named after geographical areas or inspired by nature (Fig. 11.1).[23] Some names were inspired by names presented in international color cards; others had a more Nordic feeling. The names had a great importance as they were used by the whole industry—tanners, shoe manufacturers, and shoe retailers. The names of the most popular shades also became well known among consumers. A color name could represent a certain "status" for the consumer as he or she proved that their choice of shoe color was in line with a new seasonal trend.

The NMR's color and fashion forecasts are not only interesting as testimony of actual collaboration between the countries. They are also aesthetic examples of fine graphic work from the time. No doubt there was a desire within the leather and shoe industry to be seen as a modern and forward-looking sector of the market. The trend forecasts were used to exemplify the industry's modern outlook. And they were not only used as tools of information for the industry; forecasts also served as public relations documents and information sources for the press. They were communicated to the daily and weekly newspapers as well as to the trade magazines.[24]

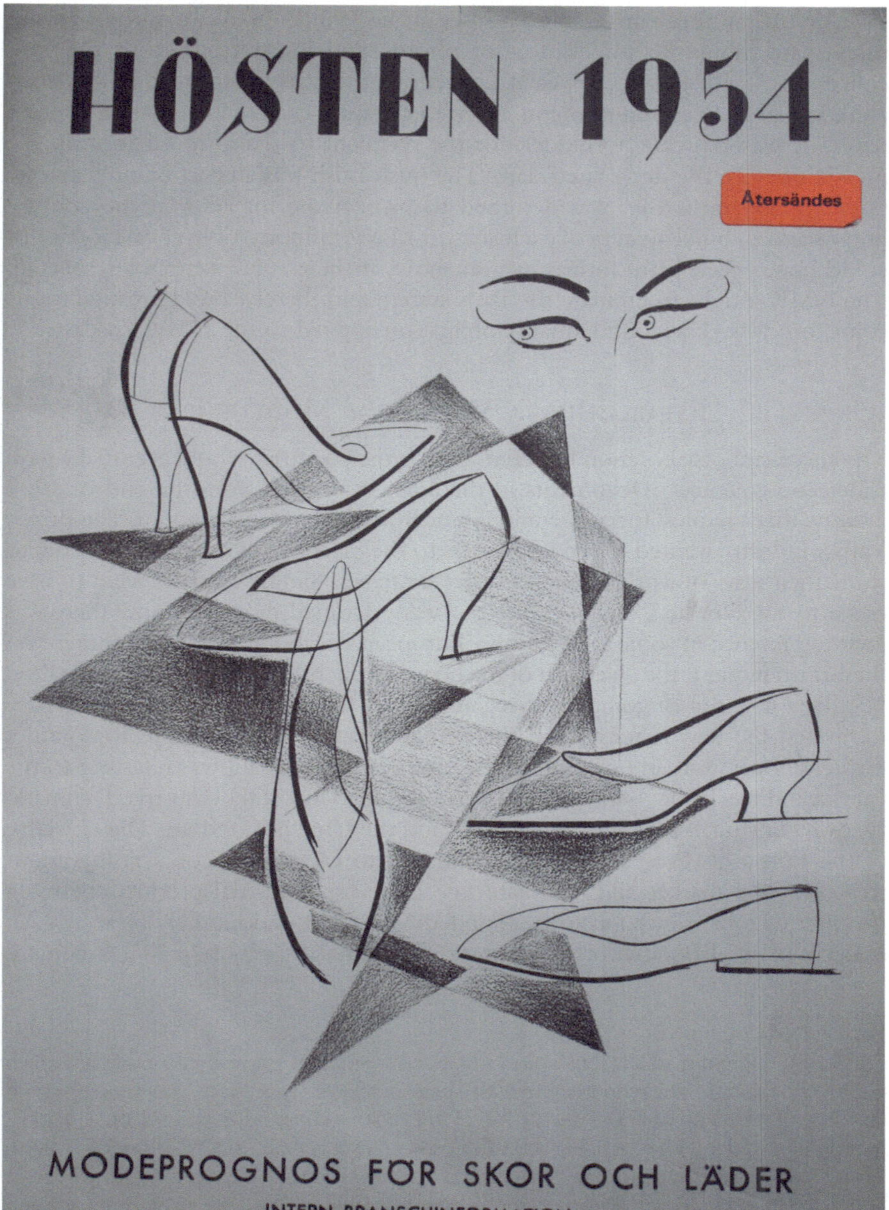

Fig. 11.1 Nordic Fashion Council, *Fashion Forecast for Shoes and Leather, Fall 1954* (front cover)

This report was produced by the Nordic Fashion Council, with the chic cover design by Aili Pekonen, the first fashion consultant of the Swedish Shoe Fashion Council (see p. 229).

Everyone visiting Paris fashion houses in the 1950s was aware of the rigorous rules concerning the publication of photos and illustrations from the new collections.[25] In advance of each collection, the Paris couture houses issued confidential press announcements and photographs, each marked with a "release date." It was expressly forbidden for the recipient to share information in the press kit before the designated date. The hush-hush was all part of an elaborate publicity apparatus that was designed to protect the interests of the couture houses and to build an aura of exclusivity for Paris fashion. A buyer or a journalist could be expelled from future fashion shows if these rules were not respected. The NMR sought to emulate the Paris system and thereby build prestige for its color forecasts. The confidentiality obligation applied to the NMR forecasts.[26]

Establishing a Model for Modeurop

The successful collaboration between the Nordic countries would eventually have wider consequences. Documents in the archives of SBR from the end of 1959 indicate that a request for cooperation came from the United Kingdom. The British leather industry wanted to send observers to the meetings of the NMR in order to study their ways of working and business strategies. Similar requests seem to have come to the Nordic Council earlier but were declined; however, now there was growing interest in some kind of intra-European collaboration. In a comment on the British request, the chairman of the board of the NMR, Åke Burendahl, wrote, "Perhaps it is the ongoing talks regarding the future 7-state market that have motivated the new request. And there might now be good reasons to consider further cooperation among European countries." Burendahl was referring to the European Free Trade Association (EFTA), founded in 1960 by Austria, Denmark, Norway, Portugal, Sweden, Switzerland, and the United Kingdom. The objective of the European Free Trade Association was to create new contacts in various sectors of the market and stimulate free trade for industrial products between member nations. The soon-to-be-founded ME could undoubtedly be seen as an example of a collaborative organization crafted with the spirit of the EFTA in mind.

Fig.11.1 (Continued)
The stylish femininity of the illustration suggests an emphasis on women's fashions, which was indeed the case. The report begins with a page of text on the subject, a couple pages with sketches of women's dresses, and a list of the colors chosen for the season (Havana, Mahogony, Kastanj, Gyllenek, Hassel, Club brown, Swedish tan, Marin, Marocko, Valnöt, Sahara, Malaga, Vallmo, Rubin, Japan Blue, Turkos, Skiffer, Tallbarr, Cypress, Tobacco, Benedictine, Pastel violet, Pastel Pink). This material is followed by color drawings and accompanying text—fourteen pages on women's shoes, one page on children's shoes, four pages on men's shoes, and five pages on ladies' handbags. The text at the very bottom of the cover indicates that the report was confidential: "Internal industry information." The red sticker declares, "to be returned," although it is unclear if this particular copy was shared within one company or between companies.

Source: Author's papers.

Its major objective and focus was to establish cooperation concerning color and leather fashion trends among manufacturers and retailers in the European countries that constituted "the Seven" members of the EFTA.

Another document from the SBR archive, probably from 1968 and entitled "A short summary of the work and development of the Swedish Shoe Fashion Council," stated, "It is worth mentioning that the Swedish Shoe Fashion Council, SBR, was the model for most shoe and leather councils founded in the 1950s in Western European countries. Also, the NMR was the model for the European color organization, founded in 1960 under the name of Modeurop. Fifteen nations now belong to this group through their national councils, one of them being the Swedish Shoe Fashion Council (SBR)."[27]

According to other sources, the model and the inspiration for the establishment of the new inter-European organization thus seems to have come when word of the Nordic council, NMR, spread in other European countries. An indication of how this might have happened comes from Leena Aro, a fashion consultant at Kenkäneuvosto in Helsinki, Finland, for many years. Aro remembers that when she joined the Finnish Shoe Council in 1975, several people present at the start of Modeurop explained its history to her. She was told that European textile experts representing the International Wool Secretariat (IWS) and the DuPont Company, the American-based chemical company that led the world in synthetic fiber production, were invited to take part in the NMR meetings in Sweden at the end of the 1950s.[28] The textile specialists from the IWS and DuPont were impressed by the high degree of collaboration in the Nordic leather and shoe industry and were eager to promote something similar among all European nations. This can be considered as one of the initial sparks behind the founding of Modeurop.[29]

Modeurop—A Color-Forecasting Hub for the European Leather and Shoe Industry

The business idea and the objective behind ME was defined at its inception in 1960—to coordinate color trends for shoes, leathers, and leather garments within the European market. ME also intended to discuss trends in leather materials.[30] Like the NMR, which inspired ME's founding, ME recognized that color was a major driving force in design and lifestyle. As one of the most important factors behind consumer choices, color was something that producers and retailers—cooperating through ME—needed to get right. To facilitate collaboration among the tanners, shoe manufacturers, and retailers in this industry, all of these groups were represented in ME from the very beginning. In this respect, too, ME had simply copied the concept and working methods of the body that already existed in the Nordic countries, the NMR.

At the same time, it should be underlined that ME's objective was never to deal with financial, market-related, or trade policy questions. The focus was on color and leather material forecasting. ME understood the importance of creating a common color vision for the European market and for those non-European nations that wanted to do business with Europe. It was a strong message from an industry that competed within its own region but at the same time had common interests vis-à-vis the external market. The decision-making was done through a group that, during its most successful years, represented almost all European nations. This pan-European collaboration lent the color forecasts an official quality and made them reliable. As we saw in Chapter 10, the Textile Color Card Association produced "American Color for the American People." In a similar spirit, Modeurop created forecasts and trend reports suited to European tastes and expectations.

Administrative and Membership Rules

According to the statutes adopted at the establishment of ME in 1960, only national organizations and councils representing the leather and shoe industry could become members. As the name indicated, this was a European group (the original name was *Euro-Mode,* which in 1963 was changed to Modeurop). Its headquarters was established in Berne, Switzerland, but was later moved to Zürich.

Though there seems to be no existing information indicating why the administration of ME was located in Switzerland, there are several possible reasons. Switzerland was a politically neutral nation, and the famous Swiss shoe manufacturer Bally was very active in promoting the founding of ME. Max Matter, the fashion director at Bally, Switzerland, was appointed the first president of ME's fashion committee.[31] Milo Legnazzi, a Swiss-Italian working at the Swiss national fashion and leather council, became the first secretary general of ME.[32] Finally, Switzerland had an advanced chemical industry, which produced the synthetic dyes and other chemicals that were widely used in leather processing and tanning.

The wider context for the establishment of ME also deserves comment. In the Nordic countries, the influence of European fashion centers in France and Italy was still important. But trends were becoming increasingly complex and harder to interpret. Paris continued to claim its hegemony as leader of the international fashion scene. However, other signals, especially around young fashion, were bubbling up as part of a new modernity in which fashion and pop music created a new arena for inspiration. London was the center of this development.[33] The early 1960s also saw the establishment in Paris of some of the most important new fashion forecasting agencies, Peclers Paris and Promostyl, both founded by female entrepreneurs in response to the growing importance of ready-to-wear in France, Germany, and elsewhere in Europe.[34] Today these are still among the most influential forecasting bureaus in the world.[35] It is likely that, due to all these new dynamics, the European leather and shoe industry felt a need to collaborate in order to send a strong message of unity, collaboration, and reliability to the market.

The key tool for this project was clear. Color!

At the launch of ME in 1960 there were thirteen member countries: Austria, Denmark, Finland, France, Italy, the Netherlands, Norway, Portugal, Spain, Sweden, Switzerland, the United Kingdom, and West Germany. Leather and shoe experts from these countries met twice a year for two to three days. The spring congress (in February) usually took place in Zürich, and the fall congress (end of September) was held in another member country. After each congress, a forecast with a new color card (aka "collection") and trends for leather materials was published for the corresponding season in the upcoming year. In keeping with this pattern, after the first ME congress in Paris in September 1960, the inaugural ME color card was produced for fall 1961. Besides color forecasting, the ME held meetings to discuss the general state of the trade and to plan industry-wide collaborations. Additionally, there was the general assembly, the most senior gathering of ME representatives, which met once a year, usually during the fall congress. Its agenda included finances, statutes, and memberships, as well as the appointment of board positions and presidents of the various subsections. A two-thirds majority of voting members was required for a resolution, with each member country having one vote.

ME was a non-profit organization, financed partly by membership fees, partly by income from the sale of seasonal color cards (Fig. 11.2). According to the former secretary of ME, Rose Marie Gresch, the approximate annual turnover in 1995 was 120,000 Swiss francs. Color cards were sold for 30 Swiss francs to the national member organizations at the end of the 1990s, and these organizations determined independently what the price of the card would be for their member companies. In the same period, the membership fee for the national organizations was around 2,200 Swiss francs (approximately 17,000 Swedish kroner or 2,500 U.S. dollars at the time). Like the Textile Color Card Association and the British Color Council, ME was a business-to-business organization, working to improve the understanding of the importance of color and color coordination between leather and shoe companies within the European market. Direct contact with consumers was not part of ME's mission.

Associated Members—But No Voting Rights

Chemical companies, which produced the dyes and needed to be consulted when choosing the right shades for coloring leather, were allowed to become associated members of ME but not to be present at the congresses as observers or to take part in the work. Nor did they have any voting rights. Their business interests, after all, overlapped with those of ME's full members but extended in many other directions too. Information regarding new colors and original leather samples was sent to the associated members after each congress. The annual fee for them was less—1,500 Swiss francs instead of 2,200 Swiss francs, in the mid-1990s, for example. Three major international companies were associated members for a long period: Ciba-Geigy, Sandoz, and Bayer Leverkusen, the first two based in Basel, Switzerland, and the last one in Leverkusen, Germany.

Around 1995, a few years before the dissolution of the original ME organization (it was later reconstructed, see below), an additional associated member was

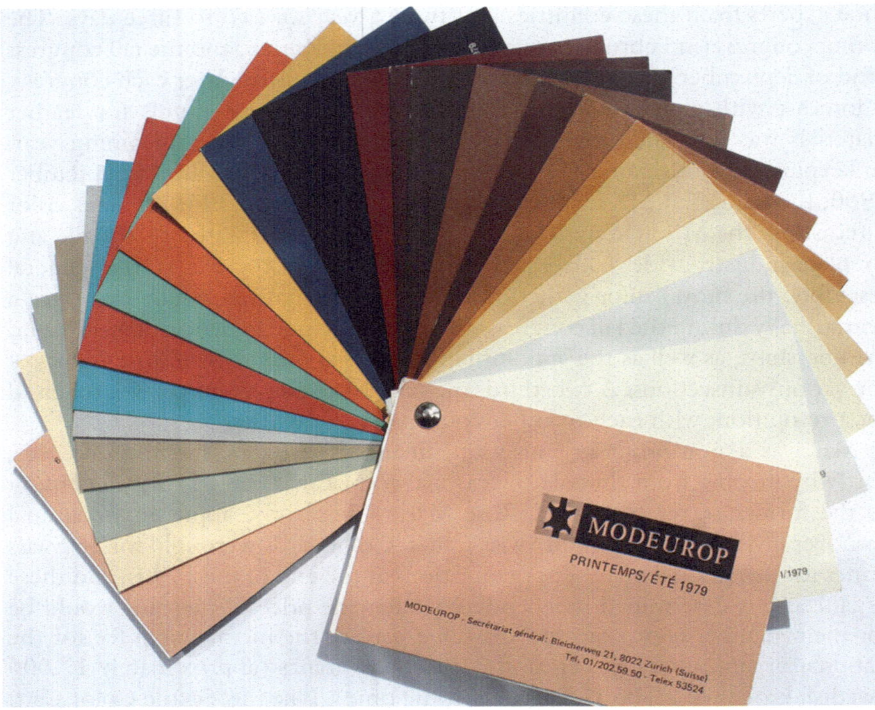

Fig. 11.2 Modeurop color card, Spring/Summer, 1979

The design of this 12 × 8-cm color card was typical of the color cards that Modeurop sold to its member organizations for further distribution to participating businesses in their respective countries. The number of colors varied from season to season, with this one containing 24 (one is hidden). Each differently colored page bears that color's name as well as the season. Behind the front cover, before the colors, is a page listing all the groups in Modeurop and all of that season's colors.

Source: Author's papers.

accepted into ME: India, as represented by the Central Leather Research Institute, or the CLRI. An exception to the rules of associated membership was also made. The Indian delegation was permitted to attend congresses, albeit without voting rights. This development represented a change in strategy and a departure from the original statutes, which had excluded non-European countries. Although India was not accepted as a full member, the new strategy was based on an understanding of changes on the global market and the growing importance of building business relationships with other parts of the world whose own leather and shoe industries were growing and becoming increasingly relevant in European markets. But the presence of India also became one of the reasons that France left ME in 1995; the French leather and shoe industry saw in India an unwelcome competitor.[36]

European Collaboration Outside Western Europe

At its inception in 1960, ME only had Western European nations as members. This was a time when the Iron Curtain—the imaginary boundary that ran through the heart of Europe to separate the Communist East Bloc countries from the "Free World" of the West—was still a hard political fact. Business relations in general were sometimes challenged by ideological, legal, and political differences. Shortly after the establishment of ME, however, applications for membership were received from Eastern European countries as well because leather production in many of them was important, and the industry there needed all the information on trends in colors and materials that it could get. The first application came from Czechoslovakia in 1969. After this, several others national trade groups from Communist Europe were accepted as members too: East Germany, Hungary, Poland, Romania, and Yugoslavia.[37]

There appears to have been no concerted opposition to opening ME to representatives from the East Bloc countries. Tanneries and shoe manufacturers in several of these nations were interesting business partners for many Western European companies.[38] On the other hand, many of these low-wage economies were attempting to compete in the more developed markets of Western Europe, which some producers in Western Europe did not view with indifference. On the contrary, the idea of letting ME fashion information in general and its color forecasts in particular automatically be used by rivals in the Eastern Bloc was seen as questionable by some Western members, including France and Spain.[39] During this period, the pros and cons of including Eastern European nations in the organization were also discussed by the UK-based International Council of Tanners (ICT), an organization whose membership included European tanners represented in ME by their respective national leather and shoe organizations. The result was similar to the decision that ME took. The promise of commercial advantages and new business prospects were seen as more important than political and ideological factors.[40]

Creating a Color Forecast

How did ME conduct its actual work? Who were the important players in the group? And what was the background and the timing for creating this kind of color information for a particular season? From its inception, ME was organized into several committees. The most important work took place in the Expert Committee, which met during every semiannual congress. Here, a color card for shoes and other accessories, such as handbags and belts, was chosen for the new season. Each national delegation had one or more representatives in the Expert Committee, each with a head who had the right to deliver the delegation's final vote. Every nation had one vote and a majority of two-thirds was required for a new color to be included in the color card.

The Expert Committee, in turn, depended on the Fashion Committee, which included a select number of representatives from member countries. The role of this committee was to present a background report of upcoming textile and fashion trends to the Expert Committee. As the shoe industry was ancillary to the textile and fashion industry, it depended directly on what was happening there as far as colors, materials, and general trends were concerned. Delegates in the Fashion Committee therefore had to possess special knowledge and information regarding future textile and fashion trends. In fact, the delegates in the Fashion committee often represented more than just the shoe and leather industry in their respective countries. The present author was not just CEO of the Swedish Shoe Fashion Council, for example, but also CEO of the Swedish Fashion Council. These ties to other industries in the fashion sector meant that the delegates to the Expert Committee had deep knowledge of all upcoming trends in fashion and textiles, which was reinforced by visits to all the textile and ready-to-wear fairs and all the other industry-produced information on upcoming fashion trends (on such fairs, see Chapter 12). This broader fashion background was essential to the work of presenting a true picture of color trends for the leather and shoe industry.[41] Specialist experts were also brought in for the men's fashion report. A third committee handled the color card for leather garments. This addition to the color forecast for shoes and accessories came around 1975. It was a decision partly based on the importance of leather garment production and tanneries in countries like Finland, Spain, and Sweden. Leather garment colors were also included in the original color card of ME from 1976 and on, as the production of leather garments grew strong, especially in Finland, Spain, and Sweden.

The start of a new season saw a meeting of the small Textile and Fashion Committee, sometimes in connection with trade fairs (for instance Première Vision in Paris or Lineapelle in Bologna) that the trend and color experts were already attending. This committee prepared a preliminary forecast for the next year's fashion trends, which it would present at the next ME congress.[42]

The Mechanics of an ME Congress: Step by Step

A congress usually lasted for two days and started with the preparation of all the leather color propositions for the new season. Whole leather hides were brought to the congress by every member nation (pigmented side leathers, aniline or semi-aniline calf or goat leathers) in new color shades. The job of providing leather samples was serious; the member who failed to bring leather samples did not have the right to vote. From the large pieces of leather, pieces of approximately 20 × 30 cm were cut out, numbered, and exhibited to the delegates in specific color groups on separate tables. The groups corresponded to the trends presented by the Fashion Committee and included three to four themes, such as basics, neutrals, spicy (warm, hot), and pop (vibrant, young).

The presentation of the new textile and fashion report formed the start of each congress as a kick-off to the work of the Expert Committee. “Mood boards” with examples of color cards from textile associations, fashion forecasting agencies, and national fashion councils decorated the walls in the meeting room, including colorful pages from fashion magazines and sketches of new fashions. Any member of the Expert Committee could comment on the textile report, but usually the fashions presented were used as a background to the new season′s leather color report.

At this point, the actual selection of the color card for the next season would begin. For several hours, sometimes continuing into the following day, delegates would circle around the tables with the new color propositions. There were private discussions, and small groups gathered around certain samples. Now and then the president of the Fashion Committee would listen to an argument, make a comment, or point out a particular color group or sample. The discussions were often lively, yet never hostile or unfriendly. But this was also the moment when national pride became a factor. A rivalry between color propositions from major fashion nations like France, Italy, and Spain was sometimes apparent.[43] Delegates occasionally took a quick look at the back of the color samples to find out where the leather originated; every sample was marked with a number indicating its place of manufacture.

Representatives also sometimes made decisions as part of country groupings. The four Nordic countries were often of the same opinion, based on the fact that market and fashion trends were similar in northern Europe. Joint Nordic decisions were also driven by the fact that industry representatives from the four countries would later have to select an NMR color card for the seasonal Nordic color program. Politically, a common Nordic agenda could also be linked to the countries’ strong regional ties that dated back centuries, as also illustrated by the frequent joint Nordic propositions and similar voting patterns in the United Nations and other international organizations.[44]

Undoubtedly there was a certain prestige in having a color proposition from one’s own country chosen; however, considerations of “national pride” never became overpowering. The objective of ME was always to choose a color card with shades that were both commercially valuable and fashionably new for the European market as a whole. For the individual tanner who delivered the color sample there could also be an image boost, increasing his status among colleagues as well as enhancing his company’s corporate image.[45] Once everyone’s mind was made up, the actual voting began, with representatives standing around the tables with the leather samples, and raising red cards for a “yes” on a new color. When two-thirds of the nations present voted in favor, the color passed. If not, it was either withdrawn, or a slightly different shade might be discussed. The same procedure was followed in the leather garment committee. Here the samples were usually presented in soft velour or nappa leathers. Considerably fewer colors were presented in this group and several nations did not attend the work of the committee because it was of interest only to countries where leather garments were produced.

The number of colors on the forecasts varied from the start of Modeurop in 1960 to the end in 1998. The very first color card, for fall and winter 1961, included only two colors, Palisander and Moresco. After that the numbers increased steadily. In the 1979 spring/summer card there were twenty-eight colors for shoes and accessories and fifteen colors for leather garments. In the mid-1990s, the number decreased again. The fall/winter card for 1996–1997 included only nine colors for shoes and accessories and eight colors for leather garments.

Once the color card was complete, the textile experts sat down to "baptize" the new shades. Finding appropriate and catchy names for the new colors became an important public relations tool, but agreeing on suitable names that would work in all countries and in different languages and cultures could be problematic. "The French tanners were furious if I came back to Paris with names that they considered not valid," explained the French representative Sylvie Lefranc.[46] References to nature, minerals, and food were popular. Political or religious references were avoided. In connection with the discussion of color, ME also worked to identify future trends in leather materials. Here, a combination of commercial and fashion aspects formed a background to detailed reports on upcoming trends.[47]

Once the color selection had been completed and the new shades named, member delegations received small samples of every new color from the original leather hides. Back home, these leather samples were cut into smaller pieces and sent to tanners in each country. To interpret the exact shade and include it in his own color collection, the tanner had to rely on the original leather sample. If necessary, he could also order a bigger color sample from the tannery responsible for the original ME sample. Lists of the tanneries whose color shades were chosen and included in the ME color collection were distributed to all members.

After each congress, the ME Color Card for the new season was produced and became an important source of income for the organization. The color card was printed on hard paper in the shape of a hand fan, usually 12 × 8 cm. It was obligatory for member countries to order a certain number of color cards for national distribution. The rules were very rigorous: color cards could only be distributed by the member nations to representatives of the leather industry in each country. Any member nation that failed to respect this rule risked exclusion from ME.[48]

A Tool for "Nation-Branding" and Social Networking

The first ME congress of the year usually took place in Zürich in February. The September congress was often arranged in one of the other member countries. It was regarded as an honor for a country to be asked to arrange a congress.

While it meant a great deal of work, it also represented a possibility to upgrade the "national brand" among other members. [49]

During congresses in member countries, delegates would always be put up in one of the top hotels. For example, the Hotel Carlton in Cannes, on the French Riviera, was the site of the spring 1975 meeting. The arrangements could be very formal. The "gala dinner" that was part of a congress outside Switzerland was sometimes an elaborate black tie affair, taking place in a posh restaurant with entertainment, music, and dancing. This can be seen as part of the zeitgeist that still existed in the 1970s and 1980s—many international congresses boasted an exquisite and traditional way of entertaining and many divisions of the fashion business valued elegance and glamour. Later on, however, the ME became much more cost-conscious.[50]

The elaborate arrangements sometimes caused problems for delegates from Eastern European countries. Their budgets were tight, and they often had to look for less expensive hotels and choose not to take part in after-work dinners. A strict political agenda lurked behind this circumstance as well. Certain representatives in the Eastern European delegations seemed more like government minders than experts from the leather industry. A sense of surveillance directed toward Western delegates was also tangible during some of the meetings held in Eastern Europe. "There was a strong control by 'secret service,' even in the hotel," remembers ME President Rolf Trüb, looking back at the congress in Prague in 1974.[51]

But there was also an informal social side to ME. During every congress an evening program was arranged for the delegates. This could be a friendly outing to a pleasant inn or a dinner in one of the traditional guild houses in Zürich. For several years, there was also a special daily program for *personnes acompagnantes* (usually wives, but once in a while also a husband). "The 'social networking' that took place during the many evenings together, under informal circumstances, should not be underestimated," recalled ME delegate Kirsten Toxvaerd, who represented the Danish Shoe Fashion Council. "Here friendships were made that lasted long after the actual ME years."[52] The informal entertainment within the ME group was meaningful for the business side too. Personal contacts between people have always been extremely important for good business relations.[53]

Financial Problems, Dissolution, and Reconstruction

Income from its color cards was vital for ME's finances. As competition from outside Europe grew increasingly fierce, many factories and production plants in the organization's European member nations had to close. This resulted in declining color card orders from the mid-1980s.[54] At the beginning of the next decade, some national member organizations left ME. In some cases, they ceased to exist; others left due to financial difficulties. Fierce competition from new actors in markets where production was less costly combined with growing imports of footwear and leathers from outside Europe was causing a large number of European shoe and leather manufacturers to go under. The 1990s also saw European textile fairs grow in importance. Première Vision in Paris, for example, added to the competition on the "trends market." Denmark, Norway, and some of the Eastern European members no longer saw the advantage of membership. By 1995, the financial situation of ME was so acute that the secretariat in Switzerland had to be shut down. The administrative functions of SE were moved to the Austrian member organization, Oestereisches Modesekretariat (The Austrian National Fashion Council) in Vienna, but the decline in member nations did not stop. France left ME in 1995, Sweden and Finland in 1997. A few nations of the former group were left, but the original idea of ME was dead.

Around 2000, hopes for the reconstruction of the organization were raised in Germany. The German Shoe Fashion Council (Deutsche Schuinstitut, or DSI) decided to try launching a new organization under the same name.[55] Today, that name stands for a group of European and non-European companies and associations working to coordinate leather color trends on the international market. The new "Modeurop" does not stand for "Fashion trends for Europe" anymore. It is not limited to national European leather councils. The objective is instead to produce color and material forecasts for the global leather market.

Measuring the Impact

The importance of ME can partly be explained by the fact that, according to its statutes, only national leather and shoe industry organizations could become members. In this way, ME hi-jacked, so to speak, the official representatives of the shoe and leather industry from each country. That is, it seems to have left no room for another intra-European organization of comparable stature. Nor was there room for individual companies or private interests in ME. This limitation lent a quasi-official stamp to the color forecasts. After all, they were produced and delivered by national experts within a nonprofit framework. The "official" character of ME's work was further underlined by the fact that it was performed during "congresses," a label indicating the semiannual gatherings were official, not mere informal conferences. The forecasts from ME relied on the broad knowledge of experts from all European countries, and through their pan-European distribution they created a common vision that made them even more important and influential in the market.

During ME's forty years of existence, however, the influence of its color forecasts undoubtedly varied. "I believe the best years were in the 1970s and the beginning of the 1980s," says Rolf Trüb, president of ME from 1985 to 1995. He also indicates that the importance of the color forecasts varied in different parts of Europe. "Northern and middle European countries would usually follow the forecasts more than countries in southern Europe." The tanneries in the northern and central European regions appreciated the standardized color card. Many shoe manufacturers also accepted the ME color trends, whereas others saw a competitive advantage in using a different color scheme.[56] However, according to Jan Ekblom, CEO of the Swedish tannery Klippans Läder, NMR president for several years, and the Swedish representative in ME, the influence of the Modeurop color card among his customers diminished the further south in Europe one went.[57]

Conclusion

ME was dissolved only a couple decades ago, but all of the records from its forty years of existence, at least in important member countries, have already been disposed of. I interpret this as a lack of understanding and respect for contemporary fashion history. A study of the background, objectives, and business model of ME offers a new understanding of one of the most efficient organizations within the European fashion industry in the latter half of the twentieth century. Further studies in this area could add new knowledge regarding a rather unknown sector of the European fashion market.

Recently the idea of the individual designer has been the subject of several works and case studies.[58] The influence of the "genius" was often seen as the main force behind fashion changes. However, the importance of fashion institutions and industrial groups within the global fashion system must not be underestimated. ME was one such organization in the area of color forecasting. It managed to coordinate the development of leather colors on the European market (both west and east) for several decades. It created a basis for decision-making and information that was reliable and influential. ME proved that color was not only a concern of individual companies. It could also become a strong tool within an industry, if it was handled by a well-organized group.

The interaction between corporate professionals and "fashion intermediaries" deserves to be noted here.[59] The fashion experts responsible for the ME Fashion Committee were highly influential with their "fashion story" as a background canvas for the ME color cards. Rolf Trüb, former president of ME, considers the work of these fashion and textile experts in the 1970s and 1980s to have been crucial to the success of ME. From a gender perspective, ME also reveals how the importance of women in the European shoe and leather industry slowly changed in the late twentieth century. For the SBR and the NMR in the 1940s and the 1950s, the only positions filled by women were fashion consultants, whereas in the ME of the 1980s and 1990s, there were several female CEOs of national member organizations, namely, from Denmark, France, and Sweden.

"I believe that an *esprit européen* was created by Modeurop among the representatives of the leather and shoe industry that did not exist in nearly the same way within the textile and fashion industry."[60] This statement by Sylvie Lefranc, former director of the Bureau de Style in France and president of the ME Fashion Committee for many years, evinced the spirit that existed within the group. Perhaps one could say that ME worked according to the ideas of the European Union long before the EU existed. Kirsten

Toxvaerd, director of the Shoe Fashion Council of Denmark, adds these final words: "There is no doubt that ME was an organization of great commercial importance for many of the member countries. And color was the unifying factor."[61]

Notes

1. In the relevant trade organization archives of former prominent member countries like Denmark, France, Germany, Sweden, and Switzerland, documents concerning the history of Modeurop (ME)—such as minutes from congresses, newsletters, financial statements, and correspondence—do not exist. To obtain reliable information, other sources had to be used, namely, a number of documents and photos from private archives belonging to people who earlier held various positions in ME. Also, press clippings from trade magazines in Denmark, Finland, and Sweden reported on some of the organization's activities.
2. The author interviewed the following people: Lenena Aro, fashion consultant at Kenkäneuvosto (The Shoe and Leather Fashion Council), Helsinki, Finland, and member of the Finnish delegation to ME, 1975–1998 (mail and telephone interview, May–June 2012); Jan Ekblom, CEO of Klippans Läderfabrik, 1958–1987; Ängelholm, Sweden, chairman of SBR and NMR, ca. 1975–1985, and member of the Swedish delegation to ME during the same period (mail and telephone interview, May 2012); Rose Marie Gresch, ME secretary, Zurich, Switzerland, 1981–1995 (mail and telephone interview, May 2012); Marga Indra-Heide, fashion consultant at Modeausschuss Schuhe, Offenbach, Germany, and member of the ME Fashion Committee for several years (mail interview, May 2012); Sylvie Lefranc, director of the Bureau de Style des Industries du Cuir, Paris, France, 1973–2001, and president of the ME Fashion Committee from 1985 (approximately) to 1995 (interview in Paris, May 9, 2012); Ernst Steiner, ME treasurer, 1960–1995 (telephone interview, June 7, 2012); Kirsten Toxvaerd, managing director at Dansk Skomoderåd (Danish Shoe Fashion Council), 1974–1981, and head of the Danish delegation to ME, 1974–1981 (interview in Helsingör, Denmark, May 4, 2012); and Rolf Trüb, CEO of Bally Arola Switzerland, president of the ME Fashion Committee, 1975–1985, and president of ME, 1985–1995 (mail and telephone interview May–June 2012). I would like to express my sincere gratitude to all former colleagues and friends for taking the time to talk to me and to share their recollections of the work of Modeurop.
3. Statistiska Centralbyrån, ed., *Statistisk årsbok för Sverige* (Stockholm, 1945 and 1960).
4. "Kristidspolitik och kristidshushållning i Sverige under och efter andra världskriget," 152:49, Statens offentliga utredningar.
5. Ibid.
6. Ibid.
7. "Skobranschrådet konstitueras," *Skohandlaren*, no. 9, 1945.
8. Minutes of SBR meeting, September 11, 1945, found in the ME file remnants in the Swedish Shoe Fashion Council (SBR) archive, Stockholm. The documents in this archive are not numbered, and the archive does not possess any finding aids.
9. Ibid.
10. "Lädertidningen presenterar Skobranschrådet," *Lädertidningen,* no. 21, 1945.

11. "Kort resumé över Skobranschrådets arbete och utveckling," ca. 1968, SBR archive.
12. Information letter to members of the SBR (probably also sent out to the media), 1946, SBR archive.
13. Aili Pekonen, Report on "The Shoe Fashion in London. Impressions from a trip to the UK 22–26 October 1946," November 1, 1946, SBR archive.
14. SBR archive.
15. Regina Lee Blaszczyk, *The Color Revolution* (Cambridge, MA, 2012).
16. See comments in Valerie Steele, *Shoes: A Lexicon of Styles* (London, 1998), 10.
17. "Färgernas psykologi i modet" (The importance of colors in fashion). In *Lädertidningen*, 22/1950, December 15, 1950.
18. SBR archive.
19. From "PM regarding the activities of the Nordic Fashion Council," February 18, 1959, SBR archive.
20. Ibid.
21. From minutes of NMR meeting in Stockholm, April 26, 1956, NMR files, SBR archive.
22. See Yuniya Kawamura, *Fashion-ology: An Introduction to Fashion Studies* (London, 2005).
23. The colors were called Havana, Mahogany, Chestnut, Golden Oak, Hazel, Club Brown, Swedish Tan, Marine, Morocco, Walnut, Sahara, Malaga, Poppy, Ruby, Japanese Blue, Turquoise, Shale, Pine, Cypress, Tobacco, Benedictine, Pastel Violet and Pastel Rose; *SBR Modeprognos Höst/vinter 1954*, SBR archive.
24. Examples can be found in "Modeprognoser 1950–60," SBR archive, Stockholm.
25. Didier Grumbach, *Histoires de la mode* (Paris, 1993), 61.
26. The end of every publication was stamped with a large "Confidential" with the following explanation: "The forecast is confidential. It is therefore of great importance that its contents are respected. The new colors and their names in the Nordic Fashion Council's Color collection may thus not be published until after the date of publication, as decided by the Council." SBR archive.
27. This document, "A short summary of the work and development of the Swedish Shoe Fashion Council" (*En kort sammanställning av arbetet och utvecklingen av Skobranschrådet*), is located in the SBR archive and is presumably from 1968, eight years after the foundation of ME.
28. On July 1, 1937, the International Wool Publicity and Research Secretariat was formed and quickly renamed the International Wool Secretariat (IWS). Based in London, the IWS had offices in every major wool-producing country by the mid-1950s. "History of the Woolmark Brand," http://www.woolmark.com/about-woolmark/history.
29. Interview with Leena Aro.
30. In the context of this book as a whole, in particular Chapter 10, it is worth recalling one instance of verified contact between the affiliated SBR—manifested in Pekonen's trip shortly after the war—and the BCC and TCCA. The last of these organizations, reports Regina Lee Blaszczyk, saw shoe and leather colors as one of its major remits already in the 1920s. At the same time, one cannot draw a straight line from the TCCA's history to that of ME, which developed from an inter-European process. Unfortunately, writing a history of transatlantic transfers and adaptations of knowledge and practices requires source material not currently available in this case.

31. A short notice in the trade magazine *Läder och Skor* (Leather and Shoes), from June 20, 1960, indicates that the Fashion Director Max Matter of Bally, Switzerland, was visiting Stockholm, Sweden in May 1960. It is likely that he met with representatives of SBR and NMR during this visit.
32. Interview with Ernst Steiner.
33. Mendes and de la Haye, *20th Century Fashion,* 158–92.
34. See Ingrid Giertz-Mårtenson, "Looking into the Future: A Study of Trend Analysis in the Fashion Industry" (MA thesis, Stockholm University, 2006).
35. The spirit that prevailed in Paris in the 1960s was the right atmosphere for the private trend business. In 1960, Maime Arnodin established an *agence de style*, later called MAFIA, in Paris. In 1970, Dominique Peclers, who worked as a stylist at the department store Printemps, opened her own "trend agency" in order to provide advice and information for the fashion industry on upcoming seasons of color and fashion trends. Her company, Peclers Paris, is still regarded as a major player in the field. The same applies to Promostyl, founded in 1966 by Françoise Vincent-Richard. Giertz-Mårtenson, "Looking into the Future."
36. Interview with Sylvie Lefranc.
37. East Germany joined in 1974. The years that the other countries joined were not preserved in the materials used for this study.
38. Interview with Jan Ekblom.
39. Interview with Sylvie Lefranc.
40. Interview with Jan Ekblom.
41. In the 1990s, some of the members of the Textile and Fashion Committee were Leena Aro, Fashion consultant Kenkäneuvosto, Finland; Susanne Galliker, Fashion consultant Swiss Textile Fashion Council and Intercolor; Ingrid Giertz-Mårtenson, CEO Swedish Fashion Council, Sweden; Marga Indra Heide, Fashion Consultant, Modeausschuss Schuhe, Germany; Sylvie Lefranc, Director Bureau de Style des Industries du Cuir, France. A special expert for Men´s fashions was Christine Grandis, Director Oestrreichisches Modesekretariat, Austria.
42. Interview with Sylvie Lefranc.
43. Interview with Kirsten Toxvaerd.
44. Interview with former UN Under Secretary General Jan Mårtenson.
45. Interview with Jan Ekblom.
46. Interview with Sylvie Lefranc.
47. See "Bulletin d´Information" from Modeurop for spring/summer 1971.
48. Interview with Rolf Trüb.
49. Sylvie Lefranc from France remembers, "Arranging a congress could be a question of doing things bigger and better than others. There was a certain competition between hosting nations. And it was a very costly event—some of it being paid by congress fees from attending delegates and a small contribution from Modeurop. But the final bill had to be paid by the hosting country." Interview with Sylvie Lefranc.
50. Interview with Kirsten Toxvaerd, who stated that ME, like many other international organizations, was watched by politicians, the media, and consumers. "Everything had to be simpler and more efficient."
51. Interview with Rolf Trüb.
52. Interview with Kirsten Toxvaerd.

53. "Such ties were developed during the informal luncheon and evening get-togethers of ME. They helped build a good business atmosphere, which can hardly be created if you do not appreciate and sympathize with the other individual." Interview with Jan Ekblom.
54. Interview with Rolf Trüb.
55. The DSI informs and coordinates trends in the German Shoe Industry, with a particular interest in children's shoes. For more, see their website at http://www.schuhinstitut.de/.
56. Interview with Jan Ekblom.
57. "When visiting a leading Italian tannery, I once saw a Modeurop color card on a wall. When I commented, "It's really good to see that you too use Modeurop," I got the following reply: "No, the color card is only there as a warning example." Interview with Jan Ekblom.
58. Kawamura, *Fashion-ology.*
59. Blaszczyk, *Color Revolution,* 6, describes fashion intermediaries as "folks often on the corporate front line, who were charged with the tasks of scoping out consumer tastes and determining the likely direction of change."
60. Interview with Sylvie Lefranc.
61. Interview with Kirsten Toxvaerd.

CHAPTER 12

Who Decides the Color of the Season? How a Trade Show Called Première Vision Changed Fashion Culture

Mary Lisa Gavenas

The silk weavers of Lyon knew that they were in trouble.

These were proud men, accustomed to being emulated and envied. For generations, their families had dealt with haute couture and royalty. But as the 1970s began, they found themselves in a world that celebrated the wash 'n' wear and wrinkle-free. When Neil Armstrong planted his flag on the moon in 1969, it had been made of nylon.[1]

During the decades following World War II, the weavers' prospects had gone from bad to worse. Asian mills churned out cheap fabrics for Asian factoriesg churning out cheap clothes. Rebuilt German factories specialized in synthetics. Americans spent fortunes promoting excrescences like Lycra and Orlon. Even the silk weavers' superintendence of aesthetics had been subverted. In the good old days, design and color trends had trickled down from Paris's *maisons de haute couture* to the rest of the world. Now merchandisers, retailers, and ready-to-wear manufacturers were unwilling to wait their turn.[2] Every Tom, Dick, and Harry was coming out with his own color card.

As fashion grew more and more global, the weavers' traditional business model grew more and more outmoded. Exports were now too important, which left trade fairs as the best way of contacting customers. But there, too, the silk weavers were thwarted. The only event that attracted fashion's major players, a twice-a-year trade fair in Frankfurt, came too late in the season to be much use to them or their customers. As for its industrial setting: well, that they found unspeakable.

M.L. Gavenas (✉)
Journalist and independent scholar, New York, NY, USA

R.L. Blaszczyk, U. Spiekermann (eds.), *Bright Modernity*, Worlds of Consumption, DOI 10.1007/978-3-319-50745-3_12

So the weavers started their own show. In the fall of 1973, fifteen French mills banded together to show their Fall 1974 collections in a downtown Lyon hotel meeting room.[3] Calling their tiny trade fair "Première Vision" because it was literally a "first look" at the next year's colors and trends, they preempted the big Frankfurt fair by over a month. They aimed not only to offer clear color trends but to offer them first—before Americans or Germans or Italians or anyone else muddied the waters. They invited their best customers from Europe, the United States, and Japan. The weavers hoped that, in return for a head start on the new season, these customers would express appreciation with larger and more lucrative orders. At least, that's the way "Première Vision" was supposed to work.

Which it did. The next year, "Première Vision Tissus de Lyon" built on its strengths by adding more promotional shade trends and moving its presentation to Paris to coincide with the prêt-à-porter shows, where the weavers' high-end clients gathered. In 1976, they made the show's color statement stronger still, ensuring that the show's color forecast was reflected in some or all of each exhibitor's offerings.

By the end of its first decade, each edition boasted over 300 exhibitors from a dozen European countries, drew over 16,000 visitors, and was an established ritual for designers, manufacturers, merchandisers, retailers, beauty companies, and everyone else whose business required knowledge of fashion—particularly color—trends.[4] From then on, its influence continued to grow.

In this case study, I examine the market forces that gave Première Vision what sociologist Lise Skov has called its "unique trend-setting function"[5] and document its development into a prime player in the globalization of the fashion industry, ending with its 2005 incorporation as Première Vision Pluriel, a Lyon-based limited company operating multiple fashion-related trade fairs on multiple continents.

As Sabine Le Chatelier, associate fashion director of Première Vision, has explained,

> People don't always understand what influences fashion. They may think everything comes from Marc Jacobs, but fashion is not only dreams and glamour.
> It's also an industrial field.[6]

What Came Before

By the 1970s, most people had stopped pretending that hemlines, shades, and silhouettes were dictates from Paris.

World War II had hastened the pace of change. After the war, cities like Florence, Rome, Milan, and London were setting themselves as design centers to rival Paris. American fashion had grown more independent and more focused on sportswear. Meanwhile, the middle classes of Africa, Asia, and South America had begun wearing Western-style, readymade clothes.

And all those factors, as an executive in the French textile industry explained, "brought a homogenization of styles in larger quantities."[7]

France's mills had problems of their own. Although French centers of textile production sustained few direct hits during World War II, the survival of that pre-war machinery proved a mixed blessing. As one industry veteran explained, "the fact that apparel factories weren't too badly damaged by the war, meant that they restarted with old machines, thus with the handicap of a prewar productivity, whereas Germany had to reconstruct and received subsidies to do so because most of its industrial centers were destroyed. In France, the renewal of machinery was a very slow process."[8]

Elsewhere in Europe, newer factories with newer equipment were better positioned to work with newer fibers. But even conventional fibers and fabrics presented problems for French mills since non-European raw materials suppliers were becoming involved in their home countries' new, vertically integrated ventures. And no matter how up-to-date their machinery, French mills couldn't compete with the lower labor costs in Asia.

At the same time, since Western-style clothes were being produced and worn in those new markets, exports became more important. French textile executive Ashley Dormeuil, fifth-generation proprietor of a mill founded in 1842, recalled, "our export in the mid-1950s was about 50 percent" and grew to about 80 percent in the following decades.[9] That may have sounded like good news, but few French mills had the financial resources to retain representatives in foreign markets.

Enter trade shows—and a whole new set of problems. For producers that prided themselves on setting trends, like the silk weavers of Lyon, the frustrations inherent in doing business at trade shows were summed up in a Frankfurt-based textile fair called Interstoff.[10] A purely commercial venture run by a company called Messe Frankfurt,[11] Interstoff was neither managed by fashion professionals nor staged in a fashion capital. Disseminating design trends was not its priority. Show management slotted Interstoff into its Frankfurt fair grounds when they were not occupied by its other shows. If that made Interstoff's timing less than optimal for textile mills and their garment-manufacturer customers, then so be it.

Under the premise that it provided one-stop shopping for apparel textiles, Interstoff put wool, acrylic, silk, rayon, cotton, polyester, and whatever else anybody wanted to sell under a single roof. The storied silk mills of Lyon peddled their pricey wares alongside copyists and cut-price commodities. The show's organization admitted no hierarchy of taste and presented no unifying fashion direction. Crowded, chaotic, and lacking glamour, Interstoff was widely regarded as an ordeal to be endured.[12]

But it was a commercial success. First staged in July of 1959, Interstoff had quickly become a semiannual ritual that, by the early 1970s, drew hundreds of exhibitors and upward of 20,000 visitors.[13] Most attended not because they enjoyed the show or were eager to spend time in its industrial exhibition halls but because everyone else in the fabric, apparel, and retail businesses was going too. Copyists exhibited next to *artistes*. Riffraff exhibited next to nobs. French and Italian textile makers, for example, attended in hopes of making export contacts. Asian mills attended in hopes of making their own export contacts or to underbid European competitors. Fiber companies—DuPont, Hoechst, Celanese, Enka, ICI—came to tout technical innovations.

No one shopped the show for color or design trends, although almost every exhibitor arrived with a color card, which presented the exhibiting company's edited range of defined shades.[14] Most claimed to offer a preview of fashionable colors for the coming season. Few came close.

Widely reviled by both exhibitors and attendees, Interstoff flourished throughout the 1960s because it had little or no competition. The show was seen as a necessary evil. Exhibitors and visitors complained about the chairs, the acoustics, and the food. "The show had an airport atmosphere," recalled denim executive Andrew Olah."[15] Paris it was not.

Because Interstoff shared the show complex with a packed schedule of other industrial fairs, Messe Frankfurt stuck to a schedule that doomed exhibitors' attempts at influencing color and design trends. Ideally, garment manufacturers would have first shopped for materials about a year before merchandise was due in stores, a timeline that allowed the label time to see the shades and design trends of the coming season and incorporate them in its line so that it would always have the latest trends ready for its customers.[16] Thus, a garment label looking for color trends for its Fall 1960 designs would benefit most by shopping for materials in the fall of 1959.

From the beginning, Interstoff's timing made that kind of fashion-conscious garment production difficult, if not impossible. Its first show, July 7–10, 1959, had been held when spring was well over, some of summer was gone, it was not yet time to work on fall, and Europeans had only a few weeks before their mills and factories closed for the annual vacation. Fall sessions convened in late November or early December—weeks after the prêt-a-porter runway shows in Paris had turned into old news and right before most production shut down for the holidays.[17] Throughout the 1960s, the show kept to a similar schedule. Thus, by the time Interstoff rolled around each season, color cards and trend reports were window dressing—major decisions on such matters having been already made in order to meet production deadlines.

After a dozen years of Interstoff, exhibitors and attendees were becoming resigned to its homogenization of style, preponderance of cheap fabrics, and lack of clear color direction. Such were the sad facts of the new fashion production cycle.

Everyone complained. Everyone kept going.

Timing Is Everything

Finally, in 1973, 15 frustrated French weavers rented a meeting room in Lyon's Sofitel for a tiny trade show called Première Vision Tissus de Lyon (PV).

> The timing and the environment of the [Interstoff] show didn't fit them as luxury products producers. They wanted a special treatment for their top-class customers. Then they decided to organize a special presentation in a hotel meeting room in Lyon for the best silk buyers from Europe, the States, Japan.... Only fifteen weavers responded to this proposal and finally it was a real success because the relationship with these quality customers was as important as the product itself.... Silk was suffering at the time, "fighting" against synthetic and new fibers whose image in the top range of products was getting stronger.[18]

"Competing friends" from Lyon and elsewhere in France joined the PV group, making about 30 exhibitors, and transferred the spring show to the Sofitel Porte de Sèvres near the Boulevard Péripherique in 1974, a site on the outskirts of Paris chosen for its convenience for overseas visitors.[19] Since the participants concentrated on silk production and their customers on high-end women's wear, PV was timed to coincide with the prêt-à-porter presentations held nearby, making attendance convenient for anyone already there on business.

Would pink be played out by next season? Would its popularity build? Would the shade soften? Or go stronger? In theory, a California-based manufacturer traveling to Paris in the fall to place orders for spring fashions could also drop by PV and get an idea of the textures, colors, and patterns available for the following fall, while his own reaction to the prêt-à-porter presentations was still fresh and he was able to discuss it with the weavers—getting a jump on his competition without incurring extra expense.

Unlike Interstoff or smaller shows sponsored by foreign trade bureaus,[20] the new show was run as a weavers' cooperative focused not on making money for the umbrella organization but on the needs of member companies and their customers. At PV, prestige was paramount. While the Frankfurt show aimed to maximize revenues by renting the greatest number of booths to the greatest number of producers, PV catered to high-end brands, celebrated *snobbisme*, and put a premium on exclusivity. Exhibitors were admitted to the PV fold on the basis of their reputation and recent collections, a vetting process similar to inclusion in a juried art show. And, although the expanded group was not strictly limited to Lyonnaise weavers, during its first years it continued under the name "Première Vision Tissus de Lyon" and used the lion that was the symbol of that city as its logo.

By the third edition of PV, in late 1974, the group was already developing promotional shade trends and sharing them before the exhibition—further distinguishing themselves from commodity mills and copyists. Months before each show, exhibiting mills had the opportunity to attend a *concertation* to share their ideas of what the coming season's trend would be. These ideas were then distilled by management and presented as a unified statement, a system that made PV radically different from both its Interstoff competition and the smaller fairs set up by trade commissions to promote local textile industries in Italy or the United Kingdom.

By 1976, with about 30 of France's most prestigious mills combining their clout each season, PV featured a single color card and trend forecast strongly presented on the show floor and amplified by the presentations in surrounding visitors' booths. Sworn to secrecy, participating weavers were given the color card before the show so that at least part of each collection would reflect that color forecast in hopes of "lending coherence to the offer, and helping to structure the market."[21] For the rest of the industry, the colors of the coming season were revealed only on the show's opening day. Release of the PV color card attained the status of an industry event.

While Interstoff stuck to its same old schedule, PV dates continued to be coordinated with the twice-a-year showing of ready-to-wear collections and circus of surrounding events that would later be known as Paris Fashion Week.[22] Its French connection helped in other ways too: Paris was a traditional capital of taste as well as a major tourist destination. Retailers and manufacturers proved as eager to go to Paris as they were reluctant to visit Frankfurt. With this new trade show, an American retailer visiting Paris in April could watch fall fashions on the runways and then stop by PV for a preview of what was coming next spring.

In October 1977, PV broadened its scope—and thus its influence—by opening to other types of fibers and fabrics, such as wool, cotton, blends, and knits. For the time being, however, it remained exclusively French. Although still using the Lyonnais lion in its logo, the show was now known as "Première Vision Tissus Création" and held adjacent to the prêt-à-porter salon at the Porte de Versailles with shuttle buses—*navettes*—running between the venues to make attendance as painless as possible.[23]

PV was already a place to see and be seen. By 1979, more than 150 French producers participated, but PV signage and brochures were trilingual (in French, German, and English) to acknowledge that at least half its visitors came from abroad. The following year, other high-end European producers who passed the jury selection were permitted to exhibit—although the show still shut out Italian mills because they were considered direct competitors to the French. At the same time, the show added trend displays specific to fabric types: without going to the bother of back-and-forth fabric development, customers could see the colors of the coming season in lace, silk, shirt fabrics, jerseys, or tweeds. Now with over 200 exhibitors, PV organized itself around its color card, which was displayed at the center of the show floor.

In 1983, after having received applications from over 100 Italian firms, PV finally invited its chief rivals, the high-end Italian companies showing at the Ideacomo, Ideabiella, and Prato Expo textile shows held later in the season, to join the PV fold. As a condition of admission, they, like all other exhibitors, subscribed to the PV color card and submitted swatches for the trend forums. The PV color card now ruled throughout Europe. In October of that year, "Tissus Création" had been dropped from the logo and signage for the first time—soon to disappear completely.

A decade after its founding, PV attracted at least 15,000 visitors to each edition. Other shows scurried to keep up. Newer fabric fairs copied PV's scheduling, and Interstoff tried to close the five-week gap between PV and its own show.[24] But PV, which dominated the high end of the fashion market, had no direct competition. No other organization gave as much attention to the development of a color card—or enhanced it with such elegant presentations.

With the opening of its "Summer 1985" show on March 17, 1984, PV moved to the newly built Parc des Expositions convention center in Villepinte near the Charles de Gaulle Airport, substantially expanding its exhibition space. With the show no longer in proximity to the Paris ready-to-wear presentations, PV management fought to maintain the show's prestige. They wanted none of the convention-style dog-and-pony shows that big fiber companies and commodity mills staged at Interstoff and other trade fairs. Among the regulations imposed at the new venue: closed booths of uniform size and design, uniform signage, standardized lighting, limits on food and beverage service, bans on any in-booth displays visible from the show floor, and bans on music.

This imposed uniformity and lack of distraction created a bland backdrop that made PV's color forecast appear all the more dramatic. Entering the huge industrial halls of the Parc des Expositions, even the most obtuse visitors immediately sensed the latest shade trends. First, they confronted a gigantic color card—sometimes twenty feet high—at the show's entrance. Then, they saw those same colors repeated in the show's carpeting, walls, and signage. They also saw show personnel dressed in uniforms that reflected the mood and colors of the coming season.

Each show's color card was further amplified in the exhibition spaces known as "trend forums," where buyers found an edited selection of swatches showing how exhibitors interpreted the next season's colors, textures, and other trends. Days before each show, the PV display team was charged with selecting fabric swatches that best represented that edition's forecast. Each exhibitor was well aware that by expending significant creative effort on interpreting the PV trend forecast received in advance of the show, his or her designs could gain valuable exposure on the show floor—a reward system that further reinforced the authority of PV forecasts.

In 1987, PV again expanded the trend forecasting that attracted so many foreign visitors, adding foreign mills and selected international forecasters to the concertation meetings that began working on the color card at least eighteen months in advance of the actual season. That same year, PV president Bernard Dupasquier emphasized the importance of leading trends rather than waiting to follow them, saying, "Our job is to bring the weaver closer and closer to the market."[25] Within a year of the new panel's first presentation, attendance was up nearly 50 percent, reaching nearly 35,000 in March of 1989—nearly 21,000 of those visitors coming from outside France. In the United States, fashion forecasters did PV-based presentations for audiences who couldn't make the trip to Paris.[26]

Each edition also had its own slogan and accompanying graphic—that edition's "visual"—to convey the mood of the coming season. Following the practice of France's fashion houses, these words and pictures tended toward the poetic rather than the literal, and no expense was spared in their production. For its Spring/Summer 1988 show, for example, PV management used the slogan *"Le Langage Secret,"* accompanied by watercolor splotches and symbols painted in a naive style. For the Fall/Winter 1989/1990 show, the theme was *"La terre est bleue comme une orange"* ("the Earth is blue like an orange"), a quotation from poet Paul Éluard illustrated by a gigantic apple with the dimpled skin of a citrus fruit. For the first Spring/Summer show of the new decade, the theme was *"Je décalque l'invisible"* ("I trace the invisible") from Jean Cocteau, illustrated by what appeared to be a raindrop. Each show was promoted with billboards around Paris, as well as display advertising in internationally distributed trade papers like Fairchild Publications' *Women's Wear Daily* and *Daily News Record.*[27]

The trade press began covering in PV in 1977, when the show expanded to include high-end wools, cottons, and other fibers in addition to its original silks. Afterward, PV's coverage in U.S. trade publications continued to build, especially once it became a steady source of advertising revenue for Fairchild Publications.[28] Twice a year, whole issues of textile publications in the United States, France, and China were devoted to analysis of PV's color card and its amplification in surrounding trend forums, where swatches of fabric from exhibiting weavers' current collections were displayed alongside photographs or videos that took the kind of poetic license meant to illustrate the mood of a particular season. For example, trend forums at the Fall/Winter 2005/2006 edition, held in September 2004, tried to convey the incongruity of a palette labeled "foggy brights" with photographs of other contradictions in terms: greenery reflected in skyscraper windows, a Louis XV fauteuil in a slum setting, and a tree sprouting from the side of an apartment building.

Coverage in the consumer press didn't take off until the 1980s. PV was, after all, deadly dull to anyone outside the fashion business and closed to the general public. So, although mainstream news outlets were never in regular attendance, reporters on the fashion or retail beats occasionally dropped in to do a story on the hidden workings of the fashion world, or they took the opportunity to nab an interview with an otherwise unforthcoming designer.

Writing in London's *Financial Times* in 1986,[29] Andrew Moreton explained to readers that PV had become so important that Lindka Cierach, who had designed the wedding dress for Sarah, the Duchess of York, earlier that year, was skipping the British fabric shows in preference to Paris—a newsmaking national insult. The next year, filing from London, Nina Hyde, the influential fashion editor of the *Washington Post*, interviewed Calvin Klein, whose trip to Europe had been prompted by Première Vision.[30] Filing a story from Paris in 1989, the *New York Times* fashion columnist Woody Hochswender listed U.S.-based designers "Ronaldus Shamask, Carmelo Pomodoro, Charlotte Neuville,

Andrew Jovine, Bill Robinson and Alexander Julian," then at the height of their careers, as well as representatives from Seventh Avenue stalwarts "Donna Karan, Calvin Klein, Anne Klein, Perry Ellis and Liz Claiborne" as being in mandatory attendance at Première Vision.[31]

Recognizing that customers shopped for fabric according to finished product rather than country of origin, the show reformatted in 1990, which further emphasized its pan-European character. Now, instead of being grouped together with compatriots selling lace or wool, Italian silk weavers were now be grouped near French silk weavers—allowing garment manufacturers to schedule appointments more efficiently. By 1996, the show's complex, multiple projection audiovisual component had been changed to a short film, although slide projections were still featured in a more topical "best of show" presentation.

By then, the PV color card and trend forums were considered so crucial to the coming season that many professionals took the RER train to Villepinte and paid PV's $25 admission fee with absolutely no intention of shopping for fabric. Some weren't even in the fashion business. "We fly to Europe because over there we have Première Vision," explained Dominique Szabo, the senior vice president of product development for beauty products manufacturer Estée Lauder, in 1997. "We saw what was going on in fabrics and decor and object and even the people, how they were dressed at the entrance. We spend one day because we want to touch, we want to look at people, we want to see what they have put on the wall. We want to look at the video."[32] The following year, the director of creative product development at the same beauty products company, Aerin Lauder Zinterhoffer, explained why attendance at PV was necessary for a business that did not use textiles: "Fabrics are very important for us. The sense of texture. Finish. Color.... Meaning when you see a lot of satin fabrics, you know you have to put that trend in your product as shine," Szabo added, "It's never an idea. Not suddenly 'oh, I like gray, let's do gray.' No. Never. It's a lot of research. A lot of slaving away. Always there is a direction. There is something."[33]

By the late 1990s, each edition of PV regularly drew over 800 exhibitors and over 40,000 attendees. Hotel rooms in Paris were fully booked months in advance of the show dates. As the new century approached, PV was no longer scheduled around Paris Fashion Week. Instead the fashion shows in Paris, London, Milan, and New York were scheduled around PV. In a story about the packed schedule of runway shows slated for the tents in New York's Bryant Park in September 2002, the *New York Times* noted, "Designers wanted to show early so they could make it to the Première Vision, the fabric fair in Paris where they shop for the next season's materials."[34] PV's role in the origination of color trends had become so central to the fashion business that many seasons saw a week-long gap in the runway schedule—generally between the season's start in New York and its resumption in Europe—while the industry adjourned en masse to the Parc des Expositions.

In the twenty-first century, PV added smaller shows in select markets. First came European PreView, which debuted in New York in 2000.[35] Next, PV launched an edition in Shanghai in 2004, intentionally limited to about 500 invitation-only attendees in an attempt to control copyists.[36] Playing up its role as a "link between the market and the producers,"[37] displays at each show used swatches only from mills exhibiting at that edition, meaning that no display was ever transferred from another show. While the trend forums of these smaller, overseas editions had nowhere near the production values of the extravaganzas in Villepinte, they served to underscore the primacy of the PV color card by making it the centerpiece of each installation.

The twenty-first century also saw PV accepting non-Europeans as exhibitors, beginning with the September 2002 show, further spreading the influence of the PV color card by guaranteeing that elite manufacturers from other continents participated. Acknowledging its de facto status as a producer of trade fairs, PV increased the leverage of its forecasting by joining forces with Expofil, a trade show for fibers and yarns, in 2004. The next year, PV annexed Indigo, a trade show for prints and surface design. In 2005, it formally annexed two more trade shows long held concurrently at the Parc des Expositions—ModAmont (for trim and findings) and Le Cuir à Paris (for leather and fur)—forming the entity known as Première Vision Pluriel.[38]

Now an umbrella organization for well over 1,000 manufacturers of fashion-related materials that encompassed everything from faux fur to sequins, PV nonetheless maintained its original snob appeal. The Première Vision Pluriel extravaganza at the Parc des Expositions may have been a huge trade show, but it remained one where business could be conducted by repairing to a specialty wine bar. Or refreshment stands selling foie gras.

Creating the PV Color Card

From its beginnings, PV put an emphasis on color forecasting that was radically different from anything done by its competition. During the first two or three shows, this may have been done simply for reasons of prestige: the Lyon weavers were, after all, at the highest end of the market, with reputations to uphold, and they were now reminding designers, the press, and buyers attending the Paris fashion shows of the weavers' role in color and design.[39]

Even today, though, no one else attempts statements as emphatic as those made at the Parc des Expositions. Back in the 1970s, few shows would have thought to bother.[40] Trend forums at textile trade shows—if they existed at all—were usually ad hoc groupings of current collections from exhibitors (who may or may not have paid an additional fee for the privilege of being highlighted), which were then stuck on a wall under a catchy rubric. In those days, each fiber company had its own full-time forecaster and sizable fabric companies had at least one full-time designer. Fashion manufacturers and retailers had access to their own forecasters: all of them purporting to predict future color trends and all producing their own color cards and shade ranges.[41]

By contrast, PV presented slick, sophisticated color trends aimed squarely at its end market: the fashion industry. "The key [to the PV color card] is closeness to the industry," said associate fashion director Le Chatelier, who spent sixteen years at a trend-forecasting firm before joining the PV team. From its beginning, the PV color card began in physical meetings or concertations, where weavers provided input based on their own knowledge of fashion cycles, customer requests, production capabilities, observed trends, and anything else that they deemed an influence on the coming season. As Le Chatelier explained, "This is not a collection of personal statements, but something based on research and industrial knowledge... [that] then becomes part of the color card, which creates trends... " In other words, "it's the story of which comes first, the chicken or the egg? Now the way that we present the trends is the way the industry has been structured."[42]

During the 1980s, PV increased its number of exhibitors and attendees dramatically.[43] In 1989, a veteran reporter for Fairchild Publications noted, "The big Première Vision show in Paris has come to be regarded internationally as a leader in providing fashion and color trend information and in helping to crystallize the mood and character of the season ahead. But nearly all of the other international shows have heightened their efforts in this area."[44]

By 2005, PV was still developing each season's color forecast in consultation with a consortium of member companies—much as it had done in the 1970s when, it was a relatively small weavers' cooperative. The process, however, was only nominally collaborative and definitely not democratic. Steered by PV fashion director Pascaline Wilhelm, a team of six full-time employees worked year-round to facilitate the process of creating the color card and putting together the trend forums for each show. "All year, they do fashion surveys and research. The look of the show, the personality, changes radically. The concept must be visible the minute you walk through the door," said Le Chatelier. "We are the only show which has a team 100 percent dedicated to fashion information."[45]

Typically, those team members have had an art school education with a specialization in textiles. For example, Wilhelm, who joined in 1998, studied textiles at ENSAD, the École Nationale Supérieure des Arts Decoratifs in Paris, and Le Chatelier attended the École Supérieure des Arts Appliqués in Paris, better known as the École Duperré. Le Chatelier emphasized the shared pragmatism of PV employees, calling the team "very professional people... not the big gurus. These are people who cannot talk about color without also talking about texture, weight, or matte versus shiny.... "[46]

In theory, each color card started from scratch. "Every six months, it's the white pages," said Le Chatelier. "The aim is to extract the creativity of the exhibitors." As the show entered its fourth decade, the next season's color card began with a series of concertations. The first, in France, was scheduled ten days after the close of the previous Parc des Expositions show. The team then invited a select group of elite exhibitors to participate in each concertation and share ideas. The purpose, said Le Chatelier, was to "try to mix people with different know-hows" and thereby "extract common points." These elected representatives came from noncompeting sectors—a denim maker might sit alongside a lace maker but would never see a rival denim maker at the same meeting—and conferred in a workshop-style forum. Those invited were not professional trend forecasters. "They came with their ideas, mixing points of view...sharing color in a very personal way," said Le Chatelier. Methods ranged from sharing "swipe" (visuals already published by magazines, brochures, or websites) to complex slide shows, computer programs, or snips of ribbon from the flea market. A member of the PV team then put together a preliminary color card based on the results of that meeting.

Three weeks after the show, the process was repeated in each of the major European countries and in Japan, with each member country arriving at its own roughed-out color card. After that, one representative from each national workshop took part in a final two-day workshop to arrive at a synthesis "of strong key stories" and "define [colors] more precisely."[47] For the spring shows scheduled for the Parc des Exposition each February, this meeting was held in mid-November. For the Fall shows staged in September, it happened at the end of April.

The final product, exclusive to PV, showed approximately twenty colors, ranging over both darks and lights. "It is quite short," explained Le Chatelier, "but big enough because each month you [a retailer or manufacturer] need to inject richness into the line."[48] Once the color card was assembled, the PV session team started work: strategizing the official theme, creating the accompanying graphic, and dreaming up evocative shade names in both French and English. The color card was printed and sent to PV participants along with explanatory iconography and written themes. By the end of May or the beginning of June, work on the September show's color card was complete and the fashion team could concentrate on preparing the show forums.

From 2000 onward, the public preview of the color card came at the two-day European PreView, the small, two-day show staged in Manhattan during the second week of July—a bonne bouche before the big September show at the Parc des Expositions. During the second week of January, the process repeated when the spring color card was shown in the lead-up to the French show in February. Since most mills did not have time to interpret the color card or work up a full line of samples, European PreView did not substitute for the larger show. Its displays were rudimentary and its trend forums were not particularly predictive of what would be seen in Villepinte. The big draws were the hour-long, audio-visual "Trend Tasting" conducted twice each day by Le Chatelier, as well as the wall-size installation of the color card. But although the colors themselves were now known, the impact of the color card wasn't fully felt until its display at the Parc des Expositions in Villepinte.

How each mill followed—or did not follow—that color card has always been one of the most misunderstood aspects of PV. Participating mills were not required to use it exclusively; although some did, especially since a really beautiful interpretation of the color card invariably landed the mill prominent placement in the show's trend forums and possible inclusion in each day's "best of show" highlights. "What we never want is uniformity," said Le Chatelier; "everyone has a different way to work with the trend. Some follow step by step. Other put themselves in opposition."[49]

Because most designers and high-end labels claimed to have exclusives on the fabrics that they used, their buying and ordering process has also been misconstrued. Representing the extreme high end, Hermès' menswear designer Véronique Nichanian never missed PV, but also never used a fabric for Hermès that was not a guaranteed exclusive.[50] She made the trip to PV not to place orders—transactions could take place at her office in Paris or in follow-up discussions—but to see PV's color card and interpretation of the season. Having gained substantial textile expertise during her early career as in-house sourcing expert for Italian-born designer Nino Cerruti, she went to the Parc des Expositions to suss out its color card and trend forums and look for technical advances from individual exhibitors, before beginning collaboration with her chosen vendors. Having the luxury of Hermès's unlimited budget, Nichanian often pushed a new fabric (for example, stretch linen) through several "developments"—the test runs of new fabrics—until she was satisfied. By the time her menswear collection debuted on the runway, its fabrics reflected both Hermès's tradition of exclusivity and Nichanian's response to the mood of that season.

As Le Chatelier puts it, "The color card is a reference point."

Giving the Card Clout

For PV to issue its own color card was nothing new, even in the 1970s.

As a device for announcing and shaping trends, the color card has changed little in the past century.[51] Color cards aimed at the garment industry must include both darks and lights as well as neutrals and brights to meet manufacturers' end needs; they rarely comprise less than a dozen shades or more than two dozen, lest the statement become diluted. In any color card for the apparel industry, the art lies not only in shade selection but in shade combination. For example, a concentration of whitened shades is a strong clue that white will dominate the next season. Or the inclusion of several variations on black may signal a season of steampunk chic. Or all the shades on a color card may look slightly dulled and gray.

From the beginning, PV made the message and mood of its color card almost impossible to miss. In an edition held in March 1988, "The overall retro character of Première Vision could be seen through the extensive use of blowups of old photographs from the late '30s used as display materials. And these also turned up in the heavily attended audiovisual presentation done by the organizers of the show."[52]

In 1989, PV received the results of a report commissioned from Axios, a French market research firm, showing that the majority of its visitors "believed that presentation on the basis of different materials would greatly improve the show."[53] For the next few years, trend forums became exponentially more elaborate, while copies of the PV color cards being sold at the show became collectible pieces of fashion publishing. For the Fall/Winter 1991/1992 show, for example, the artist Elia Kim was commissioned to produce a wooden box of lithographs called *Le Cercle Magique,* with each lithograph illustrating not only the color but the concept behind it. Some of the interpretations were literal (such as "cereal," a neutral shade illustrated by a drawing of a field of grain growing on a tabletop), others less so ("indigo," depicted by turbans on hatstands).[54]

Thereafter, each presentation came as a surprise. For the Fall/Winter 1994/1995 show, the *L'Instant de Création* color card was presented by a portfolio of fashion illustrations drawn by fashion designers including Christian Lacroix, Claude Montana, and Emanuel Ungaro. For Fall/Winter 1997/1998, there was *Audace*, a binder of all twenty-nine colors in that season's color card, each displayed on both crepe and satin silk woven with the PV logo. The next season, Spring 1998, brought *Big Bang,* interpreted with a shadowbox made of clear acrylic filled with fabric swatches and yarns. After 2000, presentations became more practical, but no less lavish. For PV's Spring 2002 edition, *Impulsion* was interpreted by four flip books named and explained in five languages.

Equal pains were taken with descriptive language. In a textbook example of what French sociologist Pierre Bourdieu called the "mastery of verbal accompaniment, preferably technical, archaic and esoteric, which separates informed tasting from mere passive consumption," even the plainest presentation of the 20 shades in the show's color card were captioned by names in both French and English that emphasized the nuance of that shade.[55] On a single color card, a strong red would be called "ketchup," pale lavender was "Turkish delight," black was "black moon," and shades that most consumers would describe as "dark gray" were specified as "meteorite," "compost," and "tar."[56] The color card itself was then described in language aimed at an audience able to decode sentences such as "The range incites to serene and energetic dialogues between softness and audacity. Placing saturated colours as anchorage points, spicing them with terrestrial darks, tempering them with muted neutral and stirring them up in hot and cold."[57]

The need for continual distinction and differentiation meant that PV never repeated colors and names. Displays were never reused. As PV entered its fourth decade, each show at the Parc des Expositions amplified that season's color card in over a dozen trend forums, which were completely re-themed, reconceived, and rebuilt with site-specific architecture each time—something all the more impressive because the PV team had only three days to install its displays at the Parc des Expositions and two days to dismantle them. "Three hours after, the show is gone," Le Chatelier said with a resigned sigh. "It is the character of the ephemeral." Depending on the season, the PV team employed everything from a carousel to a stand of bamboo to put its point across. In one of its more literal interpretations, PV pointed to the trend forum with a Las Vegas-style neon sign spelling out the word "gamme," a pun on the English "game" and the French "gamme de couleurs." Directly beneath, visitors could play one-armed bandits to see what colors were coming up for the next year.[58] The rest of the exhibition space was, as much as possible, coordinated to expand upon that theme, using everything from colored fabrics to cover the cement walls to colored carpets lining the aisles. In 2005, when shine made a strong return to the market, PV sprinkled tasteful sparkles up and down the aisles of the Parc des Expositions' Hall Five.[59]

How PV Changed Fashion Culture

The authority of PV's trend presentation reduced the market's tolerance for difference. Partly because of PV's efficiency in transmitting color trends, the fashion market's mechanism of color forecasting also changed—leaving many of the individual forecasters who had been employed by fiber companies, mills, and retailers out of a full-time job. Rather than employing a dedicated color forecaster, Wal-Mart, the world's largest retailer, simply dispatched its people to PV. "Most of them [the forecasters] go to PV," explained Roseann Forde, who lost her own job as DuPont's fashion marketing director and global colorist after nearly three decades.[60]

Early editions of PV were usually six weeks or more ahead of other fabric shows.[61] But to a less quantifiable degree, PV's method of presenting color trends also shortened the fashion cycle. When PV decreed, for example, that lavender and baby blue would be the accent shades of the season, those shades were represented in almost every booth at the show.[62] There was no lag time for buyers and manufacturers to see whether or not lavender and baby blue sold well, or which weaver would execute the idea best. Lavender and baby blue were everywhere at once. They were integrated into the PV color card, prominently featured in the trend forums, and shown in bunting, signage, and other decor. Even the carpet lining the aisles was purple. Everyone in the fashion world was suddenly on the same page at the same time.

By anticipating the needs of its customers—driving the market rather than reacting—PV allowed fashion companies to skip steps in previous models of transmitting color trends. In the twenty-first century, PV's timing, location, and accessibility made it possible for even the most inexperienced and unconnected member of the fashion world to hop on the RER line from Paris to Villepinte and gather the same information on color trends as sourcing experts, well-connected designers, and retail executives. While the silk weavers of Lyon may have started the show to strike a blow against offshore competition, their venture did more to enable it. PV's authoritative color forecasting made offshore production, which requires time allowances for shipping and customs, measurably more efficient.

Because the show centered on the textile market, which required the longest lead times and remained the most tactile segment of fashion (and therefore the most difficult to copy from print or electronic communications), PV hastened the globalization of fashion in ways that changes in media, patternmaking, and transportation never had. Nobody had to wait to watch the colors coming down the runways anymore, then wait another season to launch their own reactions and re-interpretations. At PV, trends were made equally available to both the high and low ends of the fashion market at the same time.

By the late 1980s, the PV color card had become a self-fulfilling prophecy. Fashion trades covered PV as an event, making no attempt to judge its color card or argue its interpretation. Stores, fashion labels, accessories makers, and beauty companies attended, then invested according to what they gleaned from the show—thus guaranteeing that stores were full of whatever PV predicted for the season.

High-cost and low-cost fashions were no longer distinguishable by their relative novelty, as they had been when Paris couture was regarded as the ultimate source of invention. With the same styles, shades, and silhouettes on offer at both H&M and Bergdorf Goodman, enormous differences in price were justified not by the freshness of the trend being presented but by the expense of its execution according to cost of material, country of origin, and method of production.

For this, the fashion world had Première Vision to thank.

Or blame.

Notes

1. Anne M. Platoff, "Where No Flag Has Gone Before: Political and Technical Aspects of Placing a Flag on the Moon," NASA Contractor Report 188251, August 1993, Johnson Space Center, NASA, http://www.jsc.nasa.gov/history/flag/flag.htm.
2. In *The Color Revolution* (Cambridge, MA, 2012), 286, Regina Lee Blaszczyk estimates that, before World War II, the life cycle of a color trend originating in Paris was about 7 years, adding, "By the mid 1970s, there wasn't 'time for a new color to filter down from the top.'"
3. Jacques Brunel, then president of Première Vision Pluriel, in an e-mail message to the author on April 16, 2008, dated the first gathering to October 1973.
4. Although this paper is based on interviews and historical research conducted in the Première Vision archives in Lyon, it also draws on my experience as an editor at *Glamour, InStyle, Mirabella,* and industry trade publications, especially my 2002–2007 position as Senior Textiles Editor at Fairchild, the publisher of *Women's Wear Daily* and *Daily News Record,* as well as my 2007–2012 stint as a consultant to Supima, an exhibitor at Expofil.
5. Lise Skov, "The Role of Trade Fairs in the Global Fashion Business," *Current Sociology* 54 (September 2006): 764–83.
6. Sabine Le Chatelier, interview with author, May 25, 2012. Le Chatelier joined Première Vision in 2004 after 16 years at Peclers Paris, a trend forecasting firm.
7. Première Vision president Robert Brochier quoted by Sophie d'Aulnay, "The Postwar French Revolution: 1945–1995," *Daily News Record,* December 7, 1995.
8. Ibid.

9. D'Aulnay, "The Postwar French Revolution: 1945–1995."
10. A brand name that joined the prefix for "international" with *Stoff*, the German word for "material."
11. Claudia Maurer, a press coordinator for Messe Frankfurt, in an e-mail message to the author, April 2012, explained that trade show producer Messe Frankfurt traces its lineage through the 1907 foundation of the Ausstellungs- und Festhallen-Gesellschaft mbH and situated itself in the tradition of the first documented mention of a trade fair in Frankfurt in 1150.
12. Andrew Olah, discussion with author, December 2007.
13. Attendance figures obtained from Maurer for Messe Frankfurt, e-mail to author, April 2012.
14. For an historical overview of how color cards for the apparel industry gained wider cultural capital, see Blaszczyk, *Color Revolution,* 39–43.
15. Andrew Olah in discussion with the author, December 2007.
16. For an overview of the overlapping seasonal production cycles in the U.S. fashion industry, see Irene Daria, *The Fashion Cycle* (New York, 1990), which follows several American designers as they develop and produce collections.
17. Maurer, e-mail to author, April 2012.
18. Brunel, e-mail to author, April 16, 2008.
19. Ibid.
20. In the decades following World War II, small fabric fairs, sponsored wholly or in part by national trade bureaus, were a frequent feature of the fashion textile market. See, for example, Frank Stuart, "Portuguese Offer Fabric Show," *Daily News Record,* March 21, 1986.
21. Première Vision Paris: History, http://www.premierevision.com/history/, accessed July 25, 2016.
22. Unlike haute couture shows, which were exhibitions of custom-made clothes for a rarefied clientele, French prêt-à-porter shows were regularly attended not only by the press but also by manufacturers, retailers, merchandisers, and an assortment of people in businesses related to fashion production (e.g., beauty products)—in much the same way that the contemporary New York Fashion Week remains, at its core, a business event.
23. Information on PV show dates, programs, and presentations is based on the author's research in the uncataloged archives and unsorted ephemera of Première Vision Pluriel (as it was then known), conducted in the basement of its Lyon headquarters in September 2006.
24. Frank Stuart, "Fabric Shows Add Fashion Services," *Daily News Record,* November 10, 1989; J. Russell Kraus, "Interstoff Mulling Early Spring Show," *Daily News Record,* May 11, 1983 (but Interstoff did not close the gap until 1996).
25. Frank Stuart, "Première Vision's Success Attributed to Its Strong Position on Fashion," *Daily News Record,* November 16, 1987.
26. Frank Stuart, "NAFTA Pact to Play Key Role at Fabric Show in New York," *Daily News Record,* March 17, 1993.
27. The same publisher's precursor to *Women's Wear Daily* (WWD), covering the menswear industry as a Monday through Friday daily newspaper from 1892 to 1997, then on a reduced frequency basis until its demise in 2008.
28. Due to the collapse of the U.S. textile and apparel manufacturing industries and the concomitant loss of advertising revenues, Fairchild News Service was

disbanded and, by 1997, *Daily News Record* was cut back to three-times-a-week frequency, then to its weekly format in 2001 before being discontinued altogether in 2008.
29. Andrew Moreton, "Paris Textiles Weave a Spell," *Financial Times,* October 8, 1986.
30. Nina Hyde, "From London," *Washington Post,* March 22, 1987.
31. Woody Hochswender, "Patterns: Buying What People Wear," *New York Times,* March 21, 1989.
32. Dominique Szabo, interview with author, November 20, 1997.
33. Aerin Lauder Zinterhoffer, interview with author, November 20, 1998.
34. Ginia Bellafante, "Front Row: A Jam-Packed Seventh on Sixth," *The New York Times,* September 17, 2002.
35. In its early years, European PreView (renamed Première Vision New York when the main show began accepting exhibitors from other continents), ran concurrently with textile shows that included the Turkish Fashion Fabric Exhibition, PanTextiles, Yarn Fair International, and the Lenzing-sponsored Innovation Asia.
36. Marilise Gavenas, "Third edition planned for March," *Daily News Record,* November 22, 2004. This followed "mini shows" in Japan and would be followed by efforts in Beijing and Hong Kong, although only Shanghai maintained a regular place on the show calendar.
37. Le Chatelier, interview with author, December 11, 2014.
38. Le Cuir à Paris was renamed Première Vision Leather in late 2014. See the chronology on the Première Vision Paris website, "History," http://www.premierevision.com/history, accessed July 25, 2016.
39. Former PV president Daniel Faure, discussion with author, September 21, 2006.
40. Former DuPont forecaster Roseann Forde, discussion with author, April 2003.
41. Ibid.
42. Le Chatelier, interview with author, December 11, 2014.
43. There were, for example, 18,864 visitors to its March 1982 edition, a figure that climbed to 42,437 by October 1992.
44. Stuart, "Fabric Shows Add Fashion Services."
45. Le Chatelier, interview with author, May 25, 2012. At the time, Le Chatelier had been observing PV since her student days in the early 1980s and had been on staff since 2004.
46. Le Chatelier, interview with author, May 25, 2012.
47. Ibid.
48. Ibid.
49. Le Chatelier interview with author, May 25, 2012.
50. Véronique Nichanian, interview with author, February 2004.
51. A *New York Times* brief published in 1918 announced the Textile Color Card Associations' intended March distribution of its Fall color card. Update the grammar a bit and the announcement could have appeared in this morning's *Women's Wear Daily.* See also Chapter 10 of the present volume.
52. Frank Stuart, "Première Vision Generates a Bright, Vivid Color Message for Spring'89," *Daily News Record,* March 22, 1988.
53. Fairchild News Service, "Plan Attractive New Format for Spring'90 Première Vision," *Daily News Record,* July 6, 1989.
54. Research conducted by author in PV storage facility in September 2006.

55. Quotation: Pierre Bourdieu, *Distinction: A Social Critique of the Judgement of Taste,* trans. Richard Nice (Cambridge, MA, 1984), 279.
56. As in the color card for the Fall/Winter 2004/2005 season.
57. [PV], *Autumn Winter 05/06 Press Kit: Fashion Info September 2004 Salon*, 3, author's personal papers.
58. This was for the Spring 2005 season.
59. Marilise Gavenas, "Time to Shine," *Daily News Record,* March 21, 2005.
60. Forde, interview with author, September 2006. Regina A. Blaszczyk reports that national organizations such as the Color Association of the United States (successor to the Textile Color Card Association discussed in Chapter 10) and industry-specific groups such as the leather-oriented Modeurop (Chapter 11) saw their influence wane in this context, although I never encountered them in the course of my coverage of fashion trends and markets.
61. Sophie d'Aulnay, "Interstoff's Late Timing Inhibits Men's Business," *Daily News Record,* April 12, 1994.
62. As it did in the Fall/Winter 2005/2006 edition held in February of 2005; Marilise Gavenas (unbylined), "The Lavender Mob" and "The Purple Gang," *Daily News Record,* January 17, 2005.

Index

Note: The letter 'n' following the locators refers to endnote numbers and the letter 'f' refers to figures.

R.L. Blaszczyk, U. Spiekermann (eds.), *Bright Modernity*, Worlds of Consumption, DOI 10.1007/978-3-319-50745-3

The manufacturer's authorised representative in the EU is Springer Nature Customer Service Centre GmbH, Europaplatz 3, 69115 Heidelberg, Germany. If you have any concerns regarding our products, please contact ProductSafety@springernature.com

Printed and bound by CPI Group (UK) Ltd, Croydon, CR0 4YY
25/09/2026
02222859-0017